The
Act of Writing
CANADIAN ESSAYS FOR COMPOSITION
REVISED THIRD EDITION

Ronald Conrad
Ryerson Polytechnical Institute

McGraw-Hill Ryerson Limited
Toronto Montreal New York Auckland Bogotá Caracas
Hamburg Lisbon London Madrid Mexico Milan New Delhi
Paris San Juan São Paulo Singapore Sydney Tokyo

The
Act of Writing
Canadian Essays for Composition,
Revised Third Edition

Copyright © McGraw-Hill Ryerson Limited, 1993, 1990, 1987, 1983. All rights reserved. No part of this publication may be reproduced, stored in a retrieval system, or transmitted, in any form or by any means, electronic, mechanical, photocopying, recording, or otherwise, without prior written permission of McGraw-Hill Ryerson Limited.

3 4 5 6 7 8 9 10   TRI   9 8 7 6 5 4

Printed and bound in Canada

Cover, Design, and Illustrations by Christopher Griffin

Sponsoring Editor: Susan Erickson

Production Editor: Rodney Rawlings

Permissions Editor: Norma Christensen

Care has been taken to trace ownership of copyright material contained in this text. However, the publishers will welcome information that enables them to rectify any reference or credit in subsequent editions.

Canadian Cataloguing in Publication Data

Conrad, Ronald, 1941–
The act of writing: Canadian essays for composition

Rev. 3rd ed.
ISBN 0-07-551711-6

1. English language–Rhetoric.   2. Canadian essays (English).*   I. Title.

PE1429.C66 1993   808'.0427   C93-094499-2

AUGUSTANA LIBRARY
UNIVERSITY OF ALBERTA

From the reference
library of

Tables of Contents

Contents

And then. . . .

CHAPTER 1: NARRATION   1

Writing about Myself

"There were cheers and laughter as Tivadar hit me in the
nose before I got my jacket off. It was not the first time I had
tasted my own blood, but it was the first time a Christian had
made it flow."

Writing about Others

For example. . . .

CHAPTER 2: EXAMPLE   35

It's large and yellow and. . . .

CHAPTER 3: DESCRIPTION 59

sockets. The power that I felt was not in the thing itself, but in some tremendous force behind it, that the carver had believed in."

Here's why. . . .

CHAPTER 4: CAUSE AND EFFECT   89

serpentine, with the swelling body of a single, composite creature."

It's just the opposite of. . . .

---

someone else will. Thus, as we gaze at the Stein Valley, we
see it in terms of jobs, board feet . . . and profit."

In a way, it's like. . . .

CHAPTER 6: ANALOGY AND RELATED DEVICES   173

Therefore. . . .

CHAPTER 9: ARGUMENTATION AND PERSUASION   267

Contents by Subject

CHILDHOOD AND OLD AGE

WOMEN IN SOCIETY

OUTSIDERS

THE CITY

THE ENVIRONMENT

WORK

LEISURE

VIOLENCE IN SOCIETY

SCIENCE AND TECHNOLOGY

BUSINESS AND INDUSTRY

THE MEDIA

THE ARTS

LAUGHS

PEOPLES AND PLACES

MAINLY CANADIAN

Acknowledgements

Doris Anderson: "The 51-Per-Cent Minority," Doris Anderson, *Maclean's,* January 1980. Reprinted by permission of Doris Anderson.

Margaret Atwood: "Canadians: What Do They Want?" by Margaret Atwood from *Mother Jones*, January 1982. Used by permission of *Mother Jones.*

Russell Baker: Copyright © 1979 by The New York Times Company. Reprinted by permission.

Pierre Berton: From *The Smug Minority*, 1968. By permission of the author, Pierre Berton.

June Callwood: Courtesy June Callwood, columnist, the *Globe and Mail.*

Emily Carr: From *Klee Wyck* by Emily Carr © 1941. Reprinted with the permission of Irwin Publishing, Toronto, Ontario.

Lesley Choyce: Appeared in the *Globe and Mail,* 7 March, 1987, p. D6. A revised, longer version appeared in *An Avalanche of Ocean* by Lesley Choyce (Fredericton: Goose Lane Ed., 1987).

Gregory Clark: "The Cat" by Gregory Clark. Used by permission of the Montreal Standard (1973) Limited.

Dian Cohen: From "Commodities and Collectibles" in Dian Cohen, *Money* (Prentice-Hall Canada, 1987), pp. 213–217. © 1987 Dian Cohen.

Mike Constable: Cartoon at start of Chapter 5. © 1988 Mike Constable. Reprinted and cropped by permission of the cartoonist, Mike Constable.

Donald Creighton: Excerpt from *Canada: The Heroic Beginnings*, 1974. Reproduced with permission of the Minister of Supply and Services Canada, from the publication *Canada: The Heroic Beginnings,* catalogue no. R64-82/1974-1, published by Macmillan of Canada in cooperation with Indian and Northern Affairs Canada, Parks Canada and the Canadian Government Publishing Centre, Supply and Services Canada.

Robertson Davies: From *A Voice from the Attic* by Robertson Davies. Used by permission of the Canadian publishers, McClelland and Stewart, Toronto.

Wendy Dennis: "A Tongue-Lashing for Deaf Ears" by Wendy Dennis, *Maclean's*, November 1981. Used by permission of the author.

Kildare Dobbs: © Kildare Dobbs.

Sylvia Fraser: From *My Father's House*, by Sylvia Fraser. Copyright © 1987 by Sylvia Fraser. Published by Doubleday Canada Limited. Reprinted by permission of Doubleday Canada Limited.

Robert Fulford: From *Crisis at the Victory Burlesk: Culture, Politics & Other Diversions* by Robert Fulford © copyright 1968 Oxford University Press Canada. Reprinted by permission.

George Gabori: "Coming of Age in Putnok" from *When Evils Were Most Free*, George Gabori, Deneau Publishers. Used by permission of the author.

Charles Gordon: Reprinted by permission Maclean's Magazine.

Ray Guy: Permission to use this material granted by Breakwater Books Ltd.

Roderick Haig-Brown: From *The Master and His Fish* by Roderick Haig-Brown. Used by permission of the Canadian publishers, McClelland and Stewart, Toronto.

Charles Yale Harrison: Printed courtesy Potlatch Publications Limited, Hamilton, Ontario.

Bruce Hutchison: "Cowboy from Holland" from *Canada: Tomorrow's Giant*, Bruce Hutchison, 1957. Permission granted by the author.

W. P. Kinsella: "How to Write Fiction" by W. P. Kinsella. From the *Globe and Mail*, April 27, 1985. Used by permission of the author.

Joy Kogawa: From *Obasan* by Joy Kogawa, © 1981. Reprinted by permission of Lester & Orpen Dennys Publishers Ltd., Canada.

Bonnie Laing: © 1989 Bonnie Laing. First printed in the *Globe and Mail*.

Michele Landsberg: © Michele Landsberg. Reprinted from the *Globe and Mail*, November 7, 1987, p. A2, by permission of the author.

Margaret Laurence: From *Heart of a Stranger* by Margaret Laurence. Used by permission of the Canadian publishers, McClelland and Stewart, Toronto.

Gary Lautens: "Man, You're a Great Player!" from *Laughing with Lautens* by Gary Lautens. Reprinted by permission of McGraw-Hill Ryerson Limited.

Stephen Leacock: From *Literary Lapses* by Stephen Leacock. Used by permission of the Canadian publishers, McClelland and Stewart, Toronto.

Félix Leclerc: Excerpt from *Pieds nus dans l'aube*. Coll. "Bibliothèque canadienne-française." Montreal, Fidès 1978. Translated by Philip Stratford. Permission to reprint Philip Stratford's English translation of the excerpt granted by Nelson Canada Limited.

Christie McLaren: The *Globe and Mail*, Toronto.

Hugh MacLennan: Reprinted by permission of the author and his agent, Blanche C. Gregory, Inc.

Thierry Mallet: © 1930, Thierry Mallet, as originally published in *The Atlantic Monthly*, March, 1927.

John Bentley Mays: Reprinted by permission of the *Globe and Mail*.

Mavor Moore: © 1986 Mavor Moore, used with his permission.

Farley Mowat: Excerpt from *People of the Deer* by Farley Mowat. Copyright © 1952, Farley Mowat Limited. Used by permission of the author.

Richard Needham: From *The Hypodermic Needham*, 1970. Used by permission of Richard J. Needham and the *Globe and Mail*, Toronto.

Michael Ondaatje: Copyright © Michael Ondaatje, from *Running in the Family*

(McClelland and Stewart, 1982). Used by permission of the author.

B. W. Powe: © 1987 B. W. Powe. Reprinted from the *Globe and Mail*, June 13, 1987, p. C17, by permission of the author.

Mordecai Richler: Reprinted by permission of International Creative Management Inc., copyright © 1986 by Mordecai Richler. Originally published in the *New York Times*.

Erika Ritter: From *Urban Scrawl* by Erika Ritter © 1984. Reprinted by permission of Macmillan of Canada, A Division of Canada Publishing Corporation.

Franklin Russell: From *The Hunting Animal* by Franklin Russell. Used by permission of the Canadian publishers, McClelland and Stewart, Toronto.

Judy Stoffman: "The Way of All Flesh" by Judy Stoffman, *Weekend Magazine*, September 15, 1979. Reprinted by permission of the author.

David Suzuki: "Hidden Lessons." With author's permission. "Native Peoples Liken Ruination of Nature to Church Destruction." With author's permission.

To the Student

Reading and writing are two sides of the same coin. If you read one book a year like the average Canadian, you will never really learn to write. But perhaps 80 or 90 percent of those who read habitually will become much better writers than those who don't, and because of this will succeed more easily in school and career — not to mention leading a fuller life because of what they have learned while reading.

All this is why you are using *The Act of Writing*. If you meet the challenges that a book like this poses, you can do a lot for yourself. Among these challenges:

- Read the essays with attention, and maybe reread them, to understand their topic and the techniques the author has used to present it.

- React to the argument, thinking critically, agreeing or disagreeing. And in discussion tell your classmates and teacher why. Be forceful: if you have reasoned well, your opinion is as good as anyone else's.

- Write a strong response to the topic or choice of topics suggested by your teacher. Using the essays you have studied as models, organize clearly, argue well, and polish your own language to the most powerful level you can achieve.

- To do this, reject those writing practices of the past that are inefficient or even harmful; exert yourself to learn and use the "process" approach explained and encouraged throughout this book. It may be based on today's research, but it is how most good writers have always written.

- Finally, *read more*. See the biographical introductions, which tell what else our authors have written. See the "Further Reading" suggested after each essay. And when a particular author or subject strikes your interest, choose the books you will read now, or over the holidays, or next summer. Improve your writing and enlarge your world by reading now and for the rest of your life.

R. C.

To the Teacher

We are gratified by the enthusiasm of teachers and students for *The Act of Writing* since its publication in 1983, but we have also listened to your requests for change — both in your verbal comments and in your opinions quantified by our recent user survey. The present edition delivers all your most often requested changes, while carefully preserving the qualities you liked in the first place.

The request most often voiced was for a unit on argumentation and persuasion. You now have it: our new Chapter 9 is the centrepiece of this edition, a "superchapter" offering a substantial introduction as well as eight model essays carefully selected to demonstrate a range of approaches to argumentative and persuasive writing. To make room for this major chapter without inflating the size and cost of the book, we have shortened four other chapters and dropped a fifth, the relatively little used "Extended Definition." Yet we have maintained the key chapters "Cause and Effect" and "Comparison and Contrast" at a full complement of six essays each, and have beefed them up with some fine new selections by authors like David Suzuki, Mordecai Richler, Mavor Moore, Russell

Baker, and Margaret Laurence. (We are printing Laurence's classic essay "Where the World Began," requested in the survey.)

Another frequent request was to apply more fully the introductory instruction on process in writing. We have done so. There are now 47 individual "Process in Writing" assignments throughout the book, one in response to the subject and/or approach of each selection. And at the end of every chapter, immediately after the list of 25 to 30 essay topics, is a sequence entitled "Process in Writing: Guidelines": a series of optional steps individualizing the process approach for the method of organization explored in that chapter. (By the way, every one of the 245 end-of-chapter essay topics is new, to provide you with fresh reading matter in your students' essays.)

Other requests were for more women authors, more essays on the media, and more essays on the environment. You now have them. And in general, you have easier access to more essays demonstrating each pattern of organization: systematic cross-references after each chapter introduction now identify those essays in other chapters that most strongly use the central approach of the unit your class is studying. For example, Chapter 3, "Description," reprints four essays but refers you to six more elsewhere in the book, for a total of ten selections that make strong use of description.

Another kind of cross-referencing is offered in a new feature: "Further Reading," just after each essay, suggests several book titles in a variety of genres, relating to the author and/or topic just studied — in order to encourage wide reading and facilitate independent study.

Finally, new selections are central to any edition. We have chosen ours for their impact, variety, style, polish, and clarity of organization. We hope they will stimulate debate in your classroom, and we hope that as models they will encourage critical thinking, clear organization, and careful revision in the writing of your students.

HOW TO USE THIS BOOK

The Act of Writing, Third Edition, offers flexibility and encourages individualization. The combination of four to eight essays per chapter with several more identified in cross-references will yield more selections per unit than you are likely to use. Thus you can individualize, choosing those that best suit the needs and interests of your particular class. This book also offers a range of difficulty, from essays that are easily accessible to almost all students to essays that are frankly challenging. (*Note:* The "Table of Contents and Difficulty Ranking" of your instructor's manual ranks all selections by level of difficulty, so that if you are new to this book you can more easily plan a syllabus to fit the needs of your class.) The numerous discussion topics after each selection offer you and your students a choice of theme and emphasis in classroom debate. And finally, the "Process in Writing" topic after each essay, the many end-of-chapter topics, and the optional process "Guidelines" tailored for each chapter give a wide latitude of choice for the individual teacher, the individual class, the individual student.

Note also the two tables of contents. The first lists all selections in their chapters arranged by *form of organization* (you can choose from six essays, for example, that all demonstrate organization through comparison and contrast). The second table of contents lists all essays by general *subject*, to help you choose selections of interest to your particular students.

An introductory essay, "The Act of Writing," starts the book off by putting to rest a number of widespread misconceptions about writing that plague students in the classroom, then attempts to describe what it is that an essayist actually does. It emphasizes the individuality of the writer, the importance of motivation, the role of intuition as well as logic, and a balance of spontaneity and revision in the process of writing.

The essays are all by Canadians or by persons with Canadian experience, but the scope ranges widely: some are about Canada, some are about other countries, and most are concerned with such universal themes as childhood, aging, work, technology, sport, and war. The use of Canadian essays is not a statement of nationalism. In fact, it is an attempt to bring to Canada the kind of anthology that is taken for granted in other countries: a collection of works that are mostly universal in theme but that, naturally, draw a good part of their content from the country in which the book will be used.

As we have seen, the essays are arranged in chapters that each demonstrate a fundamental and useful pattern of organization. "Narration" starts the book off, because no approach is easier or more motivating for a first assignment than writing a story, in chronological order, about oneself. "Example" and "Description" follow, because these methods of development are used to some degree in almost all writing. "Cause and Effect" and the following chapter, "Comparison and Contrast," are at the centre of the essayist's organizational repertoire. "Analogy" and "Classification" follow "Comparison and Contrast," for they are both varieties of comparison. "Process Analysis," an approach used widely across the curriculum, follows. After all these *forms*, our new chapter, "Argumentation and Persuasion," explores more fully the writer's most common and basic *purpose*, to make a point. It explores the dualities of deduction and induction, and of argumentation and persuasion, then illustrates their application with the eight model essays.

Every selection is prefaced with an introduction to the author, designed to interest the student and encourage further reading in the author's works. And each selection is followed by pedagogical material entitled "Further Reading," "Structure," "Style," "Ideas for Discussion and Writing," and in Chapter 9 "Argumentation and Persuasion." Note that in this material different questions serve different purposes. Some are directive, calling attention to major features of the essay. Some are technical, for example focussing on a specific point of language that illustrates a technique. And still others are exploratory, encouraging open-ended response. The instructor's manual offers answers to those questions that are not open-ended and suggests responses to some that are. Read the manual's introduction: it gives more suggestions for using *The Act of Writing*. For each essay, the manual also lists vocabulary that may need attention.

Each of the nine chapters begins with a discussion of how and why to use the form at hand, and ends with a selection of 25 to 30 essay topics which complement that form. These topics have been chosen with care, to tap some of the students' deepest concerns and channel them into motivation for writing. The reason for this attention to topics is that no one problem is more destructive to the performance of both student and teacher than dull or superficial subject matter. How can writing be important if its content is not? And how can a teacher enjoy or even tolerate marking without an interest in *what* the students are saying? A further "Process in Writing" topic occurs after each essay. If class members have had a good discussion about the selection, their motivation and writing performance may be greatest if they explore these topics, which draw upon both the subject and the underlying form of the essay that precedes them. And at the end of each chapter occur the optional process guidelines mentioned earlier, individualized for the specific pattern of development in that unit.

Finally, a glossary at the end defines literary terms often used in the discussion questions; when one of these terms is a key part of a passage, it appears in SMALL CAPITALS.

The instructor's manual has been revised for this edition, and will be sent gratis upon request.

I would like to thank all those who, in one way or another, helped with this project: students and colleagues who reacted to essays; teachers who gave of their time to answer our survey; John Cook, who advised on choice of selections; and Dan Bratton, who critiqued the introduction to our new chapter. Thanks also to Jocelyne and Michel Leclerc for their research in Quebec, to Mary Stevens, Win McGlone, Allan Weiss, and Karen Kitagawa, and to Norma Christensen for her detective skills in tracking down permissions. Doris Anderson, Judy Stoffman, and translator Philip Stratford took the time to update their selections, and George Gabori,

Christie McLaren, Judy Stoffman, Bonnie Laing, Charles Gordon, and Wendy Dennis gave me information to help in writing or updating their biographies. Above all I thank my wife Mary, whose good advice smoothed the way through every stage of this edition.

R. C.

Introduction: The Act of Writing

Writing is one of the most widely misunderstood of human activities. It is odd that after all the years we have spent in school, after all the hours we have spent reading other people's writing and producing our own, most of us cannot say what really happens when we write. We can describe other complicated tasks — driving a car, baking bread, building a radio, or programming a computer. But to most people the act of writing is a mystery. Not that we don't have theories, either those told us in school or those we have arrived at ourselves. But many of these theories are misconceptions that actually hinder our efforts to write. Let's look at some of them.

MISCONCEPTION: Writing is like following a blueprint: I figure it all out in advance and then just fill in the details. Of course an outline, used sensibly, will help. But some of us were taught in school that our best thinking goes into a logical and detailed outline — and that the writing itself is secondary. Thus we are reduced to carpenters or plumbers of the written word, who merely saw, cut, and fit the pieces in place once the master plan has been established. The problem with this reassuringly logical approach is that it views writing as a science, not as the art that all our practical experience tells us it is. How many of us have given up on a required outline, done our thinking mostly as we wrote the essay itself, then produced an outline by seeing what we just wrote? Or how many of us have painfully constructed a detailed outline in advance, only to find while writing the essay that our real message does not fit the plan?

Writing is exploring! We know the direction in which we will go and the main landmarks we hope to pass, but not every twist and turn of the path. What a dull trip it would be if we did! Let's leave room for discovery, because some of our best ideas occur in the act of writing. Quebec poet St.-Denys Garneau went so far as to say, "I cannot think except when writing." Many teachers now reflect the fact of writing as discovery by calling a first draft the *discovery draft.*

But while avoiding the rigor mortis of overplanning, let's not go to the opposite extreme, like Stephen Leacock's famous horseman who "rode madly off in all directions." We do work best with an outline, five or ten or fifteen lines that define the main point and how we intend to support it. But our outline should be a brief one — a compass on a journey, not a blueprint for a construction project.

MISCONCEPTION: If I don't hit it right the first time, I've failed. It's not hard to see where this idea came from: in school we write so many essays and tests within the limits of one class period that writing in a hurry begins to seem normal. But merely completing such an assignment is difficult; seriously revising it is even more difficult. Few people can "hit it right the first time." Professional writers know this; most of them take longer to write than we do. They tinker with words and sentences, they cross out and replace sections, they go through two or three or even five or ten drafts — and sometimes they throw the whole thing out and start over. These writers know by experience that writing is not a hit-or-miss affair with only one try allowed, but a *process.* They know that revision can yield astonishing results.

MISCONCEPTION: When I write, I am speaking on paper. If you have heard yourself speaking on tape, you were no doubt surprised at the number of filler words you used. "Uh," "um," "well," and "hmmm" serve to fill in the gaps between your thoughts but hardly help to carry the message. And if you listened closely, you may have been surprised at the number of incomplete statements — fragments that by themselves made little or no sense. Fillers and fragments are tolerated in speech because, after all, we are making up our message on the spot. There is no chance to plan, revise, edit, or proofread.

But in writing there is, and this fact increases the expectations of your reader far beyond those of your listener. Language in written form can be planned. It is complete. It is precise and concise. It uses standard words. It is punctuated. It follows all the rules. In short, it is a product of the time that its written form allows you to give it, not a spur-of-the-moment, hope-for-the-best effort like the speech that comes so easily from your mouth.

MISCONCEPTION: The best words are the biggest words. Variations on this theme are *If my writing looks scholarly it will impress the reader,* and even *If I make my essay so difficult that no one knows what I'm saying, everyone will believe me.* At the roots of these widespread ideas is a notion that writing is a kind of competition between writer and reader. A writer who is obscure enough will make the reader feel like a dummy and will thus win the game.

Avoiding the game altogether is difficult when so many leaders in business, education, and government play it. The first step toward open communication, though, is to think of your reader not as an opponent but as an ally. You are both working toward the same goal, which is the reader's clear understanding of your ideas. Another step is to admit that words small in size can be large in meaning. The best-loved writings in our language show a strong preference for short words. Writing made of them is more concise, more vivid, and usually more profound than writing made of the elephantine words that some of us ransack the dictionary for. When a long word conveys your meaning best — perhaps like "elephantine" above — by all means use it. But often the writer, like the architect, finds that *less is more.*

MISCONCEPTION: I don't like to write. For some unfortunate people this statement is true. But for most who say it, the truth is really "I don't like to *begin* writing." Who does? Staring at that blank page is like staring from a diving board at the cold water below. But a swimmer and a writer both work up their courage to plunge in, and soon they both experience a new sensation: they don't want to come out. Teachers whose students write journals in class see the process at work every day. As class begins, the writers are filled with stress: they chew their pens and frown as they stare at the page to be filled. But a few minutes later they are scribbling furiously away, recording in an almost trance-like state their latest experiences, feelings, and insights. And when the teacher asks them to stop, in order to begin the next activity, they are annoyed: they sigh and *keep on writing* until asked a second or third time to stop.

Let's admit that most writers — and that includes professionals — dread the beginning. Let's also admit that most writers enjoy the rest of it, hard work though it may be.

With some of the most widespread misconceptions behind us, let's take a fresh look at the act of writing. First, let's allow for personal differences. *Know yourself!* If you are the kind of person whose desk is piled a foot high with papers and books, whose closet is an avalanche waiting to happen and whose shoes have not been shined in two years, you may write best by planning little and emphasizing your spontaneity. If you are the kind of person who plans an August holiday in January, who keeps a budget right down to the penny, and who washes the car every Wednesday and Saturday whether it needs it or not, you may write best by planning fully. On the other hand, your natural tendencies may have caused you problems and may therefore need to be fought. If your spontaneity has produced writings that can't stay on topic, plan more: make a careful outline. If overorganizing has sucked the life out of your writing, free yourself up: leave more room for discovery as you write. Whatever the case, use the approach that works for *you*.

Let's allow also for differences in assignments. If you are dashing off a short personal sketch, your planning may be no more than an idea and a few moments of thought. If you are writing a long research essay, the product of days in the library, you may need an outline two pages long. No one approach works for every person and every assignment. Keep in mind, then, that the process we are about to examine is a *starting point*, a basis but not a blueprint for your own writing.

THE BEGINNINGS OF AN ESSAY CAN BE FOUND IN THE ANSWERING OF SEVERAL QUESTIONS:

1. *Why am I writing?* This most basic of questions too often goes unasked. If the answer is "to fill up five pages," "to impress," or "to get an 'A'," you are beginning with a severe handicap. The immediate reason to write may be a class assignment, but the real reason must be to communicate something of value. Otherwise your motivation is lost and so is your performance. Therefore, choose from a list of topics the one that is most significant to you. If no topic seems significant, devise a way to *make* one significant. Look at it from a new viewpoint or approach it in some unusual way. If that fails, and if your teacher is approachable, voice your concern and suggest an alternative topic. One teacher we know about always made students analyze the relative merits of chocolate and vanilla ice cream, on the theory that a dull subject will not distract a writer from the real goals: grammar and style. He was wrong. Research demonstrates

that motivation is the prime cause of improvement in writing — and motivation comes largely from writing about things that matter.

When you write on your own, as in a private journal, you may still need to answer the question *Why am I writing?* Simply recording events can be dull. Record also your feelings, your perceptions, and your conclusions about those events. If you have personal problems, as most people do, confront them on the page. The more you discover yourself and your world through writing, the more important the writing becomes.

2. *How big is my topic?* Classroom essays are shorter than most people realize. A book may contain 100,000 words; a magazine article 2000 or 5000; a classroom essay as few as 500 or even 250. Therefore narrowing the essay topic is more important than most people realize.

One student, who had been a political prisoner, decided to write about economic systems. He knew the subject well and was committed to it. But what he attempted was an analysis of communism, socialism, and capitalism — all in two pages! A lack of focus spread his very short essay so thin that it approached the state of saying nothing about everything. It was the barest scratching of the surface, a summary of basic facts that everyone already knows.

If the same person had described his arrest and imprisonment — or even one day in his cell — he might have said far more about the system he had fought against. It is in specifics that we best learn generalities. Think of writing as photography. Putting aside the wide-angle lens that includes too much at a distance, look through the telephoto lens that brings you up close to a small part of the subject. Select the part most meaningful to you, perhaps the part most characteristic of the whole, and then take the picture.

Nearly all of the essays in this book are closeups: they tend to explore one situation, one incident, one person, or one process. Yet most of them are longer than the essays you will write. Therefore, when you choose a topic, judge its size — and if you have to, *change* its size.

3. *What message am I sending?* You may know your topic well. But unless you send a message concerning it, your reader will think, *what's the point?* A message is often a value judgement: Are robots dangerous? Will they take away our jobs or someday even rule over us? Or do they help us? Will they free us at last from the dehumanizing tyranny of manual labour? Most of the essays in this book take such a stance, either pro or con, toward their subjects. Some avoid judging their subjects directly, but send other messages: one shows what it's like to be down and out; one shows how a childhood event can shape us as adults; another shows how aging is a continual, lifelong process.

If you have chosen a topic because it seems meaningful, you will no doubt have a message to send. What do you most feel like saying about the topic? Once you know, get it down in writing. This THESIS STATEMENT, as it is often called, normally comes at or near the beginning of an essay. It is an introductory sentence or passage that does more than just tell what the topic is; it clearly states, as well, what you are saying *about* the topic. It lets your reader know what is coming — and, in the process, it commits you to a purpose that all the rest of the essay must in one way or another support. It is your guide as you write.

4. *Who is my audience?* Do you talk the same way to a friend and a stranger? To an old person and a child? To a hockey coach and a professor? Probably not. Neither would you write the same way to all readers. In a private journal you can write as freely as you think, for you are the reader: omissions and excesses of all kinds will be understood and forgiven. In letters to a close friend you are nearly as free, for the reader knows you well enough to supply missing explanations or interpret remarks in the light of your personality. But your freedom shrinks when you write for others: a business person, a public official, a teacher. Now you must fight a misconception shared by many people: *Everyone is like me.*

This idea is seldom articulated but may lurk as a natural assumption in the backs of our minds. It is a form of egotism. If you assume that everyone is like you, many readers will not accept or even understand your message — because they are *not* like you. They did not grow up in your family, neighbourhood, or even country. They are older or younger, or of the opposite sex. They have had different life experiences and as a result have different knowledge and temperaments and values.

Keep these differences in mind as you write. You will not prove your point by quoting Marx to a capitalist, the Bible to an atheist, or Germaine Greer to a male supremacist. Any argument built on a partisan foundation will collapse if the reader does not accept that foundation. Instead, build from facts or ideas that your reader probably does accept: killing is bad, government is necessary, women are human beings, and so on. Is your topic controversial? Then avoid an open display of bias. Calling intellectuals "Commies" or abortionists "hired killers" will appeal only to those who shared your view in the first place. (For more on these matters, read the introduction to Chapter 9, "Argumentation and Persuasion.")

Does the reader know what you know? If you write about statistics for a statistics teacher, use any technical terms customary to the field, and avoid the insult of explaining elementary points. But if you write on the same subject for a class exercise in English or a letter to the editor, your reader will be very different: avoid most technical terms, define those you do use, and explain more fully each step of your argument.

The more open you become to the individuality of your reader, the more open your reader becomes to your message. It is a matter of mutual respect.

PREWRITING

How do we begin the act of writing: by putting those first words on a page? The philosopher Lao-Tze said, "A journey of a thousand miles begins with the first step." In a way he was right: if we never take that official first step, we will certainly never arive at our destination. But how much daydreaming, planning, and scheming do we do beforehand? Do we set out on a journey without consulting the map or the calendar or the tourist brochure or the travel guide — not to mention our bankbook? And do we write an essay without in some way resolving the questions we have just asked:

> **Why am I writing?**
> **How big is my topic?**
> **What message am I sending?**
> **Who is my audience?**

The process of writing, then, begins in thought. But thoughts do not come on command. Like the diver, we look down at the cold water and dread the plunge. Some writers try to "break the ice" by manipulating their environment: finding a quiet spot in front of a blank wall, a particularly soft or hard chair, good lighting, or a favourite pen. Others fortify themselves with a good night's sleep, food, or a cup of coffee. Still others loosen up through exercise or music. Any of these tricks may help, but they all avoid the real issue: How do we begin to *think?*

One very direct approach, a variation on the traditional technique of outlining, is *brainstorming:* once you have roughly identified your subject, simply write down words or phrases that relate in any way to it. Cover a page with these fragments. Put down anything that comes, letting one thought lead to another. Some entries will seem off-topic, trivial, or even loony, but others may be just what you need: the keys to your essay. Circle them. Put them in order. As crude as this primitive outline may seem, it has served a purpose: your thoughts have begun to arrive. The process is in motion. You have taken that first "step" before even starting the first draft.

A similar but even more powerful "icebreaker" is *freewriting*. Put a blank piece of paper on the desk with your watch beside it. Think of your topic. Now *write!* Put down anything that comes: sentences, phrases, words — logical thoughts, hasty impressions, even pure garbage. Do not cease the physical act of writing, do not even lift the pen from the page, for at least five minutes. If your next thought doesn't come, write the last one over and over until the next one does come. What you produce may surprise you.

Like brainstorming, freewriting is an exercise in free association: the flow of your thoughts, the unpredictable leaps of your intuition, will "break the ice," priming you to write. They may also do much more: as in brainstorming, you may end up with a page of scribbling that contains the main points of your essay. Try to find them. Circle them. Put them in order. See if your intuition has led the way in answering the questions: *Why am I writing? How big is my topic? What message am I sending? Who is my audience?* If all goes well, you have already begun your journey.

THE FIRST WORDS

After your thoughts are flowing comes the next step, the opening passage of your essay. In a very short composition your THESIS STATEMENT may serve also as the first words. In many longer essays it comes at the end of an introduction. Only about one-fourth of the selections in this book start right off with what could be called a thesis statement. What do the others start with?

Background information: About half the essays in this book lead off by relating the circumstances in which the topic is set. For examples, see the beginnings of our essays by Gabori (p. 4), Richler (p. 103), Laurence (p. 162), Dobbs (p. 274), and Berton (p. 289).

Anecdote: A brief story, usually of a humorous or dramatic incident, can lead into the topic. See Hutchison (p. 47), Powe, (p. 112), Leacock (p. 233), and Atwood (p. 302).

Quotation or allusion: The words of a philosopher, of a news report, of a recognized specialist in the subject, or of anyone with close experience of it can be used to break the ice. See Cohen (p. 252), Dobbs (p. 274), and Kogawa (p. 315).

Sense images: Vivid description can attract a reader's interest to the topic. See Fraser (p. 8), McLaren (p. 67), Choyce (p. 72), Carr (p. 77), and Russell (p. 123).

A striking comparison or contrast: Showing how things are like or unlike each other is a dramatic way to introduce a topic. See Moore (p. 143), Suzuki (p. 157), Laurence (p. 162), Haig-Brown (p. 209), Cohen (p. 252), and Atwood (p. 302).

Narrative: Several selections in this book begin by telling a story upon which the essay is based. See Harrison (p. 13), MacLennan (p. 221), Gordon (p. 309), and Dennis (p. 322).

An unusual or puzzling statement: Such an opening appeals to the reader's curiosity. See Fulford (p. 51), Laurence (p. 162), and Kinsella (p. 216).

Figures of speech: A striking METAPHOR, SIMILE, or PERSONIFICATION can spark the opening. See Choyce (p. 72), Leclerc (p. 194), Stoffman (p. 238), and Cohen (p. 252).

Most of these introductions are short: a couple of sentences or a paragraph or two at the most. And almost all of them are designed to *interest* the reader, for an apathetic reader may not even finish the essay, let alone like or understand it. Writing is fishing. You throw in the line. Your reader tastes the bait (your introduction), bites, is pulled through the waters of your argument, and — if the line of thought doesn't break — lands in your net.

You, the writer, may also be "hooked." Once you have hit upon a strong introduction, one that shows off the drama or importance of your topic, the beginning may carry you along with it. And once you get going, the idea embodied in your thesis statement may pull you through the essay, enabling you to write freely as one passage leads to another. You may become less and less aware of your surroundings as you become more and more immersed in your subject. By the time you develop a good beginning, you may experience the act of writing the way one student described it: "At first I couldn't start, but then I couldn't stop."

THE BODY

By itself, an introduction is a head without a body. A head gives direction, but without a body it goes nowhere. The "body" of your essay has the main work to do: following the direction set by your introduction, and especially by your thesis statement, it explains, illustrates, and sometimes attempts to prove your point. But if it ever ignores the direction set by the head, it ceases to do its job. Even the best of explanations, without a sense of direction, is like one of those unfortunate football players we sometimes hear about who complete a 90-yard run to the wrong goal. On the other hand, we know that writing is discovery. The acts of writing and revising will sometimes take us in a new direction that is better than the old one set by the introduction. When that happens, change, not the body, but the "head," so that the two will work together in the new direction.

The most obvious way to keep a direction is to base your essay on a particular form — and that is what most of this book is about. As you read and discuss the essays that follow, and as you write your own essays using the forms upon which other writers have based their oganization, you will develop a range of choices:

Narration: In simple time order, from the first event to the last event, tell a story that illustrates the point.

Example: Give one in-depth example that explains the point, or a number of shorter examples.

Description: Recreate for your reader, through the most vivid language possible, your own or someone else's experience with the subject.

Cause and Effect: Explain by showing how one situation or event causes another.

Comparison and Contrast: Explain by showing how two things are like or unlike each other.

Analogy and Related Devices: In comparing two things, use the one to explain the other.

Classification: Make a point by fitting the parts of your subject into categories.

Process Analysis: Show how something happens or how something is done.

Argumentation and Persuasion: Using any pattern that works, make your point through logic and/or emotion.

Seldom does one of these methods appear alone. A *process analysis*, for example, is usually told as a *narrative*. Here and there it may use *examples, description*, or any of the other patterns to help make its point. But these combinations occur naturally, often without the writer's knowing it. In most cases the only form deliberately chosen by a writer is the main one upon which the whole essay is structured.

How do you choose the right form? Let the subject be your guide. In architecture, form follows function. Rather than cram an office into a pre-selected structure, a designer likes to begin with the *function* of that office. How much space best serves its needs? What shape? What barriers and passageways between one section and another? What front to present to the world?

An essay is much the same: the needs of its subject, if you are sensitive to them, will in most cases suggest a form. If the main point is to show your reader what something is like, you may naturally use examples and description. If the subject is unusual or little known, you may use a comparison or contrast, or an analogy to something that the reader does know. If its parts seem important, you may discuss them one by one in a classification. And when some other need is greater, you may use still another form. If you stay open to the subject, whatever it is, this process can be so natural that you *recognize* rather than *choose* a form.

If the process is natural, then why study the forms in this book? Think of the architect again: Why does he or she study design in school? For one thing, knowing how each form is constructed assures that the building will not collapse. For another, in those cases when the choice is *not* easy, a conscious knowledge of all the possibilities will help.

Consider the longer essay — perhaps a report or research paper. A stack of notes sits on your desk. They are in chaos. Even with brainstorming or freewriting, knowing your purpose, having the facts, and completing a thesis statement, you can't think how to coordinate all those facts. First give the natural process its best chance: sort all your notes into groups of related material, using a pair of scissors if necessary to divide unrelated points. When everything is in two stacks, or five stacks or ten, let your mind work freely. How do these groups relate to each other? Does one come before another in time? Does one cause another? Does one contradict another? Are they all steps in a process or parts of a whole? Now add your conscious knowledge of the forms: Do you see narration, example, description, cause and effect, comparison and contrast, analogy, classification, or process analysis? It is the rare case when one of these forms cannot supply the basic structure to support your argument.

If you use the essay topics at the end of each chapter in this book, your choice of form will already be made. This process may seem to bypass the ideal method of letting form follow function. The topics, though, are selected to go well with the form studied in their chapter. And just as the architect practises the standard designs in school to learn their forms and functions, so can the writer deliberately practise the standard essay designs to learn *their* forms and functions. Both architect and writer will then be ready when the choice is truly open.

TRANSITIONS

We have mentioned the passageways inside a building. Without them an office would be useless: no one could move from one room to another or pass business from one stage to another. Yet some essays are built without passageways. One point ends where another begins, without even a "then" or "therefore" or "however" or "finally" to join them. Readers have to expend a great deal of effort on breaking through the walls in order to follow the writer's train of thought from one room to the next.

Help your readers. *You* know why one point follows another, but do *they*? Make sure by supplying transitions: say "although" or "but" or "on the other hand"; say "because" or "as a result" or "since"; say "first" or "next" or "last"; say "for example" or "in conclusion." And when moving readers from one major division of your essay to the next, devote a full sentence or even a paragraph to the job (one good example is paragraph 10 of Doris Anderson's essay).

Your plan may already be the right one, setting your points in their most logical order. But let that logic show: give your readers a door between every room.

THE CLOSING

We've discussed the beginning, the middle, and transitions between parts. What remains is of course the ending. Every essay has one — the point at which the words stop. But not all endings are closings. A closing is deliberate. In some clear way it tells the reader that you have not just run out of time, ink, or ideas, but that you have *chosen* to stop here. If you end at just any convenient spot, without engineering an effect to fit your ending, the essay may trail off or even fall flat. But as preachers, composers, playwrights, and film directors know, a good closing can be even stronger than a good opening. How do the essays in this book come to a close? They use a variety of devices:

Reference to the opening: Repeating or restating something from the opening gives a sense of culmination, of having come full circle. See the openings and closings by Laurence (pp. 162 and 167), Stoffman (pp. 238 and 245), Berton (pp. 289 and 294), Atwood (pp. 302 and 305), and Kogawa (pp. 315 and 318).

Contrast or reversal: This ironic device exploits the dramatic potential of the closing. See the openings and closings by Fulford (pp. 51 and 53), Moore (pp. 143 and 145), and Stoffman (pp. 238 and 245).

Question: A question and its answer, or a question calling for the reader's answer, is a common means of closing. See Davies (p. 176), Leacock (p. 235), and Dennis (p. 324).

Quotation: A good quotation, of either prose or poetry, can add authority and interest to a closing. See Haig-Brown (p. 213).

Transition signals: Words, phrases, or sentences of transition commonly signal the closing. See Gabori (p. 5) and Landsberg (p. 286).

Revealing the significance: Showing the implications or importance of the subject makes for a strong closing. See Gabori (p. 5), Clark (p. 95), Powe (p. 114), Suzuki (p. 159), Dobbs (p. 280), and Landsberg (p. 286).

Summary: About a fourth of the essays in this book give a summary, either alone or in combination with other closing techniques, but one that is always *short*. See Mallet (p. 64), Haig-Brown (p. 213), and Berton (p. 294).

Conclusion: Although "conclusion" is often a label for the closing in general, more accurately it is only one of many closing techniques — the drawing of a conclusion from the discussion in the essay. See Richler (p. 109), Mays (p. 120), Suzuki (p. 159), Laurence (p. 167), and Landsberg (p. 286).

Prediction: A short look at the subject's future can very logically close a discussion of that subject's past or present. See Hutchison (p. 48), Powe (p. 114), Suzuki (p. 159), and Landsberg (p. 286). Sometimes discussing the future takes the form of a call to action (see Dennis, p. 324).

You have probably noticed that some authors are named more than once; like openings, closings can exploit more than one technique. In fact, the more the better. Stay open to techniques that appear while you write, even as you construct a closing on the one technique you have deliberately chosen. Any of these choices will be stronger, though, when used with the most fundamental technique of all: building your whole essay toward a high point or *climax*. Put your points in order from least important to most important, from least useful to most useful, or from least dramatic to most dramatic. Then you will have made possible a closing that applies all the dramatic power of the final position.

When you get there, apply the force of that closing to a real message. Techniques used just for their own sake are cheap tricks. Do not waste them. Instead, use them to underline your basic message, to impress upon your audience one last and most convincing time that what you have to say is significant. Your closing, more than any other part of your essay, can send the reader away disappointed — or moved.

THE PROCESS: HOW MANY DRAFTS?

We have discussed the act of writing as a process in which, rather than trying to "hit it right the first time," we follow a number of steps in the journey toward a good essay. The rest of this book develops that approach. After each selection you will find an assignment called "Process in Writing" that draws on the essay you have just read, suggesting a related topic for an essay of your own. The main steps of the process are given, individualized for the particular topic.

And at the end of each chapter you will find a whole page of essay topics, designed for practice in the form of organization you have just studied. After them, in each chapter, appear sections called "Process in Writing: Guidelines" which give the steps of a process designed for the organizational form you have just studied. Whether you write from a topic given just after an essay or choose a topic from the end-of-chapter list, remember that these steps are only *guidelines* to the process; use the ones that seem best.

Our "process" of writing is flexible; it is not a blueprint like the elaborate outlines our parents and grandparents were made to construct. Above all, the process is "recursive" — that is, while you may begin with brainstorming or freewriting, go on to a discovery draft, revise your argument in a further draft or drafts, and finally edit for spelling and grammar, you may also double back or jump forward at any time. Studies show that professionals writing all kinds of documents in all kinds of fields do this. While generating their "discovery draft" they may stop here and there to improve a word choice or fix punctuation — changes that normally occur later. Or, while they are in the middle of editing or even proofreading, a fine new idea may come thundering out of their mind; so they may back up a few steps, write it out, and add it to their argument, perhaps junking something else they had thought was good. All this is consistent with the reality that *we think while writing*.

Do feel free to transgress the process "guidelines" in these ways, but not so often that you undercut the advantages of the process itself. For example, in writing your discovery draft you may detect a spelling error or a piece of dubious sentence structure. If you must, stop here to edit. But better yet, why not just circle the spot and come back to fix it later? For now, let the material keep rolling out uninterrupted. Later on, while you are editing or even proofreading, a whole new idea may come. You could go back even now to fit it in — but this means work, maybe even reorganization. Proceed only if it is a real improvement and if you have the time.

Finally, how many drafts are we talking about? The "guidelines" later on are sometimes vague on this point — because what do we mean by a draft? Is every new copy a draft? No, unless it incorporates many improvements that you wrote between the lines and in the margins of the previous draft. (Be sure to double- or triple-space in the first place, to make such revision possible.) Very seldom can you write a good essay in only one draft. On the other hand, a total of four or five or six drafts may be a sign of time wasted just recopying, not revising. You can often reach a point at least close to your best writing performance in two or three real drafts. In practice you might produce a discovery draft, cover it with revisions, then recopy all this into a second draft, cover it with editing, then recopy all this into your good version to hand in (but not until you proofread even it).

When do you reach the journey's end? You will know when you get there. It is the point where your response to a significant topic has become so direct, so exact, so forceful, that at last you know exactly what you think. It is clear that you were writing for others, but at this moment it is even clearer that you were writing for yourself.

Canapress Photo Service.

" 'You're selling tickets,' I said. 'You're a gate attraction now — not some bum who only can skate and shoot and the rest of it. Your profanity is beautiful.' "
— Gary Lautens, "Man, You're a Great Player!"

Narration

And then. . . .

Telling a story, or narrating, is one of the most appealing and natural ways
to convey information. Every time you tell a joke, trade gossip, invent a
ghost story, or tell a friend what you did on the weekend, you are
narrating. In both speech and writing, telling a story can be the most
direct way to make a point. If your idea or opinion was formed by your
experience, a clear account of that experience will often help people to
understand and even to accept your point.

How could a soldier explain the terrors of a shelling attack better than
by narrating the experience of it? Charles Yale Harrison narrates the third
selection of this chapter, "In the Trenches." He might have constructed a
logical argument to make his point. But instead he tells us how the blast
threw him into the air, how the ground heaved, how he breathed the
smoke and tasted his own blood. As his readers, we tend to identify with
him, share his experience, and, most important of all, understand his
point.

In some ways narrating is easy. The only research Harrison required
was his own experience. And his basic plan of organization was no more

complicated than the chronological order in which the events occurred. (A flashback to the past or a glance at the future may intervene, but basically a narrative is the easiest of all writing to organize.) Yet a narrative, like any other form of writing, is built on choices.

Choice of scope: Time stretches infinitely toward both the past and future — but where does your narrative most logically begin and end? Include only the part or parts that best illustrate your point. If facts about the past or future are needed, sketch them in with a few words of explanation.

Choice of details: Which details will contribute to the main point? Reject the trivial ones and seek those that represent your dominant impression or idea. Which details are most vivid? Reject the weak ones and select those that help the reader to see, hear, feel, smell, or taste — in other words, those that most encourage the reader to *experience* the events.

Choice of connections: Readers like to be "swept along" by a narrative. How is this effect achieved? Partly by an economical use of words, and partly by the use of time signals. Like road signs for the motorist, the words "at first," "next," "then," "immediately," "suddenly," "later," "finally," and "at last" show the way and encourage progress. Use these words, and others like them, wherever they fit. Choose carefully, making the right signals help to build your effect.

So far we have discussed only the first-person narrative. There are many advantages to writing about yourself. You know your subject well (in fact, is there any subject that you know better?), yet in writing about yourself you may come to new understandings of your ideas and actions. You are vitally interested in your subject and thus will be motivated to do your best in writing about it. And finally, your reader may appreciate the authenticity of a story told by the very person who experienced the event.

But it is not always possible or even desirable to limit the subject to oneself. In choosing the third-person narrative, which tells the actions of others, the writer opens up a vast area of possibilities. Only through writing about others can one discuss past eras, places one has never visited, and events one has never experienced. In the second part of this chapter, Donald Creighton uses archaeological and historical evidence to write about the Vikings, and Gary Lautens consults his imagination to produce a narrative in its freest form, fiction.

Note: Many authors in later chapters combine narration with other ways to develop their material. For more examples, see these selections:

George Gabori

Coming of Age in Putnok

Translated from the Hungarian by Eric Johnson with George Faludy

George Gabori (pronounced Gábori) runs a cab company in Toronto. But like many immigrants to this country, he has a past that he will not soon forget. Gabori was born in 1924 to a Jewish family in the village of Putnok, Hungary. His childhood was happy but short, for when the Germans occupied Hungary and threatened the existence of the Jews, he joined the resistance. He led daring sabotage raids on railyards and docks until the Gestapo sent him, still a teenager, to a concentration camp. Things did not improve when the Russians drove out the Germans; soon after his release from a Nazi camp, he found himself breaking rocks in a notorious Soviet labour camp. Always outspoken, Gabori played a part in the 1956 revolution, then escaped from Hungary and eventually wrote his memoirs in Hungarian. With the help of Hungarian poet George Faludy, Eric Johnson condensed and translated the enormous manuscript, and it was published in 1981. Since then, When Evils Were Most Free *has become a minor Canadian classic. Our selection is its opening passage.*

1   When I was nine years old my father, victorious after a long argument with my grandfather, took me out of our town's only *cheder* and enrolled me in its only public school. Overnight I was transported from the world of Hebrew letters and monotonously repeated texts to the still stranger world of Hungarian letters, patriotic slogans and walls covered with maps.

2   Grandfather rolled his eyes and predicted trouble, but it seemed he was wrong. I sat beside a boy my own age named Tivadar, a gentile — everybody was a gentile in that school except me. Tivadar and I got along famously until, after two or three weeks, he approached me in the schoolyard one day and asked me if it was true what the others were saying, that "we" had murdered Jesus.

3   Strange to tell — for this was 1933 and we were in Hungary — I had never heard about this historical episode, and I left Tivadar amicably enough, promising to ask my father about it. We met again the next morning and I told him what I had learned: that the Romans had killed

4

Jesus, and that anyway Jesus had been a Jew, like me, so what did it matter to the Christians?

"That's not true," said Tivadar menacingly.   4

"My father does not lie," I replied.   5

By now a crowd had gathered around us and there was nothing for it   6 but to fight it out. There were cheers and laughter as Tivadar hit me in the nose before I got my jacket off. It was not the first time I had tasted my own blood, but it was the first time a Christian had made it flow. Tivadar was flushed with pleasure and excitement at the applause and not at all expecting it when I lashed out with my fist and sent him sprawling backward on the cobbles. The crowd of boys groaned and shouted to Tivadar to get up and kill the Jew, but poor Tivadar did not move. Frightened, I grabbed my jacket and shoved my way through the crowd stunned into silence by this overturning of the laws of nature.

They were silent at home too when I told them what had happened.   7 My father sent for me from his office in the afternoon, and I entered cap in hand. He always wore a braided Slovak jacket at work and looked more like a peasant than a Jewish wine merchant.

"Well, who started it?" asked my father, wearing an expression I had   8 never seen on his face before. I was not at all frightened.

"He did. I told him what you said about Jesus and he challenged   9 me."

My father clamped his teeth on his cigar and nodded, looking right   10 through me.

"Jews don't fight," he finally said.   11

"Then why did you put me in a Christian school?" I asked in a loud,   12 outraged whine.

"That's why I put you there, my son," he said at last, then swept me up   13 and kissed me on the forehead. "You're learning fast; only next time don't hit him quite so hard."

Then he sent me out quickly and I stopped on the landing, startled to   14 hear loud, whooping, solitary laughter coming out of my father's office.

ΔΔΔΔΔΔΔΔΔΔΔΔΔΔΔΔΔΔΔΔΔΔΔΔΔΔΔΔΔΔΔΔΔΔΔΔΔΔΔΔΔΔΔΔΔΔΔΔΔΔΔΔΔΔΔΔΔΔΔΔΔΔΔΔ

Further Reading:

George Gabori, *When Evils Were Most Free*
George Faludy, *My Happy Days in Hell*

Structure:

1. What is the most basic pattern by which this selection is organized?

2. Point out at least ten words or phrases that signal the flow of time in this narrative.

3. Reread the first paragraph carefully. Has Gabori given us a good background to the selection? Name every fact that this introduction reveals about the setting and about the author.

Style:

1. How economical or wasteful of words is this opening passage of George Gabori's autobiography? After reading it, how well do you think you know the author and his times? Could you predict with confidence anything of his character or fate as an adult? Does this opening selection make you feel like reading the rest of the book? Why or why not?

2. Gabori's book, *When Evils Were Most Free*, is a translated and condensed version of the Hungarian original. To what extent does this fact separate us from the author's thoughts? How exact can a translation be? If you yourself speak two languages, how precisely can you express sayings from one in the other? To what extent can Gabori's translator, Eric Johnson, be thought of as the author of this selection?

3. Gabori states in paragraph 6, "It was not the first time I had tasted my own blood. . . ." Is this image effective? If so, why?

4. When Gabori refers to "poor Tivadar" (par. 6), is the word "poor" used in a special sense? What is Gabori really saying?

Ideas for Discussion and Writing:

1. What is the "overturning of the laws of nature" to which Gabori refers at the end of paragraph 6?

2. Was Gabori's father right in moving the boy from a Hebrew *cheder* to a public school? In disproving the idea that "Jews don't fight" (par. 11), has the boy learned a worthwhile lesson? Or has he merely imitated the worst traits of his opponents, thereby becoming like them?

3. Every ethnic group in Canada — including the English Canadians — is a minority. Has your minority suffered any form of persecution in Canada? If you have been a victim, narrate an actual incident and your reaction to it. Give plentiful details, as Gabori does.

4. What are autobiographies for? What do you think writing your own life story would do for you? What might your story do for others?

5. **PROCESS IN WRITING:** *Write a chapter of your own autobiography.*

Select one *key incident in your life, then freewrite on it for at least five minutes. Look over what you have produced, keep the best of it, and from this write your first draft. Have you begun and ended at just the right places, narrating the event itself but omitting parts that don't matter? Strengthen the next draft with more* IMAGES *and examples, following Gabori's example. Now share your story with a small group of classmates, and adjust anything that does not communicate with this audience. Finally, read your* narrative *aloud, with expression, to the whole class.*

Note: See also the Topics for Writing at the end of this chapter.

Sylvia Fraser

My Other Self*

*"Writing is healing," says Sylvia Fraser. Born in 1935 in Hamilton, Ontario, Fraser
by the 1980s had become an award-winning journalist and the author of five novels
(Pandora, 1972; The Candy Factory, 1975; A Casual Affair, 1978; The
Emperor's Virgin, 1980; and Berlin Solstice, 1984). But signs of trouble had
also appeared. Her seemingly happy marriage had fallen apart. Her fiction grew
darker in vision and increasingly filled with sexual violence. Then the dam broke.
Psychotherapy uncovered what Fraser's "other self" had known for decades: that from
her kindergarten year almost until the end of high school, her father had abused her
sexually. Now it was clear how her novel Berlin Solstice had acquired its intimate
and chilling insight into Nazi Germany. As Fraser put it, "Being victimized and
essentially tortured by my father, I identified with the Jews. In trying to understand
how the Germans could have done what they did, I was trying to understand my
father — and I was preparing myself for my own truth" (Globe and Mail, June 4,
1988). The memoir that followed, My Father's House (1987), startled both the
critics and the public with its honesty, clarity of style, and emotional force. The book
not only helped to "heal" its author, but ignited public debate on a hidden social
problem, encouraging many other incest victims to deal with their past. From this book
comes our selection, which dramatizes the victim's "other self" trying to emerge.*

1   The ice at Gage Park is best in the morning when it's flint-hard and
glass-smooth. All is possible. You carve out circles and eights, and
nothing exists until you put it there. Sometimes you just race around the
rink, your legs sliding like they're on elastic bands, with your breath
whistling through your teeth like steam from a locomotive, faster and
faster.

2   Soon it's noon. The rink fills with kids in red and blue parkas playing
tag or crack the whip.

3   "Hi!" It's Joe Baker from school. "Wanna skate?"

4   I prefer to play tag, but I don't want to hurt Joe's feelings and, besides,
if I say no to him, maybe Perry Lord won't ask me. Such delicate weights

---

*Editor's title.

and balances are the stuff of predating, as I am coming to know it. Giving my hand to Joe with a bright paste-on smile, I slow my racing pace to his stodgy rhythm. The sound system squawks out "Oh, How We Danced on the Night We Were Wed" as we skate around and around, like the needle on the record. Joe's silence rattles me. I make chattery conversation. "Did you see The Thing from the Deep?"

By bad luck, the record never ends. The needle hits a crack, repeats "we   5
vowed our true love we vowed our true love we vowed our true love," then jerks into "Don't Fence Me In." Now Joe links arms, forcing me to even greater intimacy and an even slower beat, *and making my other self very, very nervous. She cannot bear to be held or confined.* The game of tag is breaking up. Joe speaks his only sentence, and it is a lethal one. "Can I ah take you home if ah you're not doing anything?"

At the word "home" a cold shiver passes through me. I ransack my   6
head for an explanation for the unpleasant way I am feeling and, failing that, an excuse. "I'll check with Arlene. We came together."

The clubhouse is crowded and noisy and steamy, as always. We jostle   7
for a place on the splintery benches closest to the wood stove. The air stinks of charred wool — someone's icy mittens left too long on top. Joe helps me off with my skates, then unlaces his own while I inform Arlene. "Joe wants to take me home."

"He's cute. You have all the luck."   8

I study Joe through the lens of Arlene's enthusiasm: brown cowlick in   9
wet spikes from his cap, earnest face bent over the task of knotting skate laces. Cute? Now that I know how I'm supposed to feel, I am reassured. Well, maybe.

We leave the rink just as the gang takes off in a gossipy pinwheel for the   10
Kozy Korner. I think about suggesting we go too, but I'm afraid Joe doesn't have any money and I don't want to seem like a gold digger. Perry Lord tosses a snowball at Cooky Castle but hits Arlene instead. Tonya Philpott zings one back overhand, the way a boy would. I yearn to take up the challenge, but being with a boy obliges me to conform to more ladylike standards. Trapped, I stick my fists in my pockets.

Crunch crunch crunch. Skates knotted over Joe's shoulder, we trudge   11
through the chalky snow. I've already told Joe the plot of The Thing from the Deep, and since I saw it uptown it wasn't a double feature. The silence lengthens with the shadows. Joe doesn't seem to mind. I do.

"Arlene says you got a hundred in arithmetic."   12

"Yeah. So did you."   13

"Yeah. But our test was easier."   14

I make the mistake of taking my hand out of my pocket to brush a   15
snowflake. Joe commandeers it. *My other self panics.* How long before I can brush another snowflake and get it back without seeming rude? As I am

working out the etiquette of this, two dogs rush the season by attempting to "do it" on the path in front of us. *My other self slips toward hysteria.* I burst into giggles. The blood rises up Joe's protruding ears. He fumbles with his backside: "Are you laughing at the rip in my ski pants?"

16   "No, it isn't that." But I can't stop giggling.

17   "Joker Nash cut it with his skate."

18   "Honest, I didn't even notice." I stifle more giggles in a sneeze. "Ah-choo !"

19   We are approaching my house. The giggles stop. Now my anxiety grows so intense I'm afraid I'll faint. Snatching my hand from Joe's, I pick up a stick and drag it ping ping ping along the fence around St. Cecilia's Home the way I used to as a kid, pretending this is the most important thing in the world. How can I let you hold my hand when I am busy doing this?

20   We turn the corner. Now I see it — a sour-cream frame listing with snow like a milk bottle with the cap frozen off. *Home.* I stop, rooted to the spot. For reasons I can't explain, it's essential that Joe go no farther. I reach for my skates. "I live only a couple of doors away."

21   "I don't mind. I'll carry them to the — "

22   "No!" I yank the skates from Joe's neck, almost beheading him. "I've got to go — by myself."

23   Again Joe blushes from his neck through his ears. "Is it because of the rip in my ski pants? You don't want your parents to see — "

24   "No!" Then more humanely: "Honest. It has nothing to do with you." Pushing past him, I sprint for my father's house, clearing the steps in a single bound. As I open the storm door, the wind catches it.

25   "Don't slam the door!" roars my father from his armchair.

26   *My other self bursts into hysterical weeping.*

27   "What's wrong?" asks my mother.

28   Again, I find myself overcome by an emotion for which I must find a reason. Hurling my skates at her feet, I shout: "Why do I have to wear these old things? They hurt my feet."

29   Wiping her hands on her apron, my mother rallies. "Those skates were new last winter."

30   "Secondhand from Amity. You said I could have new skates for Christmas."

31   "You needed other things." By now I'm racked with weeping I can't control. Not about the skates, though I hear a voice I hardly recognize go on and on about them. "I hate these skates." Rage pours out of me like lava, devastating everything in its path. It flows around my father, implacable in his asbestos armchair.

32   It's a relief to be sent upstairs without supper. Flinging myself onto my

bed, I pound the pillow till my body is seized with convulsions, *releasing the rage my other self can no longer control.*

ΔΔΔΔΔΔΔΔΔΔΔΔΔΔΔΔΔΔΔΔΔΔΔΔΔΔΔΔΔΔΔΔΔΔΔΔΔΔΔΔΔΔΔΔΔΔΔΔΔΔΔΔΔΔΔΔΔΔ

Further Reading:

Sylvia Fraser,
> *My Father's House*
> *Pandora*
> *Berlin Solstice*

Ruth Kempe, *The Common Secret: Sexual Abuse of Children and Adolescents*

Structure:

1. Does Sylvia Fraser *narrate* "My Other Self" in straight chronological order?
2. Fraser opens this sequence with ice (par. 1) and closes it with lava (par. 31). Explain how her progression of IMAGES parallels her progression of emotion. Explain also how these progressions add force to her narrative.
3. What does Fraser achieve by putting all references to her "other self" in italics?

Style:

1. Like Charles Yale Harrison later in this chapter, Fraser narrates in the present tense. Why? Would "My Other Self" have been stronger or weaker in the past tense? Why? Have you ever narrated in the present tense?
2. Where does Fraser use IMAGES that appeal to our senses of sight, touch, hearing, and smell? Point out one good example of each.
3. In paragraph 9 our narrator says, "I study Joe through the lens of Arlene's enthusiasm. . . ." Point out at least two more METAPHORS in this selection. In paragraph 31 she says, "Rage pours out of me like lava. . . ." Point out at least two more SIMILES. What do these FIGURES OF SPEECH contribute to the total effect?

Ideas for Discussion and Writing:

1. Fraser has stated in an interview, "I think of child abuse as being the AIDS of the emotional world. You cripple that child's emotional system so it can't deal with life" (*Globe and Mail*, June

4, 1988). Point out all the ways in which our selection dramatizes her comment.

2. Why does Fraser refer to her "other self" in the third person, as "she"? What does this usage seem to imply about young Fraser's mental state?

3. Some studies have suggested that sexual abuse has become an epidemic, with as many as one out of every three or four children victimized (*Globe and Mail*, April 15, 1989). Why does it happen? What could be done to reduce the incidence of these crimes? To rehabilitate the victims? To rehabilitate the offenders?

4. Fraser has linked her fascination with the Holocaust to her feelings about her father (see the introduction to this selection). To what extent do you believe our relationship to our parents becomes a model for our perceptions of the world? For example, do children of authoritarian parents grow up to resent other authority in the form of employers, police, or government?

5. If you have read the previous narrative, "Coming of Age in Putnok," compare the forces of suppression experienced by young George Gabori and by Sylvia Fraser.

6. Have you shared Fraser's experience of writing as healing? Analyze how the process might occur when we write an angry letter to tear up, when we send a letter to the editor, when we write a poem, or when we keep a personal journal.

7. PROCESS IN WRITING: *Think of an occasion when you got carried away by your own emotions. Experience it again by freewriting, never stopping the motion of your pen for several minutes. Use the present tense, as Fraser does, to heighten the immediacy of your account. Now narrate a first draft, incorporating the best of your prewriting. In the next draft add more SENSE IMAGES and FIGURES OF SPEECH (remembering the "ice" and the "lava" of "My Other Self"). Have you moved the action along with time signals such as "then," "next," "suddenly," or "at last"? Have you trimmed out deadwood? If you report dialogue, have you used quotation marks, and have you begun a new paragraph for each change of speaker? Finally, test your prose aloud before writing the final version.*

Note: See also the Topics for Writing at the end of this chapter.

Charles Yale Harrison

In the Trenches

Charles Yale Harrison (1898–1954) was born in Philadelphia and grew up in Montreal. His independent spirit revealed itself early: in grade four he condemned Shakespeare's The Merchant of Venice *as anti-Semitic, and when his teacher beat him he quit school. At 16 he went to work for the* Montreal Star *and at 18 joined the Canadian army. As a machine gunner in France and Belgium during 1917 and 1918, Harrison witnessed the gruesome front-line scenes he was later to describe in fiction. He was wounded at Amiens and decorated for bravery in action. After the war Harrison returned to Montreal but soon left for New York, where he began a career in public relations for the labour movement and for numerous humanitarian causes. He also wrote several books, both nonfiction and fiction. By far the best is* Generals Die in Bed, *an account of trench warfare that shocked the public and became the best seller of 1930. Spare in style, biting and vivid, this autobiographical novel was described by the* New York Evening Post *as "the best of the war books." From it comes our selection.*

We leave the piles of rubble that was once a little Flemish peasant town and wind our way, in Indian file, up through the muddy communication trench. In the dark we stumble against the sides of the trench and tear our hands and clothing on the bits of embedded barbed wire that runs through the earth here as though it were a geological deposit. 1

Fry, who is suffering with his feet, keeps slipping into holes and crawling out, all the way up. I can hear him coughing and panting behind me. 2

I hear him slither into a water-filled hole. It has a green scum on it. Brown and I fish him out. 3

"I can't go any farther," he wheezes. "Let me lie here, I'll come on later." 4

We block the narrow trench and the oncoming men stumble on us, banging their equipment and mess tins on the sides of the ditch. Some trip over us. They curse under their breaths. 5

6   Our captain, Clark, pushes his way through the mess. He is an Imperial, an Englishman, and glories in his authority.

7   "So it's you again," he shouts. "Come on, get up. Cold feet, eh, getting near the line?"

8   Fry mumbles something indistinctly. I, too, offer an explanation. Clark ignores me.

9   "Get up, you're holding up the line," he says to Fry.

10   Fry does not move.

11   "No wonder we're losing the bloody war," Clark says loudly. The men standing near-by laugh. Encouraged by his success, the captain continues:

12   "Here, sergeant, stick a bayonet up his behind — that'll make him move." A few of us help Fry to his feet, and somehow we manage to keep him going.

13   We proceed cautiously, heeding the warnings of those ahead of us. At last we reach our positions.

ΔΔΔ

14   It is midnight when we arrive at our positions. The men we are relieving give us a few instructions and leave quickly, glad to get out.

15   It is September and the night is warm. Not a sound disturbs the quiet. Somewhere away far to our right we hear the faint sound of continuous thunder. The exertion of the trip up the line has made us sweaty and tired. We slip most of our accouterments off and lean against the parados. We have been warned that the enemy is but a few hundred yards off, so we speak in whispers. It is perfectly still. I remember nights like this in the Laurentians. The harvest moon rides overhead.

16   Our sergeant, Johnson, appears around the corner of the bay, stealthily like a ghost. He gives us instructions:

17   "One man up on sentry duty! Keep your gun covered with the rubber sheet! No smoking!"

18   He hurries on to the next bay. Fry mounts the step and peers into No Man's Land. He is rested now and says that if he can only get a good pair of boots he will be happy. He has taken his boots off and stands in his stockinged feet. He shows us where his heel is cut. His boots do not fit. The sock is wet with blood. He wants to take his turn at sentry duty first so that he can rest later on. We agree.

19   Cleary and I sit on the firing-step and talk quietly.

20   "So this is war."

21   "Quiet."

22   "Yes, just like the country back home, eh?

23   We talk of the trench; how we can make it more comfortable.

24   We light cigarettes against orders and cup our hands around them to

hide the glow. We sit thinking. Fry stands motionless with his steel helmet shoved down almost over his eyes. He leans against the parapet motionless. There is a quiet dignity about his posture. I remember what we were told at the base about falling asleep on sentry duty. I nudge his leg. He grunts.

"Asleep?" I whisper. 25

"No," he answers, "I'm all right." 26

"What do you see?" 27

"Nothing. Wire and posts." 28

"Tired?" 29

"I'm all right." 30

The sergeant reappears after a while. We squinch our cigarettes. 31

"Everything O.K. here?" 32

I nod. 33

"Look out over there. They got the range on us. Watch out." 34

We light another cigarette. We continue our aimless talk. 35

"I wonder what St. Catherine Street looks like — " 36

"Same old thing, I suppose — stores, whores, theaters — " 37

"Like to be there just the same — " 38

"Me too." 39

We sit and puff our fags for half a minute or so. 40

I try to imagine what Montreal looks like. The images are murky. All 41
that is unreality. The trench, Cleary, Fry, the moon overhead — this is real.

In his corner of the bay Fry is beginning to move from one foot to 42
another. It is time to relieve him. He steps down and I take his place. I look into the wilderness of posts and wire in front of me.

After a while my eyes begin to water. I see the whole army of wire posts 43
begin to move like a silent host towards me.

I blink my eyes and they halt. 44

I doze a little and come to with a jerk. 45

So this is war, I say to myself again for the hundredth time. Down on 46
the firing-step the boys are sitting like dead men. The thunder to the right has died down. There is absolutely no sound.

I try to imagine how an action would start. I try to fancy the 47
preliminary bombardment. I remember all the precautions one has to take to protect one's life. Fall flat on your belly, we had been told time and time again. The shriek of the shell, the instructor in trench warfare said, was no warning because the shell traveled faster than its sound. First, he had said, came the explosion of the shell — then came the shriek and then you hear the firing of the gun. . . .

From the stories I heard from veterans and from newspaper reports I 48
conjure up a picture of an imaginary action. I see myself getting the Lewis

gun in position. I see it spurting darts of flame into the night. I hear the roar of battle. I feel elated. Then I try to fancy the horrors of the battle. I see Cleary, Fry and Brown stretched out on the firing-step. They are stiff and their faces are white and set in the stillness of death. Only I remain alive.

49   An inaudible movement in front of me pulls me out of the dream. I look down and see Fry massaging his feet. All is still. The moon sets slowly and everything becomes dark.

50   The sergeant comes into the bay again and whispers to me:

51   "Keep your eyes open now — they might come over on a raid now that it's dark. The wire's cut over there — " He points a little to my right.

52   I stand staring into the darkness. Everything moves rapidly again as I stare. I look away for a moment and the illusion ceases.

53   Something leaps towards my face.

54   I jerk back, afraid.

55   Instinctively I feel for my rifle in the corner of the bay.

56   It is a rat.

57   It is as large as a tom-cat. It is three feet away from my face and it looks steadily at me with its two staring, beady eyes. It is fat. Its long tapering tail curves away from its padded hindquarters. There is still a little light from the stars and this light shines faintly on its sleek skin. With a darting movement it disappears. I remember with a cold feeling that it was fat, and why.

58   Cleary taps my shoulder. It is time to be relieved.

△△△

59   Over in the German lines I hear quick, sharp reports. Then the red-tailed comets of the *minenwerfer*° sail high in the air, making parabolas of red light as they come towards us. They look pretty, like the fireworks when we left Montreal. The sergeant rushes into the bay of the trench, breathless. "Minnies," he shouts, and dashes on.

60   In that instant there is a terrific roar directly behind us.

61   The night whistles and flashes red.

62   The trench rocks and sways.

63   Mud and earth leap into the air, come down upon us in heaps.

64   We throw ourselves upon our faces, clawing our nails into the soft earth in the bottom of the trench.

65   Another!

66   This one crashes to splinters about twenty feet in front of the bay.

67   Part of the parapet caves in.

°*minenwerfer*: mine-throwing trench mortars.

We try to burrow into the ground like frightened rats.   68

The shattering explosions splinter the air in a million fragments. I taste   69
salty liquid on my lips. My nose is bleeding from the force of the
detonations.

SOS flares go up along our front calling for help from our artillery. The   70
signals sail into the air and explode, giving forth showers of red, white and
blue lights held aloft by a silken parachute.

The sky is lit by hundreds of fancy fireworks like a night carnival.   71

The air shrieks and cat-calls.   72

Still they come.   73

I am terrified. I hug the earth, digging my fingers into every crevice,   74
every hole.

A blinding flash and an exploding howl a few feet in front of the   75
trench.

My bowels liquefy.   76

Acrid smoke bites the throat, parches the mouth. I am beyond mere   77
fright. I am frozen with an insane fear that keeps me cowering in the
bottom of the trench. I lie flat on my belly, waiting. . . .

Suddenly it stops.   78

The fire lifts and passes over us to the trenches in the rear.   79

We lie still, unable to move. Fear has robbed us of the power to act. I   80
hear Fry whimpering near me. I crawl over to him with great effort. He is
half covered with earth and debris. We begin to dig him out.

To our right they have started to shell the front lines. It is about half a   81
mile away. We do not care. *We* are safe.

Without warning it starts again.   82

The air screams and howls like an insane woman.   83

We are getting it in earnest now. Again we throw ourselves face   84
downward on the bottom of the trench and grovel like savages before this
demoniac frenzy.

The concussion of the explosions batters against us.   85

I am knocked breathless.   86

I recover and hear the roar of the bombardment.   87

It screams and rages and boils like an angry sea. I feel a prickly   88
sensation behind my eyeballs.

A shell lands with a monster shriek in the next bay. The concussion rolls   89
me over on my back. I see the stars shining serenely above us. Another
lands in the same place. Suddenly the stars revolve. I land on my
shoulder. I have been tossed into the air.

I begin to pray.   90

"God — God — please. . ."   91

I remember that I do not believe in God. Insane thoughts race through   92
my brain. I want to catch hold of something, something that will explain

this mad fury, this maniacal congealed hatred that pours down on our heads. I can find nothing to console me, nothing to appease my terror. I know that hundreds of men are standing a mile or two from me pulling gun-lanyards, blowing us to smithereens. I know that and nothing else.

93   I begin to cough. The smoke is thick. It rolls in heavy clouds over the trench, blurring the stabbing lights of the explosions.

94   A shell bursts near the parapet.

95   Fragments smack the sandbags like a merciless shower of steel hail.

96   A piece of mud flies into my mouth. It is cool and refreshing. It tastes earthy.

97   Suddenly it stops again.

98   I bury my face in the cool, damp earth. I want to weep. But I am too weak and shaken for tears.

99   We lie still, waiting. . . .

ΔΔΔΔΔΔΔΔΔΔΔΔΔΔΔΔΔΔΔΔΔΔΔΔΔΔΔΔΔΔΔΔΔΔΔΔΔΔΔΔΔΔΔΔΔΔΔΔΔΔΔΔΔΔΔΔΔΔΔΔ

Further Reading:

Charles Yale Harrison, *Generals Die in Bed*
Erich Maria Remarque, *All Quiet on the Western Front* (novel)
Ernest Hemingway, *A Farewell to Arms* (novel)
Timothy Findley, *The Wars* (novel)
Heather Robertson, ed., *A Terrible Beauty: The Art of Canada at War*

Structure:

1. Does this narrative ever deviate from chronological order? If so, where and how?
2. This selection contains a great many short paragraphs, some only a word or two long. Examine paragraphs 25–30, 53–56, and 60–68, determining in each passage why the paragraphs are so short.
3. This account of an artillery attack ends with the words "We lie still, waiting. . . ." Is the ending effective, and if so, how?

Style:

1. What degree of CONCISENESS has Harrison achieved in this selection?
2. Discuss the horror of this statement about the rat and how

Harrison achieves such horror in so few words: "I remember with a cold feeling that it was fat, and why" (par. 57).

3. An apparently simple account of events can sometimes carry great power. Discuss the sources of power in paragraph 89: "A shell lands with a monster shriek in the next bay. The concussion rolls me over on my back. I see the stars shining serenely above us. Another lands in the same place. Suddenly the stars revolve. I land on my shoulder. I have been tossed into the air."

4. Harrison makes war come alive for us by attacking our five senses. Find at least one example each of a strong appeal to our senses of sight, hearing, touch, taste, and smell.

5. This narrative is filled with FIGURES OF SPEECH. Point out at least one good SIMILE and one good METAPHOR.

6. Why is "In the Trenches" told in the present tense, even though the book in which it appeared was published years after the war?

Ideas for Discussion and Writing:

1. Our narrator relates his first experience of war. Has it taught him anything?

2. Have you read books or seen films that show war in a positive light? Name them. In what ways does "In the Trenches" differ from those accounts?

3. "In the Trenches" is part of a book entitled *Generals Die in Bed.* Discuss the implications of this title.

4. In paragraph 48, our narrator imagines what the attack will be like: "I see Cleary, Fry and Brown stretched out on the firing-step. They are stiff and their faces are white and set in the stillness of death. Only I remain alive." Do many people think this way, expecting to survive though others may not? Do we secretly feel immortal, despite knowing intellectually that we are not? If so, can you think of reasons why?

5. If you have read "Coming of Age in Putnok," compare the conflict described by George Gabori with that described by Harrison. Does hostility between individuals in any way contribute to hostility between nations?

6. PROCESS IN WRITING: *If you have been to war as our narrator has, or if you have been through another dangerous or frightening experience that taught you something, tell the story in a narrative, using chronological order and the present tense, as Harrison does. In your second draft, develop more fully your appeals to at least three of the five senses: sight,*

hearing, touch, taste, and smell. Then cut out every word of deadwood as you develop your final draft.

Note: See also the Topics for Writing at the end of this chapter.

Donald Creighton

The Western Way*

Donald Creighton (1902–1979) has been one of Canada's most widely read historians. He was born in Toronto, held numerous degrees both earned and honorary, had a distinguished career as history professor at the University of Toronto from 1927 to 1970, and wrote numerous and varied works of history that brought him both scholarly and popular acclaim. The most important of these are The Commercial Empire of the St. Lawrence *(1937); his massive biography in two volumes,* John A. Macdonald: The Young Politician *(1952) and* John A. Macdonald: The Old Chieftain *(1955); and* The Forked Road: Canada 1939–1957 *(1976). In his later years Creighton was seen by some as overly conservative, writing history that favoured the powerful and slighted the weak, while he was seen by others as anti-American, anti-Quebec, and overly nationalistic. But if his interpretation was at times controversial, his research was massive and solid. Others criticized him for his style, often so vivid and dramatic that it seemed more typical of fiction than of history. But it is this very style that enabled the general public as well as specialists to read and appreciate his work. Creighton's colourful and at times even racy prose is nowhere better displayed than in our selection, which appeared in* Canada: The Heroic Beginnings *(1974), a book aimed at the general public.*

I t was the Norsemen who first fought their way westward across the North Atlantic and gained the earliest footholds on the shore of what is now Canada. Their precarious lodgement at the edge of the New World was the ultimate achievement of a vast expansion of the Scandinavian peoples. Driven forth by the pressure of over-population and the hope of spacious lands and easy riches, the Vikings of Norway and Denmark first burst out of their restricted homelands towards the end of the eighth century. Their assault on western Europe and the islands beyond, maintained for more than 200 years of raids, pillage, conquest, and colonization, was the greatest movement of people that the West had known since the Germanic barbarians had overwhelmed the Roman Empire five centuries earlier. The Franks and the Goths had travelled

1

*Editor's title.

westward by land; but the Vikings, "the dark red seabirds", came by sea, and a large part of the surprise and terror of their coming lay in the swift mobility of their ships.

2   Their typical warship, the Viking "long-ship", was a long, low, graceful vessel, clinker-built with overlapping planks of oak, a single, square, brightly coloured sail, and carved and ornamented dragon prows. Sixty or seventy warriors, their shields hung on the bulwarks of the vessels, their barbaric costumes adorned with brooches and bracelets, would man the long-ship, sail or row it across the North Sea or down the Channel, beach it on some shore or drive it up an estuary or river, and then, with bow and sword and battle-axe, descend upon the countryside and its helpless villages.

3   These savage pirates and marauders followed two main routes. One ran north-westward to Scotland, to the Orkney, Shetland, and Faroe Islands, and beyond to Iceland. The other led south-westward towards England, the Netherlands, France, Spain, and Portugal and into the Mediterranean. The second route, which was soon distinguished by such Viking triumphs as the founding of the Danelaw in England and the conquest of Normandy in France, became the more frequented and the more famous of the two; but the north-west route, the "western way" as it was called, which swept in a great arc across the North Atlantic and ended in North America, had its own special interest and importance.

4   Although almost everything the Vikings did was marred by violence and stained with blood, the advance along the "western way" was marked, not so much by warfare and conquest, as by discovery and colonization. The Norwegians had found and peacefully settled the Orkney, Shetland, and Faroe Islands before the violent Viking onslaught on western Europe began; and during the latter part of the ninth century, they discovered and occupied Iceland, a volcanic island, much of it a desolate wilderness of lava and glacier. Like the long-ships, the ships of these Norwegian colonists were clinker-built, but in other respects they differed radically from the Viking war vessels; they were cargo boats, decked fore and aft, with a wide beam and a deep draft, and roomy enough to carry passengers, animals, and cargo, as well as crew. Unlike the ornately garbed warriors who terrorized England and Europe, the mariners of the "western way" wore plain hooded gowns made of a coarse woollen cloth called wadmal, and carried sleeping bags of sheepskin or cowhide.

5   On good days, as one looked out from the west coast of Iceland, a faint line of mountains could be seen in the remote distance; and to Eric the Red, the violent son of a savage father, they offered both a way of escape and a promise of adventure. Thorwaldr, the father, outlawed from Norway for manslaughter, had fled to Iceland; Eric, outlawed in his turn

for homicide, determined to find his refuge in the unknown country to the west. In 982 he sailed west, discovered a huge ice-covered island, and wintered on its farther coast. He could not return home for good, nor did he want to: instead, he decided to found a colony on the land of his discovery. He called it Greenland, a boldly fraudulent advertisement intended to attract prospective immigrants; and in 986, triumphantly leading a fleet of twenty-four ships, he set sail again, reached the west coast of his island once more in safety, and laid the bases of two settlements.

Even yet the westward urge had not spent itself. The drive that had brought Thorwaldr to Iceland and Eric to Greenland was still strong and insistent enough to carry Leif, Eric's son, to the end of the "western way" and to the New World. About 1000, he captained a planned expedition to the west and south. He found first a barren land of flat rock and glacier, which he called Helluland (Flagstone Land), and then a very different country, heavily forested, with white sandy beaches, which he named Markland (Forestland). A strong north-east wind drove the ship on for two days; and finally, on the bright morning of the third, it brought the voyagers to a beautiful land, with ample pasture, and grape vines, and the biggest salmon they had ever seen. Leif called their discovery Vinland (Wineland), and there he and his men built houses and started a permanent settlement. The good reports they brought home stimulated the interest of the Greenlanders, and during the next fifteen years, there were several voyages to Vinland, two by Leif's brothers and one by his illegitimate daughter, Freydis, as ferocious a murderess as any in Viking history. There was at least an attempt at large-scale colonization, but in fact the settlement did not endure.

Helluland was probably the southern shore of Baffin Island, and there can be little doubt that Markland formed part of the Labrador coast. The location of Vinland is much more uncertain. The topographical indications in the Norse Sagas are confused and at times seemingly contradictory. Vinland, the beautiful land of the Greenlanders, has been located all the way from Newfoundland to New England; but until 1960, no archaeological evidence had been found to prove the truth of any of these conjectures. In that year, a Norwegian, Helge Ingstad, discovered the buried foundations of a number of pre-Columbian houses at L'Anse aux Meadows, on Epaves Bay, part of Sacred Bay, a much larger body of water, at the northern tip of Newfoundland.

Epaves Bay is a broad, gently curving bay facing the entrance to the Strait of Belle Isle and so shallow that at low tide it is dry a long way out from the shore. A wide, green, grassy plain, level or slightly undulating, springy to the step with peat turf, stretches away inland on every side. A rich variety of small bushes, plants, and grasses — mountain ash, prostrate juniper, iris, angelica, Labrador tea, blueberries, and partridge and bakeapple berries — covers the plain with a dense shaggy coat; and through it, ending in the bay, winds a tumultuous little river, picturesquely named the Black Duck Brook. A little way in from the shore, the land rises slightly in an ancient marine terrace; and along it, in a straggling line, lie the foundations, made of layers of turf, of eight houses of different sizes, and the remnants of boat sheds and of cooking and charcoal pits. Most of these sites, including the largest, where a structure of six rooms once stood, are north of Black Duck Brook; but one, which was evidently a smithy, is situated on the south side of the little river; and since bog iron is available near by, a Norse smith may have smelted ore here as well as worked iron. A Norse woman must have sat spinning in one of the rooms in the largest house, for a soapstone spindle whorl, of characteristic Norse design, was found there, as well as a bronze pin with a ring in its head and several iron rivets.

9   The Norse sagas date the discovery and occupation of Vinland at the beginning of the eleventh century, and radio carbon tests place the ruins at L'Anse aux Meadows in approximately the same period. The L'Anse aux Meadows site may not be Vinland; but there can be no doubt that the Norse men and women who built and inhabited these houses were among the first Europeans who ever lived in North America.

ΔΔΔΔΔΔΔΔΔΔΔΔΔΔΔΔΔΔΔΔΔΔΔΔΔΔΔΔΔΔΔΔΔΔΔΔΔΔΔΔΔΔΔΔΔΔΔΔΔΔΔΔΔΔΔΔΔ

Further Reading:

Donald Creighton, *Canada: The Heroic Beginnings*
Helge Ingstad, *Westward to Vinland*
Farley Mowat, *Westviking: The Ancient Norse in Greenland and North America*

Structure:

1. Why does Creighton discuss the violence of Viking expansion in Europe before he describes in detail Viking expansion in the New World?
2. To what extent does this selection analyze the *causes* of Norse exploration and settlement along the "western way"? Name all the major causes identified by Creighton.
3. In what sense are paragraphs 1–4 a narrative? What is the story being narrated?
4. What is the main difference in focus between the opening

narrative and the narrative found in paragraphs 5 and 6?
5. In what sense do paragraphs 7–9 form a narrative?
6. Creighton's paragraphs are unusually clear in their organization and fully developed in their content. Examine especially paragraphs 3, 5, and 6: analyze how each develops the point stated in its opening "topic sentence."
7. What similarity do you find between the opening and the closing of this selection?

Style:

1. Our selection is typical of historical writing in its narrative form, but certainly not in its STYLE. Point out at least five passages which, in their vivid or even racy style, seem more typical of FICTION than of history.
2. Reread carefully the opening paragraph of this selection, then point out all the ways in which it appeals to the reader's interest.
3. In what way does the beginning of paragraph 5 appeal to the reader?
4. What effect is sought in the words "Leif, Eric's son" (par. 6)?
5. How long would Creighton's paragraphs be if you wrote them out? Do you ever write paragraphs as long as his? Should his be shorter? Why or why not?

Ideas for Discussion and Writing:

1. Name as many reasons as you can for the study of history.
2. Napoleon defined history as "a set of lies agreed upon." Oscar Wilde defined it as "gossip" and Henry Ford as "bunk." What motives do you think might lead some historians to falsify history? If falsification occurs, is it deliberate or unconscious? Can you think of an example of history as "bunk"?
3. Why do historians pay more attention to the "discovery" of the New World by Europeans than to the original discovery of the New World by Asians who crossed the Bering Strait to Alaska?
4. Both the Scandinavians and the French had colonized what is now Canada long before the British arrived. In what major ways can you imagine your present life would be different if the Vikings had established the dominant culture of our country? If the French had established it?
5. PROCESS IN WRITING: *Write a* narrative *history of one branch of your family, from your earliest known ancestor to yourself. First ask a parent or grandparent for facts, then arrange this information*

chronologically in a first draft. Check it over: Is everything in time order?
Do TRANSITIONS signal the movement from one generation to the next?
Do ancestors come alive through IMAGE and EXAMPLE? In your further
drafts, revise until these goals are met. If you realize that you lack
material, ask your source of information for more. Be sure to check
accuracy by showing that person at least one draft, and finally, give him
or her a good copy to keep.

Note: See also the Topics for Writing at the end of this chapter.

Gary Lautens

Man, You're a Great Player!

"An old English teacher of mine," writes Gary Lautens, "once said she'd drop dead if I ever made a living as a writer. Now, if she's a good sport, she'll keep her end of the bargain." In fact Lautens did go on to make his living by writing. Born in 1928 in Fort William, Ontario, he graduated from McMaster University in 1950 with a B.A. in history — then spent the next 13 years as a sports columnist with the Hamilton Spectator. *Moving to the* Toronto Star *in 1962, he wrote a column of zany humour which became so popular that selections from it were reprinted in books:* Laughing with Lautens *(1964),* Take My Family — Please! *(1980), and* No Sex Please . . . We're Married *(1983). In both 1981 and 1984 Lautens won the Leacock Medal for Humour. But the high point of his journalistic career was a period as executive managing editor of the* Toronto Star, *from 1982 to 1984. Our selection, from* Laughing with Lautens, *reflects Lautens' experience both as a sports writer and as a humourist.*

O ccasionally I run into sports figures at cocktail parties, on the street, or on their way to the bank.   1

"Nice game the other night," I said to an old hockey-player pal.   2

"Think so?" he replied.   3

"You've come a long way since I knew you as a junior."   4

"How's that?"   5

"Well, you high-stick better for one thing — and I think the way you clutch sweaters is really superb. You may be the best in the league."   6

He blushed modestly. "For a time," I confessed, "I never thought you'd get the hang of it."   7

"It wasn't easy," he confided. "It took practice and encouragement. You know something like spearing doesn't come naturally. It has to be developed."   8

"I'm not inclined to flattery but, in my book, you've got it made. You're a dirty player."   9

"Stop kidding."   10

"No, no," I insisted. "I'm not trying to butter you up. I mean it. When you broke in there were flashes of dirty play — but you weren't consistent.   11

That's the difference between a dirty player and merely a colourful one."

12   "I wish my father were alive to hear you say that," he said quietly. "He would have been proud."

13   "Well, it's true. There isn't a player in the league who knows as many obscene gestures."

14   "I admit I have been given a few increases in pay in recent years. Management seems to be treating me with new respect."

15   "You're selling tickets," I said. "You're a gate attraction now — not some bum who only can skate and shoot and the rest of it. Your profanity is beautiful."

16   "C'mon."

17   "No, I'm serious. I don't think anyone in the league can incite a riot the way you can."

18   "I've had a lot of help along the way. You can't make it alone," he stated generously.

19   "No one does," I said.

20   "Take that play where I skate up to the referee and stand nose-to-nose with my face turning red. It was my old junior coach who taught me that. He was the one who used to toss all the sticks on the ice and throw his hat into the stands and pound his fist on the boards."

21   "You were lucky to get that sort of training. A lot of players never learn the fundamentals."

22   "I think there are a few boys in the league who can spit better than me."

23   "Farther, perhaps, but not more accurately," I corrected.

24   "Well, thanks anyway. I've always considered it one of my weaknesses."

25   "That last brawl of yours was perfectly executed. Your sweater was torn off, you taunted the crowd, you smashed your stick across the goalposts. Really a picture Donnybrook."

26   "The papers gave me a break. The coverage was outstanding."

27   "Do you ever look back to the days when you couldn't cut a forehead or puff a lip or insult an official?"

28   "Everyone gets nostalgic," he confessed. "It's a good thing I got away from home by the time I was fifteen. I might never have been any more than a ham-and-egger, you know, a twenty-goal man who drifts through life unnoticed."

29   "What was the turning point?"

30   "I had heard prominent sportsmen say that nice guys finish last, and that you have to beat them in the alley if you hope to beat them in the rink. But it didn't sink in."

31   "Nobody learns overnight."

"I wasted a few years learning to play my wing and to check without   32
using the butt of the stick. But I noticed I was being passed by. I skated
summers to keep in shape, exercised, kept curfew."

"Don't tell me. They said you were dull."   33

"Worse than that. They said I was clean. It's tough to live down that   34
sort of reputation."

I nodded.   35

"Anyway, during a game in the sticks, I was skating off the ice — we had   36
won five-one and I had scored three goals. The home crowd was pretty
listless and there was some booing. Then it happened."

"What?"   37

"My big break. My mother was in the stands and she shouted to me. I   38
turned to wave at her with my hockey stick and I accidentally caught the
referee across the face. He bled at lot — took ten stitches later."

"Is that all?"   39

"Well someone pushed me and I lost my balance and fell on the poor   40
man. A real brawl started. Luckily, I got credit for the whole thing — went
to jail overnight, got a suspension. And, talk about fate! A big league scout
was in the arena. He offered me a contract right away."

"It's quite a success story," I said.   41

"You've got to get the breaks," he replied, humbly.   42

ΔΔΔΔΔΔΔΔΔΔΔΔΔΔΔΔΔΔΔΔΔΔΔΔΔΔΔΔΔΔΔΔΔΔΔΔΔΔΔΔΔΔΔΔΔΔΔΔΔΔΔΔΔΔΔΔΔΔΔΔ

Further Reading:

Gary Lautens, *Laughing with Lautens*
Ken Dryden, *The Game*
Peter Gzowski, *The Game of Our Lives*

Structure:

1.   What proportion of this selection do you estimate is DIALOGUE?
     And what function is served by the parts that are not dialogue?
2.   What is the most basic way in which the dialogue is organized?
     Are there major divisions within it? If so, where, and how do
     the parts differ?
3.   Should this selection be labelled ESSAY or FICTION? In what
     sense might it be both?

Style:

1.   Why are there so many paragraph breaks in this short
     selection?
2.   In paragraph 9 the narrator tells his friend, "I'm not inclined

to flattery but, in my book, you've got it made. You're a dirty player." Discuss the IRONY that underlies this comment. How important is Lautens' ironic TONE to the humour and the message of this selection as a whole? In particular, examine the use of irony in the title and in paragraphs 1, 8, 12, 15, 20, 21, 34, and 40.

3.   Do you think the humorous approach chosen by Lautens has made the point strongly? Would a serious approach, like that of the other narratives in this chapter, have worked as well?

4.   Point out at least five COLLOQUIAL or SLANG terms that seem more at home in the dialogue of this selection than they would in a typical essay.

Ideas for Discussion and Writing:

1.   As the saying puts it, "I went to the fights and a hockey game broke out." To what extent do people watch hockey for the fights and to what extent do they watch it for the traditional skills of the game? Is violence necessary to attract fans? How could hockey be made more interesting without resorting to fights?

2.   In this selection that criticizes violence in hockey, where does Lautens blame parents? Fans? Coaches? Management? Sports writers?

3.   It is said that soccer originated in warfare: villagers would kick the severed head of an enemy, like a ball, from one end of the village to the other. Think of the sports you play. What resemblances, if any, do you see between competition on the playing field and competition on the battlefield?

4.   Must a sport be based on conflict, as in two teams each moving a puck or ball in the opposite direction? Name or devise a sport that is free of conflict. Can such a sport be interesting?

5.   PROCESS IN WRITING: Narrate *a violent incident that you witnessed at a sports event, either in person or on television. First freewrite, then channel your momentum into a quick first draft. In further versions add more time signals to speed the action, and more SENSE IMAGES to bring it alive for your reader. Is your TONE consistent (comic, earnest, ironic, or tragic all the way through)? Have you begun and ended at the right moments, so as to waste no words? Have you read aloud, to fine-tune your style?*

Note: See also the Topics for Writing at the end of this chapter.

Topics for Writing

CHAPTER 1: NARRATION

WRITING ABOUT MYSELF

Choose one of these topics as the basis of a narrative about yourself. Tell a good story: give colourful details and all the facts needed to help your reader understand and appreciate the event. (See also the guidelines that follow.)

1. My traffic accident
2. The day I learned to be honest
3. My moment as a sports hero
4. The day I learned to recognize people of the opposite sex as equals
5. My visit to the dentist
6. My brush with the law
7. An occasion when I surprised myself
8. My first date
9. The day I learned to like (or dislike) school
10. The day I was a victim of prejudice
11. The day I learned to tell the truth
12. The day I got lost
13. The day I realized what career I wanted
14. My escape from another country
15. The day I realized I was an adult

WRITING ABOUT OTHERS

From this list of events, choose one that you witnessed in person. Narrate it, giving colourful details and all the facts needed to help your reader understand and appreciate the event. (See also the guidelines that follow.)

16. A brush with death
17. A rescue
18. An incident of sexism
19. A catastrophe
20. An example of charity in action
21. An assault
22. An historical event
23. A major failure of communication
24. An important event in the life of a child
25. An important event in the life of an elderly person
26. A violent incident at a sporting event

27. A practical joke that backfired
28. An alarming mob scene
29. An example of courage in action
30. A success in the life of a teacher

Note also the Process in Writing topic after each selection in this chapter.

Process in Writing: Guidelines

Follow at least some of these steps in the act of writing your narrative (your teacher may suggest which ones).

1. *If you keep a journal, search it for an incident that could develop one of our topics.*

2. *When you have chosen a topic, freewrite on it for at least five minutes, never letting your pen stop. The results will show whether your choice is good. If it is, incorporate the best parts into your first draft. If it is not, try another topic.*

3. *Write your first draft rapidly, spilling out the story onto the paper. Double-space, to leave room for revision. But do not stop now to fix things like spelling and grammar, for you will lose momentum. Consider narrating in the present tense, making the action seem to happen now.*

4. *Look over this draft: Does it begin and end at just the right places, narrating the event itself but omitting parts that don't matter? If you see deadwood, chop it out.*

5. *In your second draft, add more SENSE IMAGES to heighten the realism. Add more time signals, such as "first," "next," "then," "suddenly," and "at last," to speed up the action.*

6. *Read a draft to family members, friends, or classmates. Does it sound good? Revise awkward passages. Does it communicate with your AUDIENCE? Revise any part that does not.*

7. *Finally, edit for spelling, grammar, and other aspects of "correctness" before writing and proofreading the final copy. (If you use a computer, save this version on disk in case your teacher suggests further revision.)*

Crombie McNeill, Toronto.

"What feeds we used to have. Not way back in the pod auger days, mind you. That was before my time. I mean not long ago, just before the tinned stuff and the packages and the baker's bread started to trickle into the outports."

— Ray Guy, "Outharbor Menu"

Example

For example. . . .

Many an audience, after trying in vain to understand a speaker's message, has been saved from boredom or even sleep by those powerful words, "FOR EXAMPLE." Heads lift up, eyes return to the front, and suddenly the message is clear to everyone. Writers, as well as speakers, need to use examples. Pages of abstract reasoning, of generalizations, of theory without application, will only confuse, bore, and finally alienate your reader. But the same ideas supported by well-chosen examples will much more easily interest and even convince your reader. Examples take many forms:

Personal experience: To illustrate your point, narrate an incident that you have experienced. Did an earthquake or tornado or flood show you the power of nature? Did an accident illustrate the danger of drinking and driving, or a fire the danger of smoking in bed? Did a major success or failure demonstrate the importance of work or planning or persistence?

The experience of others: To illustrate your point, narrate an incident that you have seen yourself or heard about from other sources. Did your neighbour's unloved child run away from home or rob a milk store or get married at age 16? Did your uncle lose his job because of automation or recession or imports? Did a famous person succeed despite a physical handicap or a deprived childhood?

Hypothetical examples: In a future-oriented society like ours, many arguments speculate about what might happen *if*. . . . Since the event or situation has not yet come to pass, use your best judgement to imagine the results. What would happen if children had the vote? If street drugs were legalized? If shopping were done by computer? If gasoline were five dollars a litre? If a woman became prime minister? If a world government were adopted?

Quotations: If the words of a poet, politician, scientist, or other prominent person illustrate your point clearly and authoritatively, quote them and of course state who said them. What did Aristotle, Shakespeare, Machiavelli, Freud, Marx, or John Diefenbaker say about love or power or sex or money or old age or war? Start with the index of *Bartlett's Familiar Quotations* or *Colombo's Canadian Quotations* to find an apt statement on almost any important topic.

Statistics: Numerical examples lend a scientific, objective quality to your argument. Tell what percentage of marriages will end in divorce or how many minutes each cigarette takes off your life or how much energy a person consumes travelling by car as opposed to train, bus, or airplane. Five good sources of statistics are *Information Please Almanac, The World Almanac and Book of Facts, The Corpus Almanac of Canada, Canada Year Book,* and any good atlas. Be scrupulously honest, because almost everyone knows how statistics are sometimes made to lie (remember the statistician who drowned in the river that averaged two feet deep!).

Other devices: Later chapters in this book discuss cause and effect, comparison and contrast, and analogy. These devices may be used not only to plan the structure of an entire essay, but also to construct short and vivid examples within the essay.

Almost all good writing contains examples, but some writing contains so many that it uses examples as a means of organizing as well as to illustrate. Ray Guy's essay "Outharbor Menu" has a brief introduction, a one-sentence closing, and a body made up of nothing but examples. Such a collection could be a mere list of trivia, but Ray Guy — like anyone who writes well — has chosen his examples carefully for their colour and for the support which they give to his point.

Another technique is to use one long, well-developed example — in effect, a narrative. Bruce Hutchison does so in "Cowboy from Holland":

EXAMPLE 37

focussing almost totally on the little Dutch boy, he gives us one long example to represent the millions of other immigrants who have become Canadians. Of course one example — or twenty — will prove nothing. Statistics come close to proof, especially when based on a large and carefully designed study. But in general an example is not a device of proof; it is a device of illustration and therefore an aid to both understanding and enjoyment.

Note: Many authors in other chapters use examples extensively, along with different ways to develop their material. See especially these selections:

Michele Landsberg, "West Must Confront Anonymous Misery of the World's Children," p. 284

Judy Stoffman, "The Way of All Flesh," p. 238

Margaret Atwood, "Canadians: What Do They Want?," p. 302

Charles Gordon, "A Guided Tour of the Bottom Line," p. 309

Doris Anderson, "The 51-Per-Cent Minority," p. 138

Pierre Berton, "The Dirtiest Job in the World," p. 289

Ray Guy

Outharbor Menu

Although Ray Guy has been Newfoundland's favourite writer for some years, he is only now being discovered by the rest of Canada. Guy was born in 1939 at Arnold's Cove, an outport on Placentia Bay. As a child he learned to value the self-reliance of traditional Newfoundland life. After two years at Memorial University he went to Toronto, where in 1963 he earned a diploma in journalism at Ryerson Polytechnical Institute. Upon his return to Newfoundland he began reporting for the St. John's Evening Telegram, *but found that reporting was not enough. His distaste for the Liberal government of Joey Smallwood, and especially for its policy of closing down the outports where for centuries Newfoundlanders had lived by fishing, led Guy to become a political columnist. His satirical attacks on Smallwood were so devastating that some people credit him with Smallwood's defeat in the provincial election of 1971. Leaving the* Telegram *when it was bought by the Thomson chain, Guy went freelance, continuing to pour satire on his targets. Guy's newest departure is writing plays, yet even in a new genre his salty humour is much like that of his columns. His best writings are collected in* You May Know Them as Sea Urchins, Ma'am *(1975);* That Far Greater Bay *(1976), which won the Leacock Medal for Humour; and* Ray Guy's Best *(1987). Our selection comes from* That Far Greater Bay.

1   What feeds we used to have. Not way back in the pod auger days,° mind you. That was before my time. I mean not long ago, just before the tinned stuff and the packages and the baker's bread started to trickle into the outports.

2   Out where I come from the trickle started when I was about six or seven years old. One day I went next door to Aunt Winnie's (that's Uncle John's

---

°the pod auger days: a common Newfoundland expression meaning "the old days." A pod auger is an auger with a lengthwise groove.

Aunt Winnie) and she had a package of puffed rice someone sent down from Canada.°

She gave us youngsters a small handful each. We spent a long time 3 admiring this new exotic stuff and remarking on how much it looked like emmets' eggs. We ate it one grain at a time as if it were candy, and because of the novelty didn't notice the remarkable lack of taste.

"Now here's a five cent piece and don't spend it all in sweets, mind." 4 You never got a nickel without this caution attached.

Peppermint knobs. White capsules ringed around with flannelette pink 5 stripes. Strong! You'd think you were breathing icewater. They're not near as strong today.

Chocolate mice shaped like a crouching rat, chocolate on the outside 6 and tough pink sponge inside. Goodbye teeth. Bullseyes made from molasses. And union squares — pastel blocks of marshmallow.

Those mysterious black balls that were harder than forged steel, had 7 about 2,537 different layers of color and a funny tasting seed at the centre of the mini-universe.

Soft drinks came packed in barrels of straw in bottles of different sizes 8 and shapes and no labels. Birch beer, root beer, chocolate, lemonade, and orange.

Spruce beer, which I could never stomach, but the twigs boiling on the 9 stove smelled good. Home brew made from "Blue Ribbon" malt and which always exploded like hand grenades in the bottles behind the stove.

Rum puncheons. Empty barrels purchased from the liquor control in 10 St. John's. You poured in a few gallons of water, rolled the barrel around, and the result was a stronger product than you put down $7.50 a bottle for today.

Ice cream made in a hand-cranked freezer, the milk and sugar and 11 vanilla in the can in the middle surrounded by ice and coarse salt. I won't say it was better than the store-bought stuff today but it tasted different and I like the difference.

Rounders (dried tom cods) for Sunday breakfast without fail. Cods 12 heads, boiled sometimes, but mostly stewed with onions and bits of salt pork.

Fried cod tongues with pork scruncheons.° Outport soul food. Salt 13 codfish, fish cakes, boiled codfish and drawn butter, baked cod with savoury stuffing, stewed cod, fried cod.

°from Canada: Newfoundland did not join Confederation until 1949, after the time Ray Guy describes.
°pork scruncheons: crisp slices of fried pork fat.

14   Lobsters. We always got the bodies and the thumbs from the canning factories. When eating lobster bodies you must be careful to stay away from the "old woman," a lump of bitter black stuff up near the head which is said to be poisonous.

15   I was always partial to that bit of red stuff in lobster bodies but never went much on the pea green stuff although some did.

16   We ate turrs° (impaled on a sharpened broomstick and held over the damper hole to singe off the fuzz), some people ate tickleaces° and gulls but I never saw it done.

17   We ate "a meal of trouts," seal, rabbits that were skinned out like a sock, puffin' pig (a sort of porpoise that had black meat), mussels and cocks and hens, otherwise known as clams, that squirt at you through air holes in the mud flats.

18   Potatoes and turnips were the most commonly grown vegetables although there was some cabbage and carrot. The potatoes were kept in cellars made of mounds of earth lined with sawdust or goosegrass. With the hay growing on them they looked like hairy green igloos.

19   A lot was got from a cow. Milk, certainly, and cream and butter made into pats and stamped with a wooden print of a cow or a clover leaf, and buttermilk, cream cheese. And I seem to remember a sort of jellied sour milk. I forget the name but perhaps the stuff was equivalent to yogurt.

20   There was no fresh meat in summer because it wouldn't keep. If you asked for a piece of meat at the store you got salt beef. If you wanted fresh beef you had to ask for "fresh meat."

21   Biscuits came packed in three-foot long wooden boxes and were weighed out by the pound in paper bags. Sultanas, Dad's cookies, jam jams, lemon creams with caraway seeds, and soda biscuits.

22   Molasses was a big thing. It was used to sweeten tea, in gingerbread, on rolled oats porridge, with sulphur in the spring to clean the blood (eeeccchhhh), in bread, in baked beans, in 'lassie bread.

23   It came in barrels and when the molasses was gone, there was a layer of molasses sugar at the bottom.

24   Glasses of lemon crystals or strawberry syrup or limejuice. Rolled oats, farina, Indian meal. Home-made bread, pork buns, figgy duff,° partridgeberry tarts, blanc mange, ginger wine, damper cakes.°

25   Cold mutton, salt beef, peas pudding, boiled cabbage, tinned bully beef

---

°turr: a term applied to both the razor-billed auk and the murre, in this case probably the auk.
°tickleace: the kittiwake, a kind of gull.
°figgy duff: boiled raisin pudding.
°damper cakes: a kind of bannock made on the damper (upper surface) of a cookstove.

for lunch on Sunday, tinned peaches, brown eggs, corned caplin.°

And thank God I was twelve years old before ever a slice of baker's   26
bread passed my lips.

ΔΔΔΔΔΔΔΔΔΔΔΔΔΔΔΔΔΔΔΔΔΔΔΔΔΔΔΔΔΔΔΔΔΔΔΔΔΔΔΔΔΔΔΔΔΔΔΔΔΔΔΔΔΔΔΔΔΔΔΔΔΔΔΔΔ

Further Reading:

Ray Guy,
  That Far Greater Bay
  Ray Guy's Best
Farley Mowat, *This Rock Within the Sea: A Heritage Lost*
Al Pittman, *Once When I Was Drowning: Poems*

Structure:

1. Point out everything that Ray Guy's first sentence tells us
    about the essay which will follow.
2. In his last sentence Ray Guy exclaims, "And thank God I was
    twelve years old before ever a slice of baker's bread passed my
    lips." What does this sentence achieve that qualifies it to
    conclude the essay?
3. What percentage of this essay do you estimate consists of
    examples? Are there enough to illustrate the point? Are there
    too many?
4. Why does Ray Guy relate the incident of the puffed rice (pars.
    2 and 3)?

Style:

1. How wastefully or economically does Ray Guy use words in
    this essay? Explain.
2. Point out sentence fragments in this essay. Why do you think
    Guy uses them?
3. Point out the expressions that most strongly give "Outharbor
    Menu" a TONE that is folksy and COLLOQUIAL. Is this tone
    appropriate to the topic?
4. In paragraph 18 Guy describes the root cellars: "With the hay
    growing on them they looked like hairy green igloos." Where
    else has he used SIMILES — comparisons that describe one thing
    in terms of another?

°caplin: a small and edible ocean fish often used by cod fishermen as bait (see "The
Capelin," by Franklin Russell).

Ideas for Discussion and Writing:

1. How nostalgic is Ray Guy about his topic? To what extent do you think he exaggerates or presents a one-sided picture because he is writing about his childhood? Is nostalgia desirable in our lives? Can it ever work against us?

2. In his newspaper columns, Ray Guy strongly opposed governmental measures to move people from Newfoundland's outports — such as the one described in this essay — to centralized locations where they would work in factories instead of fishing. To what extent do you think the traditional life of a culture should be preserved? Is a government ever justified in deliberately changing it? If so, under what conditions?

3. In the last few decades, fast-food chains have been standardizing the eating habits not only of Canada but also of many other countries. In this process what have we gained? What have we lost?

4. In paragraph 13 Guy uses the expression "outport soul food." To what does "soul food" usually refer? Do we all prefer a kind of "soul food" that we ate while growing up?

5. PROCESS IN WRITING: *In an essay, describe the "soul food" of your own childhood. Take notes for several days, letting one memory lead to the next. Then write a draft, packing in large numbers of examples. In further drafts increase the SENSE IMAGES and FIGURES OF SPEECH, to bring this cuisine alive for readers who may have grown up elsewhere. Finally, read the whole thing aloud, to detect and iron out any repetition or other awkwardness of style, before writing the good draft.*

Note: See also the Topics for Writing at the end of this chapter.

Richard Needham

A Sound of Deviltry by Night

Richard Needham is a journalist who for over two decades, until his retirement in the late 1980s, wrote a column of aphorisms, puzzles, riddles, and satire for the Toronto Globe and Mail. *He has been one of our few genuine cynics, a writer who delighted in attacking sacred cows — and who, for this reason, tended to provoke either love or hatred in his readers. Needham was born in 1912 in Gibraltar, grew up in India, Ireland, and England, and at age 16 left home to come to Canada. After working as a farm hand, he found his first writing job at the* Toronto Star. *Through the years he worked also at the Hamilton* Herald, *the Sudbury* Star, *the Calgary* Herald, *and — for most of the time from 1951 until his retirement — the* Globe and Mail. *His short satires have been collected in* Needham's Inferno *(1966), which won the Stephen Leacock Medal for Humour,* The Garden of Needham *(1968),* A Friend in Needham *(1969),* The Wit & Wisdom of Richard Needham *(1977), and* You and All the Rest *(1982). Our selection typifies Needham's ironical tone, his love of puns, and his extraordinarily concise style. It appears in* The Hypodermic Needham *(1970) in slightly different form.*

I n the city, you can go broke on $20,000 a year; but in the suburbs, you can do it on $30,000. Suburbanites accomplish this in some measure by staging lavish cocktail parties at which matrons gobble pizza as they discuss their weight problem, and men get smashed out of their skulls while they boast how they gave up smoking.

What function these parties serve (outside of plunging the host and hostess further into debt) has long baffled sociologists. My theory — true for myself, at least — is that the cocktail party is a form of shock treatment comparable to the snake pit of earlier times. So great is the horror of it, so keen the sense of relief at escaping, that all one's other sufferings and problems are reduced to triviality.

Finding myself beset by fortune's slings and arrows not long ago, I subjected myself to the ordeal by guzzle, gabble and gorge at a home so far north of the city that several of the guests greeted each other by rubbing noses. The usual cocktail-party types were on hand — languid immigrants, inferior decorators, insulting engineers, gloomy dames, misplaced trustees, impractical nurses, a dean of women who had been fired for having men in her room at all hours of the day and night, a marriage counsellor who announced that his third wife had just left him for the fifth time, and a psychiatrist who kept getting down on his hands and knees and frisking about the place, nipping at the women's heels.

4   It is customary at these gatherings to have the phonograph on at full blast; this forces people to shout and scream at each other, which in turn dries out their throats, which in turn causes them to get bagged more quickly, which is why they went to the party in the first place. Having no opinions or information worth bellowing, I customarily listen to those of others. Standing near a group of women, I caught the following fragments:

5   'The only thing I have against men is me ... *The Naked Ape* is disgusting, I stayed up all night reading it ... I don't know how old she is exactly, but she does enjoy a nice hot cup of tea ... Even a newspaperman is better than no man at all ... We eventually had to leave Picton; the pace was too fast ... I keep having this awful nightmare; a big brute of a man is chasing me, and I escape ... I found out early on Bay Street that all men are married, but some are less married than others ... I didn't mind Jack's cruelty and extravagance; what finished it off was the way he kept clearing his throat every five minutes.'

6   Going out in the garden, I found a young man who told me, 'I hate university but I have to stay there so I can graduate and get a good job, and pay back the money I borrowed to go to university.' The young woman with him said she had a different problem. 'It's my parents. They're so good and kind and trusting, and I'm so rotten. When I come home drunk at two in the morning with my clothes torn, and tell them I was in a car accident, they believe me. This makes me feel guilty, and so I become twice as rotten. I wish I had parents like Jill; her father drinks his pay, and her mother runs around with every man on the block, so she doesn't have to feel guilty about being even more rotten than I am.'

7   Going back into the house, I listened in on a group of men: 'I've always thought of Highway 7 as the square root ... When the postal strike ends, how will people be able to tell? ... I've at last figured it out, Doris Day is her own grandmother ... I know beer's the drink of moderation, that's why I hate it ... When your plane lands in Toronto, you have to set your watch back thirty years ... Liquor at the C.N.E.? It's enough to make Judge Robb turn over in his grave ... I'm still looking for a woman who measures down to my standards ... I didn't mind Marge's boozing and infidelity; what drove me out was that she never changed the blade after shaving her legs with my razor.'

It seemed at this point I'd had enough, so I finished the   8
Scotch-and-tonic someone had pressed on me, said farewell to the hostess,
and made an inglorious exit by tripping over the dachshund. Still, I was
safely out; I wouldn't need to do it again for a long time; and I walked
steadily south until the crumbling tenements, polluted air, garbage-lit-
tered streets, and screams of hold-up victims informed me I was back in
civilization.

△△△

Further Reading:

Richard Needham,
  Needham's Inferno
  The Hypodermic Needham

Structure:

1. Which paragraph states the main point of this selection?
2. Does the fact that the main point is made through SATIRE detract in any way from its importance as the organizational focus of this essay?
3. What do paragraphs 5, 6, and 7 achieve through presenting a rapid profusion of very short *examples*? What is the overall effect?
4. Paragraph 5 consists of comments by women, paragraph 6 of comments by one couple, and paragraph 7 of comments by men. What purpose does this grouping serve?
5. To what extent does *narration*, as well as example, help to structure this selection?

Style:

1. Richard Needham was a journalist. Do you see ways in which this selection resembles or differs from a news article?
2. Needham uses words playfully. In paragraph 3, what is he doing when he refers to "languid immigrants," "inferior decorators," and "insulting engineers"?
3. Pick out examples of COLLOQUIAL or SLANG words used by Needham, and discuss the effects of this very informal language. In what kinds of writing would you not use such words?
4. Needham is known for his ability to condense an idea or a characterization into a one-sentence EPIGRAM. In paragraph 7 a guest says, "I know beer's the drink of moderation, that's why I hate it." How many more epigrams do you find?

5. When in paragraph 7 a guest says, "I've always thought of Highway 7 as the square route," what device of humour is Needham using?

6. Do you think that Needham's devices of light humour trivialize the argument? Or do they enhance the argument by making it entertaining?

7. In the phrase "beset by fortune's slings and arrows" (par.3), Needham is alluding to Hamlet's famous speech:

> To be, or not to be: that is the question:
> Whether 'tis nobler in the mind to suffer
> The slings and arrows of outrageous fortune,
> Or to take arms against a sea of troubles,
> And by opposing end them?

Is the ALLUSION appropriate? Should we be thinking of Hamlet's serious problems and his contemplation of suicide in a sentence that continues with Needham's "ordeal by guzzle, gabble and gorge"?

Ideas for Discussion and Writing:

1. Is Needham's only aim to amuse us, or is he at least partly serious in portraying a cocktail party as "a form of shock treatment"?

2. Are there topics so serious that they cannot be developed through SATIRE?

3. Why do people go to parties? Give some good reasons. Give some bad reasons.

4. What STEREOTYPES do you recognize in Needham's thumbnail portraits of the guests?

5. Does the narrator hate only cocktail parties, or does he seem cynical about humanity in general? Give reasons for your answer.

6. PROCESS IN WRITING: *Think of either the best or the worst party you have ever attended. Freewrite on the topic for five or ten minutes, to discover your TONE (serious, humorous, satirical, etc.) and to begin recording examples. Now write a first draft, let it cool off for a day, then go back to add more examples. Are there enough? Do they all reinforce your chosen tone and your value judgement? Do they enable your reader to "see" the event? Now trim deadwood ruthlessly to produce a final version that, like Needham's writing, is fast-moving and concise.*

Note: See also the Topics for Writing at the end of this chapter.

Bruce Hutchison

Cowboy from Holland

Bruce Hutchison, born in 1901 in Prescott, Ontario, has had a very long and full career as a journalist. Considered the dean of political commentators in Canada, Hutchison has covered every prime minister since Wilfrid Laurier. He has written over a dozen books, won three National Newspaper Awards and three Governor General's Literary Awards. Hutchison began reporting in Ottawa, was associate editor of the Winnipeg Free Press *from 1944 to 1950, editor of the Victoria* Daily Times *from 1950 to 1963, and, from 1963 until his retirement in 1979, editorial director of the* Vancouver Sun. *With a writing schedule that at times has reached 10,000 words a day, Hutchison has not stopped at newspaper work: he has also produced books of history, fiction, biography, geography, and politics. His best-known are* The Unknown Country: Canada and Her People *(1942) and* Canada: Tomorrow's Giant *(1957). Our selection, which is from the latter book, exemplifies the colourful and even impassioned nature of Hutchison's prose, and his ongoing quest to define our national identity.*

The great myth of Canada and the essential ingredient of the nation 1
recently hurtled into my garden on a tricycle. It was ridden by a golden-haired boy of five years just out from Holland. I do not know his name. He has yet to master the English language. But he has learned the first word of the myth. The word, of course, is "cowboy." He shouted it through my gate, brandished two toy pistols, and whipped his three-wheeled horse over my flower beds.

Though my young friend knows little about Canada, he has hit 2
unerringly on its true content and oldest instinct. He has joined that long procession which started out of Europe in the first days of the seventeenth century, crossed an ocean and a continent, and marched westward to another ocean. He has grasped, by the deep wisdom of childhood, the primal force forever driving the Canadian westward against the wilderness. After the trim postage stamp of Holland he has seen the limitless space of a new land. He has breathed the west and become a

cowboy. We are witnessing in our neighborhood the birth of a Canadian.

3   The other day the carefree cowboy got down to the serious business of Canada. He became, by hereditary impulse, a farmer. His father, who had long cultivated the soil of Holland and acquired a Canadian farm only a month ago, gave the boy a set of tools, a little tin spade, rake, and hoe. Immediately the horse and pistols were laid aside.

4   As I drove down our country lane, the boy was digging up the roadside, smoothing it with his rake, and preparing to sow his first crop. There, in that small figure, was the genius of an ancient farm people transplanted across ocean and continent.

5   He shouted at me, in his own tongue, to observe his labors. They didn't amount to much beside his father's long spring furrows near by, but they were a beginning. The seeds of Holland would germinate in the Canadian soil, and the seeds of Canada in the boy.

6   Soon, I suppose, he will forget his native land and his father's language. Within a year or so of entering a Canadian school he will be indistinguishable from other young Canadians in appearance, speech, and mind. Yes, but he, and other boys from foreign lands, carry with them certain invisible baggage that no customs inspector will discern. They carry, like the first French Canadians, the English, the Scots, the Irish, and the rest of us, a fraction of the old world. It is of such fractions, mixed together and smoothed by environment, that Canada is made.

7   Yesterday some boys born in Canada jeered at the Dutch immigrant and trampled his new seed bed. When he sought refuge in my garden, I tried to tell him that the Canadians were only demonstrating, by a perverse method, their pride in Canada. They acted, I said, like boys everywhere and much like the world's statesmen.

8   I tried to tell the immigrant about another boy of his own age who reached Upper Canada in 1820, the son of a Scots storekeeper with a habit of unprofitable speculation and an addiction to strong drink. That boy seemed to have less chance in life than the boy from Holland. Yet he died as the first prime minister of Canada and the idol of his people.

9   John Alexander Macdonald, as I attempted to explain, was an immigrant. So were the French before him and the Indians before them. All Canadians were immigrants a few generations back, and so diverse in blood that no racial stock could now claim to be a national majority. We are a nation of immigrants and minorities, slowly combining and issuing in what we call the Canadian breed.

10   The Dutch boy listened, but he didn't understand. Repeating the only Canadian word in his vocabulary, he said he was a cowboy. Well, that would serve well enough for a start. He had begun to get to the root of the matter. And today I observed the next chapter in an old story — the native

Canadian boys were teaching an immigrant the art of baseball, the secret of a robin's nest in an apple tree, the green mysteries of a swamp.

ΔΔΔΔΔΔΔΔΔΔΔΔΔΔΔΔΔΔΔΔΔΔΔΔΔΔΔΔΔΔΔΔΔΔΔΔΔΔΔΔΔΔΔΔΔΔΔΔΔΔΔΔΔΔΔΔΔΔΔΔΔ

Further Reading:

Bruce Hutchison, *The Far Side of the Street*
Frederick Philip Grove, *Settlers of the Marsh* (novel)
John Marlyn, *Under the Ribs of Death* (novel)
Adele Wiseman: *The Sacrifice* (novel)

Structure:

1. In what ways and to what degree does this extended *example* of one immigrant develop the topic of immigration to Canada?
2. To what extent does this essay use short examples, in addition to the one long example of the Dutch boy?
3. Is the last sentence effective as a conclusion? What does it accomplish?

Style:

1. The "three-wheeled horse" mentioned in paragraph 1 is of course not a horse but a tricycle. Point out at least three more METAPHORS, figures of speech that are literally false but poetically true.
2. Is Hutchison's approach to his topic mainly OBJECTIVE or SUBJECTIVE? Give reasons for your answer. In what ways might his essay be different if he had used the opposite approach?

Ideas for Discussion and Writing:

1. This selection first appeared in 1957 as part of Bruce Hutchison's book *Canada: Tomorrow's Giant*. Has the author's prophecy come true? In the years since 1957 has Canada become a "giant"? Might it be a "giant" in some ways but not in others? Give examples to support your answer.
2. Hutchison states in paragraph 3 that farming is "the serious business of Canada." If he had written his essay today, what do you think the immigrant boy would learn as "the serious business of Canada"?
3. To what extent is the myth of the cowboy still with us in Canada? Does it affect our lives in any concrete way? Do you view its influence, if any, as positive or negative? Give examples to support your answers.

4. **PROCESS IN WRITING:** *If you have moved here from another country, write the story of your own first days in Canada, as an* example *of the opportunities and/or pitfalls of immigration. If you were born in Canada, write a similar essay about moving to a new neighbourhood, school, town, city, or province.*

First take a page of notes. Discard any irrelevant items, and from the rest write a quick first draft. In your second draft you will probably recall more examples: *specific facts and* IMAGES. *Add them, to help your reader experience your story. Read aloud to detect and revise wordy or awkward passages, then produce your final copy.*

Note: See also the *Topics for Writing* at the end of this chapter.

Robert Fulford

Where, Exactly, Are This Book's Readers?

A high school dropout and former copy boy at the Toronto Globe and Mail, *Robert Fulford has risen to become the nation's most respected journalist writing in English. He has reported, edited, and been columnist for several newspapers and magazines, as well as hosting radio broadcasts for the CBC and the* Realities *series for* TVOntario. *But Fulford began his greatest contribution to Canadian public life when in 1968 he was named editor in chief of the nation's oldest magazine. For 19 years his editorial abilities and his penetrating and well-written columns helped to make* Saturday Night *into English Canada's best magazine of culture and public affairs. But when financier Conrad Black bought the venerable publication in its centennial year, Fulford quit rather than accept restrictions on his editorial freedom. Through the years Fulford has collected the best of his columns and articles into books, such as* Crisis at the Victory Burlesk: Culture, Politics & Other Diversions *(1968), from which our selection comes. Upon leaving* Saturday Night *he began a column for the* Financial Times, *and in 1988 he told his story in* Best Seat in the House: Memoirs of a Lucky Man.

There's always the possibility, of course, that the world already has   1
enough books; may, in fact, have *too many* books. This thought has
never occurred to a publisher; it has probably occurred to only a minority
of authors; but certainly it has occurred at one time or another to every
book reviewer in the world.

For the fact is that book reviewers spend their lives surrounded by piles   2
of books they will never read and they can't imagine anyone else reading.
Every morning a young man comes into my office with a pile of half a
dozen books, and on the average three of them fall into this category.

Take one that turned up yesterday: *They Gave Royal Assent,* subtitled   3
The Lieutenant-Governors of British Columbia. Imagine it. Not just a book on
lieutenant-governors — a subject with truly monumental possibilities for

producing boredom — but a book on *British Columbia* lieutenant-governors.

4   Now the thing about lieutenant-governors is that, in general, they don't do anything. They just sort of *preside*. Their lives lack, not to put too fine a point on it, drama. So who will read this book? If you were lieutenant-governor of British Columbia you might well want to read it, and if you aspired to that office you would almost certainly be anxious to obtain a copy. But surely that makes a limited market. In addition there are descendants and other connections of lieutenant-governors; but this, too, must be a comparatively small group. Will the author, D. A. McGregor ('veteran journalist, editor and history-researcher,' the jacket says) meet friends who have read his book and who will congratulate him on it? 'Nice job on the lieutenant-governors, old man,' one imagines them saying. But who would they be?

5   The publishers, Mitchell Press of Vancouver, have dutifully sent out review copies. Why? Because publishers do this — they operate automatically on the I-shot-an-arrow-into-the-air theory of publicity. They just send out books at random, whether anybody wants them or not. It gives them some queer sense of satisfaction. They feel they are playing their part.

6   So here are all these books floating around in the mails and then ending up on the desks of people who view them with apathy if not distaste. Any book reviewer can at any moment, and to his horror, look around his office and instantly spot three books on the Quebec crisis, four histories of Ontario counties, five books on how to diet, two authorized biographies of Teilhard de Chardin, and one book by a man who lived six months with a colony of apes and didn't find out anything.

7   Right now I have here, in front of me: *The Bahamas Handbook* (547 pages, would you believe it?); *One of Our Brains is Draining*, a novel by someone named Max Wilk; *The Nation Keepers*, a book of essays by the likes of Wallace McCutcheon and John Robarts; *Brant County, A History, 1784–1945; Success at the Harness Races*, by Barry Meadow, 'a practical guide for handicapping winners'; *Churchill, His Paintings*, a gift book priced at only $12.50 and worth, anyway, a nickel; *Vigor for Men Over 30*, as depressing a title as any I've encountered this season, by Warren Guild, M.D., Stuart D. Cowan, and Samm Sinclair Baker (a slim book, but it took three men to write it); *A History of Peel County, 1867–1967; Nineteenth Century Pottery and Porcelain in Canada*; and *Great True Hunts*, a $17.95 picture book all about how various famous men — such as the Shah of Iran, Tito, and Roy Rogers — go out and kill beautiful animals for fun.

8   I can't get a copy of the new John O'Hara novel, no matter how hard I try, but I have all these other books around me, and they're piling up,

piling up. A man came to my office yesterday and claimed he couldn't find me. I was there all the time, but hidden. The situation, as it often does in December, is reaching a critical phase.

But what about those Vancouver publishers? What exactly did they have in mind when they sent out those review copies of their lieutenant-governor book? Did they think people would *read* it, and then *write* something about it? Did they anticipate that soon they would begin receiving clippings, full of praise for their courage, imagination, and resourcefulness in publishing this significant volume? One can imagine the quotes: 9

   '*A stimulating and indeed an engrossing account of. . . in places thrilling, in others richly analytical . . . abrasive, tough, probing . . . profound and moving in its depiction of . . . a very badly needed contribution to the history of. . . . full of those insights we have come to expect from . . .*'   10

Or did they, retaining some grasp on reality, know all the time what would happen — that one book editor after another across the country would silently pass the book along to his paper's library, hoping that someday someone on the staff — for some unthinkable reason — would want to know something about the lieutenant-governors of British Columbia?   11

The notion that perhaps there may be too many books in the world, that perhaps it is more creative *not* to write a book than to write one, occurred to me when I returned the other day from two weeks of leave and began wading through a pile of books on Christian revival, books on space exploration, and books on nineteenth-century Canada. . . . But I immediately set that whole subversive idea aside. Because after all I'd just spent the previous two weeks, uh, writing a book.   12

ΔΔΔΔΔΔΔΔΔΔΔΔΔΔΔΔΔΔΔΔΔΔΔΔΔΔΔΔΔΔΔΔΔΔΔΔΔΔΔΔΔΔΔΔΔΔΔΔΔΔΔΔΔΔΔΔΔΔΔΔΔΔΔ

Further Reading:

Robert Fulford,
   Best Seat in the House: Memoirs of a Lucky Man
   An Introduction to the Arts in Canada

Structure:

1.   Where is Fulford's main point first stated?
2.   Why do you think Fulford devotes six paragraphs to *They Gave Royal Assent: The Lieutenant-Governors of British Columbia*, but only a few words to each of the many other books he names?
3.   How convincing are Fulford's examples? Would you want to read any of the books that he makes fun of?

4. What effect is achieved in the final sentence where Fulford confesses that he himself has just written a book?

Style:

1. When did you first realize that this is a humorous essay?
2. People say "uh" but hardly ever write it. Why does Fulford use it in his final sentence? Point out other places where he uses INFORMAL, conversational language and discuss the effects he achieves in doing so.
3. In paragraph 7 Fulford tells us that *Vigor for Men Over 30* is "a slim book, but it took three men to write it." Point out other examples of IRONY, in which we hear the opposite of what we might have expected.
4. Why do you think Fulford wrote paragraph 7 as one long sentence?
5. What do Fulford's imagined book review quotations in paragraph 10 make fun of?

Ideas for Discussion and Writing:

1. Fulford begins his essay by stating, "There's always the possibility, of course, that the world already has enough books; may, in fact, have *too many* books." Do you agree? How do you feel in a large library with thousands of books around you? Can you think of reasons why a library might collect the books Fulford criticizes?
2. What kinds of books do you own? Name your favourites. How do you choose a book to buy?
3. Why do people write books? What are some bad reasons? What are some good reasons?
4. PROCESS IN WRITING: *Review a book you have recently read, illustrating your argument profusely with* examples. *First freewrite for several minutes to get your thoughts flowing. Now, looking at what you have produced, decide on your* THESIS, *your* AUDIENCE, *and your* TONE. *Do a discovery draft, then look it over. Is your point of view clear? Are there enough examples? Does every example support the thesis? Whatever your tone, is it consistent? In further drafts, revise until all these goals are met.*

Note: See also the Topics for Writing at the end of this chapter.

EXAMPLE   55

Topics for Writing

CHAPTER 2: EXAMPLE

If one of these traditional or popular sayings expresses an important lesson you have learned about life, illustrate it in an essay developed through extensive use of example. (See also the guidelines that follow.)

1. Experience is the best teacher.
2. Money cannot buy happiness.
3. The best defence is a good offence.
4. You have to like yourself before you can like others.
5. Practice makes perfect.
6. True wealth is measured by what you can do without.
7. If you try to please the world, you will never please yourself.
8. Time is money.
9. Virtue is its own reward.
10. No pain, no gain.
11. Beauty is only skin-deep.
12. Money is the root of all evil.
13. Nothing ventured, nothing gained.
14. The more you have, the more you want.
15. Love is blind.

If your answer to one of the following is based on strong experience, support it in an essay developed through extensive use of example. (See also the guidelines that follow.)

16. The (best/worst) program on television is _____.
17. _____ is the best book I've ever read.
18. The (best/worst) spectator sport of all is _____.
19. One kind of music I really detest is _____.
20. _____ is the (best/worst) restaurant I've ever tried.
21. My favourite newspaper is _____.
22. _____ is the most practical computer for my needs.
23. My favourite musician is _____.
24. The very (best/worst) film I have ever seen is _____.
25. _____ is my favourite holiday spot.
26. _____ is my best subject this term.
27. The radio station I prefer is _____.
28. _____ is the best teacher I've ever had.

29. The political leader I most admire is _____.
30. _____ is my favourite city.

Note also the Process in Writing topic after each selection in this chapter.

EXAMPLE   57

Process in Writing: Guidelines

Follow at least some of these steps in developing your essay through examples (your teacher may suggest which ones).

1. *Choose a topic you think you like, and try it out through brainstorming or freewriting. Do you have something to say? Can you supply examples? If not, try another topic.*

2. *Visualize your audience: What level of language, what* TONE, *what examples, will communicate with this person or persons? (Look over the kinds of examples listed in our chapter introduction.)*

3. *Do a rapid "discovery draft," double-spaced. Do not stop now to fix things like spelling and grammar; just get the material down on paper.*

4. *The next day, look this draft over. Are there enough examples? Or: Is your one long example explained in depth? If not, add more. Does each example support your main point? If not, revise. Are examples in order of increasing importance? If not, consider rearranging to build a climax.*

5. *Check your second draft for* TRANSITIONS, *and add if necessary. Test your prose by reading aloud, then revise awkward or unclear passages. Now reach for the dictionary and a grammar book if you need them.*

6. *Proofread your final copy slowly, word by word (if your eyes move too fast, they will "see" what should be there, not necessarily what is there).*

Christie McLaren.

" 'I bum on the street. I don't like it, but I have to. I have to survive. The only pleasure I got is my cigaret. . . . It's not a life.' "

— Christie McLaren, "Suitcase Lady"

Description

It's large and yellow and. . . .

Consider the writer's tools: words in rows on the page. The writer cannot use gestures, facial expression, or voice as the public speaker does. The writer cannot use colour, shape, motion, or sound, as the filmmaker does. Yet words on the page can be powerful. We have all seen readers so involved in a book that they forget where they are; they will fail to hear their own name called or they will pass their own stop on the bus or subway. These readers have passed into another world, living at second-hand what the writer has lived or at least imagined at first-hand. How does writing convey experience so vividly? One way is through description.

In simulating direct experience, description makes frequent appeals to our senses:

Sight
Hearing
Touch
Smell
Taste

59

Of course, it would be clumsy for a writer to march one by one through all five senses in the same passage. More often he or she will evoke strongly only one or two of the senses, then later move on to others. We see this approach in Lesley Choyce's description of winter surfing: "I can hear the blood pounding in my ears over top of the roar of the winter sea collapsing all around." Later he moves from our sense of hearing to our sense of touch: "I'm bouncing over rocks but they're all round and soft with seaweed. It doesn't hurt. ...." Emily Carr appeals to our senses of smell and sight together when she writes "Smell and blurred light oozed thickly out of the engine room, and except for one lantern on the wharf everything else was dark." Then in the next paragraph she moves on to hearing and touch: "Every gasp of the engine shook us like a great sob."

In a description not all words are equal. Use the short and strong ones, not the long and flabby ones. Do we write "perspiration" or "sweat"? "Expectorate" or "spit"? "Ambulate" or "walk"? "Vertiginous" or "dizzy"? "Altercation" or "fight"? The answer is usually clear.

Choose words that convey the right feeling as well as the right dictionary meaning. One student ended a pretty description of the ocean by saying that the water was "as still as a pan full of oil." The image of water as oil may imply stillness, but this water is not exactly something we would want to swim in or even watch at sunset — we'd be too busy thinking of pollution! Another student described forest trees in autumn as being the colour of a fire engine. While the colour may be right, we are left with the distracting image of a fire engine, a product of urban society, in the forest. Spend the time, then, to sense the emotional as well as logical meanings of your words. Search your first draft for weak or inexact or inappropriate words, and replace them. If the right word doesn't come, find it in a dictionary or thesaurus.

Figures of speech — such as the similes and metaphors discussed in Chapter 6 — are powerful tools of description. When Emily Carr writes that a man's face is "greeny-brown and wrinkled like a baked apple," or when Thierry Mallet writes that a woman's throat, "thin and bare as a vulture's neck, showed the muscles like cords," the idea of old age is swiftly and powerfully conveyed. Onomatopoetic language — words like "scuttled," "slithered," "grated," and "ooze" — describes by sounding like what it means. Emily Carr enriches her description with these and many others.

Behind every descriptive choice you make, behind every image you supply to your reader, is an overall purpose. In a warmup exercise such as freewriting, or even as you begin a "discovery draft," you may not yet know that purpose. But the act of writing will soon make it clear: Is your subject scary, inspiring, pitiful, exasperating, ugly, beautiful, calm, or violent? Once you are sure, help your audience to be sure as well.

Sometimes the main point, the overall impression, is announced in a thesis statement. Other times it is only implied. But whichever is the case, keep this main point firmly in mind as you choose each detail, each image, each word. Apply it thoroughly again as you revise. By the time you finish, your description will function much like a standard essay: whether it has a thesis statement or not, it will work towards one main purpose from beginning to end. In other words, it will convey a *message*.

Note: Many authors in other chapters use description to help make their point. See especially these examples:

Margaret Laurence, "Where the World Began," p. 162
Charles Yale Harrison, "In the Trenches," p. 13
Hugh MacLennan, "A Sound beyond Hearing," p. 221
Franklin Russell, "The Capelin," p. 123
Joy Kogawa, "Grinning and Happy," p. 315
John Bentley Mays, "What You Get Is Not Always What You See,"
    p. 117

AUGUSTANA LIBRARY
UNIVERSITY OF ALBERTA

Thierry Mallet

The Firewood Gatherers*

Thierry Mallet joined the French fur company Revillon Frères as an apprentice trader, and went on to establish and oversee a large group of trading posts in the Barrens of the Canadian arctic. Through each of the 20 years before our selection was published, Mallet had travelled through the region, sometimes at great risk, inspecting those posts. His intimate knowledge of the land and of the people who lived on it led him to write a small book, Plain Tales of the North. *Then in 1930 appeared his second small volume,* Glimpses of the Barren Lands. *Both books were published in New York by Revillon Frères. Mallet's style is spare but powerful, as if to reflect the arctic itself. Our selection comes from* Glimpses of the Barren Lands.

1   Our camp had been pitched at the foot of a great, bleak, ragged hill, a few feet from the swirling waters of the Kazan River. The two small green tents, pegged down tight with heavy rocks, shivered and rippled under the faint touch of the northern breeze. A thin wisp of smoke rose from the embers of the fire.

2   Eleven o'clock, and the sun had just set under a threatening bank of clouds far away to the northwest. It was the last day of June and daylight still. But the whole country seemed bathed in gray, boulders, moss, sand, even the few willow shrubs scattered far apart in the hollows of the hills. Half a mile away, upstream, the caribou-skin topeks of an Eskimo settlement, fading away amid the background, were hardly visible to the eye.

3   Three small gray specks could be seen moving slowly above our camp. Human shapes, but so puny, so insignificant-looking against the wild rocky side of that immense hill! Bending down, then straightening up, they seemed to totter aimlessly through the chaos of stone, searching for some hidden treasure.

4   Curiosity, or perhaps of touch of loneliness, suddenly moved me to

---

*Editor's title.

62

leave camp and join those three forlorn figures so far away above me near the sky line.

Slowly I made my way along the steep incline, following at first the bed of a dried-up stream. Little by little the river sank beneath me, while the breeze, increasing in strength, whistled past, lashing and stinging my face and hands. I had lost sight momentarily of the three diminutive figures which had lured me on to these heights. After a while a reindeer trail enabled me to leave the coulee and led me again in the right direction, through a gigantic mass of granite which the frost of thousands of years had plucked from the summit of the hill and hurled hundreds of feet below.

At last I was able to reach the other side of the avalanche of rocks and suddenly emerged comparatively in the open, on the brim of a slight depression at the bottom of which a few dead willow bushes showed their bleached branches above the stones and the gray moss. There I found the three silent figures huddled close together, gathering, one by one, the twigs of the precious wood. Two little girls, nine or ten years old, so small, so helpless, and an aged woman, so old, so frail, that my first thought was to marvel at the idea of their being able to climb so far from their camp to that lonely spot.

An Eskimo great-grandmother and her two great-granddaughters, all three contributing their share to the support of the tribe. Intent on their work, or most probably too shy to look up at the strange white man whom, until then, they had only seen at a distance, they gave me full opportunity to watch them.

All were dressed alike, in boots, trousers, and coats of caribou skin. The children wore little round leather caps reaching far over their ears, the crown decorated with beadwork designs. One of them carried on the wrist, as a bracelet, a narrow strip of bright red flannel. Their faces were round and healthy, the skin sunburned to a dark copper color, but their cheeks showed a tinge of blood which gave them, under the tan, a peculiar complexion like the color of a ripe plum. Their little hands were bare and black, the scratches caused by the dead twigs showing plainly in white, while their fingers seemed cramped with the cold.

The old woman was bareheaded, quite bald at the top of the head, with long wisps of gray hair waving in the wind. The skin of her neck and face had turned black, dried up like an old piece of parchment. Her cheeks were sunken and her cheek bones protruded horribly. Her open mouth showed bare gums, for her teeth were all gone, and her throat, thin and bare as a vulture's neck, showed the muscles like cords. Her hands were as thin as the hands of a skeleton, the tip of each finger curved in like a claw. Her eyes, once black, now light grey, remained half closed, deep down in their sockets.

10   She was stone blind.

11   Squatting on her heels, she held, spread in front of her, a small reindeer skin. As soon as the children dropped a branch beside her, she felt for it gropingly; then, her hands closing on it greedily, like talons, she would break it into small pieces, a few inches long, which she carefully placed on the mat at her feet.

12   Both little girls, while searching diligently through the clumps of dead willows for what they could break off and carry away, kept absolutely silent. Not only did they never call to one another when one of them needed help, but they seemed to watch each other intently whenever they could. Now and then, one of them would hit the ground two or three times with the flat of her hand. If the other had her head turned away at the time, she appeared to be startled and always wheeled around to look. Then both children would make funny little motions with their hands at one another.

13   The little girls were deaf and dumb.

14   After a while they had gathered all the wood the reindeer skin could contain. Then the children went up to the old woman and conveyed to her the idea that it was time to go home. One of them took her hands in hers and guided them to two corners of the mat, while the other tapped her gently on the shoulder.

15   The old, old woman understood. Slowly and carefully she tied up the four corners of the caribou skin over the twigs, silently watched by the little girls. Groaning, she rose to her feet, tottering with weakness and old age, and with a great effort swung the small bundle over her back. Then one little girl took her by the hand, while the other, standing behind, grasped the tail of her caribou coat. Slowly, very slowly, step by step they went their way, following a reindeer trail around rocks, over stones, down, down the hill, straight toward their camp, the old woman carrying painfully for the young, the deaf and dumb leading and steering safely the blind.

ΔΔΔΔΔΔΔΔΔΔΔΔΔΔΔΔΔΔΔΔΔΔΔΔΔΔΔΔΔΔΔΔΔΔΔΔΔΔΔΔΔΔΔΔΔΔΔΔΔΔΔΔΔΔΔΔΔΔ

Further Reading

Maurice Metayer, ed. and trans., *I, Nuligak* (autobiography)
Dorothy Eber, ed., *Pitseolak: Pictures out of My Life*
Penny Petrone, ed., *Northern Voices: Inuit Writing in English*
Farley Mowat, *People of the Deer*
Yves Thériault, *Agaguk* (novel)

Structure:

1. "The Firewood Gatherers" is *narrated* in chronological order. Point out at least fifteen words or phrases that signal the flow of time.
2. Which paragraphs are devoted so fully to *description* that they interrupt completely or almost completely the flow of time?
3. To what extent is the effect of "The Firewood Gatherers" based upon *comparisons and contrasts*?
4. In what way does the last sentence summarize the entire selection?

Style:

1. How CONCRETE or ABSTRACT is the language of this selection? Point out three or four passages that illustrate your answer.
2. How economical or wasteful is Mallet's use of words? Does the large amount of description cause this passage to be wordy? Why or why not?
3. Mallet's description of the old woman, in paragraph 9, makes extensive use of SIMILE. For example, her throat is "thin and bare as a vulture's neck. . . ." Point out all the other similes in this paragraph.
4. In paragraph 5, Mallet writes of "a gigantic mass of granite which the frost of thousands of years had plucked from the summit of the hill and hurled hundreds of feet below." Where else in this selection does he use the device of PERSONIFICATION, in which inanimate things are described in human terms?

Ideas for Discussion and Writing:

1. Judging by the evidence in "The Firewood Gatherers," how do this traditional society and our modern society differ in their views of the old and the handicapped? What do you imagine the old blind woman and her deaf and dumb great-granddaughters would be doing if they lived today in your town or city?
2. When will you retire if you have the choice? And what will you do in retirement to retain a sense of your own worth?
3. What are some advantages and disadvantages of the extended family? If you live in the same house as your grandparents, describe what they do for you that your parents cannot do. Describe also the problems, if any, that their presence creates.

When you grow old, will you prefer to live with your
descendants or in a home for the aged? Why?

4. If you have read "Suitcase Lady," by Christie McLaren,
compare the two women. If you had to be one or the other,
would you choose to be the Eskimo great-grandmother of the
Barrens or the homeless "suitcase lady" of Toronto? Why?

5. PROCESS IN WRITING: *Go to see either the oldest or the youngest
person you know. Take notes. At home or at school, draft a vivid
description. Then in subsequent drafts, sharpen the word choice, the*
IMAGES, *and the* FIGURES OF SPEECH, *to give an exact and strong
impression of your subject. Test your prose aloud before writing the final
version.*

Note: See also the Topics for Writing at the end of this chapter.

Christie McLaren

Suitcase Lady*

When Christie McLaren wrote "Suitcase Lady" she was a student at the University of Waterloo, reporting for the Toronto Globe and Mail *as a part of her English co-op work experience. After graduation she spent a year and a half at the* Winnipeg Free Press, *then returned to the* Globe, *where since 1984 she has reported on a variety of issues. An avid hiker, skier, and canoeist, McLaren channelled her love of the outdoors into several years of reporting on forestry, energy, and other environmental issues. Another of McLaren's interests is photography (she took the portrait used at the beginning of this chapter). Though a professional journalist, she says that "writing . . . is nothing but pain while you're doing it and nothing but relief when it's done. Any joy or satisfaction, I think, is a bit of fleeting luck." McLaren spent several nights with "the Vicomtesse" before hearing the story she reports in this selection. The article and photograph first appeared in 1981 in the* Globe.

Night after night, the woman with the red hair and the purple dress sits   1
in the harsh light of a 24-hour doughnut shop on Queen Street
West.

Somewhere in her bleary eyes and in the deep lines of her face is a story   2
that probably no one will ever really know. She is taking pains to write
something on a notepad and crying steadily.

She calls herself Vicomtesse Antonia The Linds'ays. She's the suitcase   3
lady of Queen Street.

No one knows how many women there are like her in Toronto. They   4
carry their belongings in shopping bags and spend their days and nights
scrounging for food. They have no one and nowhere to go.

---

*Editor's title.

5   This night, in a warm corner with a pot of tea and a pack of Player's, the Vicomtesse is in a mood to talk.

6   Out of her past come a few scraps: a mother named Savaria; the child of a poor family in Montreal; a brief marriage when she was 20; a son in Toronto who is now 40. "We never got along well because I didn't bring him up. I was too poor. He never call me mama."

7   She looks out the window. She's 60 years old.

8   With her words she spins herself a cocoon. She talks about drapes and carpets, castles and kings. She often lapses into French. She lets her tea get cold. Her hands are big, rough, farmer's hands. How she ended up in the doughnut shop remains a mystery, maybe even to her.

9   "Before, I had a kitchen and a room and my own furniture. I had to leave everything and go."

10   It's two years that she's been on the go, since the rooming houses stopped taking her. "I don't have no place to stay."

11   So she walks. A sturdy coat covers her dress and worn leather boots are on her feet. But her big legs are bare and chapped and she has a ragged cough.

12   Yes, she says, her legs get tired. She has swollen ankles and, with no socks in her boots, she has blisters. She says she has socks — in the suitcase — but they make her feet itch.

13   As for money, "I bum on the street. I don't like it, but I have to. I have to survive. The only pleasure I got is my cigaret." She lights another one. "It's not a life."

14   She recalls the Saturday, a long time ago, when she made $27, and laughs when she tells about how she had to make the money last through Sunday, too. Now she gets "maybe $7 or $8," and eats "very poor."

15   When she is asked how people treat her, the answer is very matter-of-fact: "Some give money. Some are very polite and some are rude."

16   In warm weather, she passes her time at the big square in front of City Hall. When it's cold she takes her suitcase west to the doughnut shop.

17   The waitresses who bring food to the woman look upon her with compassion. They persuaded their boss that her sitting does no harm.

18   Where does she sleep? "Any place I can find a place to sleep. In the park, in stores — like here I stay and sit, on Yonge Street." She shrugs. Sometimes she goes into an underground parking garage.

19   She doesn't look like she knows what sleep is. "This week I sleep three hours in four days. I feel tired but I wash my face with cold water and I feel okay." Some questions make her eyes turn from the window and stare hard. Then they well over with tears. Like the one about loneliness. "I don't talk much to people," she answers. "Just the elderly, sometimes, in the park."

Her suitcase is full of dreams.   20

Carefully, she unzips it and pulls out a sheaf of papers — "my   21
concertos."

Each page is crammed with neatly written musical notes — the careful   22
writing she does on the doughnut shop table — but the bar lines are
missing. Questions about missing bar lines she tosses aside. Each
"concerto" has a French name — Tresor, La Tempete, Le Retour — and
each one bears the signature of the Vicomtesse. She smiles and points to
one. "A very lovely piece of music. I like it."

She digs in her suitcase again, almost shyly, and produces a round   23
plastic box. Out of it emerges a tiara. Like a little girl, she smooths back
her dirty hair and proudly puts it on. No one in the doughnut shop seems
to notice.

She cares passionately about the young, the old and the ones who suffer.   24
So who takes care of the suitcase lady?

"God takes care of me, that's for sure," she says, nodding thoughtfully.   25
"But I'm not what you call crazy about religion. I believe always try to do
the best to help people — the elderly, and kids, and my country, and my
city of Toronto, Ontario."

ΔΔΔΔΔΔΔΔΔΔΔΔΔΔΔΔΔΔΔΔΔΔΔΔΔΔΔΔΔΔΔΔΔΔΔΔΔΔΔΔΔΔΔΔΔΔΔΔΔΔΔΔΔΔΔΔΔΔΔΔΔΔΔ

Further Reading:

Ian Adams, *The Poverty Wall*
George Orwell, *Down and Out in Paris and London*

Structure:

1. "Suitcase Lady" appeared as a feature article in the Toronto
   Globe and Mail. Name all the ways that you can think of in
   which, as a piece of newspaper journalism, it differs from the
   typical ESSAY in this book.
2. What does McLaren achieve in the opening description?
3. How do the frequent quotations help McLaren to build her
   description?
4. McLaren's photograph of "the Vicomtesse" originally
   accompanied McLaren's article in the *Globe and Mail*. Does a
   descriptive piece of writing like "Suitcase Lady" need an
   illustration? What does the photograph do that the article
   cannot do? And what does the article do that the photograph
   cannot do?
5. How does McLaren employ IRONY in the closing?

Style:

1. How difficult or easy is the vocabulary used in "Suitcase Lady" compared with that of most of the essays you have read in this book? Why?
2. "With her words she spins herself a cocoon," states McLaren in paragraph 8. Point out another vivid METAPHOR, a statement that is literally false but poetically true.
3. Of the many concrete details, point out those that you think most strongly convey the flavour of this suitcase lady's life, and discuss why these particular details are effective.

Ideas for Discussion and Writing:

1. If you have read "The Firewood Gatherers," by Thierry Mallet, compare the hardships faced by the aboriginal great-grandmother in the arctic with those faced by the suitcase lady in Toronto. In what ways is each of these two persons better off? In what ways is each worse off? If you had to be one of these two women, which would you choose to be, and why?
2. "It's not a life," says "the Vicomtesse" in paragraph 13. Is our society doing enough, either through acts of individuals or acts of institutions such as church and government, to make it "a life" for the homeless? What prevents society from doing more?
3. How do you react to people who, like the suitcase lady, "bum on the street"? Do you divide them into categories? When do you give and when do you not give? How does the giving or not giving make you feel, and why? How do you think it makes them feel, and why?
4. In paragraph 6, the suitcase lady speaks of her son in Toronto: "We never got along well because I didn't bring him up. I was too poor. He never call me mama." Discuss the effects of poverty on family life. In the area where you live, how much money does a family need to stay together? To avoid quarrels over money? To feel hopeful about the future?
5. If you have read the selection "The Country of the Poor" by June Callwood, compare Callwood's broad treatment of the homeless in Canada with McClaren's in-depth treatment of one homeless person. What does each approach achieve that the other cannot?
6. PROCESS IN WRITING: *Tape an interview with a person who in economic status, age, culture, values, or some other respect is radically different from you. Then write a profile. Following McLaren's example, characterize your subject by quoting some of his or her best comments. In*

the next draft add more IMAGES *of physical appearance. When your final draft is done, read it aloud, with feeling, to the class.*

Note: See also the Topics for Writing at the end of this chapter.

Lesley Choyce

The Waves of Winter

One day in 1977 as Lesley Choyce was walking down Forty-Second Street in New York City, a taxi backfired. "A hundred people around me dropped to the ground," he later wrote. "They automatically assumed it was a sniper. I was beginning to get the feeling that there were better places on the planet to while away my time." Choyce's "better place" is now Porter's Lake, Nova Scotia. Choyce had loved the rural New Jersey into which he was born in 1951, but a "ravenous suburbanization" had consumed it. After studying English at Rutgers University and at Montclair College, he began doctoral work at the City University of New York, but his experience of America's largest city only increased his alienation from urban and industrial society. He now writes, "my inevitable move to Nova Scotia was, without a doubt, a return to my primitive, innocent, pre-suburban past." Since his immigration Choyce has established himself as the author of a dozen books (fiction, science fiction, poetry, and essays), as a TV talk-show host, teacher, editor, and anthologist, and as director of Pottersfield Press, which publishes his works and those of other Maritimers. As an essayist he is brash, irreverent, and polemical, a foe of nuclear power plants and the arms race, and an enemy of urbanization and industrialization. But he is also genial, fascinated both by human nature and by the natural world which he describes in our selection. "The Waves of Winter" appeared in the Toronto Globe and Mail *of March 7, 1987 and was collected in his 1987 book of essays,* An Avalanche of Ocean: The Life and Times of a Nova Scotia Immigrant.*

1 Picture this. It's the third day of February in Nova Scotia. Along the Atlantic coast, arctic ghosts swirl up into the frigid air from the sea. The water, a tropical minus 2 degrees Celsius, is steaming up into the minus 18-degree atmosphere. A light north wind has recently arrived from Hudson Bay and stirs the morning sea wraiths into a vertical dance, then chases them off to sea.

2 I arrive at the Lawrencetown Headland in my old Pinto stationwagon. Looking out to sea I find near-perfect, six-foot-high waves breaking beyond the tip of the land. The short drive to this sacred spot has not allowed my engine to warm up enough to provide any semblance of heat.

In fact, the engine had only groaned when I first urged it to turn over. It was sound asleep, hibernating. Winter wanted us all to freeze up into absolute zero mobility. But man is restless. He wants to get on with business, school, work. Some of us, however, just want to go surfing.

I put on my surfing gear in the house: socks, long underwear, hand-knitted gloves made of Alpaca hair from Peru. Then I climb into my drysuit. A surfing drysuit is just a big rubber bag shaped like a human body. You wear clothes underneath, a three-piece suit if you like. It's supposed to keep you dry but mine leaks a little so I have to wear old plastic bags over my gloves and socks as I slide my feet and hands into the drysuit. Next I pop my head through the neck seal. The fit has to be snug, so the feeling is that of a relatively mild Halifax nightclub bouncer trying to choke you to death.   3

Then it's outside into the frozen wasteland to find my board, buried by last night's snow storm. I find it's frozen into a minor glacier that has formed beneath the snow overnight, so I go back into the house to get a hammer. I have to literally mine my surfboard out of the ice.   4

By the time I get to the beach, my once warm body is already cold. But the waves are beautiful. The sun is out. The water is blue, clean, cracking cold hard tubes of Atlantic Ocean with immaculate precision beyond the stony shoreline.   5

I carry my board down the embankment, wading through drifted snow as high as my chest. Along the shoreline there is no snow, but each black and grey boulder is frozen over with a formidable headgear of ice. Slippery going: I have to half crawl, half walk over the frozen rocks. I remind myself that even salt-water freezes if it isn't stirred around and if the temperature has dropped below minus 20 degrees overnight.   6

At last my rubber feet find the open ocean. My board is still heavy with ice cakes and I soak it in the sea until they drift off. Now I'm wading through the shallows, walking over kelp and barnacle-laden rocks. The sun is in my face as I hop up onto my board and begin to knee-paddle to sea. It almost feels warm. The water is so clear I see everything on the bottom: fish, swaying kelp, rockweed, sea urchins, mussels, barnacles sharp as razor blades. I am at home here, happy, in love with being alive.   7

Past the tip of the headland I arrive at where the hungry waves are peaking and peeling off in two directions. From here I'll find my spot, paddle hard down the face of a bulging heave of sea, then go right or left, east or west, into the sunrise or off toward Halifax. Instead I sit for a minute, watch my breath turn to white ice as I breathe out. Ten feet away a blubbery harbor seal pops up and checks me out as a candidate for breakfast or mating. I'm never sure which. He has the head of a giant dog with foot-long whiskers. He's well insulated with fat, and the part of him   8 under water that I can't see probably weighs about 800 pounds. As usual, he's just curious. His eyes are deep and dark with the mysteries of the sea and you can tell he's never sold insurance.

9   He points his head to the sky, then slips back beneath the surface. I see my wave on the horizon, shift further west to be at the precise point of the peak. Three deep strokes and I'm off, dropping down the face of a pristine, blue North Atlantic wave. I dig in my back foot hard and turn the board so that I'm sliding parallel to the wave. I'm moving east at the speed of light straight into the burning heart of the early morning sun. I tuck down because I see the wave is about to break over my head. And then, for a brief but eternal instant, I'm inside the tube. The wave is leaping out over my head, my feet are still firmly planted on the board and I'm surrounded on five sides by water. I'm ecstatically inside the ocean and for the moment completely dry. The sun itself is perfectly positioned in the doorway of the only way out. I can hear the blood pounding in my ears over top of the roar of the winter sea collapsing all around. The trick now is to find the hidden key to the front door and burst out into oxygen and blue sky.

10   But the warden sneaks up from behind, pulls me two critical inches further back into the tunnel and, with indifferent violence, the wave sucks me into its throat, gobbles me up, drags me to the top of the wave, then slams me to the bottom where I'm brutally thrashed around. It's like being a mouse and getting thrown into somebody's washing machine during a heavy rinse cycle. Only it's much cooler. Seconds under water in the winter stretch out into hours. When you pay your dues for hedonistic winter pleasures, the interest rates are extremely high.

11   I tell myself as usual to relax. The wave has always lost its appetite for me before, and vomited me back up into the world of air-breathing creatures. But first I'm punched around a few times until the oxygen is long gone from my lungs and I begin to see colors. Fortunately my arms are working of their own accord to send me to the surface.

12   I'm bouncing over rocks but they're all round and soft with seaweed. It doesn't hurt, but I feel a bit like a silver ball in an old pinball machine. My lungs are ordering my chest to breathe, but my brain relays the news that seawater will not suffice for air. Then finally I feel the wave give up its grip and I'm out of the turbulent whitewater. I stick my head up into the air and breathe. My heart is pounding and my lungs are working overtime. I start to swim, my surfboard in tow, out of the way of the next incoming wave. I swim hard and sneak over top of the feathering wall just as the ice-cream headache sets in.

13   An ice-cream headache is what happens after your head has been exposed to very cold water for more than three seconds. I wear a wetsuit hood over my head, but it's not quite enough to keep out the demons of

cold. Once your brain is assaulted with below-zero water, it starts getting real angry at your skull and starts wanting out. The pain doesn't last long, maybe 30 seconds. But think about the worst migraine you could ever have, served up with a cherrybomb. That's what an ice-cream headache feels like. Fortunately, it goes away quite quickly and somehow you immediately forget that it happened. So you paddle back out to sea and hope to do it all over again. Maybe this time you'll make it through the tube.

ΔΔΔΔΔΔΔΔΔΔΔΔΔΔΔΔΔΔΔΔΔΔΔΔΔΔΔΔΔΔΔΔΔΔΔΔΔΔΔΔΔΔΔΔΔΔΔΔΔΔΔΔΔΔΔΔΔΔΔΔΔΔΔΔ

Further Reading:

Lesley Choyce,
> *An Avalanche of Ocean: The Life and Times of a Nova Scotia Immigrant*
> *Downwind* (novel)
> *Fast Living* (poems)
> *The End of Ice* (poems)

Structure:

1. Why does Lesley Choyce begin "The Waves of Winter" by saying "Picture this"?
2. Identify Choyce's THESIS STATEMENT.
3. Point out five paragraphs that make especially strong use of *description.* Can you find a paragraph that does not?
4. To what extent is this selection a *narrative?* Does it ever deviate from straight chronological order?
5. Which paragraphs employ *process analysis* — showing how something is done?
6. Analyze Choyce's closing strategy in his last two sentences.

Style:

1. If this event occurred on "the third day of February," why does Choyce cast it in the present tense? What are the effects? Have you tried this device of style yet?
2. Study Choyce's use of SENSE IMAGES. Point out examples (one of each) of strong appeals to our senses of sight, of hearing, and of touch.
3. Choyce employs the device of PERSONIFICATION so strongly that the ocean and its waves emerge as a sort of monster bent on destroying the surfer. Point out at least two paragraphs in which he achieves this effect.
4. Read aloud the following sentence from paragraph 5: "The

water is blue, clean, cracking cold hard tubes of Atlantic Ocean with immaculate precision beyond the stony shoreline." Describe the effects of its rhythm, and name the device that produces the effects.

5. Point out all the reasons why this sentence from paragraph 9 is effective: "I'm moving east at the speed of light straight into the burning heart of the early morning sun."

Ideas for Discussion and Writing:

1. "You can tell he's never sold insurance," Choyce writes of the harbour seal he encounters in the ocean. Toward what larger truths may this cryptic and seemingly absurd remark point? What does it tell us about the author himself?

2. On a February day in Nova Scotia, surfing must be one of the pastimes we would least expect to see. Point out all the evidence you can find in this selection showing why Lesley Choyce does it.

3. Why does danger appeal to us? Why do we go skiing, mountain climbing, spelunking, scuba diving, or even skydiving? Why do we ride the roller coaster? Why do we watch war movies, police shows, adventure and horror films?

4. Do you try to ignore and escape our northern climate, or do you try to experience and enjoy it? Whichever way you answer, describe your favourite techniques for achieving the goal.

5. PROCESS IN WRITING: *Think of the most adventurous thing you have ever done. Freewrite on the topic for five minutes, generating material and motivation. Now from this starting point write a narrative in which you vividly describe the event and its setting. Use Choyce's present-tense technique to make the action seem to happen right now. In your next draft, fine-tune your descriptive passages by adding SENSE IMAGES and by manipulating word choice and sentence rhythm to achieve sound-effect language (ONOMATOPOEIA). Add any missing time signals, especially at the beginnings of paragraphs, to keep the action moving. Finally, test your prose aloud before writing the final copy. Your audience should be able to "hear" your effects, just as you "heard" Lesley Choyce's, even while reading silently.*

Note: See also the Topics for Writing at the end of this chapter.

Emily Carr

D'Sonoqua

Although Emily Carr (1871–1945) was born to a conservative family in the restrictive atmosphere of 19th-century Victoria, British Columbia, she emerged as one of the nation's most original painters and writers. Strong-willed and independent, she turned down several offers of marriage because she believed men "demanded worship" and would only hold her back. Instead she pursued her goal to San Francisco, London, and Paris, where she studied art. Home again, with a new way of seeing inspired by post-impressionist artists in France, she embarked alone on expeditions to remote Indian villages along the mainland coast and in the Queen Charlotte Islands, where she expressed on canvas the power she felt in the ruins of ancient cultures. Our selection describes three such trips. The public laughed at her bold and free art, but she kept on. Around 1929 Carr shifted focus to the paintings for which she is now best known, her looming, energetic and explosive visions of the coastal rain forest itself. Emily Carr spent most of her life in poverty, for recognition was late in coming. She managed a rooming house for many years, and would sometimes paint on cardboard because canvas cost too much. In her last years, plagued by ill health, she abandoned painting for writing. Our selection comes from her first and best book, published in 1941, Klee Wyck *(the title is her name, "Laughing One," given her by the Nootka Indians).* Klee Wyck *is an extension of her painting: a collection of word sketches in which language is at once rich and suggestive, yet pared down to the bone. During her lifetime she published two more books,* The Book of Small *(1942) and* The House of All Sorts *(1944). Others did not appear until after her death:* Growing Pains *(autobiography, 1946),* The Heart of a Peacock *(1953),* Pause: A Sketch Book *(1953), and finally her journals, published as* Hundreds and Thousands *(1966).*

I was sketching in a remote Indian village when I first saw her. The village was one of those that the Indians use only for a few months in each year; the rest of the year it stands empty and desolate. I went there in one of its empty times, in a drizzling dusk.

When the Indian agent dumped me on the beach in front of the village,

1

2

he said "There is not a soul here. I will come back for you in two days." Then he went away.

3   I had a small Griffon dog with me, and also a little Indian girl, who, when she saw the boat go away, clung to my sleeve and wailed, "I'm 'fraid."

4   We went up to the old deserted Mission House. At the sound of the key in the rusty lock, rats scuttled away. The stove was broken, the wood wet. I had forgotten to bring candles. We spread our blankets on the floor, and spent a poor night. Perhaps my lack of sleep played its part in the shock that I got, when I saw her for the first time.

5   Water was in the air, half mist, half rain. The stinging nettles, higher than my head, left their nervy smart on my ears and forehead, as I beat my way through them, trying all the while to keep my feet on the plank walk which they hid. Big yellow slugs crawled on the walk and slimed it. My feet slipped, and I shot headlong to her very base, for she had no feet. The nettles that were above my head reached only to her knee.

6   It was not the fall alone that jerked the "Oh's" out of me, for the great wooden image towering above me was indeed terrifying.

7   The nettle-bed ended a few yards beyond her, and then a rocky bluff jutted out, with waves battering it below. I scrambled up and went out on the bluff, so that I could see the creature above the nettles. The forest was behind her, the sea in front.

8   Her head and trunk were carved out of, or rather into, the bole of a great red cedar. She seemed to be part of the tree itself, as if she had grown there at its heart, and the carver had only chipped away the outer wood so that you could see her. Her arms were spliced and socketed to the trunk, and were flung wide in a circling, compelling movement. Her breasts were two eagle heads, fiercely carved. That much, and the column of her great neck, and her strong chin, I had seen when I slithered to the ground beneath her. Now I saw her face.

9   The eyes were two rounds of black, set in wider rounds of white, and placed in deep sockets under wide, black eyebrows. Their fixed stare bored into me as if the very life of the old cedar looked out, and it seemed that the voice of the tree itself might have burst from that great round cavity, with projecting lips, that was her mouth. Her ears were round, and stuck out to catch all sounds. The salt air had not dimmed the heavy red of her trunk and arms and thighs. Her hands were black, with blunt finger-tips painted a dazzling white. I stood looking at her for a long, long time.

10   The rain stopped, and white mist came up from the sea, gradually paling her back into the forest. It was as if she belonged there, and the mist were carrying her home. Presently the mist took the forest too, and, wrapping them both together, hid them away.

"Who is that image?" I asked the little Indian girl, when I got back to the house. 11

She knew which one I meant, but to gain time, she said, "What image?" 12

"The terrible one, out there on the bluff." The girl had been to Mission School, and fear of the old, fear of the new, struggled in her eyes. "I dunno," she lied. 13

I never went to that village again, but the fierce wooden image often came to me, both in my waking and in my sleeping. 14

Several years passed, and I was once more sketching in an Indian village. There were Indians in this village and in a mild backward way it was "going modern." That is, the Indians had pushed the forest back a little to let the sun touch the new buildings that were replacing the old community houses. Small houses, primitive enough to a white man's thinking, pushed here and there between the old. Where some of the big community houses had been torn down, for the sake of the lumber, the great corner posts and massive roof-beams of the old structure were often left, standing naked against the sky, and the new little house was built inside, on the spot where the old one had been. 15

It was in one of these empty skeletons that I found her again. She had once been a supporting post for the great centre beam. Her pole-mate, representing the Raven, stood opposite her, but the beam that had rested on their heads was gone. The two poles faced in, and one judged the great size of the house by the distance between them. The corner posts were still in place, and the earth floor, once beaten to the hardness of rock by naked feet, was carpeted now with rich lush grass. 16

I knew her by the stuck-out ears, shouting mouth, and deep eye-sockets. These sockets had no eye-balls, but were empty holes, filled with stare. The stare, though not so fierce as that of the former image, was more intense. The whole figure expressed power, weight, domination, rather than ferocity. Her feet were planted heavily on the head of the squatting bear, carved beneath them. A man could have sat on either huge shoulder. She was unpainted, weather-worn, sun-cracked, and the arms and hands seemed to hang loosely. The fingers were thrust into the carven mouths of two human heads, held crowns down. From behind, the sun made unfathomable shadows in eye, cheek and mouth. Horror tumbled out of them. 17

I saw Indian Tom on the beach, and went to him. 18

"Who is she?" 19

The Indian's eyes, coming slowly from across the sea, followed my pointing finger. Resentment showed in his face, greeny-brown and wrinkled like a baked apple, — resentment that white folks should pry into matters wholly Indian. 20

21   "Who is that big carved woman?" I repeated.

22   "D'Sonoqua." No white tongue could have fondled the name as he did.

23   "Who is D'Sonoqua?"

24   "She is the wild woman of the woods."

25   "What does she do?"

26   "She steals children."

27   "To eat them?"

28   "No, she carries them to her caves; that," pointing to a purple scar on the mountain across the bay, "is one of her caves. When she cries 'OO-oo-oo-oeo', Indian mothers are too frightened to move. They stand like trees, and the children go with D'Sonoqua."

29   "Then she is bad?"

30   "Sometimes bad . . . sometimes good," Tom replied, glancing furtively at those stuck-out ears. Then he got up and walked away.

31   I went back, and, sitting in front of the image, gave stare for stare. But her stare so over-powered mine, that I could scarcely wrench my eyes away from the clutch of those empty sockets. The power that I felt was not in the thing itself, but in some tremendous force behind it, that the carver had believed in.

32   A shadow passed across her hands and their gruesome holdings. A little bird, with its beak full of nesting material, flew into the cavity of her mouth, right in the pathway of that terrible OO-oo-oo-oeo. Then my eye caught something that I had missed — a tabby cat asleep between her feet.

33   This was D'Sonoqua, and she was a supernatural being, who belonged to these Indians.

34   "Of course," I said to myself, "I do not believe in supernatural beings. Still — who understands the mysteries behind the forest? What would one do if one did meet a supernatural being?" Half of me wished that I could meet her, and half of me hoped I would not.

35   Chug — chug — the little boat had come into the bay to take me to another village, more lonely and deserted than this. Who knew what I should see there? But soon supernatural beings went clean out of my mind, because I was wholly absorbed in being naturally seasick.

36   When you have been tossed and wracked and chilled, any wharf looks good, even a rickety one, with its crooked legs stockinged in barnacles. Our boat nosed under its clammy darkness, and I crawled up the straight slimy ladder, wondering which was worse, natural seasickness, or supernatural "creeps." The trees crowded to the very edge of the water,

and the outer ones, hanging over it, shadowed the shoreline into a velvet smudge. D'Sonoqua might walk in places like this. I sat for a long time on the damp, dusky beach, waiting for the stage. One by one dots of light popped from the scattered cabins, and made the dark seem darker. Finally the stage came.

We drove through the forest over a long straight road, with black pine trees marching on both sides. When we came to the wharf the little gas mail-boat was waiting for us. Smell and blurred light oozed thickly out of the engine room, and except for one lantern on the wharf everything else was dark. Clutching my little dog, I sat on the mail sacks which had been tossed on to the deck. [37]

The ropes were loosed, and we slid out into the oily black water. The moon that had gone with us through the forest was away now. Black pine-covered mountains jagged up on both sides of the inlet like teeth. Every gasp of the eingine shook us like a great sob. There was no rail round the deck, and the edge of the boat lay level with the black slithering horror below. It was like being swallowed again and again by some terrible monster, but never going down. As we slid through the water, hour after hour, I found myself listening for the OO-oo-oo-oeo. [38]

Midnight brought us to a knob of land, lapped by the water on three sides, with the forest threatening to gobble it up on the fourth. There was a rude landing, a rooming-house, an eating-place, and a store, all for the convenience of fishermen and loggers. I was given a room, but after I had blown out my candle, the stillness and the darkness would not let me sleep. [39]

In the brilliant sparkle of the morning when everything that was not superlatively blue was superlatively green, I dickered with a man who was taking a party up the inlet that he should drop me off at the village I was headed for. [40]

"But," he protested, "there is nobody there." [41]

To myself I said, "There is D'Sonoqua." [42]

From the shore, as we rowed to it, came a thin feminine cry — the mewing of a cat. The keel of the boat had barely grated in the pebbles, when the cat sprang aboard, passed the man shipping his oars, and crouched for a spring into my lap. Leaning forward, the man seized the creature roughly, and with a cry of "Dirty Indian vermin!" flung her out into the sea. [43]

I jumped ashore, refusing his help, and with a curt "Call for me at sundown," strode up the beach; the cat followed me. [44]

When we had crossed the beach and come to a steep bank, the cat ran ahead. Then I saw that she was no lean, ill-favoured Indian cat, but a sleek aristocratic Persian. My snobbish little Griffon dog, who usually [45] refused to let an Indian cat come near me, surprised me by trudging beside her in comradely fashion.

46   The village was typical of the villages of these Indians. It had only one street, and that had only one side, because all the houses faced the beach. The two community houses were very old, dilapidated and bleached, and the handful of other shanties seemed never to have been young; they had grown so old before they were finished, that it was then not worth while finishing them.

47   Rusty padlocks carefully protected the gaping walls. There was the usual broad plank in front of the houses, the general sitting and sunning place for Indians. Little streams ran under it, and weeds poked up through every crack, half hiding the companies of tins, kettles, and rags, which patiently waited for the next gale and their next move.

48   In front of the Chief's house was a high, carved totem pole, surmounted by a large wooden eagle. Storms had robbed him of both wings, and his head had a resentful twist, as if he blamed somebody. The heavy wooden heads of two squatting bears peered over the nettle-tops. The windows were too high for peeping in or out. "But, save D'Sonoqua, who is there to peep?" I said aloud, just to break the silence. A fierce sun burned down as if it wanted to expose every ugliness and forlornness. It drew the noxious smell out of the skunk cabbages, growing in the rich black ooze of the stream, scummed the water-barrels with green slime, and branded the desolation into my very soul.

49   The cat kept very close, rubbing and bumping itself and purring ecstatically; and although I had not seen them come, two more cats had joined us. When I sat down they curled into my lap, and then the strangeness of the place did not bite into me so deeply. I got up, determined to look behind the houses.

50   Nettles grew in the narrow spaces between the houses. I beat them down, and made my way over the bruised dank-smelling mass into a space of low jungle.

51   Long ago the trees had been felled and left lying. Young forest had burst through the slash, making an impregnable barrier, and sealing up the secrets which lay behind it. An eagle flew out of the forest, circled the village, and flew back again.

52   Once again I broke silence, calling after him, "Tell D'Sonoqua —" and turning, saw her close, towering above me in the jungle.

53   Like the D'Sonoqua of the other villages, she was carved into the bole of a red cedar tree. Sun and storm had bleached the wood, moss here and there softened the crudeness of the modelling; sincerity underlay every stroke.

She appeared to be neither wooden nor stationary, but a singing spirit,   54
young and fresh, passing through the jungle. No violence coarsened her;
no power domineered to wither her. She was graciously feminine. Across
her forehead her creator had fashioned the Sistheutl, or mythical
two-headed sea serpent. One of its heads fell to either shoulder, hiding the
stuck-out ears, and framing her face from a central parting on her
forehead which seemed to increase its womanliness.

She caught your breath, this D'Sonoqua, alive in the dead bole of the   55
cedar. She summed up the depth and charm of the whole forest, driving
away its menace.

I sat down to sketch. What was this noise of purring and rubbing going   56
on about my feet? Cats. I rubbed my eyes to make sure I was seeing right,
and counted a dozen of them. They jumped into my lap and sprang to my
shoulders. They were real — and very feminine.

There we were — D'Sonoqua, the cats and I — the woman who only a   57
few moments ago had forced herself to come behind the houses in
trembling fear of the "wild woman of the woods" — wild in the sense that
forest-creatures are wild — shy, untouchable.

△△

Further Reading:

Emily Carr,
  Klee Wyck
  The Book of Small
Maria Tippett, *Emily Carr: A Biography*
Doris Shadbolt, *The Art of Emily Carr*
Paula Blanchard, *The Life of Emily Carr*
Germaine Greer, *The Obstacle Race*

Structure:

1. Emily Carr's opening sentence is, "I was sketching in a remote
    Indian village when I first saw her." Why are we not shown
    "her" identity until paragraph 6?
2. How many basic parts form this *description*? Where do they join
    each other and how do they differ?
3. Are the images of D'Sonoqua merely different from each other
    or do they form a progression?
4. Since each image is in a different location, the sections of the
    description are separated by travel. In addition to its
    organizational function, does the travel have a symbolic
    function? Consider this passage from paragraph 38:

There was no rail round the deck, and the edge of the boat lay level with the black slithering horror below. It was like being swallowed again and again by some terrible monster, but never going down. As we slid through the water, hour after hour, I found myself listening for the OO-oo-oo-oeo.

Style:

1. Although Emily Carr is respected as a writer, she is known primarily as a painter. What aspects of her prose remind you of the visual arts? Point out passages that illustrate your answers.
2. What effect is achieved by Carr's use of the words "scuttled" (par. 4), "slithered" (par. 8), "grated" (par. 43), and "ooze" (par. 48)?
3. Carr plays with words. Instead of describing the walk as "slimy," she writes that the slugs "slimed" the walk. Where else do you find words used in unusual and fresh ways?
4. When Carr describes the wharf as having "crooked legs stockinged in barnacles" (par. 36), what FIGURE OF SPEECH is she using? Where else does it occur? What effect does it have on the description?
5. Emily Carr is noted for the extreme CONCISENESS of her writing. Identify some of the techniques through which she achieves it, and point out examples of their use.

Ideas for Discussion and Writing:

1. In paragraph 31 Carr states of the second D'Sonoqua: "The power that I felt was not in the thing itself, but in some tremendous force behind it, that the carver had believed in." And in paragraph 53, she states of the third D'Sonoqua: "sincerity underlay every stroke." Is skill itself insufficient to create art? Must the artist believe in some "tremendous force"?
2. What is art for? As you seek answers to this far-reaching question, think of various manifestations of art:
   — Monumental architecture, as in cathedrals, banks, and large train stations
   — Pretty paintings and photographs on living room walls
   — Heroic sculptures of politicians and generals riding their horses or standing on pedestals in parks
   — "Unrealistic" art in its many forms: impressionism, cubism, surrealism, expressionism, etc.
   — The images of D'Sonoqua described by Emily Carr

3. The narrator, the little girl, and Indian Tom are all afraid of D'Sonoqua. Do humans create monsters because they crave something to fear? To hate? To test themselves against? Think of Polyphemus, Grendel, Frankenstein's monster, Dracula, Moby Dick, King Kong, witches, ghosts, and "the bogeyman."

4. If you have read "What You Get Is Not Always What You See," by John Bentley Mays, compare the ways in which art interprets nature in the paintings of the Group of Seven and in the images of D'Sonoqua described by Carr.

5. **PROCESS IN WRITING:** *Write a vivid and detailed description of any one work of art that you see every day (it could be a well-designed building; a public sculpture; a photograph, poster, or painting on your wall; etc.). First take notes or brainstorm, to generate material and to choose an overall effect. After a quick "discovery draft," deliberately add more and more FIGURES OF SPEECH and SENSE IMAGES. Then, like Carr, trim every single word that does not in some way contribute to your overall main effect.*

Note: See also the Topics for Writing at the end of this chapter.

Topics for Writing

CHAPTER 3: DESCRIPTION

Describe one of the following as vividly as you can. (See also the guidelines that follow.)

1. The crowd at a rock concert
2. Cottage country in autumn
3. The kitchen of a fast-food restaurant
4. Your favourite painting or sculpture
5. A factory assembly line
6. A polluted river or lake
7. A building that you love or detest
8. Your room
9. Your pet
10. The subway platform during rush hour
11. A garden in July
12. The midway at night
13. A New Year's Eve party
14. Your favourite gallery of a local museum
15. A fitness club on a busy day
16. The terminal of an airport
17. A garage sale
18. A nightclub on a Saturday night
19. A hologram
20. A wedding reception
21. The interior of a barn
22. A highrise building under construction
23. The race track on a busy day
24. The interior of a bus station or train station
25. A professional wrestling match

Note also the Process in Writing topic after each selection in this chapter.

Process in Writing: Guidelines

Follow at least some of these steps in the act of writing your description (your teacher may suggest which ones).

1. *If you can, take eyewitness notes for your description. If you cannot, at least choose a topic you know well enough to make very specific notes from memory.*

2. *Look these notes over. What is the dominant impression, your main feeling or idea of the subject? Put it into a sentence (this will be your THESIS, whether or not you will actually state it in the description).*

3. *With your notes and thesis before you, write a rapid first draft, double-spaced. Get it all down on paper, rather than stopping now to revise.*

4. *When your first draft has "cooled off," look it over. Does every aspect of your description contribute to the main overall effect? If not, revise. Does each word "feel" right? When one does not, consult your thesaurus for another.*

5. *In the next draft increase the SENSE IMAGES — appeals to sight, hearing, touch, smell, and maybe even taste. Add more TRANSITIONS. Read aloud to detect and revise awkwardnesses hidden to the eye.*

6. *Finally, look over the spelling and grammar before writing your good copy. Afterward, proofread word by word. If you have used a computer, save the essay on disk in case your teacher suggests further revision.*

Lambert/Miller Comstock Inc.

When we look out the cottage window at, say, a sunset smoldering over the sparkling waves, exactly *what are we seeing? Is it Nature, redolent with raw, primordial beauty? Or do we see Nature that's been subtly colonized by landscape paintings?*
— *John Bentley Mays, "What You Get Is Not Always What You See"*

Cause and Effect

Here's why. . . .

One of our most human traits is a desire to make sense of things by asking *"why?"* If something good happens, we naturally want to know *why* so we can repeat it. If something bad happens, we want to know *why* so we can avoid it in the future. And other times we want to know *why* out of plain curiosity. These motives are so strong that cause and effect reasoning is one of our chief ways of thinking — and one of our best ways to organize an essay.

When you investigate causes and effects, try to get them right. Some years ago, a church in Florida began a campaign to burn records by Elton John and other rock stars. A survey had reported that 984 out of 1000 girls who had become pregnant out of wedlock had "committed fornication while rock music was played." The assumption was automatic: rock music causes pregnancy. Before they lit the first match, though, the church members might have asked what *other* causes contributed to the effect. How many of the music lovers had also taken alcohol or drugs? How many had failed to use means of birth control? Was the music played because "fornication" generally takes place inside a building, where sound systems also happen to be? The church might also have investigated causes further in the past: What kinds of family backgrounds and what influences of society prepared the fornicators to enter the situation in the first place? And, finally, the church might have asked how often people in this age group listened to Elton John and his friends while *not* fornicating. Rock music may still be to blame — but who knows without a more objective and thorough search of causes? When you trace causes and effects, consider these principles:

Just because one event follows another, don't assume the first causes the second. If a black cat crosses the road just before your car blows up, put the blame where it belongs: not on the cat but on the mechanic who forgot to replace your crankcase oil.

Control your prejudices. If the bank manager refuses to give you a loan, is it because bankers are capitalist exploiters who like to keep the rest of us down? Or is it because this one had to call the collection agency the last time you took out a loan?

Explore causes behind causes. Your employer promoted you because you work hard. But why do you work hard: because you are afraid of being fired? Because you need the money to pay off your car? Because your parents set a workaholic example for you? Or because in fact you like the job?

Many events have multiple causes and multiple effects:

In addition, each of these causes may have one or more causes behind it, and each of these effects may produce further effects, leading to an infinite chain of causality receding into the past and reaching into the future. Where, then, do you draw the boundaries as you plan an essay of cause and effect? The answer lies in your own common sense: include enough to make your point clearly and fairly, then stop. If your parents are workaholics, a description of their behaviour may help a reader to understand your own. But do we need to hear about your grandparents as well? If we do, would a quick summary be enough, since we've already heard the details in your parents' case?

All the essays in this chapter show at least one clear-cut cause and at least one clear-cut effect. But while some pay equal attention to both, others focus down to emphasize *mostly* cause or *mostly* effect. And while some show only one major cause or one major effect, others show a great number of causes or a great number of effects. As you choose your own approach to the organization of a cause-and-effect essay, remember above all your *purpose*: What arrangement will most strongly explain and emphasize your main point? Use it.

Note: Many essays in other chapters use cause and effect to help make their point. See especially these:

Judy Stoffman, "The Way of All Flesh," p. 238

Margaret Atwood, "Canadians: What Do They Want?" p. 302

David Suzuki, "Native Peoples Liken Ruination of Nature to Church Destruction," p. 157

John Bentley Mays, "What You Get Is Not Always What You See," p. 117

Catharine Parr Traill, "Remarks of Security of Person and Property in Canada," p. 148

Gregory Clark

The Cat

Greg Clark (1892–1977) was a storyteller. For many years on the inside back page of Weekend Magazine *he told a story each week about the war, or his hunting and fishing pals, or characters he knew, or the odd events that came his way in Toronto. And in his last years, living in Toronto's old King Edward Hotel, he would delight staff and friends in the dining room by spinning tales from a long and colourful life. Hardly believing that so may things could happen to one person, his readers or listeners often wondered if the stories were true. "What a question to ask!" Clark would reply. He was born in Toronto and was a journalist — reporter, feature writer and columnist — for over 60 years. He began with the paper his father edited, the* Toronto Star. *When the First World War came, he tried several times to enlist but was turned down for being too small. When Clark finally got into the army, though, he rose from private to major and won the Military Cross for courage under fire at Vimy Ridge. Afterwards he returned to the* Star, *where he worked with Ernest Hemingway, Morley Callaghan, and Gordon Sinclair. During the next war, he served as a war correspondent until his own son was killed in action. Clark's greatest popularity came with the column he wrote for* Weekend Magazine *from 1952 almost to the end of his life. Many of these pieces — short, funny, warmhearted, and full of homely wisdom — were gathered in books, among them* Hi There! *(1963), from which our selection comes.*

1   As far, far back as I could remember, I had a dread of cats. Dread, I think, is the word. Not fear. Not hatred. Not revulsion. Just dread.

2   One time, my fishing companion, W. C. Milne, asked me to pick up his fishing tackle at his house, and gave me the key. His wife was out of town.

3   I didn't know the Milnes had acquired a cat. I opened the front door and started through the vestibule for the living room, where the tackle was heaped on a chair. I froze in my tracks.

4   Somebody was in the house!

"Margaret?" I called.

No answer.

From a golf bag in the vestibule I took an iron.

Everything in my nature told me SOMEBODY was in the house. As an old soldier, though only 30, I had an instinct for danger. I could FEEL it.

From wall to wall, I slid to the back door, finding it locked. With the niblick ready to throw or to swing, I sidled up the stairs, knowing any instant I would have to strike. In those days, I was not afraid of men.

Along the hall, into one room, then another, I moved, all tight as a stretched elastic band. In the front bedroom, on the bed was a black-and-yellow cat, arching aristocratically on being disturbed. I yelled, and chased it from the room and down the stairs and out the back door, which I opened, banging the golf stick.

"Ah, yes," said Billy Milne, when I told him. "That's our new cat."

But as I remember it, it never came home.

As a child, I used to cross the street, on my way to school, if I saw a cat in my path. In my teens, at the age when we look for chosen friends, I lost sundry friends because they had a cat in the house. In World War I, as a young fellow with the lives of thirty-eight men on my mind and soul, I led a night patrol into a ruined farmhouse and made an utter ass of myself because I let fly with a Very light pistol into a black cellar empty save for a poor mangy cat.

But I was certain it had been the enemy.

It took me weeks to restore the faith of my thirty-eight men.

Ah, cats!

"It," said my doctor friends, consolingly, "is one of those mysterious, unexplainable phobias. . . ."

I was in the back half of my fifties when I visited my Aunt Minnie Greig, in Seaforth, Ont. She was my stylish aunt, a beautiful woman.

We sat on her veranda, rocking; and she, being my elder by twenty or more years, was regaling me with stories of times past.

"You were an awful little shrimp," she said.

"Was I?" I regretted.

"So timid," said Aunt Min.

"Was I?" I muttered.

"Do you remember your white cat?" she asked.

"MY white cat?" I barely whispered.

"Joe, your dad," said Aunt Minnie, rocking idly, "bought you a white cat, since your mother wouldn't have a dog in the house. It was a beauty, that cat. Snow white."

I had a strange feeling, as I sat watching Aunt Minnie rocking, that I was in the act of taking off a heavy coat, a coat with pockets full of things.

28   "How old was I?" I said.

29   "Two," said Aunt Minnie. "You still had diapers. Do you remember what the back yard was like?"

30   "Yes," I said. "I was eight when we left there. There was a grape vine on the fence at the far end."

31   "Right," said Aunt Minnie. "A grape arbor."

32   "And over that fence," I said, "was Lilley's greenhouses."

33   "Good for you !" cried Aunt Minnie. "The Lilleys were the florists, and they had those greenhouses. . . ."

34   "What," I interrupted cautiously, "about the cat?"

35   "I'm coming to that," said Aunt Minnie. "Well, the Lilleys had trouble with mice and rats in the greenhouses. So they used to put out poison."

36   "Did I," I asked, "like the cat? The white cat?"

37   "LIKE it!" cried Aunt Minnie. "There you'd go, staggering around with that cat draped over your skinny little arm."

38   "I . . ." I said, and stopped.

39   "You took the cat to BED with you," said Aunt Min. "I told your mother, Sarah Louisa, never, never to let a cat in bed with an infant. But there you were with that blamed cat on the pillow beside your head."

40   "Well, I . . ." I tried again, my body prickling, my back hair creeping as it did in that ruined farmhouse in Flanders.

41   "The cat," said Aunt Min, "seemed as attached to you as you were to it. It followed you everywhere, around the house, out the door, in the back yard."

42   I pressed my back against the back of my chair.

43   "It was white?" I asked.

44   "Snow white, I told you," said Aunt Min. "Well, here's what happened. Your lovely white cat disappeared!"

45   "Disappeared?"

46   "I was staying with your mother at the time," said Aunt Min. "The cat vanished. It was gone all night. It didn't come home the next day. You kept toddling around, hunting for it, upstairs, downstairs, out the door, all around the yard, back in the door, upstairs, downstairs, until we were sick of the sight of you."

47   "Did I cry?"

48   "No, you just went wandering around, looking under everything. It was kind of pitiable, really."

49   "So?" I said, my back no longer twitching.

50   "We were sitting in the kitchen, having a cup of tea," said Aunt Minnie.

"Your mother, Mamie Armour, Mrs. Taylor from next door, and your Aunt Mart.

"Then," said Aunt Min, "up the back steps from the yard you came, CARRYING your white cat!" 51

I tightened. 52

"It was DEAD!" cried Aunt Min. "STIFF dead! It had been dead two 53 days. Poisoned from Lilley's greenhouses. Its tail was sticking out stiff. Its white fur was all matted, damp. And you were HUGGING it to your little chest, your chin over it."

"What happened?" I got the question out. 54

"Why, we all screamed!" said Aunt Min. "Your mother was first to 55 reach you, and she snatched the cat from you so violently, you fell back on the steps; and she THREW it half way down the yard, and we were all screaming and yelling, and Aunt Mart had a fainting spell, and you were howling, and your mother was grabbing at you. . . ."

ΔΔΔ

Do you know what I wish you for a Happy New Year? 56

I wish you the luck to find YOUR Aunt Min, and have her tell you 57 anecdotes about your childhood.

For in them, you may find, as I found, absolution from ancient fears, 58 and mysterious dreads, and the strange darknesses that lie beyond the horizon of consciousness.

To know is to understand, even yourself. 59

ΔΔΔΔΔΔΔΔΔΔΔΔΔΔΔΔΔΔΔΔΔΔΔΔΔΔΔΔΔΔΔΔΔΔΔΔΔΔΔΔΔΔΔΔΔΔΔΔΔΔΔΔΔΔΔΔΔΔ

Further Reading:

Gregory Clark, *Hi There!*
Jock Carroll, *The Life & Times of Greg Clark*

Structure:

1. Point out several effects achieved by the introduction (par. 1–17).
2. Is Clark's "dread" of cats caused by only one event? Or is there a chain of *cause and effect*? If so, point out all the links in the chain.
3. Most of this selection takes the form of *narration*. Why are there two narrators?
4. Gregory Clark's usual way of exploring a subject was to tell a story. Do you think the cause and effect analysis of this

selection is helped or harmed by the narrative form in which it appears?

Style:

1. Although this selection is short, it contains 59 paragraphs. Give as many reasons as you can for their short length.
2. How FORMAL or INFORMAL is the STYLE of this selection? Refer to passages that illustrate your answer.
3. Explain the effect of paragraph 27: "I had a strange feeling, as I sat watching Aunt Minnie rocking, that I was in the act of taking off a heavy coat, a coat with pockets full of things."

Ideas for Discussion and Writing:

1. For many years the inside back page of *Weekend Magazine* featured Clark's "shorties," as he called them. When he was first offered that page to fill, he wondered if he could write anything in so few words. "It's quite simple," his editor said. "Write about small things." Is Clark's story of the cat a "small thing"? In what ways may it be larger than it seems at first?
2. Discuss the emotions that the women exhibit to young Clark in paragraph 55. How would you have reacted if you had been one of those women, and why?
3. The process that Clark describes is similar to that of psychoanalysis: learning about oneself in order to find "absolution from ancient fears, and mysterious dreads, and the strange darknesses that lie beyond the horizon of consciousness" (par. 58). Clark found his "absolution." Do you believe that self-knowledge always has a good result? How does self-knowledge help us in life?
4. Do you have unexplained "dreads," like Clark's dread of cats? Name one or two and invent possible *causes* for them. Join class members in inventing possible causes of each other's dreads.
5. PROCESS IN WRITING: *Visualize your own worst "dread." Now probe its causes by first writing its name in the middle of a page, then adding near it other words that it brings to mind. Draw lines of connection. Now take the best insights from this cluster outline and use them in the first draft of an essay that traces the actual or probable causes of your attitude. In the second draft add more IMAGES and examples to help us "see" your subject. Have you used transitions like "because," "since," "so," and "as a result" enough to emphasize the cause and effect? Have*

you trimmed deadwood? Have you tested your prose aloud before writing the final version?

Note: See also the Topics for Writing at the end of this chapter.

David Suzuki

Hidden Lessons*

Like Joy Kogawa (see p. 323), David Suzuki was born in Vancouver (1936) of Japanese ancestry and during the Second World War was interned as an "enemy alien." Since then, like Kogawa, he has made a major contribution to the life of the country that once persecuted him. Suzuki earned a Ph.D. at the University of Chicago (1961), specializing in genetics, then began to teach at the University of British Columbia. He swiftly gained an international reputation for his genetic research on fruit flies, and in 1969 won a prize as "outstanding research scientist in Canada." Since then he has won many other awards, grants, and honorary degrees. He lectures internationally, writes a syndicated newspaper column, and in addition to his scholarly publications has written books for a larger audience: Metamorphosis *(his autobiography, 1987), and* Looking at Insects/Looking at Plants *(1987, for children). But he has won his greatest prominence as host of the CBC's popular and long-lived television series* The Nature of Things. *Though some scientists think he is wasting his talents in broadcasting, Suzuki believes that research and scholarly publication are not enough: the effects of science and technology on our daily lives are so vast, so pervasive, so full of both hope and danger for all of us, that they must be explained to the general public. In performing this service for his viewers and readers, Suzuki has become a moralist as well as a scientist, urging week after week that we share this planet more generously with its other species. Our selection, from the February 7, 1987* Toronto Globe and Mail, *makes the point in an especially concrete way. (See also p. 157 for more discussion of Suzuki and another sample of his work.)*

1   In spite of the vast expanse of wilderness in this country, most Canadian children grow up in urban settings. In other words, they live in a world conceived, shaped and dominated by people. Even the farms located around cities and towns are carefully groomed and landscaped for human convenience. There's nothing wrong with that, of course, but in such an environment, it's very easy to lose any sense of connection with nature.

---

*Editor's title.

In city apartments and dwellings, the presence of cockroaches, fleas, ants, mosquitoes or houseflies is guaranteed to elicit the spraying of insecticides. Mice and rats are poisoned or trapped, while the gardener wages a never-ending struggle with ragweed, dandelions, slugs and root-rot. We have a modern arsenal of chemical weapons to fight off these invaders and we use them lavishly.

We worry when kids roll in the mud or wade through a puddle because they'll get "dirty." Children learn attitudes and values very quickly and the lesson in cities is very clear — nature is an enemy, it's dirty, dangerous or a nuisance. So youngsters learn to distance themselves from nature and to try to control it. I am astonished at the number of adults who loathe or are terrified by snakes, spiders, butterflies, worms, birds — the list seems endless.

If you reflect on the history of humankind, you realize that for 99 per cent of our species' existence on the planet, we were deeply embedded in and dependent on nature. When plants and animals were plentiful, we flourished. When famine and drought struck, our numbers fell accordingly. We remain every bit as dependent upon nature today — we need plants to fix photons of energy into sugar molecules and to cleanse the air and replenish the oxygen. It is folly to forget our dependence on an intact ecosystem. But we do whenever we teach our offspring to fear or detest the natural world. The urban message kids get runs completely counter to what they are born with, a natural interest in other life forms. Just watch a child in a first encounter with a flower or an ant — there is instant interest and fascination. We condition them out of it.

The result is that when my 7-year-old daughter brings home new friends, they invariably recoil in fear or disgust when she tries to show them her favorite pets — three beautiful salamanders that her grandfather got for her in Vancouver. And when my 3-year-old comes wandering in with her treasures — millipedes, spiders, slugs and sowbugs that she catches under rocks lining the front lawn — children and adults alike usually respond by saying "yuk."

I can't overemphasize the tragedy of that attitude. For, inherent in this view is the assumption that human beings are special and different and that we lie outside nature. Yet it is this belief that is creating many of our environmental problems today.

Does it matter whether we sense our place in nature so long as we have cities and technology? Yes, for many reasons, not the least of which is that virtually all scientists were fascinated with nature as children and retained that curiosity throughout their lives. But a far more important reason is that if we retain a spiritual sense of connection with all other life forms, it can't help but profoundly affect the way we act. Whenever my daughter sees a picture of an animal dead or dying, she asks me fearfully,

"Daddy, are there any more?" At 7 years, she already knows about extinction and it frightens her.

8   The yodel of a loon at sunset, the vast flocks of migrating waterfowl in the fall, the indomitable salmon returning thousands of kilometres — these images of nature have inspired us to create music, poetry and art. And when we struggle to retain a handful of California condors or whooping cranes, it's clearly not from a fear of ecological collapse, it's because there is something obscene and frightening about the disappearance of another species at our hands.

9   If children grow up understanding that we are animals, they will look at other species with a sense of fellowship and community. If they understand their ecological place — the biosphere — then when children see the great virgin forests of the Queen Charlotte Islands being clearcut, they will feel physical pain, because they will understand that those trees are an extension of themselves.

10   When children who know their place in the ecosystem see factories spewing poison into the air, water and soil, they will feel ill because someone has violated their home. This is not mystical mumbo-jumbo. We have poisoned the life support systems that sustain all organisms because we have lost a sense of ecological place. Those of us who are parents have to realize the unspoken, negative lessons we are conveying to our children. Otherwise, they will continue to desecrate this planet as we have.

11   It's not easy to avoid giving these hidden lessons. I have struggled to cover my dismay and queasiness when Severn and Sarika come running in with a large wolf spider or when we've emerged from a ditch covered with leeches or when they have been stung accidentally by yellowjackets feeding on our leftovers. But that's nature. I believe efforts to teach children to love and respect other life forms are priceless.

ΔΔΔΔΔΔΔΔΔΔΔΔΔΔΔΔΔΔΔΔΔΔΔΔΔΔΔΔΔΔΔΔΔΔΔΔΔΔΔΔΔΔΔΔΔΔΔΔΔΔΔΔΔΔΔΔΔΔΔ

Further Reading:

David Suzuki, *Metamorphosis*
Rachel Carson, *Silent Spring*
Annie Dillard, *Pilgrim at Tinker Creek*
Henry David Thoreau, *Walden*

Structure:

1.   What rhetorical device does David Suzuki use in his opening sentence, and how does it begin to introduce his subject?

2.   Which does Suzuki explore more thoroughly, the *causes* of children's positive or negative attitudes toward nature or the

effects of these attitudes? Point out which paragraphs analyze mostly *causes* and which analyze mostly *effects*. Is Suzuki right to discuss the causes first and the effects afterward?

3. How long a chain of cause and effect does Suzuki show us? Point out each link.

4. Suzuki no doubt hopes his argument will spur us to action. Does his closing help to achieve that goal? When he admits in paragraph 11 that "It's not easy to avoid giving these hidden lessons," do you feel discouraged or challenged?

Style:

1. Describe Suzuki's prose: Is it like that of Franklin Russell's essay in this chapter, full of deliberate strategies and devices calculated to affect us? Or is it a plain and direct means to express a message? Is either of these approaches better? Which do you prefer to read? Which do you use in your own writing, and why?

2. Why is paragraph 6 the shortest paragraph of the essay?

Ideas for Discussion and Writing:

1. Do you share the negative attitudes discussed by Suzuki? Do you dread or fear insects, worms, snakes, mice, or weeds? If so, how did you learn these attitudes? How similar are they to those of your parents? And what dangers, if any, do these life forms actually pose to you?

2. In paragraph 8 Suzuki writes, "there is something obscene and frightening about the disappearance of another species at our hands." Yet elsewhere he has claimed that two species an hour disappear from the earth, mostly because we "develop" natural habitats for our own profit. How important to you is a new paper mill, a logging project in the rain forest, a highway, dam, housing project, ski resort, oil well, or aluminum smelter — compared to the existence of a species? Defend your view with reasons.

3. First we learned to shun *racism*, and then *sexism*. Is *speciesism* next? Argue why we should or why we should not continue to regard ourselves as far more important than other members of our ecosystem.

4. Our exploitation of nature has often led to economic growth. To what extent is this exchange desirable? If we could save the rivers, the lakes, the rain forests, and our other ecosystems on earth by consuming less, how would you react? How large a

cut in income would you accept to achieve the goal: 10 percent, 25 percent, 50 percent, or none at all? Defend your answer with arguments.

5. If it is now tree-planting season (early to middle spring, or late fall), buy a tree at a nursery, then plant it in a good location (perhaps in the garden of your parents or other relations). Now write an essay tracing the future *effects* of this act upon our own species. In your second draft, make sure you have analyzed the effects of effects, as you look into the future.

6. PROCESS IN WRITING: *Find an article about an environmental problem, in a current issue of your favourite newspaper or newsmagazine. In response, write a short but hard-hitting letter to the editor exposing the* effects *of the problem. Since editors like conciseness, edit your second or third draft painstakingly so that every word counts. Cut deadwood. Replace vague or weak words with exact and strong ones. Do not "tell" at great length, but "show" with quick and vivid images or examples. Now try a draft out on an "audience" of three or four classmates; incorporate the best of their suggestions before mailing your final copy to the editor. Then watch the next issues to see whether your message is printed. If the editor has cut any part of your letter, analyze why: Was it wordy? Weak? Off the topic?*

Note: See also the Topics for Writing at the end of this chapter.

Mordecai Richler

1944: The Year I Learned to Love a German

Mordecai Richler is one of our most widely read novelists and one of the best Canadian essayists of his generation. His carefully crafted, funny, ruthlessly satirical prose devastates its targets: hypocrisy, pretension, self-righteousness, prejudice, provincialism, and nationalism (he attacks all these things in our selection). Richler was born in 1931 to a working-class family in the Jewish quarter of Montreal. In 1951 he left to spend two years in Paris, where he wrote his first novel. He returned to work at the CBC, then from 1954 to 1972 lived and worked in England. Since 1972 he has made his home in Montreal. Richler has maintained a steady output of novels: The Acrobats *(1954),* Son of a Smaller Hero *(1955),* A Choice of Enemies *(1957),* The Apprenticeship of Duddy Kravitz *(1959),* The Incomparable Atuk *(1963),* Cocksure *(1968),* St. Urbain's Horseman *(1971), and* Joshua Then and Now *(1980). Both* Duddy Kravitz *and* Joshua *have been made into films, as well as his children's book* Jacob Two-Two Meets the Hooded Fang *(1975). Many of Richler's more than 300 essays and articles, published in journals both here and abroad, have been collected in books:* Hunting Tigers under Glass *(1968),* Shovelling Trouble *(1972),* Notes on an Endangered Species *(1974),* The Great Comic Book Heroes *(1978) and* Home Sweet Home: My Canadian Album *(1984). Our selection is from the* New York Times Book Review *of February 2, 1986. It is Richler's adaptation of his introduction to the Book-of-the-Month-Club edition of Remarque's novel. This fine example of Richler's thought and style has been reprinted elsewhere in abbreviated form, but is presented here in its entirety.*

R eading was not one of my boyhood passions. Girls, or rather the absence of girls, drove me to it. When I was 13 years old, short for my age, more than somewhat pimply, I was terrified of girls. They made me feel sadly inadequate. As far as I could make out, they were attracted only to boys who were tall or played for the school basketball team or at least shaved. Unable to qualify on all three counts, I resorted to subterfuge. I set out to call attention to myself by becoming a character. Retreating into high seriousness, I acquired a pipe, which I chewed on ostentatiously, and made it my business to be seen everywhere, even at school basketball games, absorbed by books of daunting significance. Say, H. G. Wells's "Short History of the World" or Paul de Kruif's "Microbe Hunters" or John Gunther inside one continent or another. I rented these thought-provoking books for three cents a day from a neighborhood lending library that was across the street from a bowling alley where I used to spot pins four nights a week.

2   Oh, my God, I would not be 13 again for anything. The sweetly scented girls of my dreams, wearing lipstick and tight sweaters and nylon stockings, would sail into the bowling alley holding hands with the boys from the basketball team. "Hi," they would call out, giggly, nudging one another, even as I bent over the pins, "how goes the reading?"

3   The two women who ran the lending library, possibly amused by my pretensions, tried to interest me in fiction.

4   "I want fact. I can't be bothered with *stories*," I protested, waving my pipe at them, affronted. "I just haven't got the time for such nonsense."

5   I knew what novels were, of course. I had read "Scaramouche," by Rafael Sabatini, at school, as well as "Treasure Island" and some Ellery Queens and a couple of thumpers by G. A. Henty. Before that there had been Action Comics, Captain Marvel, Batman and — for educational reasons — either Bible Comics or Classic Comics. All these treasures I bought under the counter, as it were. They were passed hand to hand on dark street corners. Contraband. Our samizdat. The reason for this being that in 1943 the dolts who prevailed in Ottawa had adjudged American comic books unessential to the war effort, a drain on the Canadian dollar.

6   Novels, I knew, were mere romantic make-believe, not as bad as poetry, to be fair, but bad enough. Our high school class master, a dedicated Scot, had been foolish enough to try to interest us in poetry. A veteran of World War I, he told us that during the nightly bombardments on the Somme he would fix a candle to his steel helmet so that he could read poetry in the trenches. A scruffy lot, we were not moved. Instead we exchanged knowing winks behind that admirable man's back. Small wonder, we agreed, that he had ended up no better than a high school teacher.

7   My aunts consumed historical novels like pastries. My father read Black Mask and True Detective. My mother would read anything on a Jewish subject, preferably by I. J. Singer or Sholem Asch, though she

would never forgive the latter for having written "The Nazarene," never mind "Mary" and "The Apostle." My older brother kept a novel, "Topper Takes a Trip," secure under his mattress in the bedroom we shared, assuring me that it was placed at just such an angle on the springs that if it were moved so much as a millimeter in his absence he would know and bloody well make me pay for it.

I fell ill with a childhood disease. I no longer remember which, but obviously I meant it as a rebuke to those girls in tight sweaters who continued to ignore me. Never mind, they would mourn at my funeral, burying me with my pipe. Too late, they would say, "Boy, was he ever an intellectual!"   8

The women from the lending library, concerned, dropped off books for me at our house. The real stuff. Fact-filled. Providing me with the inside dope on Theodor Herzl's childhood and "Brazil Yesterday, Today, and Tomorrow." One day they brought me a novel: "All Quiet on the Western Front" by Erich Maria Remarque. The painting on the jacket that was taped to the book showed a soldier wearing what was unmistakably a German Army helmet. *What was this*, I wondered, *some sort of bad joke?*   9

Nineteen forty-four that was, and I devoutly wished every German left on the face of the earth an excruciating death. The Allied invasion of France had not yet begun, but I cheered every Russian counterattack, each German city bombed, and — with the help of a map tacked to my bedroom wall — followed the progress of the Canadian troops fighting their way up the Italian boot. Boys from our street had already been among the fallen. Izzy Draper's uncle, Harvey Kugelmass's older brother. The boy who was supposed to marry Gita Holtzman.   10

"All Quiet on the Western Front" lay unopened on my bed for two days. A time bomb ticking away, though I hardly suspected it. Rather than read a novel, a novel written by a German, I tuned in to radio soap operas in the afternoons: "Ma Perkins," "Pepper Young's Family." I organized a new baseball league for short players who didn't shave yet, appointing myself commissioner, the first Canadian to be so honored. Sifting through a stack of my father's back issues of Popular Mechanics, I was sufficiently inspired to invent a spaceship and fly to Mars, where I was adored by everybody, especially the girls. Finally, I was driven to picking up "All Quiet on the Western Front" out of boredom. I never expected that a mere novel, a stranger's tale, could actually be dangerous, creating such turbulence in my life, obliging me to question so many received ideas. About Germans. About my own monumental ignorance of the world. About what novels were.   11

At the age of 13 in 1944, happily as yet untainted by English 104, I   12 couldn't tell you whether Remarque's novel was

a. a slice of life
b. symbolic
c. psychological
d. seminal.

13   I couldn't even say if it was well or badly written. In fact, as I recall, it
didn't seem to be "written" at all. Instead, it just flowed. Now, of course, I
understand that writing that doesn't advertise itself is art of a very high
order. It doesn't come easily. But at the time I wasn't capable of making
such distinctions. I also had no notion of how "All Quiet on the Western
Front" rated critically as a war novel. I hadn't read Stendhal or Tolstoy
or Crane or Hemingway. I hadn't even heard of them. I didn't know that
Thomas Mann, whoever he was, had praised the novel highly. Neither
did I know that in 1929 the judges at some outfit called the
Book-of-the-Month Club had made it their May selection. But what I did
know is that, hating Germans with a passion, I had read only 20, maybe
30, pages before the author had seduced me into identifying with my
enemy, 19-year-old Paul Baumer, thrust into the bloody trenches of
World War I with his schoolmates: Müller, Kemmerich and the reluctant
Joseph Behm, one of the first to fall. As if that weren't sufficiently
unsettling in itself, the author, having won my love for Paul, my enormous
concern for his survival, then betrayed me in the last dreadful paragraphs
of his book:

14   "He fell in October 1918, on a day that was so quiet and still on the
whole front, that the army report confined itself to the single sentence: All
quiet on the Western Front.

15   "He had fallen forward and lay on the earth as though sleeping.
Turning him over one saw that he could not have suffered long; his face
had an expression of calm, as though almost glad the end had come."

16   The movies, I knew from experience, never risked letting you down like
that. No matter how bloody the battle, how long the odds, Errol Flynn,
Robert Taylor, even Humphrey Bogart could be counted on to survive
and come home to Ann Sheridan, Lana Turner or — if they were sensitive
types — Loretta Young. Only character actors, usually Brooklyn Dodger
fans, say George Tobias or William Bendix, were expendable.

17   Obviously, having waded into the pool of serious fiction by accident, I
was not sure I liked or trusted the water. It was too deep. Anything could
happen.

18   There was something else, a minor incident in "All Quiet on the
Western Front" that would not have troubled an adult reader but, I'm
embarrassed to say, certainly distressed that 13-year-old boy colliding
with his first serious novel.

Sent out to guard a village that has been abandoned because it is being   19
shelled too heavily, Katczinsky, the incomparable scrounger, surfaces
with suckling pigs and potatoes and carrots for his comrades, a group of
eight altogether:

"The suckling pigs are slaughtered. Kat sees to them. We want to make   20
potato-cakes to go with the roast. But we cannot find a grater for the
potatoes. However, that difficulty is soon got over. With a nail we punch a
lot of holes in a pot lid and there we have a grater. Three fellows put on
thick gloves to protect their fingers against the grater, two others peel the
potatoes, and the business gets going."

The business, I realized, alarmed — no, *affronted* — was the making of   21
potato latkes, a favorite of mine as well as Paul Baumer's, a dish I had
always taken to be Jewish, certainly not a German concoction.

What did I know? Nothing. Or, looked at another way, my real   22
education, my lifelong addiction to fiction, began with the trifling
discovery that the potato latke was not of Jewish origin, but something
borrowed from the Germans and now a taste that Jew and German
shared in spite of everything.

I felt easier about my affection for the German soldier Paul Baumer   23
once I was told by the women from the lending library that when Hitler
came to power in 1933 he had burned all of Erich Maria Remarque's
books and in 1938 he took away his German citizenship. Obviously Hitler
had grasped that novels could be dangerous, something I learned when I
was only 13 years old. He burned them. I began to devour them. I started
to read at the breakfast table and on streetcars, often missing my stop, and
in bed with benefit of a flashlight. It got me into trouble. I grasped, for the
first time, that I didn't live in the center of the world but had been born
into a working-class family in an unimportant country far from the cities
of light: London, Paris, New York. Of course this wasn't my fault, it was
my inconsiderate parents who were to blame. But there was, I now
realized, a larger world out there beyond St. Urbain Street in Montreal; a
world that could be available to me, even though — to my mother's
despair — I had been born left-handed, ate with my elbows on the table
and had failed once more to lead the class at school.

Preparing myself for the *Rive Gauche*,° I bought a blue beret, but I   24
didn't dare wear it outside, or even in the house if anybody else was at
home. I looked at but lacked the courage to buy a cigarette holder. But
the next time I took Goldie Zimmerman to a downtown movie and then
out to Dinty Moore's for toasted tomato sandwiches, I suggested that

---

°*Rive Gauche*: the "Left Bank" of Paris, traditional quarter of students and intellectuals.

instead of milkshakes we each order a glass of *vin ordinaire*. "Are you crazy?" she asked.

25   As my parents bickered at the supper table, trapped in concerns now far too mundane for the likes of me — what to do if Dworkin raised the rent again, how to manage my brother's college fees — I sat with but actually apart from them in the kitchen, enthralled, reading for the first time, "All happy families are alike but an unhappy family is unhappy after its own fashion."

26   Erich Maria Remarque, born in Westphalia in 1897, went off to war, directly from school, at the age of 18. He was wounded five times. He lost all his friends. After the war he worked briefly as a schoolteacher, a stonecutter, a test driver for a tire company and an editor of Sportbild magazine. His first novel, "Im Westen Nichts Neues," was turned down by several publishers before it was brought out by the Ullstein Press in Berlin in 1928. "All Quiet on the Western Front" sold 1,200,000 copies in Germany and was translated into 29 languages, selling some four million copies throughout the world. The novel has been filmed three times; the first time, memorably, by Lewis Milestone in 1930. The Milestone version, with Lew Ayres playing Paul Baumer, won Academy Awards for best picture and best direction.

27   Since "All Quiet on the Western Front" once meant so much to me, I picked it up again with a certain anxiety. After all this time I find it difficult to be objective about the novel. Its pages still evoke for me a back bedroom with a cracked ceiling and a sizzling radiator on St. Urbain Street, mice scrabbling in the walls, a window looking out on sheets frozen stiff on the laundry line, and all the pain of being too young to shave, an ignorant and bewildered boy of 13.

28   Over the years the novel has lost something in shock value. The original jacket copy of the 1929 Little, Brown & Company edition of "All Quiet on the Western Front" warns the reader that it is "at times crude" and "will shock the supersensitive by its outspokenness." Contemporary readers, far from being shocked, will be amused by the novel's discretion, the absence of explicit sex scenes, the unbelievably polite dialogue of the men in the trenches.

ΔΔΔ

29   The novel also has its poignant moments, both in the trenches and when Paul Baumer goes home on leave, an old man of 19, only to find insufferably pompous schoolmasters still recruiting the young with mindless prattle about the fatherland and the glory of battle. Strong characters are deftly sketched. Himmelstoss, the postman who becomes a

crazed drillmaster, Tjaden, the peasant soldier, Kantorek, the school-master. On the front line the enemy is never the Frogs or the Limeys, but the insanity of the war itself. It is the war, in fact, and not even Paul Baumer, that is the novel's true protagonist. In a brief introduction to the novel Remarque wrote: "This book is to be neither an accusation nor a confession, and least of all an adventure, for death is not an adventure to those who stand face to face with it. It will try simply to tell of a generation of men who, even though they may have escaped its shells, were destroyed by the war."

Since World War I we have become altogether too familiar with larger   30
horrors. The Holocaust, Hiroshima, the threat of a nuclear winter. Death by numbers, cities obliterated by decree. At peace, as it were, we live with the daily dread of the missiles in their silos, ours pointed at them, theirs pointed at us. None of this, however, diminishes the power of "All Quiet on the Western Front," a novel that will endure because of its humanity, its honor and its refusal to lapse into sentimentality or strike a false note. It is a work that has earned its place on that small shelf of World War I classics alongside "Goodbye to All That," by Robert Graves, and Ernest Hemingway's "A Farewell to Arms."

△△△

Further Reading:

Mordecai Richler,
> *The Apprenticeship of Duddy Kravitz*
> *The Street* (short stories)

Erich Maria Remarque, *All Quiet on the Western Front*
Charles Yale Harrison, *Generals Die in Bed* (novel)
Ernest Hemingway, *A Farewell to Arms* (novel)

Structure:

1. Through his long introduction, how does Mordecai Richler prepare us for the argument that follows? Specifically, what do paragraphs 1 and 2 achieve? What do paragraphs 3–6 achieve?
2. Why does Richler devote such a short portion of his argument to the original *causes* of his reading, and such a large portion to the *effects*?
3. Point out all the *effects* on young Richler of reading novels, as shown especially in paragraph 11, paragraphs 13–17, paragraphs 18–22, and paragraph 23.
4. Do you like Richler's technique of using spaces to divide the parts of his essay? Have you ever tried this? In short essays or in long essays?

5. What closing technique does Richler employ when in paragraph 30 he refers to nuclear weapons?

Style:

1. Richler's message is obviously serious. Why, then, does he poke fun at adolescence, at his own and others' reading habits, at high school English, at the movies, and other targets? Do Richler's humour and even SATIRE strengthen or weaken his argument? Defend your answer with reasons.
2. One of the most reliable techniques of both novelists and essayists is to clothe abstractions in concrete IMAGES — to "show, don't tell." Analyze how Richler applies this principle in paragraphs 11, 24, and 27.
3. Explain Richler's IRONY in calling Paul Baumer "an old man of 19" (par. 29). Using this example and its context, explain how irony can produce CONCISENESS.
4. Point out all the ways in which the METAPHOR of Remarque's novel as a "time bomb" (par. 11) is appropriate to this topic.

Ideas for Discussion and Writing:

1. Almost all well-known writers share with Richler the fact of having at some time read voraciously. Analyze this apparent *cause-and-effect* relationship: Why does reading other people's writing help us improve our own? Have you read enough? Analyze the *causes* of your attitude towards reading. Analyze also the *effects*.
2. Richler admits that, as a Jewish boy growing up during the Second World War, he "devoutly wished every German left on the face of the earth an excruciating death" (par. 10). Why *every* German? Describe the STEREOTYPE that underlies this passage. Does it apply to those Germans who hid persecuted Jews? To those who fled Hitler's power, or even tried to assassinate him? Does it apply to Erich Maria Remarque? To Paul Baumer? If this stereotype is unreliable, then what about other stereotypes: of women, teenagers, old people, Newfoundlanders, Quebeckers, Jews, Russians?
3. After reading 20 to 30 pages of *All Quiet on the Western Front*, Richler is "seduced" by the author into "identifying" with his "enemy," and even feels "betrayed" when, at the end, Paul Baumer dies. Cite one example from elsewhere in the essay, to show how fiction changes us by breaking down STEREOTYPES.
4. "I never expected that a mere novel, a stranger's tale, could

actually be dangerous," says Richler in paragraph 11. In what ways can a novel be "dangerous"? Why did Hitler burn this one and strip its author of German citizenship (par. 23)? Name other well-known books that have been burned, censored, or refused publication. What do these reactions reveal about the power and importance of the writer in society?

5. Apply Richler's experience to other media. List the five or ten films you have most recently seen, and list several TV serials you have followed. Which were "dangerous," challenging established attitudes? Which were "safe," reinforcing established attitudes? Defend your judgements with specific examples.

6. **PROCESS IN WRITING:** *Choose either a "dangerous" or a "safe" film or TV series from the previous question. Now in an essay of cause and effect, analyze how the chosen work affected your attitude: Did it change your mind about something? Or did it reinforce your existing attitude? Begin with a page of notes: jot down specific scenes in which the work disturbed or reassured you. Now use the best of this material in your first draft. Did the act of writing awaken pertinent details you had forgotten? Add them. Did the act of writing even change your opinion about whether the work is "dangerous" or "safe"? If so, change your thesis and adjust your examples. In successive drafts strengthen your transitions to speed your argument and highlight the causality. Cut deadwood. Finally, test your prose aloud before writing the final version.*

Note: See also the Topics for Writing at the end of this chapter.

B. W. Powe

Book Ends?

As a writer in an age of electronic media, B. W. Powe considers himself a "solitary outlaw," an outsider fighting the currents of his time. Born in 1955 in Ottawa, he studied at York University and at the University of Toronto, where he was profoundly influenced by the concept of media theorist Marshall McLuhan that electronic media are turning the world into a "global village." Although McLuhan and his followers once saw a potential for democracy in this process, Powe believes that in the "post-literate" global village, we surrender our individual judgement to the group and thus lose control of our destiny. In his highly charged prose, Powe warns readers over and over that the only way to retain independence is to perform the solitary acts of reading and thinking. This perspective underlies his 1984 book of literary criticism A Climate Charged, *and especially his 1987 book of essays* The Solitary Outlaw, *in which he holds up for inspection the examples of five literate and therefore independent public figures, among them Canadians Pierre Trudeau, Glenn Gould, and Marshall McLuhan himself. Powe works as a media consultant as well as writing articles, reviews, essays, stories, and books. Our selection first appeared in the June 13, 1987 Toronto* Globe and Mail.

1   An editor once called me on the telephone to verify copy changes in an article I had written.

2   "I've corrected the typos in the manuscript," he explained, "including the one in your name. You left the two Ls off of Powell."

3   Indignant, I answered: "Do you think I'd misspell my own name?"

4   "Well, how was I to know?" he said. "You spelled Hemingway with only one m."

5   This true story may be indicative of a decay in the publishing industry. The perhaps insignificant event may speak of the shift we are now experiencing from literate awareness to what I have called post-literacy. This is the decay of the role of the word in the electronic society. It is a decay that can affect writers, readers, publishers, editors and book-designers — the structure of the means of production of the printed word, of what we call a book.

On record are the opinions of a book-lover. Call it a partisan   6
enthusiasm. Whatever this love may be, I can still walk into a bookstore
(well stocked with recent work, reprints of old) and feel replenished, as if I
have been out with old, loyal friends. I am not objective about this issue. I
am prepared to be impolite.

Only now I suspect that the great days of publishing may be past,   7
vaporized by the twin attacks of the post-literate sensibility and the
hypnotism of new machines (word-processors and desk-top publishing,
all wired into electric speed); that the word has been pushed out from the
centre of cultural concern; that a lack of imaginative foresight rules how
we respond to the printed page. For the writer, reader and publisher alike
are caught in the devaluation of the book. Post-literate publishing
dominates the dissemination of the word. Publishers and writers do not
seem to know they are contributing to the dissolution of literacy; what is
worse, many do not seem to care.

I should make it clear that illiteracy (a hot subject of debate in the press   8
and the electronic media) is a separate issue. If you cannot read and write,
then the question of what happens to books and their readership is an
esoteric one. In post-literacy, those who grew up in our school systems can
read and write to a degree; but the ability to wholly comprehend the
printed word has declined. We are in the electronic fire of VCRs, stereos
and laser printers, and no one is immune from the fallout.

When is a book not a book? When it's a disk. There we begin our   9
research into the post-literate impact on how we think, feel and
respond.

Stress effects: 10

Books change into coffee-table books (furniture), posters, scrolls, tapes,   11
non-books and paperback originals designed for fast sales and early
obsolescence. In the publishing houses, editing dies as an art.
Proof-reading skills become a rarity because few people can concentrate
for any length of time. Conformity of tone and style will be the case
because computer systems can allow only as much as they have been
programmed for. Typos continue to be an epidemic; but since most
people don't read, what does it matter if there are mistakes?

In post-Gutenberg or post-Caxton technology, the resolution of the   12
letter undergoes a profound change. Type is adjusted for the television
eye. Desk-top publishing (DTP) printers produce letters of lower density
than photo-typesetting. There are few dots per letter. The consequence: a
loss of the firm character. Low-resolution type is appropriate for scanning
and skimming rather than for considered reading.

More post-literate fallout: the vanishing reader. Educational texts   13
boom in a market that competes for the last captive crowd: students.
Trade publishers depend on patronage; government support is necessary

when the public is small. But when patronage is the standard in society, clubhouse writing (coteries) take over: 200 copies of a book sold will constitute a bestseller.

14   In the large publishing houses, when the publishers and editors no longer read, then it won't matter what they produce. The main concern is going to be the package (the appearance) and the market. Eccentric writing is consigned to a box labelled "Uptown." If the formula book becomes the rule, anything that demands an independent response (an intelligent point of view) will be branded reactionary or elitist.

15   Paradoxically, as computer speed and imagery become the attributes of book production, the industry could find itself rendered static. Faster speeds bring confusion and burnout. Thus the industry sees a greater turnover of staff and more technological experimentation. But the latest computer technology has not yet been successfully integrated into the old system of gentleman publishing. The promise of increased production with decreased costs may be a myth: prices continue to rise; remainder counters fill; and government commissions and writers' unions still ask, "What's wrong?"

16   Indulge me in a conspiracy theory. DTP is not just a creative addition, not merely a way of increasing efficiency, not "the way of the future," but it is the first attack by computer companies on the book itself. After the breakdown of the fully formed character comes the home terminal: the screen replaces the page. A disk can be stored to last; libraries can be discarded; screens offer movement, imagery and illusions of creativity; everyone can be a publisher, with the possible end of the circulation of most printed material.

17   What is the future of the book under such circumstances? The blurb, Marshall McLuhan said, the half-read text, the 900-page work meant only to be adapted for a TV mini-series. What may vanish with these transformations are the habits of privacy, individual thought and will, the ability to reason and concentrate, the solitary voice and the separate imagination.

18   Let's be blunt: perhaps the school systems, the corporations, and the electronic media want us to be deadened. The rulers do not want us to challenge the currents and signals. For writing and reading do threaten to become the property of the few. Then that few run the risk of becoming so isolated that all ideas, perceptions and differing opinions will one day be of no concern to anyone.

19   Well, while those of us in the skin trade keep our ink running and typewriters oiled, the word-processors rush and the input/output flows on. You can only express your present fears, and hope that a thing you love is not in its death throes.

20   We have yet to see whether we stand at the finish or at the renewal of

the literate tradition, whether the book (cracked and yellowing from private use) will soon be a relic of a lost civilization, with the printed word itself to be pondered and remembered for a spell it was once said to hold.

ΔΔΔΔΔΔΔΔΔΔΔΔΔΔΔΔΔΔΔΔΔΔΔΔΔΔΔΔΔΔΔΔΔΔΔΔΔΔΔΔΔΔΔΔΔΔΔΔΔΔΔΔΔΔΔΔΔΔΔΔ

Further Reading:

B. W. Powe,
  The Solitary Outlaw
  A Climate Charged
Brian Fawcett, *Cambodia: A Book for People Who Find Television Too Slow*
Marshall McLuhan, *Understanding Media*
Allan Bloom, *The Closing of the American Mind*
George Orwell, *1984*

Structure:

1. Does B. W. Powe's opening ANECDOTE succeed in attracting your attention? Does it lead directly to his subject?
2. Powe's argument is an overall web of *cause and effect*, developed by smaller chains of causality throughout. Point out all the causes and effects Powe traces in paragraphs 7–8; in paragraph 11; in paragraph 12; in paragraph 14; in paragraphs 16–18. In summary, what are the original *causes*? What are the ultimate *effects*?
3. After exposing an ominous chain of cause and effect, in which a decline of the book leads to a decline in personal independence, Powe concludes, "We have yet to see whether we stand at the finish or at the renewal of the literate tradition . . ." (par. 20). Does this admission weaken his argument, letting it trail off into uncertainty? Or, in portraying the effects of electronic publishing as still in the balance, does he heighten the poignancy of his argument?

Style:

1. In paragraph 6 Powe frankly states: "I am not objective about this issue. I am prepared to be impolite." Identify at least one passage where he is "impolite." Can anger and bluntness produce effective writing? Have they here?
2. Point out the IRONIES of Powe's opening ANECDOTE. To what extent does irony underlie the rest of Powe's essay? Identify three more good examples of it.

Ideas for Discussion and Writing:

1. Do you love books, as Powe does? Or are you the average Canadian who reads less than one book a year? Identify the *causes* of your attitude towards reading.

2. Do you share Powe's view that, in "post-literacy," the book may be doomed? A generation from now, will your children be reading the tenth edition of this book on a computer screen? Or will they be reading anything at all? Defend your answer with reasons.

3. As published in the *Globe and Mail*, Powe's essay contained a spelling error — "obsolecence" for "obsolescence" — in the very paragraph that tells how "proof-reading skills become a rarity" and "Typos continue to be an epidemic" (par. 11). Do you imagine the author planted this "error" as an ironic gesture to illustrate the point? Or was it an accident, which in even more ironic fashion illustrates his point?

4. In *Cambodia: A Book for People Who Find Television Too Slow*, Brian Fawcett theorizes that the medium of television systematically destroys both our memory and imagination, leaving us prey to political and economic forces that wish to rule us. Do you agree with Fawcett — and with Powe, who in paragraphs 16–18 lances a similar "conspiracy theory"? Have these angry social critics gone too far? Or do you sense that a nice evening of TV dulls your own "individual thought and will" (par. 17)? And can you imagine "rulers" who wish us to be "deadened" so we will not "challenge the currents and signals" (par. 18)?

5. **PROCESS IN WRITING:** *Do you write with a computer? When you went electronic, what were the effects? Do you now write better? Worse? Faster? Slower? Do you exploit the editing powers of this medium? With what result? In an essay, explain these and any other effects of word processing. First brainstorm a page of notes, then apply the best of these to a first draft, either written longhand or keyed directly into the machine. Print out at least two successive drafts, double- or triple-spaced, to revise and edit by hand, before entering the improvements each time. Are the transitions specific? Do they highlight your logic? Have you tested your prose aloud before printing out the good version? Finally, save the essay on disk in case your teacher requests further revision.*

Note: See also the Topics for Writing at the end of this chapter.

John Bentley Mays

What You Get Is Not Always What You See

John Bentley Mays is one of the nation's liveliest and most respected art critics. Born in Louisiana, he came to Canada to teach in the Humanities Division of York University, but in 1973 quit to become a writer. Since that time he has published a novel (The Spiral Stair, *1977), an operatic libretto, art criticism for* Maclean's *magazine, and since 1980 a regular column on art for the Toronto* Globe and Mail. *He appears often on radio and television, and has lectured across Canada. As an art critic Mays is direct and outspoken. In a field so subjective that it almost seems to invite vague commentary, Mays writes a vivid prose that can praise or devastate with equal ease. The combination of his clear language, his incisive judgement, and his encyclopedic knowledge of the field produces an art criticism that, in the words of one reader, "connects with reality." His essay, from the August 22, 1987* Globe, *tells how the nation's most cherished movement in art has changed the way we see the world around us.*

E ven if you love big city life the way Howard Hughes° loved his oxygen   1
tent, chances are you've given in to the invitations and cajolings of
your friends, and done some time in cottage country this summer.

Beshorted in awful cabbage-green Bermudas picked up at Towers on   2
the way out of town, with a gym bag full of books you think really ought to
be plowed through some day — say, the novels of Edith Wharton — and
armed with a vat of bug-off, you join the tense, sluggish flow of cars
northward on the expressway.

It takes about three hours, two pit-stops for the kids, and one milkshake   3
spilled all over the back seat, and you're there.

As things pleasantly turn out, *there* happens to be Fairy Lake, a broad,   4
lovely sheet of water sheltered by low, green hills, and set in rolling

---

°Howard Hughes: an eccentric American billionaire who spent the last part of his life in an
oxygen tent.

countryside near Huntsville, Ont. The cottage itself is a charming storybook house built in the 1930s, nestled among the blue and golden flowers of late summer. You are bewitched by a hammock slung between tall pines on a broad lawn sloping down to the shore. Three days after touch-down, not one Edith Wharton book has been opened, there's sand in your Florsheims and, despite all, cottage country has worked its old dreamy spell, melting away city knots you didn't even know you had.

5   At Fairy Lake, anyway, there may be more to that spell than just the usual warm sun and sparkling blue water. The lake was given its unusual name by the first European settlers in the area, who had heard from the native people that spirits haunted the waters. Early lakeside dwellers reported strange voices in the night, and mysterious lights skittering over the surface.

6   But whether or not the lake's magic has ever drawn people with mediumistic concerns, it has surely touched the imagination of some of Canada's most down-to-earth modern artists.

7   Tom Thomson, the extraordinary Canadian landscape painter, dropped by Fairy Lake in 1912 on one of his early sketching trips into Ontario's north woods. A result of that stop was an oil called Fairy Lake, now in the McMichael Canadian Collection at Kleinburg. Both Arthur Lismer and A.Y. Jackson, who later became founding members of the pioneering Group of Seven landscape painters, visited Thomson at Fairy Lake, and may have sketched with him there.

8   As often happens when the art-minded venture into the Ontario north so notably chronicled by the Group, thoughts turn almost automatically to an interesting puzzle of Canadian culture. When we look out the cottage window at, say, a sunset smoldering over the sparkling waves, *exactly* what are we seeing? Is it Nature, redolent with raw, primordial beauty? Or do we see Nature that's been subtly colonized by landscape paintings? Is that a glorious sunset, or a sunset that looks glorious because it looks like one we've seen, painted gloriously and unforgettably by a Group member?

9   After all, the visual education of native Ontarians, if not other Canadians, is saturated with Group pictures, in real or in reproduction. Each year, some 45,000 school children are trucked off to the Art Gallery of Ontario, to look at Canada's most famous landscape paintings, among others. Those who grow up to become gallery-goers will certainly be seeing that art, in different settings (ranging from special exhibits to permanent displays), every year, probably forever.

10   And even those who won't ever set foot in a gallery after graduation will probably never quite escape the calenders and posters, postcards and greeting cards. Or the established view that the Group of Seven gave Canadians the first definitively nationalist view of the north. Or the

bottom-line fact that Group works remain among the most highly valued works of Canadian art, usually selling well, often fetching absolute top dollar, and predictably making auction-room news a couple of times each season.

There's no scientific way to tell how much of Fairy Lake is nature, and how much is art. Or if there is a way, it lies through the realm of the philosophical discipline known as epistemology, and quite beyond the ken of the present writer. But sitting on the dock on a Saturday afternoon, with your toes in the waters of Fairy Lake, you make certain common-sense observations that may have a bearing on the case.

The day is muggily hot, hazy and still, with a thin grey scrim covering the sky. The hills across the lake are dull olive-green; a tiny, rocky island between this side and the far shore is an angular blackish-brown sherd against the gun-metal water.

You shouldn't be surprised if you catch yourself thinking: "It's just not a Group of Seven kind of day." The view off the dock surely doesn't look like a typical picture by Thomson or the Group, who liked their lakes raked by dramatic sunlight or lashed by summer storms. What *is* odd is the way Fairy Lake, overcast and calm, tends to disappear, or become strangely remote, even as you look at it. The absence of the standard codes of Group work, such as wind-shredded clouds, wind-chopped lake surfaces, bright colors and so forth, makes the scene before your eyes appear to lack what might be called "essential cottage-countryhood." The lake doesn't look much different from Lake Ontario on a dog day afternoon.

In reality, of course, a hot, muggy day in Muskoka during August is not all that unusual. Despite the regional tourist hype, the stuffy weather farther south often creeps up north of Orillia. This condition may be disappointing to those who have fled Toronto for what they believe will be cooler climes — but definition, not disappointment, is what I'm talking about here. A hot, becalmed Fairy Lake seems to disappear *as cottage country* at the precise moment it no longer evokes the nationalist, nativist, vitalistic mystique of Group painting — and seems to become cottage country again as soon as the wind whips up, the clouds get ragged and the water begins to lash the boathouse. Which, in fact, is just what happened the next day, with exactly the predicted result.

Now, it may strike you as a bit strange how the codes of wildness, freeness, urgency, the primitive and such have become the basis of our visual doctrine about what's really cottage country and what isn't — especially since the Muskoka spectacle of endless electrified, plumbered, septic-tanked little houses quickly accessible from Toronto by paved roads is not exactly a vision of the Forest Primeval. But our eyes forget old things slowly, and learn new things only with a struggle. For

11

12

13

14

15

them (if not for our minds), Muskoka is, or should be, the Muskoka that appears in the painting of the Group. If it doesn't fit, our eyes tend to ignore it, and scan the horizon to find what does fit.

16   It would be foolish to underestimate the staying power of the Group's ways of seeing. There have been notable recent attempts to revision the Ontario landscape in painting, by Jeff Spalding, Douglas Kirton, Richard Storms, among others. But whatever their interest to art-world professionals — and the interest is often keen — these attempts to debunk or displace or revise the Group's visual myths haven't worked — not, at least, on the level of those 45,000 school children who are frog-marched through the AGO each year, or the myriads for whom Canadian art *is* Group art, and Group art is the only true nationalist art. So it happens that this weekend, as usual during he summer, *tout* Toronto will hit the road north, expecting to see (and actually seeing) a world constructed by a few magnificent paintings done about 70 years ago.

ΔΔΔΔΔΔΔΔΔΔΔΔΔΔΔΔΔΔΔΔΔΔΔΔΔΔΔΔΔΔΔΔΔΔΔΔΔΔΔΔΔΔΔΔΔΔΔΔΔΔΔΔΔΔΔΔΔΔΔΔ

Further Reading:

John Berger, *Ways of Seeing*
Gabrielle Roy, *The Hidden Mountain* (novel)
Peter Mellen, *The Group of Seven*
Joan Murray and Lawren Harris, *The Best of the Group of Seven*

Structure:

1. Why does John Bentley Mays open his essay with the grotesque IMAGE of Howard Hughes and his oxygen tent? Does this in some way begin to introduce Mays' subject? Explain.
2. Mays does not reveal his main point, the effect of art on our perception of nature, until paragraph 8. Analyze how each preceding paragraph advances his introduction to that point.
3. In Mays' argument that we tend to see nature through eyes conditioned by art, what *causes* does he cite in paragraph 9? In paragraph 10? In paragraphs 12 through 14? In paragraph 15? In the closing paragraph? Are these separate causes or are they linked in a chain of cause and effect? Explain.
4. Give at least two reasons why the final sentence of the essay refers to the kind of trip north that Mays began with in his opening?

Style:

1. In paragraph 1 Mays slyly compares Ontario's cottage country to a prison, by speculating that we have "done some time"

there. Point out the ALLUSION made by each of the these other expressions, and the IRONY that it achieves:

A. "plowed through" (par. 2)

B. "pit-stops" (par. 3)

C. "subtly colonized" (par. 8)

D. "bottom-line fact" (par. 10)

2. In most of his writing on art, Mays adopts the light, irreverent, satirical TONE that we have seen in even the first line of this essay. Does it work? Is a serious tone necessarily best for a serious topic, or has Mays shown otherwise? Explain.

3. Draw up a profile of the audience Mays is trying to address in his essay. Who are these people? What is their level of intelligence, of education, of income? What vehicle do you suppose they drive, what sports do they play, and what periodicals do they read (besides of course the *Globe and Mail*)? In his level and in his general approach, do you believe Mays has reached this audience? Explain.

Ideas for Discussion and Writing:

1. How extensively have you been exposed to Group of Seven art? Do you recognize the work of Franklin Carmichael, Lawren Harris, A. Y. Jackson, Franz Johnston, Arthur Lismer, J. E. H. MacDonald, F. H. Varley, or their friend Tom Thomson? What IMAGES of the Canadian landscape has their work prepared you to see? And do these images correspond to the Canada you know? Explain.

2. Do countries need a "nationalist art," as Mays calls it in paragraph 16? Do they need "visual myths"? Does Canada? How do you think the ways of seeing embodied in Group of Seven art have affected Canada as a whole?

3. "If some countries have too much history, we have too much geography," said Prime Minister W. L. Mackenzie King in 1936. What exactly do you think he meant? In what ways do you think he was right or wrong? Does Group of Seven art in any way illustrate his view?

4. If you have read Emily Carr's "D'Sonoqua," compare the "way of seeing" encouraged by the art of Northwest Coast totem pole carvers to that of the Group of Seven as described by Mays.

5. In discussing the "codes" of our "visual doctrine" (par. 15), Mays states that "our eyes forget old things slowly, and learn new things only with a struggle." Examine the visual "codes" of one earlier period or school of art: for example, prehistoric

cave painting, Egyptian murals, classical Greek or Roman sculpture, Byzantine icons, Romantic painting, impressionist painting, cubism, or surrealism. Analyze the ways in which one of these "visual doctrines" may have "colonized" real life by making people see things in certain ways.

6.   **PROCESS IN WRITING:** *Develop an essay of cause and effect on the above topic. At the museum or library, examine and react to works of the period or school of art you have chosen. Take notes. Brainstorm or freewrite. Share a draft with classmates, then incorporate their suggestions into your final version.*

Note: See also the Topics for Writing at the end of this chapter.

Franklin Russell

The Capelin

Once a professional hunter, Franklin Russell is now a naturalist and an internationally respected writer about nature. He was born in 1922 in New Zealand, but he has also lived in Australia, Great Britain, Canada (he is a Canadian citizen), and, since 1963, the United States. Having been a farmer, hunter, forester, and erosion control specialist, and having travelled to most parts of the globe, Russell has experienced nature first-hand in a multitude of environments. It is from these experiences that he has written a succession of vivid and wise books about nature — among them Watchers at the Pond *(1961),* The Secret Islands *(1965) and* Searchers at the Gulf *(1970). Margaret Laurence once stated, "Franklin Russell is one of the very few writers who can communicate the essential fact that the planet is totally alive." In a prose of rare power, Russell demonstrates this gift in the present selection, which is a chapter from his book* The Hunting Animal *(1983).*

B eyond the northern beach, a grey swell rolls in from Greenland and runs softly along the shore. The horizon is lost in a world of gray, and gulls glide, spectral in the livid air. Watching, I am enveloped in the sullen waiting time and feel the silence, drawn out long and thin. I wait for the sea to reveal a part of itself. 1

A capelin is perhaps the best-hunted creature on earth. It is not more than five inches long, about the size of a young herring, and un-distinguished in appearance, except that when it is freshly caught, it is the color of mercury. As the capelin dies, its silvery scales tarnish and the glitter goes out like a light, ending a small allegory about nature, a spectacle of victims, victors, and an imperative of existence. Its death illuminates a dark process of biology in which there are shadows of other, more complex lives. 2

The capelin are born to be eaten. They transform oceanic plankton into flesh which is then hunted greedily by almost every sea creature that swims or flies. Their only protection is fecundity. One capelin survives to 3 adulthood from every ten thousand eggs laid, and yet a single school may stir square miles of sea.

4   In mid-June, the capelin gather offshore. They can be seen everywhere and at all times in history, symbols of summer and fertility, of Providence and danger. I see them along the shores of Greenland, Iceland, Norway, and near Spitsbergen. I follow them across the northern coast of Russia. Chill air, gray seas, the northern silences, are the capelin's world in Alaska, in the Aleutians, around Hudson Bay, and along the northeastern shores of North America. But the capelin of the Newfoundland coast are the most visible. Here, they spawn on the beaches rather than in deep water offshore, and I have to see their rush for eternity.

5   They gather a thousand feet offshore, coalescing into groups of a hundred thousand to break the water's surface with bright chuckling sounds. They gather, and grow. Soon they are in the millions, and with other millions swimming up from the offshore deeps. They gather, now in the billions, so densely packed together in places that the sea shimmers silver for miles and flows, serpentine, with the swelling body of a single, composite creature.

6   The fish do, in fact, possess a common sense of purpose. Nothing can redirect their imperative to breed. I once swam among them and saw them parting reluctantly ahead of me, felt their bodies flicking against my hands. Looking back, I saw them closing in, filling up the space created by my passage. The passive fish tolerated me, in their anticipation of what they were about to do.

7   At this time of the year they are so engrossed that they barely react when a host of creatures advances to kill them. Beneath and beyond them, codfish pour up out of the deep. They overtake the capelin, eat them, plunge their sleek dark bodies recklessly into shallow water. Some have swum so rapidly from such depths that their swim bladders are distended by the sudden drop in water pressure. The cod are gigantic by comparison with the capelin. Many weigh one hundred pounds or more, and will not be sated until they have eaten scores of capelin each. The water writhes with movement and foam where cod, headlong in pursuit, drive themselves above the surface and fall back with staccato slaps.

8   The attack of the codfish is a brutal opening to a ritual, and a contradiction in their character. Normally, they are sedentary feeders on the sea floor. Now, however, they are possessed. Their jaws rip and tear; the water darkens with capelin blood: the shredded pieces of flesh hang suspended or rise to the surface.

9   Now a group of seabirds, the parrotlike puffins, clumsy in flight, fly above the capelin, their grotesque, axlike beaks probing from side to side as they watch the upper layers of the massacre. They are joined by new formations of birds until several thousand puffins are circling. They are

silent, and there is no way of knowing how they were summoned from their nestling burrows on an island that is out of sight. They glide down to the water — stub-winged cargo planes — land awkwardly, taxi with fluttering wings and stamping, paddling feet, then dive.

At the same time, the sea view moves with new invasions of seabirds. 10 Each bird pumps forward with an urgency that suggests it has received the same stimulus as the cod. The gulls that breed on cliffs along a southern bay come first, gracefully light of wing, with raucous voice as they cry out their anticipation. Beneath them, flying flat, direct, silent, come murres, black-bodied, short-tailed, close relatives of the puffins. The murres land and dive without ceremony. Well offshore, as though waiting confirmation of the feast, shearwaters from Tristan da Cunha turn long pointed wings across the troughs of waves and cackle like poultry.

The birds converge, and lose their identity in the mass thickening on 11 the water. Small gulls — the kittiwakes, delicate in flight — screech and drop and rise and screech and drop like snowflakes on the sea. They fall among even smaller birds, lighter than they, which dangle their feet and hover at the water's surface, almost walking on water as they seek tiny pieces of shredded flesh. These are the ocean-flying petrels, the Mother Carey's chickens of mariners' legends, which rarely come within sight of land. All order is lost in the shrieking tumult of hundreds of thousands of birds.

Underwater, the hunters meet among their prey. The puffins and 12 murres dive below the capelin and attack, driving for the surface. The cod attack at mid-depth. The gulls smother the surface and press the capelin back among the submarine hunters. The murres and puffins fly underwater, their beating wings turning them rapidly back and forth. They meet the cod, flail their wings in desperate haste, are caught, crushed, and swallowed. Now seabirds as well as capelin become the hunted. Puffin and murre tangle wings. Silver walls of capelin flicker, part, re-form. Some seabirds surface abruptly, broken wings dangling. Others, with a leg or legs torn off, fly frantically, crash, skitter in shock across the water.

I see the capelin hunters spread across the sea, but also remember them 13 in time. Each year, the hunters are different, because many of them depend on a fortuitous meeting with their prey. A group of small whales collides with the capelin, and in a flurry of movement, they eat several tons of them. Salmon throw themselves among the capelin with the same abandon as the codfish, and in the melee become easy victims for a score of seals which kill dozens of them, then turn to the capelin and gorge themselves nearly stuporous. They rise, well beyond the tumult of the seabirds, their black heads jutting like rocks from the swell, to lie with distended bellies and doze away their feast. Capelin boil up around them for a moment but now the animals ignore them.

14   The capelin are hosts in a ceremony so ancient that a multitude of species have adapted to seeking a separate share of the host's bounty. The riotous collision of cod, seal, whale, and seabird obscures the smaller guests at the feast. Near the shore are small brown fish — the cunner, one of the most voracious species. Soon they will be fighting among themselves for pieces of flesh as the capelin begin their run for the beach, or when the survivors of the spawning reel back into deep water, with the dead and dying falling to the bottom. If the water is calm and the sun bright, the cunner can be seen working in two fathoms, ripping capelin corpses to pieces and scattering translucent scales like silver leaves in a wind of the sea.

15   Closer inshore, at the wave line, the flounder wait. They know the capelin are coming and their role is also predetermined. They cruise rapidly under the purling water in uncharacteristic excitement. They are not interested in capelin flesh. They want capelin eggs, and they will eat them as soon as spawning starts.

16   Now the most voracious of all the hunters appears. Fishing vessels come up over the horizon. They brought the Portuguese of the fifteenth century, who anchored offshore, dropped their boats, and rowed ashore to take the capelin with hand nets, on beaches never before walked by white men. They brought Spaniards and Dutchmen, Englishmen and Irish, from the sixteenth to the twentieth centuries. Americans, Nova Scotians, Gloucestermen, schoonermen, bankermen, long-liner captains, have participated in the ritual. All of them knew that fresh capelin is the finest bait when it is skillfully used, and can attract a fortune in codfish flesh, hooked on the submarine banks to the south.

17   But presently, these hunters are Newfoundlanders. They bring their schooners flying inshore like great brown-and-white birds, a hundred, two hundred, three hundred sail. They heel through the screaming seabirds, luff, anchor, and drop their dories with the same precision of movement of the other figures in the ritual. In an hour, three thousand men are at work from the boats. They work as the codfish work, with a frenzy that knots forearms and sends nets spilling over the sterns to encircle the capelin. They lift a thousand tons of capelin out of the sea, yet they do not measurably diminish the number of fish.

18   Meanwhile, landbound hunters wait for the fish to come within range of their lead-weighted hand nets. Women, children, and old people crowd the beach with the ablebodied men. The old people have ancestral memories of capelin bounty. In the seventeenth and eighteenth centuries, when food was often short, only the big capelin harvest stood between the shore people and starvation during the winter.

19   Many of the shore people are farmers who use the capelin for fertilizer

as well as for food. Capelin corpses, spread to rot over thin northern soils, draw obedient crops of potatoes and cabbages out of the ground, and these, mixed with salted capelin flesh, become winter meals.

The children, who remember dried capelin as their candy, share the 20 excitement of waiting. They case one another up and down the beach and play with their own nets and fishing rods. Some are already asleep because they awoke before dawn to rouse the village, as they do every capelin morning, with the cry: "They've a-come, they've a-come!"

At the top of the beach, old women lie asleep or sit watching the 21 seabirds squabbling and the dorymen rowing. They are Aunt Sadie and Little Nell and Bessie Blue and Mother Taunton, old ladies from several centuries. They know the capelin can save children in hard winters when the inshore cod fishery fails. They get up at two o'clock in the morning when the capelin are running, to walk miles to the nearest capelin beach. They net a barrel of fish, then roll the barrel, which weighs perhaps a hundred pounds, back home. They have finished spreading the fish on their gardens, or salting them, before the first of their grandchildren awakes.

They have clear memories of catching capelin in winter, when the sea 22 freezes close inshore and the tide cracks the ice in places. Then millions of capelin, resting out the winter, rise in the cracks. An old woman with a good net can take tons of passive fish out of the water for as long as her strength lasts and the net can still reach them.

A cry rises from the beach: "Here they come!" 23

The ritual must be played out, according to habit. The dorymen and 24 the seabirds, the rampaging cod and cunner, cannot touch or turn the purpose of the capelin. At a moment, its genesis unknown, they start for the shore. From the top of some nearby cliffs I watch and marvel at the precision of their behavior. The capelin cease to be a great, formless mass offshore. They split into groups that the Newfoundlanders call wads — rippling gray lines, five to fifty feet wide — and run for the shore like advancing infantry lines. One by one, they peel away from their surviving comrades and advance, thirty to forty wads at a time.

Each wad has its discipline. The fish prepare to mate. Each male 25 capelin seeks a female, darting from one fish to another. When he finds one, he presses against her side. Another male, perhaps two males, press against her other side. The males urge the female on toward the beach. Some are struck down by diving seabirds but others take their places. Cod dash among them and smash their sexual formations; they re-form immediately. Cunner rise and rip at them; flounder dart beneath them toward the beach.

The first wad runs into beach wavelets, and a hundred nets hit the 26 water together; a silver avalanche of fish spills out on the beach. In each breaking wavelet the capelin maintain their formations, two or three males pressed tightly against their female until they are all flung up on the beach. There, to the whispering sound of tiny fins and tails vibrating, the female convulsively digs into the sand, which is still moving in the wake of the retreating waves. As she goes down, she extrudes up to fifty thousand eggs, and the males expel their milt.

27   The children shout; their bare feet fly over the spawning fish; sea boots grind down; the fish spill out; gulls run in the shallows under the children's feet; the flounder gorge. A codfish, two feet long, leaps out of the shallows and hits the beach. An old man scoops it up. The wads keep coming. The air is filled with birds. The dorymen shout and laugh.

28   The flood of eggs becomes visible. The sand glistens, then is greasy with eggs. They pile in drift lines that writhe back and forth in each wave. The female capelin wriggle into masses of eggs. The shallows are permeated with eggs. The capelin breathe eggs. Their mouths fill with eggs. Their stomachs are choked with eggs. The wads keep pouring onward, feeding the disaster on the beach.

29   Down come the boots and the nets, and the capelin die, mouths open, and oozing eggs. The spawning is a fiasco. The tide has turned. Instead of spawning on the shore with the assurance of rising water behind them, each wad strikes ashore in retreating water. Millions are stranded, but the wads keep coming.

30   In the background, diminished by the quantity of fish, other players gasp and pant at their nets. Barrels stack high on the beach. Horses whinny, driven hard up the bank at the back of the beach. Carts laden with barrels weave away. Carts bringing empty barrels bounce and roar down. The wads are still coming. Men use shovels to lift dead and dying fish from drift lines that are now two and three feet high. The easterly wind is freshening. The wavelets become waves. The capelin are flung up on the beach without a chance to spawn. They bounce and twist and the water flees beneath them.

31   It is twilight, then dark; torches now spot the beach, the offshore dories, and the schooners. The waves grow solidly and pile the capelin higher. The men shovel the heaps into pyramids, then reluctantly leave the beach. Heavy rain blots out beach and sea.

32   I remain to watch the blow piling up the sea. At the lowest point of the tide, it is driving waves high up on the beach, roiling the sand, digging up the partially buried eggs, and carrying them out to sea. By dawn most of the eggs are gone. The capelin have disappeared. The seabirds, the schooners, the cod, flounder, cunner, seals, whales, have gone. Nothing remains except the marks of human feet, the cart tracks on the high part of the beach, the odd pyramid of dead fish. The feast is done.

33   The empty arena of the beach suggests a riddle. If the capelin were so

perfectly adapted to spawn on a rising tide, to master the task of burying eggs in running sand between the waves, to know when the tide was rising, why did they continue spawning after the tide turned? Was that, by the ancient rules of the ritual, intentional? If it was, then it indicated a lethal error of anticipation that did not jibe with the great numbers of the capelin.

I wonder, then, if the weak died and the strong survived, but dismiss the notion after recalling the indiscriminate nature of all capelin deaths. There was no Darwinian selection for death of the stupid or the inexperienced. Men slaughtered billions, this year and last year and for three hundred years before, but the capelin never felt this pinpricking of their colossal corporate bodies. Their spawning was a disaster for reasons well beyond the influence of man. 34

A nineteenth-century observer, after seeing a capelin spawning, recorded his amazement at "the astonishing prosperity of these creatures, cast so willfully away." It was in the end, and indeed throughout the entire ritual, the sheer numbers of capelin that scored the memory. The prosperity of the capelin preceded the disaster but then, it seemed, created it. Prosperity was not beneficial or an assurance of survival. The meaning of the ritual was slowly growing into sense. Prosperity unhinges the capelin. It is a madness of nature. Prosperity, abundance, success, drive them on. They become transformed and throw themselves forward blindly. . . . 35

I turn from the beach, warm and secure, and take a blind step forward. 36

ΔΔΔΔΔΔΔΔΔΔΔΔΔΔΔΔΔΔΔΔΔΔΔΔΔΔΔΔΔΔΔΔΔΔΔΔΔΔΔΔΔΔΔΔΔΔΔΔΔΔΔΔΔΔΔΔΔΔΔΔΔΔΔΔ

Further Reading:

Franklin Russell,
The Hunting Animal
Searchers at the Gulf
Watchers at the Pond
Farley Mowat, *Sea of Slaughter*

Structure:

1. This "ritual" of the capelin's spawning and death is organized roughly by time sequence. Point out the major steps in Russell's chronology. Is every step in chronological order? Why or why not?

2. In paragraph 4 Russell states that the capelin "can be seen everywhere and at all times in history" and in paragraph 13 he

writes, "I see the capelin hunters spread across the sea, but also remember them in time." In describing fishing schooners and persons long dead as if he sees them in the present with his own eyes, is Russell violating our sense of realism? Or in distorting time does he seek a greater effect? If so, what? Does he succeed?

3. Although we are discussing "The Capelin" as an example of development by cause and effect, Russell supports his argument with *description* as vivid as any in this book. Select the two or three paragraphs of description that most strongly affect you, and point out their most vivid words or phrases.

4. The climactic *effect* of Russell's account is the "disaster" — the seemingly needless death of countless spawning capelin as a falling tide leaves them stranded on the beach. What possible *causes* for this disaster does he reject in paragraphs 33 and 34? Which *cause* does he accept in paragraph 35? And in what way does he relate that cause to his own actions in the closing sentence? What are the overall implications for the human race?

5. Through this long examination of the capelin's mating and death, Russell waits until the very last two paragraphs to reveal the *cause* of the "disaster." Why? And are there smaller examples of *cause and effect* along the way? If so, point out the most vivid ones.

Style:

1. On a scale of one to ten, with OBJECTIVE as one and SUBJECTIVE as ten, where would you rank "The Capelin"? Do you approve of Russell's approach? Is it scientific? Is it interesting or even dramatic? Can writing be both scientifically valid and dramatic at the same time?

2. Why does Russell use the pronoun "I" in this essay? Have you ever been told not to? If so, have you always followed that rule? Or does choice of first-person or third-person narration depend on the situation? If so, what are some factors in our choice?

3. Read paragraph 27 aloud in class. Raise your hand to signal each SENSE IMAGE (each appeal to our senses of sight, hearing, touch, taste, and smell).

4. Read paragraph 28 aloud. What word is deliberately repeated several times, and why?

5. In paragraph 9 puffins are called "stub-winged cargo planes." Find at least five more METAPHORS in this selection. In

paragraph 14 cunner are described "ripping capelin corpses to pieces and scattering translucent scales like silver leaves in a wind of the sea." Find at least five more SIMILES in this selection. What is the overall effect of so many FIGURES OF SPEECH?

Ideas for Discussion and Writing:

1. Russell's introduction states that the capelin's death "illuminates a dark process of biology in which there are shadows of other, more complex lives" (par. 2). Shadows of whose lives? Do you sense any connection between this statement and the fact that Russell seems so personally involved in the capelin's "rush for eternity"? Explain.

2. If we view "The Capelin" as an ALLEGORY of the human race, what forces may we see as propelling us on our own "rush for eternity"?

3. In paragraph 16 Russell calls humans "the most voracious of all the hunters." After his description of voracious fish and birds slaughtering capelin, is this judgement accurate? In what ways are we more or less "voracious" than other species?

4. Franklin Russell reacts emotionally to nature. Do you? If so, describe a specific reaction that you had. Tell its *cause* or *causes*. Tell its *effect* or *effects*.

5. PROCESS IN WRITING: *Russell has discussed the effects of "prosperity" (his term for density of population) among the capelin. Now write your own essay analyzing the effects of overpopulation among humans (if the human race is too large a group, focus on a subgroup: a nation, city, town, neighbourhood, or even family).*

   Start by freewriting: let your imagination soar, putting down anything that comes, never stopping the pen for at least five minutes. Now use the best of this material in your first draft. Pack further drafts with the kinds of SENSE IMAGES and FIGURES OF SPEECH that power Russell's prose. Are your TRANSITIONS plentiful and clear? If not, add terms like "because," "since," or "as a result" to highlight cause and effect; add time signals like "then," "next," "soon," and "finally" to speed your argument. Finally, test your prose aloud before writing the final version.

Note: See also the Topics for Writing at the end of this chapter.

Topics for Writing

CHAPTER 4: CAUSE AND EFFECT

Analyze the cause(s) and/or effect(s) of one of the following. (See also the guidelines that follow.)

1. Marrying as a teenager
2. Use of steroids in sports
3. The high price of housing
4. Being adopted
5. Being a twin
6. Being the oldest, youngest, or middle child of a family
7. Use of the drug "crack"
8. Lying
9. Free trade between Canada and the United States
10. Getting into debt
11. Violence in a particular sport
12. Clearcutting of a forest
13. The housing shortage
14. Drought
15. Private ownership of handguns
16. Hitchhiking
17. Racial discrimination
18. Extensive reading
19. The proliferation of fax machines
20. Cheating in school
21. The high price of car insurance
22. The widespread increase in municipal recycling
23. Working while being a student
24. Eating junk food
25. Coffee addiction

Note also the Process in Writing topic after each selection in this chapter.

Process in Writing: Guidelines

Follow at least some of these steps in writing your essay of cause and effect (your teacher may suggest which ones).

1. *In the middle of a piece of paper, write the subject you wish to explore in your essay of cause and effect. Near it write many other words that it brings to mind. Connect related items with lines, then use what you see in this cluster outline to focus your argument.*

2. *Write a first draft rapidly, double-spaced, getting it all down on paper without stopping yet to revise.*

3. *When this version has "cooled off," analyze it: Have you begun and ended at just the right places in the chain of causality? If not, cut or add. Have you identified the real causes and the real effects? If not, revise.*

4. *In your next draft sharpen the* TRANSITIONS, *using expressions like "since," "although," "because," and "as a result" to clearly signal each step of your logic.*

5. *Share this draft with a small group of classmates. Revise any places where this audience does not follow your logic.*

6. *Now edit for things like spelling and grammar, and write your good copy. Proofread. If you have used a computer, save the essay on disk in case your teacher suggests further revision.*

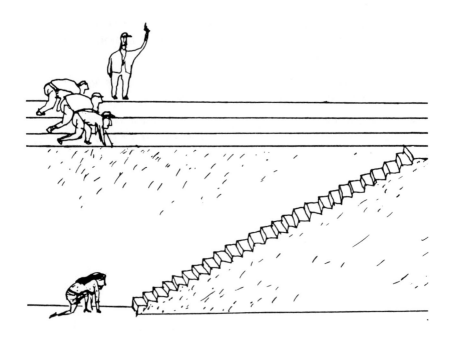

Mike Constable.

Women workers earn, on an average, only 64 cents for every $1 a man gets — even though on an average, women are better educated than men.
                                            — Doris Anderson, "The 51-Per-Cent Minority"

Comparison and Contrast

It's just the opposite of....

One of the most dramatic ways to make an argument is to compare and contrast. The term "comparison" is often used to mean the showing of both similarities and differences, but in its narrower sense refers only to the showing of similarities. A "contrast" shows differences. Of the two, contrast is the more dramatic and the more frequently used in essays.

You have experienced contrast to the fullest if you have ever known culture shock. As you arrive in a new country, the look of the buildings and streets, the smells in the air, the sounds, the language and customs, all seem strange — because you are contrasting them to what you just left. And if you stay a long time, the same thing happens in reverse when you come back: home seems strange because you are contrasting it to the place where you've just been. The cars may seem too big, the food too bland, the pace of life too fast. Travel is one of the great educational experiences: through contrast, one culture puts another in perspective.

In writing an essay you can show similarities only, or show both similarities and differences, or show differences only. Do whatever best fits your subject and your point. But whichever way you go, *choose subjects of the same general type*: two countries, two sports, two poems, or two solutions to the housing problem. For example, in our chapter, Russell Baker focusses on two cities, Toronto and New York, systematically comparing their taxis, noise, garbage, dogs, subway, vandalism, and other aspects of urban life. Despite his comic tone, and despite any disagreements we might have as to his verdict, by the time Baker gets done we have the impression of having read a logical argument. After all, Toronto and New York are in the same category: big cities.

But suppose that instead of comparing two cities, Baker had compared a city and an anthill. After all, there are similarities: both are crowded, both are highly organized, both have housing with many rooms located off corridors, etc. But no matter how much fun he might have had or what insights he might have got across, he would *prove* nothing — because people are not insects. His argument would be an *analogy*, a more imaginative but less logical kind of argument, which we will explore in the next chapter.

Once you have chosen your two subjects of the same general type, you face another choice: how to arrange them. There are two basic ways:

Divide the essay into halves, devoting the first half to Toronto and the second to New York. This sytem is natural in a very short essay, because your reader remembers everything from the first half while reading the second half. It is also natural when for some reason it seems the items are most clearly discussed as a whole rather than in parts.

Divide the subjects into separate points. First compare taxis in both cities, then noise in both cities, then garbage in both cities, and so on through your whole list of points. This system is most natural in long essays: putting related material together helps the reader to grasp comparisons or contrasts without the strain of recalling every detail from ten pages back.

Baker organizes by "separate points" even in his brief essay, because the approach fits his way of poking fun at New York: in describing how Toronto controls its garbage, he implies, without even naming his own city, that New York is full of litter. He could not have achieved this degree of conciseness had he isolated the two sides of each topic into their own "halves" of the essay.

Although "halves" are often best for short papers and "separate points" are often best for long papers, be open to the needs of your particular subject, treatment, and purpose. As Russell Baker has done, choose the approach that will most strongly deliver your message.

Note: Many essays in other chapters use comparison and contrast to help make their point. See especially these:

Bonnie Laing, "An Ode to the User-Friendly Pencil," p. 297 (a strong example of comparison and contrast developed through "separate points")

Kildare Dobbs, "The Scar," p. 274

Stephen Leacock, "How to Live to Be 200," p. 233

Judy Stoffman, "The Way of All Flesh," p. 238

Thierry Mallet, "The Firewood Gatherers," p. 62

Joy Kogawa, "Grinning and Happy," p. 315

Doris Anderson

The 51-Per-Cent Minority

Doris Anderson is one of Canada's leading advocates of women's rights. She was born in Calgary in 1925. After earning her B.A. at the University of Alberta in 1945, she wrote radio scripts, worked in advertising, then in 1951 joined the staff of Chatelaine. *As editor-in-chief from 1958 to 1977, Anderson added to the magazine's family emphasis an advocacy of higher social and economic status for women. She served as president of the Canadian Advisory Council on the Status of Women. Her sudden resignation from the council in 1981, in protest against the government's interference and its reluctance to guarantee equality of men and women in the Constitution, sparked a campaign by women that did achieve a constitutional guarantee of their rights. From 1982 to 1984 she was president of the Natonal Action Committee on the Status of Women, an umbrella group that represents over three million women in 600 organizations. Anderson has published novels,* Two Women *in 1978,* Rough Layout *in 1981 and* Affairs of State *in 1988, in addition to her many editorials and articles. "The 51-Per-Cent Minority" first appeared in* Maclean's *in 1980. Anderson has revised and updated this classic feminist essay for our present edition.*

1   In any Canadian election the public will probably be hammered numb with talk of the economy, energy and other current issues. But there will always be some far more startling topics that no one will talk about at all.

2   No one is going to say to all new Canadians: "Look, we're going through some tough times. Three out of four of you had better face the fact that you're always going to be poor. At 65 more than likely you'll be living below the poverty level."

3   And no one is going to tell Quebeckers: "You will have to get along on less money than the rest of the country. For every $1 the rest of us earn, you, because you live in Quebec, will earn 64 cents."

4   I doubt very much that any political party is going to level with the Atlantic provinces and say: "We don't consider people living there serious prime workers. Forget about any special measures to make jobs for you.

In fact in future federal-provincial talks we're not even going to discuss your particular employment problems."

And no politician is going to tell all the left-handed people in the country: "Look, we know it looks like discrimination, but we have to save some money somewhere. So, although you will pay into your company pension plan at the same rate as everyone else, you will collect less when you retire." 5

And no one is going to say to Canadian doctors: "We know you do one of the most important jobs any citizen can perform, but from now on you're going to have to get along without any support systems. All hospital equipment and help will be drastically reduced. We believe a good doctor should instinctively know what to do — or you're in the wrong job. If you're really dedicated you'll get along." 6

As for blacks: "Because of the color of your skin, you're going to be paid less than the white person next to you who is doing exactly the same job. It's tough but that's the way it is." 7

As for Catholics: "You're just going to have to understand that you will be beaten up by people with other religious beliefs quite regularly. Even if your assailant threatens to kill you, you can't do anything about it. After all, we all need some escape valves, don't we?" 8

Does all of the above sound like some nihilistic nightmare where Orwellian forces have taken over? Well, it's not. It's all happening right now, in Canada. 9

It's not happening to new Canadians, Quebeckers, residents of the Atlantic provinces, left-handed people, doctors, blacks or Indians. If it were, there would be riots in the streets. Civil libertarians would be howling for justice. But all of these discriminatory practices are being inflicted on women today in Canada as a matter of course. 10

Most women work at two jobs — one inside the home and one outside. Yet three out of four women who become widowed or divorced or have never married live out their old age in poverty. And the situation is going to get worse. 11

Women workers earn, on an average, only 64 cents for every $1 a man gets — even though on an average, women are better educated than men. 12

And when companies base pension plans on how long people live, women will pay the same rates as men but will collect less. 13

What politician could possibly tell doctors to train each other and get along without all their high technology and trained help? Yet a more important job than saving lives is surely creating lives. But mothers get no training, no help in the way of more than a token family allowance, inadequate day-care centres, and almost nonexistent after-school programs. 14

15   No politician would dream of telling blacks they must automatically earn less than other people. But women sales clerks, waitresses and hospital orderlies almost always earn less than males doing the same jobs. It would be called discrimination if a member of a religious group was beaten up, and the assailant would be jailed. But hundreds of wives get beaten by their husbands week in and week out, year after year. Some die, yet society acts as though it isn't happening at all.

16   Women make up 51 per cent of the population of this country. Think of the kind of clout they could have if they used it at the polls. But to listen to the political parties, the woman voter just doesn't exist. When politicians talk to fishing folk they talk about improved processing plants and new docks. When they talk to wheat farmers they talk of better transportation and higher price supports. When they talk to people in the Atlantic provinces they talk about new federal money for buildings and more incentives for secondary industry. When they talk to ethnic groups they talk about better language training courses. But when they think of women — if they do at all — they assume women will vote exactly as their husbands — so why waste time offering them anything? It's mind-boggling to contemplate, though, how all those discriminatory practices would be swept aside if, instead of women, we were Italian, or black, or lived in Quebec or the Atlantic provinces.

△△△

Further Reading:

Simone de Beauvoir, *The Second Sex*
Virginia Woolf, *A Room of One's Own*
Germaine Greer, *The Female Eunuch*
Margrit Eichler, *The Double Standard*
G. H. Nemiroff, ed., *Women and Men*
Ethel Wilson, *Swamp Angel* (novel)
Alice Munro, *Lives of Girls and Women* (novel)

Structure:

1.   Is Doris Anderson's argument mainly a comparison or a contrast?
2.   Is the essay organized "point by point" or by "halves"?
3.   Point out the passage of transition between Anderson's description of minorities and her description of women.
4.   In this feminist essay, why does Anderson never mention women until halfway through? How does this tactic help her reach the potentially hostile 49 percent of her audience that is composed of males?

5. If you have read *1984* or *Animal Farm*, both by George Orwell, tell how the reference to Orwell in paragraph 9 helps to explain Anderson's point.

6. Why does the closing bring in a series of new examples? And why are these examples so short?

Style:

1. How important is the title of an essay? What should it do? How effective is this one, and why?

2. Anderson's essay appeared in *Maclean's*, a magazine for the general reader. Name all the ways you can think of in which her essay seems designed for that person.

Ideas for Discussion and Writing:

1. Explain the IRONY of Anderson's claim: in what sense are women, 51 percent of the population, a "minority" in Canada?

2. Anderson states in paragraph 11, "Most women work at two jobs — one inside the home and one outside." Suppose that at some time you and your spouse both have full-time jobs. If you are a woman, how much of the housework will you expect your husband to do? If you are a man, how much of the housework will you expect your wife to do? Defend your answer with reasons.

3. "The 51-Per-Cent Minority" first appeared in 1980. Revising it for this edition a decade later, Anderson was able to raise from 61 cents to 64 cents the amount that a woman earns for every dollar a man earns. At this rate of change, equal pay will not arrive until 2110 A.D., 130 years after the essay was written. Give as many reasons as you can to explain why.

4. In paragraph 16 Anderson writes, "Women make up 51 per cent of the population of this country. Think of the kind of clout they could have if they used it at the polls." Do you agree that women have not yet used their voting power to best advantage? If so, why haven't they? And how could they begin to?

5. In "Canadians: What Do They Want?" Margaret Atwood points out that war and rape are "two activities not widely engaged in by women" (par. 1). Do you think our world would be different if it were run by women? If so, why and in what ways? If not, why not?

6. **PROCESS IN WRITING:** *Write an essay in which you* contrast *the way society trains girls to be women with the way society trains boys to be men. First divide a page into halves, one for each sex, and fill each half with examples. Now from these notes choose contrasting pairs. Decide whether to organize the pairs by "halves" or point by point, then write a rapid first draft, double-spaced. In your next draft strengthen the transitions, especially signals such as "but," "on the other hand," "however," and "yet," which point out contrast. Share a draft with classmates in small groups, to see if all parts work. Revise any that do not. Finally, read your good draft aloud to the whole class, and be prepared to answer questions asked from other points of view.*

Note: See also the Topics for Writing at the end of this chapter.

Mavor Moore

The Roar of the Greasepaint, the Smell of the Caucus

Actor, playwright, and producer, Mavor Moore is also one of our most authoritative commentators on the nation's arts and media. He was born in Toronto in 1919, studied at the University of Toronto, and since then has virtually lived the history of Canada's stage, radio, and television. He has produced and directed over 50 plays for the stage, and many others for radio and television; has written librettos for musical comedies and for the opera Louis Riel *(1967); and for many years produced and directed the annual review* Spring Thaw. *Moore was a founder of the Stratford Shakespearean Festival, was the CBC's chief producer in the early days of television, was founding chairperson of the Charlottetown Festival, and has served as chairperson of the Canada Council. In recent years, in reaction to the spread of American programming in our media, and to governmental cutbacks of public broadcasting, Moore has emerged as a defender of the arts in Canada. For several years his column in the Toronto* Globe and Mail *carried this message, in a polished and concise prose, arguing week after week that the arts are vital not only to the nation's cultural survival but even to its sovereignty. In our selection, from the August 2, 1986* Globe, *Moore turns his attention to the politicians and their own use of the media arts.*

The distaste with which many politicians approach theatre has been matched only by their eagerness to embrace it. The similarities are too obvious, too close to the knuckle and too damaging. Both deal in drama, ritual, scenarios, role-playing, speeches, spell-binding and persuasion. But theatre is supposed to be for fun, politics for real. Theatre is illusion, deception, fakery, a trick of sound and light. Isn't it? Politics is substance, honesty, actuality, natural light. Isn't it? 1

Throughout history, governors — like soldiers, lawyers, priests and priestesses, physicians, police, academics and many laborers — have worn costumes, carried "props," and produced ceremonies. When occasion demanded, rulers have not hesitated to hire hairdressers and ghost writers, musicians and decorators to improve their god-given presence. 2

But this is called pomp, and is not to be confused in the public mind with the duplicity that characterizes theatre. The thing is perfectly clear to any self-respecting politician. Or is it?

3   Then came radio to provoke this ambivalence more sharply. In the twenties and thirties, radio was the perfect way to reach the whole electorate simultaneously and a foolproof way to fudge the difference between illusion and reality: you cannot see who is speaking. If, before, few voters had actually met a candidate, now most of them became close friends of the candidate's voice. Actors' techniques of faking sincerity were suddenly in great demand.

4   One of the earliest political crises in Canadian broadcasting arose from campaign use of unidentified actors, reading from scripts, who posed as "real voters" — a practice that many advertisers still find blameless. An unprepossessing Canadian expatriate, Father Charles Coughlin, convinced millions of Americans that he was the voice of God.

5   Soon after the Second World War came television. Like radio, it offered widespread simultaneous coverage; but since seeing is believing, television had even greater potential for persuasion. Once we persuaded ourselves that the most vivid evidence of reality is what appears through this prism, it became television fare that largely determined our perceptions.

6   The manipulation of "reality" became not only a temptation but politically mandatory; if you failed to take advantage of the new mass medium, your rivals were sure to seize it. The techniques for managing impressions may have been more complex than those of stage or radio, but the stakes were higher. The simulation of artlessness had to be even more clever.

7   This realization led to wholesale intimacy between politicians and "consultants." In times gone by, I myself have coached a prime minister, assorted Cabinet ministers and a rogues' gallery of notables in how to outwit the camera. I know speech teachers who have patiently exercised nominees out of a low accent into a high, or vice versa — all in the interest of plain dealing. But this is only the beginning.

8   Every time a politician goes on television, his or her public relations team springs into action: experts to choose the setting, select the wardrobe, see that the tinted hair behaves, the make-up is *comme ci* and the lights *comme ça*. If spectacles are worn, they should be casually removed at some point, as if barely necessary for such sharp eyes — but contact lenses are best: one to read the TelePrompter and one to glance at the script occasionally to indicate that there is no TelePrompter.

9   You must have noticed, also, how the script, written by a battery of the ablest wordsmiths influence can buy, is always held loosely in the speaker's hands to show who owns it. But the owner really doesn't need it.

The words come straight from the heart. If the prompter breaks down, another take is always possible.

Perhaps, of course, the public will eventually see through it all. But at the moment politicians may have to accept an unwontedly inferior status. When it comes to promoting causes on television, raising support for the United Appeal or teaching the public its moral duty in war and peace, it's obvious whom the people trust: not our political, religious or educational leaders, but our entertainers.   10

Television inclines us to believe entertainers, who normally show little ambition to take over the real world, and to mistrust politicians, who attempt the tricks of entertainers to achieve power. The illusionist comes across as more honest than the realist.   11

Doubtless this has chilling implications for the future of government. But it may explain why some democracies would sooner elect actors who learn politicking than politicians who bridle at acting. If, that is, they notice much difference between the two.   12

∆∆

Further Reading:

Marshall McLuhan, *Understanding Media*
B. W. Powe, *The Solitary Outlaw*
Brian Fawcett, *Cambodia: A Book for People Who Find Television Too Slow*
George Orwell, *1984* (novel)
Jerzy Kosinski, *Being There* (novel)

Structure:

1. How do you react to Mavor Moore's title? Does it attract your interest? Does it reveal Moore's subject? To what familiar saying does it allude, and how does he twist that saying to introduce his point of view?
2. Moore both introduces and closes this essay with examples of his principal device, *comparison and contrast*. Does paragraph 1 mostly compare? Contrast? Or does it do both? Do paragraphs 10–11 mostly compare? Contrast? Or do they do both?
3. Do paragraphs 2–9, the body of this essay, depict politicians through *comparisons* or through *contrasts* to actors? Defend your answer with examples.
4. In Chapter 7 we will study *classification*, in which the divisions of a subject are discussed one by one. To what extent has Moore used this means of organizing? Which paragraphs of his argument does he devote to politics in the days before electronic media? To politics influenced by radio? To politics

influenced by television? And why does he dwell longest on the last category?

5. Is Moore's *comparison and contrast* organized by "halves" or "point by point"? Explain.

Style:

1. In paragraph 7 Moore admits that he himself has "coached" a "rogues' gallery of notables in how to outwit the camera." How frequently does he colour his argument with emotionally loaded words such as these? Give examples.

2. In paragraph 5 Moore calls television a "prism." Analyze what this METAPHOR implies about television as a medium.

Ideas for Discussion and Writing:

1. How do you, the AUDIENCE, react when in paragraph 7 Moore describes his having "coached" politicians in the art of the actor? In admitting to the very activity he criticizes, does the author lower his credibility, or in documenting his experience does he raise it?

2. Does Moore imply that modern leaders are less honest than the earlier leaders of paragraph 2? Or have the media of radio and television simply made the art of "illusion" easier to practise?

3. What powers did radio give politicians (par. 3–4)? What powers has television added, and why are they greater (par. 5–12)?

4. Do you believe that you, personally, can judge the character of a public figure by seeing him or her on television? Or in our electronic age is the phrase "seeing is believing" obsolete? Defend your view with at least one good example.

5. Some critics say that television gives an unfair advantage to those already in power, especially during an election campaign when the wealthiest party can buy the most television time. Others say television has a democratizing effect, as in the election debates offered by the CBC equally to each party. What is your own view? Defend it with examples.

6. Entertainers now give benefit concerts in support of native peoples, conservation of the rain forests and other natural sites, world peace, the fight against famine, and other causes. Does this illustrate Moore's concept that we trust our entertainers more than our "political, religious or educational leaders" (par. 10)?

7. **PROCESS IN WRITING:** Contrast *two Canadian political leaders, one who comes across well on television and another who does not. First divide a page in half, and make notes about each politician. Be specific, describing voice, manner, appearance, gestures, etc. Now let these notes suggest whether organization by "halves" or "point by point" would be more natural, and make a brief outline accordingly. Write a rapid first draft, double-spaced. When it "cools off," add any further examples and IMAGES needed. In your next draft sharpen word choice. Heighten TRANSITIONS. Finally, edit for details of spelling and grammar before writing the good copy. Proofread word by word.*

Note: *See also the Topics for Writing at the end of this chapter.*

Catharine Parr Traill

Remarks of Security of Person and Property in Canada

Catharine Parr ("Kate") Traill (1802–1899) exemplifies the best of Canadian pioneering life. She spent her early years in England, where she enjoyed the refinements of her father's estate near Southwold and published several books for children. But a reversal of family fortunes and her marriage to a retired half-pay officer meant immigration. In 1832 the Traills joined Catharine's brother Samuel Strickland (who would later write Twenty-Seven Years in Canada West*) near present-day Lakefield, Ontario, and before long they were joined by Catharine's sister Susanna Moodie and her husband (see Moodie's selection on page 256 of this book). Like her sister, who described pioneering life in* Roughing It in the Bush *and other books, Catharine wrote of her own experience in Upper Canada. A collection of letters to her mother appeared in 1836 as* The Backwoods of Canada, *and in 1854 appeared* The Female Emigrant's Guide, *her collection of advice and handbook of techniques. Traill continued to write children's books, and her professionalism as a botanist was widely recognized when in 1868 she published* Canadian Wild Flowers, *and in 1885* Studies of Plant Life in Canada. *All of Kate Traill's writing exemplifies her own life: she was curious, observant, self-reliant — and above all optimistic about life in the New World. These qualities shine through our selection, which comes from* The Female Emigrant's Guide.

1   There is one thing which can hardly fail to strike an emigrant from the Old Country, on his arrival in Canada. It is this, — The feeling of complete security which he enjoys, whether in his own dwelling or in his journeys abroad through the land. He sees no fear — he need see none. He is not in a land spoiled and robbed, where every man's hand is against his fellow — where envy and distrust beset him on every side. At first indeed he is surprised at the apparently stupid neglect of the proper means of security that he notices in the dwellings of all classes of people, especially in the lonely country places, where the want of security would really invite rapine and murder. "How is this," he says, "you use neither bolt, nor lock,

nor bar. I see no shutter to your windows; nay, you sleep often with your doors open upon the latch, and in summer with open doors and windows. Surely this is fool-hardy and imprudent." "We need no such precautions," will his friend reply smiling; "here they are uncalled for. Our safety lies neither in bars nor bolts, but in our consciousness that we are among people whose necessities are not such as to urge them to violate the laws; neither are our riches such as to tempt the poor man to rob us, for they consist not in glittering jewels, nor silver, nor gold."

"But even food and clothes thus carelessly guarded are temptations." 2

"But where others possess these requisites as well as ourselves, they are not likely to steal them from us." 3

And what is the inference that the new comer draws from this statement? 4

That he is in a country where the inhabitants are essentially honest, because they are enabled, by the exertion of their own hands, to obtain in abundance the necessaries of life. Does it not also prove to him that it is the miseries arising from poverty that induce crime. — Men do not often violate the law of honesty, unless driven to do so by necessity. Place the poor Irish peasant in the way of earning his bread in Canada, where he sees his reward before him, in broad lands that he can win by honest toil, and where he can hold up his head and look beyond that grave of a poor man's hope — the parish work house — and see in the far-off vista a home of comfort which his own hands have reared, and can go down to his grave with the thought, that he has left a name and a blessing for his children after him: — men like this do not steal. 5

Robbery is not a crime of common occurrence in Canada. In large towns such acts will occasionally be committed, for it is there that poverty is to be found, but it is not common in country places. There you may sleep with your door unbarred for years. Your confidence is rarely, if ever, abused; your hospitality never violated. 6

When I lived in the backwoods, out of sight of any other habitation, the door has often been opened at midnight, a stranger has entered and lain down before the kitchen fire, and departed in the morning unquestioned. In the early state of the settlement in Douro, now twenty years ago, it was no uncommon occurrence for a party of Indians to enter the house, (they never knock at any man's door,) leave their hunting weapons outside, spread their blankets on the floor, and pass the night with or without leave, arise by the first dawn of day, gather their garments about them, resume their weapons, and silently and noiselessly depart. Sometimes a leash of wild ducks hung to the door-latch, or a haunch of venison left in the kitchen, would be found as a token of gratitude for the warmth and shelter afforded them. 7

8   Many strangers, both male and female, have found shelter under our roof, and never were we led to regret that we had not turned the houseless wanderer from our door.

9   It is delightful this consciousness of perfect security: your hand is against no man, and no man's hand is against you. We dwell in peace among our own people. What a contrast to my home, in England, where by sunset every door was secured with locks and heavy bars and bolts; every window carefully barricaded, and every room and corner in and around the dwelling duly searched, before we ventured to lie down to rest, lest our sleep should be broken in upon by the midnight thief. As night drew on, an atmosphere of doubt and dread seemed to encompass one. The approach of a stranger we beheld with suspicion; and however great his need, we dared not afford him the shelter of our roof, lest our so doing should open the door to robber or murderer. At first I could hardly understand why it happened that I never felt the same sensation of fear in Canada as I had done in England. My mind seemed lightened of a heavy burden; and I, who had been so timid, grew brave and fearless amid the gloomy forests of Canada. Now, I know how to value this great blessing. Let the traveller seek shelter in the poorest shanty, among the lowest Irish settlers, and he need fear no evil, for never have I heard of the rites of hospitality being violated, or the country disgraced by such acts of cold-blooded atrocity as are recorded by the public papers in the Old Country.

10   Here we have no bush-rangers, no convicts to disturb the peace of the inhabitants of the land, as in Australia. No savage hordes of Caffres to invade and carry off our cattle and stores of grain as at the Cape; but peace and industry are on every side. "The land is at rest and breaks forth into singing." Surely we ought to be a happy and a contented people, full of gratitude to that Almighty God who has given us this fair and fruitful land to dwell in.

ΔΔΔΔΔΔΔΔΔΔΔΔΔΔΔΔΔΔΔΔΔΔΔΔΔΔΔΔΔΔΔΔΔΔΔΔΔΔΔΔΔΔΔΔΔΔΔΔΔΔΔΔΔΔΔΔΔΔΔΔΔ

Further Reading:

Catharine Parr Traill,
  The Female Emigrant's Guide
  The Backwoods of Canada
Susanna Moodie, *Roughing It in the Bush*
Margaret Atwood, *The Journals of Susanna Moodie* (poems)
Marian Fowler, *The Embroidered Tent: Five Gentlewomen in Early Canada*

Structure:

1.   The long first paragraph states all the main ideas of this essay.

What, then, does the rest of the essay do?

2. In this contrast between the dangers of life in England and the security of life in Canada, why is so much more of the argument devoted to Canada than to England?

3. The main contrast, between Canada and England, occurs in paragraphs 7–9. Why is this detailed contrast followed, in the last paragraph, by very brief contrasts to Australia and the Cape?

Style:

1. Catharine Parr Traill published *The Female Emigrant's Guide* in 1854. Does her style in this selection seem much different from the style of contemporary writers? Discuss the following:
    A. Word choice
    B. Sentences
    C. Paragraphs
    D. TONE

2. Discuss the meaning of "want" in the phrase "want of security" (middle of par. 1). Do you see other words in this essay that have changed in meaning since 1854?

3. In paragraph 7, Traill writes that Indians "never knock at any man's door." In paragraph 9, she states that "your hand is against no man, and no man's hand is against you." In fact, she mentions men so often that only once in the essay does she specifically refer to women — yet she entitled her book *The Female Emigrant's Guide*. Discuss your feelings about our traditional male-centred grammar. Is the generic "he" still accepted at all? What is the easiest way of changing it to avoid sexist language?

4. In exactness, in vividness, and in poetic power, has our language improved or deteriorated since the time of Catharine Parr Traill?

Ideas for Discussion and Writing:

1. Does modern Canada more closely resemble the new land which Traill describes in this essay, or the old land she left behind?

2. If you have moved to Canada from another country, as Traill did, have you experienced any of the benefits she describes?

3. Traill states that "it is the miseries arising from poverty that induce crime" (par. 5). Do you agree? Or does crime have other causes as well?

4. Traill states, "I, who had been so timid, grew brave and fearless amid the gloomy forests of Canada" (par. 9). The frontier has always been regarded as a place to make a new start, leaving one's problems in the past. In our increasingly crowded and industrialized world, do frontiers remain?

5. Can a "frontier" exist in the city? Are there new ways of living in old places, by which people can free themselves from problems of the past?

6. PROCESS IN WRITING: *Write an essay that* compares and/or contrasts *life in two countries, provinces, cities, towns, or neighbourhoods. First divide a page in half with a vertical line; jot down facts about item A on the left and item B on the right. Looking over these notes, decide now on your THESIS STATEMENT and choose either the "halves" or the "point by point" method of organizing. After a rapid first draft, fine-tune your organization and add more concrete details in further drafts. Now read your paper aloud, to detect repetition and any other flaws of style, before doing the final version.*

Note: See also the Topics for Writing at the end of this chapter.

Russell Baker

A Nice Place to Visit

Russell Baker is one of America's favourite humourists, author of the "Observer" column in the New York Times. *It was a month's stay in Toronto that gave him the material for this contrast of cities. Those who have read Baker already will recognize his distinctive approach: the zany and inventive humor, the satire on human foibles, and the mocking imitations of formal, scholarly, or scientific language. Basic to all this is his stance as "observer": he has a keen eye for the telling details that breathe life into writing. Baker was born in 1925 in Virginia. After a degree at Johns Hopkins in 1947, and employment from 1947 to 1954 at the* Baltimore Sun, *he did political reporting for the* New York Times. *A columnist since 1962, he now takes the whole of American life for his subject, but especially his own city, "the Big Apple." Hundreds of Baker's columns have been collected in books, among these* No Cause for Panic *(1964),* Poor Russell's Almanac *(1972), and* The Rescue of Miss Yaskell and Other Pipe Dreams *(1983). His autobiography* Growing Up *won a Pulitzer Prize in 1983. Our selection appeared first in the* New York Times, *then in Baker's book* So This Is Depravity *(1980).*

Having heard that Toronto was becoming one of the continent's noblest cities, we flew from New York to investigate. New Yorkers jealous of their city's reputation and concerned about challenges to its stature have little to worry about. 1

After three days in residence, our delegation noted an absence of hysteria that was almost intolerable and took to consuming large portions of black coffee to maintain our normal state of irritability. The local people to whom we complained in hopes of provoking comfortably nasty confrontations declined to become bellicose. They would like to enjoy a gratifying big-city hysteria, they said, but believed it would seem ill-mannered in front of strangers. 2

Extensive field studies — our stay lasted four weeks — persuaded us that this failure reflects the survival in Toronto of an ancient pattern of social conduct called "courtesy." 3

"Courtesy" manifests itself in many quaint forms appalling to the New 4

153

Yorker. Thus, for example, Yankee fans may be astonished to learn that at the Toronto baseball park it is considered bad form to heave rolls of toilet paper and beer cans at players on the field.

5   Official literature inside Toronto taxicabs includes a notification of the proper address to which riders may mail the authorities not only complaints but also compliments about the cabbie's behavior.

6   For a city that aspires to urban greatness, Toronto's entire taxi system has far to go. At present, it seems hopelessly bogged down in civilization. One day a member of our delegation listening to a radio conversation between a short-tempered cabbie and the dispatcher distinctly heard the dispatcher say, "As Shakespeare said, if music be the food of love, play on, give me excess of it."

7   This delegate became so unnerved by hearing Shakespeare quoted by a cab dispatcher that he fled immediately back to New York to have his nerves abraded and his spine rearranged in a real big-city taxi.

8   What was particularly distressing as the stay continued was the absence of shrieking police and fire sirens at 3 A.M. — or any other hour, for that matter. We spoke to the city authorities about this. What kind of city was it, we asked, that expected its citizens to sleep all night and rise refreshed in the morning? Where was the incentive to awaken gummy-eyed and exhausted, ready to scream at the first person one saw in the morning? How could Toronto possibly hope to maintain a robust urban divorce rate?

9   Our criticism went unheeded, such is the torpor with which Toronto pursues true urbanity. The fact appears to be that Toronto has very little grasp of what is required of a great city.

10   Consider the garbage picture. It seems never to have occurred to anybody in Toronto that garbage exists to be heaved into the streets. One can drive for miles without seeing so much as a banana peel in the gutter or a discarded newspaper whirling in the wind.

11   Nor has Toronto learned about dogs. A check with the authorities confirmed that, yes, there are indeed dogs resident in Toronto, but one would never realize it by walking the sidewalks. Our delegation was shocked by the presumption of a town's calling itself a city, much less a great city, when it obviously knows nothing of either garbage or dogs.

12   The subway, on which Toronto prides itself, was a laughable imitation of the real thing. The subway cars were not only spotlessly clean, but also fully illuminated. So were the stations. To New Yorkers, it was embarrassing, and we hadn't the heart to tell the subway authorities that they were light-years away from greatness.

13   We did, however, tell them about spray paints and how effectively a few hundred children equipped with spray-paint cans could at least give their subway the big-city look.

It seems doubtful they are ready to take such hints. There is a   14
disturbing distaste for vandalism in Toronto which will make it hard for
the city to enter wholeheartedly into the vigor of the late twentieth
century.

A board fence surrounding a huge excavation for a new highrise   15
building in the downtown district offers depressing evidence of Toronto's
lack of big-city impulse. Embedded in the fence at intervals of about fifty
feet are loudspeakers that play recorded music for passing pedestrians.

Not a single one of these loudspeakers has been mutilated. What's   16
worse, not a single one has been stolen.

It was good to get back to the Big Apple. My coat pocket was bulging   17
with candy wrappers from Toronto and — such is the lingering power of
Toronto — it took me two or three hours back in New York before it
seemed natural again to toss them into the street.

ΔΔΔΔΔΔΔΔΔΔΔΔΔΔΔΔΔΔΔΔΔΔΔΔΔΔΔΔΔΔΔΔΔΔΔΔΔΔΔΔΔΔΔΔΔΔΔΔΔΔΔΔΔΔ

Further Reading:

Russell Baker,
>   *Poor Russell's Almanac*
>   *Growing Up*

Structure:

1. How important to this selection are its *examples?* What
    proportion of the essay do they take up? Point out three or four
    that work especially well, and tell why they do.
2. What considerations do you think led Russell Baker to
    organize his *contrast* not by "halves" but rather "point by
    point"? Do you agree with his choice?
3. Why does Baker not always show the New York side of each
    point? Do you think these omissions are accidental or
    deliberate? Do they hinder or help us as readers? Explain.

Style:

1. Baker's title, "A Nice Place to Visit," is unfinished. What is the
    rest of this common expression, and why are we left to
    complete it ourselves?
2. How soon did you detect Baker's heavy use of IRONY? Where is
    the first place you realized he means the opposite of what he
    says?
3. Elsewhere Baker has stated his admiration for Toronto; does
    his actual opinion come through strongly in "A Nice Place to

Visit," or does his humour lead us to take his comments less seriously?

4. In paragraph 9 Baker writes, "Our criticism went unheeded, such is the torpor with which Toronto pursues true urbanity." Why is the language so FORMAL in this and other passages of his humorous essay? What effect does Baker achieve?

5. Explain the IRONY in each of the following passages:
   A. "comfortably nasty confrontations" (par. 2)
   B. "a gratifying big-city hysteria" (par. 2)
   C. "bogged down in civilization" (par. 6)
   D. "a robust urban divorce rate" (par. 8)
   E. "the vigor of the late twentieth century" (par. 14)

6. In his closing paragraph Baker refers to New York as "the Big Apple." Explore the CONNOTATIONS of this METAPHOR.

Ideas for Discussion and Writing:

1. Baker confines his contrast of Toronto and New York to the relatively minor topics of taxis, noise, garbage, dogs, the subway, and vandalism. Either in class discussion or on paper, extend his contrast to more serious urban problems such as pollution, drugs, disease, poverty, and violent crime.

2. Statistics regularly reveal more murders in American cities than in Canadian ones of equal size; the difference sometimes reaches proportions as high as ten to one. Give all the reasons you can think of to explain this contrast.

3. If you have read Richard Needham's essay "A Sound of Deviltry by Night," which appears in Chapter 2, contrast his view of Toronto to that of Russell Baker.

4. PROCESS IN WRITING: *Take some spare moments during the next week to record in a journal your main impressions of the city or town around you. On other pages, record your memories of another city or town you know elsewhere. Then freewrite on this material for five or ten minutes to make sure which place you prefer. Next write a draft of an essay that contrasts the two, showing through examples why you prefer one of them. Use Baker's point-by-point approach. Choose your own TONE, humorous or serious, and maintain it throughout. Finally discuss your first or second draft with three or four other students, then, incorporating their best suggestions, write your final version.*

Note: See also the Topics for Writing at the end of this chapter.

David Suzuki

Native Peoples Liken Ruination of Nature to Church Destruction

David Suzuki is a scientist who, as host of the CBC's popular and long-lived television series The Nature of Things, *has become one of Canada's best-known public figures. (See p. 98, where his background and work are described in the introduction to another essay.) Although he himself has done internationally recognized genetic research on cell division in fruit flies, Suzuki rejects the narrowness that sometimes underlies the specialized vision of the research scientist. Instead, he uses his broadcasts and syndicated newspaper column as platforms from which to educate the larger public about both the promise and the dangers of science. More often than not it is the dangers he exposes: the application of little-understood technologies; unchecked economic and industrial expansion; and the consequent devastation of other plant and animal species through our consumption of their habitat. In the essay that follows (from the August 27, 1988 Toronto* Globe and Mail*), Suzuki broadens his scope from that of scientist to that of moralist, as he looks at our planet through the eyes of another culture.*

A t the fourth annual Stein Festival near Lytton, B.C., almost 4,000   1
people gathered to celebrate the physical and spiritual values of the
Stein Valley, the last untouched watershed in southwestern British
Columbia.

The participants were also there to show their support to the Lytton   2
and Mt. Currie Indian bands, which are fighting to prevent logging in the
Stein River watershed.

During the three-day celebration, two young Indian men indepen-   3
dently described what the Stein meant to them in strikingly similar terms.
Each referred to the valley as a "church" or "cathedral" where he could
go to find spiritual sustenance and restoration. "When I come out of that
valley," one of them said, "I feel that all my troubles are gone. I feel
cleansed and refreshed, the way I do when I come out of my sweat
house."

The festival this year was held on the grounds of the Christian church   4
where for more than half a century, native boys and girls. including

157

Lytton band chief Ruby Dunstan, were forced to come and receive their education in the Residential Schools.

5   As we left the festival site, we passed a lovely church nestled on the hills between the decaying dormitories and sheds.

6   That church brought to mind the great Christian cathedrals of Europe, the Soviet Union and North America. Many are stunning expressions of art and architecture. The music of organs and choirs echoes through these magnificent edifices, adding to the elaborate paraphernalia of worship. In contrast to the Stein Valley, these temples are essentially celebrations of *humanity*, of our species' creativity, originality and cleverness. Our cathedrals are an affirmation that we are special, we are God's chosen.

7   In contrast, in most native cultures, it is the *land* that is sacred and everything in it — rivers, fish, trees, rocks — was put there by the Creator. Thus, to bulldoze away a sacred rock so a road can be built, to clearcut a watershed or to reroute a creek, is tantamount to sacrilege.

8   In a human-oriented religion in which all of nature is seen as God's gift to us as the chosen species, an untouched watershed becomes an opportunity. "Go forth and multiply, and fill the earth and subdue it. — And have dominion over the fish of the sea, the birds of the air and every living thing that creepeth upon the earth."

9   This notion of our special relationship with God, with the earth as a storehouse for our use, is the foundation of Western attitudes and values, even though we are no longer aware of it today.

10   The major survival trait of our species is an immense and complex brain. We are a clever and inventive species. And so we are able to think up all kinds of things to do with what we see around us.

11   In this century, our brain has brought the West an unprecedented level of health and material comfort. Our ingenuity now expressed through science and technology is taking us to places that were hitherto unreachable — outer space, the bottom of the oceans, deep into the earth.

12   Within our Western perspective, the conception of a use for our surroundings is sufficient justification for acting on it. This is particularly striking in the application of scientific knowledge — we feel that if it can be done, it *must* be done. It is not so much a matter of hubris° as it is a sacred imperative. Today, the "success" of western science has become the model for the world.

13   Now we have set our sights on colonizing outer space, engineering organisms for release into the wild, creating intelligent machines,

---

°hubris: arrogant pride, as in the flawed tragic heroes of classical Greek drama.

constructing biological weapons and developing more elaborate machines of destruction.

Once an idea is conceived, we cannot refrain from pressing on. We justify it with the rationalization that if we don't do it, someone else will. Thus, as we gaze at the Stein Valley, we see it in terms of jobs, board feet (a lumber measure) and profit. We look to harvesting mineral nodules from the ocean depths, tapping oil and gas from deep beneath the Arctic ice, exporting freshwater that flows "uselessly" to the sea. Once we have imagined a possibility for use of these "resources," to refrain from doing so is a waste, a sacrilege, a sin against a generous God.

But the Judeo-Christian exhortation to subdue the earth is only one expression of our connection with nature. We needn't look to mystical religions in the Far East for inspiration; there are other passages in the Bible that speak of sharing, stewardship and belonging.

Jesus Christ himself needed no impressive temple or elaborate robes to worship God. His temple was in the open on the mountainsides, the shore of Galilee or the desert. A profound Western interpretation was expressed by St. Francis of Assisi, who recognized the kinship of all life. He felt at peace in fraternity with nature, and through that harmony, worshipped God.

Thinking about the significance of the Stein Valley and other wilderness areas like it suggests that therein lies the potential for a reinspection and reinterpretation of our Western roots.

ΔΔΔΔΔΔΔΔΔΔΔΔΔΔΔΔΔΔΔΔΔΔΔΔΔΔΔΔΔΔΔΔΔΔΔΔΔΔΔΔΔΔΔΔΔΔΔΔΔΔΔΔΔΔΔΔΔΔΔΔΔΔΔ

Further Reading:

David Suzuki, *Metamorphosis*
Michael M'Gonigle and Wendy Wickwire, *Stein: The Way of the River*
Hugh Brody, *Maps and Dreams*
Robert Ornstein and Paul Ehrlich: *New World, New Mind*
Henry David Thoreau, *Walden*

Structure:

1. As he begins his argument David Suzuki *compares* the wilderness and a church building as places of worship. But he then poses a dramatic *contrast* and from it develops all the rest of his argument. What is this underlying contrast, and in which two paragraphs is it introduced?
2. In paragraph 8 Suzuki quotes the well-known passage from Genesis 1:28 that grants humans "dominion" over nature. Point out all the *effects* of this philosophy, as Suzuki traces them in the paragraphs that follow. What proportion of his

argument is developed by *cause and effect*? And does this rhetorical strategy strengthen or weaken Suzuki's overall *contrast*?

3. Which paragraphs most strongly develop Suzuki's argument through *example*?

4. In his closing, Suzuki suggests a more nature-friendly interpretation of Christianity. Is this final strategy a comparison, a contrast, or both? Explain.

Style:

1. Point out the SIMILES of paragraph 3 and analyze how they help to introduce Suzuki's argument.

2. Explore the IRONY of gazing at the Stein Valley "in terms of jobs, board feet . . . and profit" (par. 14).

Ideas for Discussion and Writing:

1. Whatever your culture or religion, have you ever experienced nature as holy? Describe the setting and occasion.

2. The forest in particular has been linked with religion. Early cults met in sacred groves, the columns of many temples and cathedrals represent tree trunks, and the very word "cathedral" is almost a cliché to describe a grove of trees. Yet the Americans have sawn most of their redwoods into boards, we have clearcut almost all the giant red cedars of our West Coast, and Brazilian ranchers clear land by setting fire each year to vast tracts of virgin Amazon rain forest. Following Suzuki's example, analyze how the teachings of your own religion could help to restore our reverence for trees and all nature.

3. Paragraphs 11, 12, and especially 13 portray science as a cause of our self-centred use of nature. Debate the role of the scientist: Is his or her job simply to pursue discovery wherever it leads? Or should scientists also evaluate the impact of new discoveries — like Leonardo da Vinci who invented the submarine, but then kept the idea secret because he thought it would destroy shipping and cause war?

4. In paragraph 16 Suzuki gives the example of Jesus, a non-materialist at home in nature, as an alternative to the older tradition of "subduing" the earth. Suggest five concrete things the average person in our society could also do to consume less and to live in closer harmony with nature.

5.   **PROCESS IN WRITING**: *Suzuki opens his argument with the Stein Valley logging controversy. Choose your own environmental controversy, either local, national, or international. Gather information from periodicals or from environmental groups, then make notes on the issue — "pro" on one half of the page and "con" on the other. Now choose a side and a thesis. Write an essay that* contrasts *the alternatives, either by "halves" or "point by point," arguing for the side you prefer. With each draft add more examples and concrete images, to build a hard-hitting argument like Suzuki's. Before doing your final copy, read the essay aloud to detect repetitious or awkward passages to revise.*

Note: See also the Topics for Writing at the end of this chapter.

Margaret Laurence

Where the World Began

Margaret Laurence's untimely death in 1987 was mourned across the nation by readers who had seen their own humanity reflected in her novels, and by many writers who had lost a generous friend. Born in 1926 in the prairie town of Neepawa, Manitoba and educated in Winnipeg, Laurence spent 1950 to 1957 in Somalia and Ghana with her engineer husband. There she began to write some of the best fiction yet produced by a Canadian about the Third World. Laurence later separated from her husband, and in 1962 moved with her children to England. But in her writing she returned to western Canada. Renaming her hometown "Manawaka" and recasting it in fiction, she completed what is probably our best-loved Canadian novel, The Stone Angel *(1964). It is the story of proud and stubborn Hagar Shipley, one of many strong women who would be central to Laurence's fiction. More novels followed:* A Jest of God *(1966),* The Fire-Dwellers *(1969), and* The Diviners *(1974). These, along with her book of collected short stories* A Bird in the House *(1970), made of "Manawaka" and its people a celebrated microcosm of the larger world. By the early seventies Laurence had returned to Canada, settling in Lakefield, Ontario. But* The Diviners *was to be her last novel. She now turned to activism as a feminist, as a human rights advocate, and above all as a foe of the nuclear arms race. "It is my feeling," she said, "that as we grow older we should become not less radical but more so." In her last years she worked tirelessly to save the planet that she had first come to know "where the world began." Our selection is from Laurence's 1976 book of essays,* Heart of a Stranger.

1   A strange place it was, that place where the world began. A place of incredible happenings, splendours and revelations, despairs like multitudinous pits of isolated hells. A place of shadow-spookiness, inhabited by the unknowable dead. A place of jubilation and of mourning, horrible and beautiful.

2   It was, in fact, a small prairie town.

3   Because that settlement and that land were my first and for many years my only real knowledge of this planet, in some profound way they remain my world, my way of viewing. My eyes were formed there. Towns like

162

ours, set in a sea of land, have been described thousands of times as dull, bleak, flat, uninteresting. I have had it said to me that the railway trip across Canada is spectacular, except for the prairies, when it would be desirable to go to sleep for several days, until the ordeal is over. I am always unable to argue this point effectively. All I can say is — well, you really have to live there to know that country. The town of my childhood could be called bizarre, agonizingly repressive or cruel at times, and the land in which it grew could be called harsh in the violence of its seasonal changes. But never merely flat or uninteresting. Never dull.

In winter, we used to hitch rides on the back of the milk sleigh, our   4
moccasins squeaking and slithering on the hard rutted snow of the roads, our hands in ice-bubbled mitts hanging onto the box edge of the sleigh for dear life, while Bert grinned at us through his great frosted moustache and shouted the horse into speed, daring us to stay put. Those mornings, rising, there would be the perpetual fascination of the frost feathers on windows, the ferns and flowers and eerie faces traced there during the night by unseen artists of the wind. Evenings, coming back from skating, the sky would be black but not dark, for you could see a cold glitter of stars from one side of the earth's rim to the other. And then the sometime astonishment when you saw the Northern Lights flaring across the sky, like the scrawled signature of God. After a blizzard, when the snowploughs hadn't yet got through, school would be closed for the day, the assumption being that the town's young could not possibly flounder through five feet of snow in the pursuit of education. We would then gaily don snowshoes and flounder for miles out into the white dazzling deserts, in pursuit of a different kind of knowing. If you came back too close to night, through the woods at the foot of the town hill, the thin black branches of poplar and chokecherry now meringued with frost, sometimes you heard coyotes. Or maybe the banshee wolf-voices were really only inside your head.

Summers were scorching, and when no rain came and the wheat   5
became bleached and dried before it headed, the faces of farmers and townsfolk would not smile much, and you took for granted, because it never seemed to have been any different, the frequent knocking at the back door and the young men standing there, mumbling or thrusting defiantly their requests for a drink of water and a sandwich if you could spare it. They were riding the freights, and you never knew where they had come from, or where they might end up, if anywhere. The Drought and Depression were like evil deities which had been there always. You understood and did not understand.

Yet the outside world had its continuing marvels. The poplar bluffs and   6
the small river were filled and surrounded with a zillion different grasses, stones, and weed flowers. The meadowlarks sang undaunted from the

twanging telephone wires along the gravel highway. Once we found an old flat-bottomed scow, and launched her, poling along the shallow brown waters, mending her with wodges of hastily chewed Spearmint, grounding her among the tangles of yellow marsh marigolds that grew succulently along the banks of the shrunken river, while the sun made our skins smell dusty-warm.

7   My best friend lived in an apartment above some stores on Main Street (its real name was Mountain Avenue, goodness knows why), an elegant apartment with royal-blue velvet curtains. The back roof, scarcely sloping at all, was corrugated tin, of a furnace-like warmth on a July afternoon, and we would sit there drinking lemonade and looking across the back lane at the Fire Hall. Sometimes our vigil would be rewarded. Oh joy! Somebody's house burning down! We had an almost-perfect callousness in some ways. Then the wooden tower's bronze bell would clonk and toll like a thousand speeded funerals in a time of plague, and in a few minutes the team of giant black horses would cannon forth, pulling the fire wagon like some scarlet chariot of the Goths, while the firemen clung with one hand, adjusting their helmets as they went.

8   The oddities of the place were endless. An elderly lady used to serve, as her afternoon tea offering to other ladies, soda biscuits spread with peanut butter and topped with a whole marshmallow. Some considered this slightly eccentric, when compared with chopped egg sandwiches, and admittedly talked about her behind her back, but no one ever refused these delicacies or indicated to her that they thought she had slipped a cog. Another lady dyed her hair a bright and cheery orange, by strangers often mistaken at twenty paces for a feather hat. My own beloved stepmother wore a silver fox neckpiece, a whole pelt, *with the embalmed (?) head still on*. My Ontario Irish grandfather said, "sparrow grass," a more interesting term than asparagus. The town dump was known as "the nuisance grounds," a phrase fraught with weird connotations, as though the effluvia of our lives was beneath contempt but at the same time was subtly threatening to the determined and sometimes hysterical propriety of our ways.

9   Some oddities were, as idiom had it, "funny ha ha"; others were "funny peculiar." Some were not so very funny at all. An old man lived, deranged, in a shack in the valley. Perhaps he wasn't even all that old, but to us he seemed a wild Methuselah figure, shambling among the underbrush and the tall couchgrass, muttering indecipherable curses or blessings, a prophet who had forgotten his prophesies. Everyone in town knew him, but no one knew him. He lived among us as though only occasionally and momentarily visible. The kids called him Andy Gump, and feared him. Some sought to prove their bravery by tormenting him. They were the mediaeval bear baiters, and he the lumbering bewildered

bear, half blind, only rarely turning to snarl. Everything is to be found in a town like mine. Belsen,° writ small but with the same ink.

All of us cast stones in one shape or another. In grade school, among the vulnerable and violet girls we were, the feared and despised were those few older girls from what was charmingly termed "the wrong side of the tracks." Tough in talk and tougher in muscle, they were said to be whores already. And may have been, that being about the only profession readily available to them.

The dead lived in that place, too. Not only the grandparents who had, in local parlance, "passed on" and who gloomed, bearded or bonneted, from the sepia photographs in old albums, but also the uncles, forever eighteen or nineteen, whose names were carved on the granite family stones in the cemetery, but whose bones lay in France. My own young mother lay in that graveyard, beside other dead of our kin, and when I was ten, my father, too, only forty, left the living town for the dead dwelling on the hill.

When I was eighteen, I couldn't wait to get out of that town, away from the prairies. I did not know then that I would carry the land and town all my life within my skull, that they would form the mainspring and source of the writing I was to do, wherever and however far away I might live.

This was my territory in the time of my youth, and in a sense my life since then has been an attempt to look at it, to come to terms with it. Stultifying to the mind it certainly could be, and sometimes was, but not to the imagination. It was many things, but it was never dull.

The same, I now see, could be said for Canada in general. Why on earth did generations of Canadians pretend to believe this country dull? We knew perfectly well it wasn't. Yet for so long we did not proclaim what we knew. If our upsurge of so-called nationalism seems odd or irrelevant to outsiders, and even to some of our own people (*what's all the fuss about?*), they might try to understand that for many years we valued ourselves insufficiently, living as we did under the huge shadows of those two dominating figures, Uncle Sam and Britannia. We have only just begun to value ourselves, our land, our abilities. We have only just begun to recognize our legends and to give shape to our myths.

There are, God knows, enough aspects to deplore about this country. When I see the killing of our lakes and rivers with industrial wastes, I feel rage and despair. When I see our industries and natural resources increasingly taken over by America, I feel an overwhelming discouragement, especially as I cannot simply say "damn Yankees." It should never

°Belsen: a notorious Nazi death camp.

be forgotten that it is we ourselves who have sold such a large amount of our birthright for a mess of plastic Progress.° When I saw the War Measures Act being invoked in 1970, I lost forever the vestigial remains of the naive wish-belief that repression could not happen here, or would not. And yet, of course, I had known all along in the deepest and often hidden caves of the heart that anything can happen anywhere, for the seeds of both man's freedom and his captivity are found everywhere, even in the microcosm of a prairie town. But in raging against our injustices, our stupidities, I do so *as family*, as I did, and still do in writing, about those aspects of my town which I hated and which are always in some ways aspects of myself.

16   The land still draws me more than other lands. I have lived in Africa and in England, but splendid as both can be, they do not have the power to move me in the same way as, for example, that part of southern Ontario where I spent four months last summer in a cedar cabin beside a river. "Scratch a Canadian, and you find a phony pioneer," I used to say to myself in warning. But all the same it is true, I think, that we are not yet totally alienated from physical earth, and let us only pray we do not become so. I once thought that my lifelong fear and mistrust of cities made me a kind of old-fashioned freak; now I see it differently.

17   The cabin has a long window across its front western wall, and sitting at the oak table there in the mornings, I used to look out at the river and at the tall trees beyond, green-gold in the early light. The river was bronze; the sun caught it strangely, reflecting upon its surface the near-shore sand ripples underneath. Suddenly, the crescenting of a fish, gone before the eye could clearly give image to it. The old man next door said these leaping fish were carp. Himself, he preferred muskie, for he was a real fisherman and the muskie gave him a fight. The wind most often blew from the south, and the river flowed toward the south, so when the water was wind-riffled, and the current was strong, the river seemed to be flowing both ways. I liked this, and interpreted it as an omen, a natural symbol.

18   A few years ago, when I was back in Winnipeg, I gave a talk at my old college. It was open to the public, and afterward a very old man came up to me and asked me if my maiden name had been Wemyss. I said yes, thinking he might have known my father or my grandfather. But no. "When I was a young lad," he said, "I once worked for your great-grandfather, Robert Wemyss, when he had the sheep ranch at Raeburn." I think that was a moment when I realized all over again

---

°for a mess of plastic Progress: allusion to Genesis 25, in which the hunter Esau sells his birthright to his brother Jacob for a mess of "pottage."

something of great importance to me. My long-ago families came from Scotland and Ireland, but in a sense that no longer mattered so much. My true roots were here.

I am not very patriotic, in the usual meaning of that word. I cannot say "My country right or wrong" in any political, social or literary context. But one thing is inalterable, for better or worse, for life. [19]

This is where my world began. A world which includes the ancestors — both my own and other people's ancestors who become mine. A world which formed me, and continues to do so, even while I fought it in some of its aspects, and continue to do so. A world which gave me my own lifework to do, because it was here that I learned the sight of my own particular eyes. [20]

△△△

Further Reading:

Margaret Laurence,
> *The Stone Angel*
> *The Diviners*
> *A Bird in the House*

Clara Thomas, *The Manawaka World of Margaret Laurence*
Alice Munro, *Lives of Girls and Women* (novel)
Sinclair Ross, *As for Me and My House* (novel)

Structure:

1. What organizational goals does Margaret Laurence achieve by repeating her title phrase in both the opening and the closing paragraphs?
2. Laurence's THESIS STATEMENT follows the common pattern of directly stating the main point early in the essay. Identify it.
3. In making her point, does Laurence mostly *compare* or *contrast* her small prairie town to the nation as a whole?
4. Point out at least three specific qualities of her home town that Laurence later sees in her nation — or even in the world as a whole. Cite a passage to illustrate each *comparison*.
5. What is the organizational importance of paragraphs 12, 13, and 14 to Laurence's overall argument?
6. Point out at least three paragraphs that support this essay primarily through *description*. Which one do you think most strongly conveys the flavour of Laurence's small-town childhood? Point out several of its best IMAGES and analyze why they are effective.
7. Why does this essay end with the word "eyes"?

Style:

1. Why does Laurence begin her essay with pairs of opposites ("A place of jubilation and of mourning, horrible and beautiful" — par. 1)?

2. Like Emily Carr in "D'Sonoqua," Laurence plays with words and phrases. Discuss the effects of these examples: "zillion" (par. 6), "wodges" (par. 6), "clonk" (par. 7), "cannon forth" (par. 7), and "gloomed" (par. 11).

3. To describe winter in a prairie town, paragraph 4 gives us a profusion of SENSE IMAGES. While one person reads this passage aloud, other class members can raise their hand every time they detect an appeal to their sense of sight, hearing, or touch. What is the total effect of these images?

4. In paragraph 3 the prairie is "a sea of land." Covered with snow in paragraph 4, it becomes "white dazzling deserts." Find at least five other FIGURES OF SPEECH in this essay, and analyze the impact of each.

Ideas for Discussion and Writing:

1. "Why on earth did generations of Canadians pretend to believe this country dull?" Laurence asks in paragraph 14. How would you answer her? How dull or exciting do you consider your corner of Canada? Defend your answer with examples.

2. "Everything is to be found in a town like mine. Belsen, writ small but with the same ink," Laurence writes in paragraph 9. Give one image of "Belsen, writ small" that you saw in your own childhood town or neighbourhood. Name one time and place in Canada where "Belsen" has been "writ large."

3. In paragraph 15 Laurence calls her home town a "microcosm" (literally a "small world"). As you think of the town or the city neighbourhood of your own childhood (whether in Canada or elsewhere), does it also seem a microcosm of the world? Does it illustrate Laurence's idea that "anything can happen anywhere" (par. 15)? And as you imagine other "microcosms" around the world, do you see mostly *differences* or mostly *similarities* to the people in your own?

4. PROCESS IN WRITING: *Write your own essay of comparison, entitled "Where My World Began," showing your childhood town or neighbourhood as a microcosm of the nation — or, if you like, of the world as a whole. First brainstorm to produce a page of notes, in any order. Now choose the best, put them in ascending order of importance (to create an effect of climax), and from them write your first draft. In your*

next draft add more SENSE IMAGES *to convey a sense of place (as Laurence does), and add any examples needed to illustrate your points. Now read your argument aloud to a small group of classmates, and apply the best of their suggestions as you revise toward the final version. Read the finished essay aloud, with expression, to the whole class.*

Note: See also the Topics for Writing at the end of this chapter.

Topics for Writing

CHAPTER 5: COMPARISON AND CONTRAST

Compare and/or contrast one of the following pairs. (See also the guidelines that follow.)

1. A newborn and an elderly person
2. Front-wheel-drive and rear-wheel-drive cars
3. The newspaper and the TV newcast
4. Cats and dogs
5. Renting and owning your home
6. Using credit and using cash
7. Touring bikes and mountain bikes
8. The novel and the short story
9. Any two martial arts
10. The classical music fan and the rock music fan
11. A Canadian city and an American city of the same size
12. A wedding and a funeral
13. Writing on paper and using a word processor
14. Natural and synthetic fabrics
15. The authoritarian parent and the permissive parent
16. Luxury cars and economy cars
17. Speaking and writing
18. Community college and university
19. The analogue watch and the digital watch
20. A team sport and an individual sport
21. Sales tax and income tax
22. Glasses and contact lenses
23. Driving a motorcycle and driving a car
24. Two newspapers that you know
25. Large families and small families

Note also the Process in Writing topic after each selection in this chapter.

Process in Writing: Guidelines

Follow at least some of these steps in writing your essay of comparison and contrast (your teacher may suggest which ones).

1. *Spend enough time with the topic list to choose the item that best fits your interest and experience.*

2. *Draw a line down the middle of a blank page. Now brainstorm: jot down notes for subject "A" on the left and for subject "B" on the right. Join related items with lines, then take stock of what you have: Is A better than B? Is it worse? Similar? Opposite? Or what? Express their relationship to each other in a thesis statement.*

3. *Now choose either "halves" or "separate points" to organize your argument, depending on the nature and size of your subject, then work your notes into a brief outline.*

4. *Write a rapid first draft, double-spaced, not stopping now to revise or edit.*

5. *Later analyze what you have produced: Does it follow your outline? If not, is the new material off-topic, or is it a worthwhile addition, an example of "thinking in writing"? Revise accordingly.*

6. *In your second draft cut all deadwood. Sharpen word choice. Add any missing examples. Strengthen* TRANSITIONS.

7. *Test your prose aloud before writing the good copy. If you have used a computer, save the essay on disk in case your teacher suggests further revision.*

S.S.C. Photo Centre/Image No. 001-015-010-002.

"We were all, brothers and sisters alike, born in a long three-storey wooden house, a house as humped and crusty as a loaf of homemade bread, as warm and clean inside as the white of the loaf."

— Félix Leclerc, "The Family House"

Analogy and Related Devices

In a way, it's like....

One student wrote this memory of his childhood in Toronto:

> I heard and felt a rumbling from the ground, looked up and saw a huge
> red metallic monster with a tail on the end approach us. "Run, run," I
> said, "before it eats us." My mother reassured me that no fear was
> necessary. The monster slowly rolled up beside us, opened its mouth,
> and we went in.

As adults, we know that monsters have not roamed the shores of Lake
Ontario for many millions of years, and that they were not red but green!
We also know that monsters and streetcars have little in common. Yet who
would say that this *analogy* does not clearly explain the child's first
encounter with a streetcar? It may even help us, as adults, to view with
new eyes something that we have taken for granted.

In the last chapter, we discussed how two items from the same
category — say, two cities — can be explained logically through comparison and contrast. By seeing how Toronto and New York are alike or
unlike, we gain a clearer understanding of both. An *analogy*, though, brings
together two apparently unlike items from different categories. And
instead of using the two items to explain each other, it more often uses one
as a device to explain the other. It is not the monster we care about but the
monstrous aspects of the streetcar.

In the last chapter, we speculated whether, instead of comparing two

173

cities, we could compare a city and an anthill. To those of us who live in chambers along the corridors of apartment buildings or who each day crowd into holes in the ground to take the subway, the similarities may be all too clear. We see right away that such an argument is hardly logical, for the very good reason that people are not insects. Yet the analogy may be a fresh, thought-provoking way to describe some aspects of life in a city.

One analogy from the late eighties, the "computer virus," was so vivid and timely that it swept the world. This electronic "disease" "contaminates" computer programs, "spreading" an "epidemic" of "contagion." The "outbreaks" of various "strains" can "infect" programs, erase memory, or even attack hardware. Of course "antiviral" software to "vaccinate" against infection has been developed, with brand names like "Flu Shot +," "Data Physician," "Antidote," "Virus RX," "ViruSafe" and "Vaccine 1.0." In addition, "safe computing practices" are now recommended to avoid infection by viruses such as "PC AIDS" (*Time*, September 26, 1988). What makes this analogy powerful is not just its originality, but also its extent. The further you can develop an analogy by drawing links between the two items (in this case a destructive computer program and a virus), the better your analogy.

Yet even a brief statement, such as "A destructive computer program is like a virus," can have value. As a *simile*, it is not much of an argument in itself but is a vivid statement that can be used in support of another argument. While a *simile* states that one thing is *like* another, a *metaphor* states that one thing *is* another ("A destructive computer program is a virus"). Both devices occur often in poetry and in fiction, and both are effective in essays. The last selection in this chapter, Félix Leclerc's description of his boyhood home, contains a steady stream of similes and metaphors that convey a vividly poetic sense not only of the place but also of the author's feelings about the place. Perhaps nothing objective has been proven, but a message has certainly been given.

Note: For more examples of analogy and related devices, see these essays in other chapters:

Analogy:
Erika Ritter, "Bicycles," p. 204
Simile, metaphor, and other figures of speech:
Franklin Russell, "The Capelin," p. 123
Emily Carr, "D'Sonoqua," p. 77
Joy Kogawa, "Grinning and Happy," p. 315
Margaret Laurence, "Where the World Began," p. 162
Pierre Berton, "The Dirtiest Job in the World," p. 289

Robertson Davies

The Decorums of Stupidity

The grand old man of Canadian letters, Robertson Davies has been actor, playwright, scholar, teacher, journalist, essayist — and above all, novelist. Born in 1913 in Thamesville, Ontario, he studied at Queen's and then at Oxford. After acting briefly with England's Old Vic Company, he returned to become editor of the Peterborough Examiner, *a post he graced with his polished and urbane columns. A career as English professor at the University of Toronto followed, from 1963 to his retirement in 1981. Today Davies' plays, such as* Eros at Breakfast *(1948) and* Fortune, My Foe *(1949) may seem less appealing than his many collected essays — witty, urbane, and highly polished pieces on many subjects but especially the arts (our selection comes from one of these collections,* A Voice from the Attic, *1960). Even more widely appreciated are his novels. His early "Salterton Trilogy" was well received, but it is his "Deptford Trilogy," now translated into 12 languages, that has produced his international reputation:* Fifth Business *(1970, the best of all his novels),* The Manticore *(1972), and* World of Wonders *(1975). In these novels, as in most of his literary works, one event influences another until the characters are entrapped in a web of causality. Continuing the pattern of threes, Davies' latest trilogy consists of the novels* The Rebel Angels *(1981),* What's Bred in the Bone *(1985) and* The Lyre of Orpheus *(1988).*

N ot all rapid reading is to be condemned. Much that is badly written and grossly padded must be read rapidly and nothing is lost thereby. Much of the reading that has to be done in the way of business should be done as fast as it can be understood. The ideal business document is an auditor's report; a good one is finely edited. But the memoranda, the public-relations pieces, the business magazines, need not detain us. Every kind of prose has its own speed, and the experienced reader knows it as a musician knows Adagio from Allegro. All of us have to read a great deal of stuff which gives us no pleasure and little information, but which we cannot wholly neglect; such reading belongs in that department of life which Goldsmith called "the decorums of stupidity." Books as works of art are no part of this duty-reading.

1

175

2   Books as works of art? Certainly; it is thus that their writers intend them. But how are these works of art used?

3   Suppose you hear of a piece of recorded music which you think you might like. Let us say it is an opera of Benjamin Britten's — *The Turn of the Screw.* You buy it, and after dinner you put it on your record player. The scene is one of bustling domesticity: your wife is writing to her mother, on the typewriter, and from time to time she appeals to you for the spelling of a word; the older children are chattering happily over a game, and the baby is building, and toppling, towers of blocks. The records are long-playing ones, designed for 33 revolutions of the turntable per minute; ah, but you have taken a course in rapid listening, and you pride yourself on the speed with which you can hear, so you adjust your machine to play at 78 revolutions a minute. And when you find your attention wandering from the music, you skip the sound arm rapidly from groove to groove until you come to a bit that appeals to you. But look — it is eight o'clock, and if you are to get to your meeting on time, Britten must be choked off. So you speed him up until a musical pause arrives, and then you stop the machine, marking the place so that you can continue your appreciation of *The Turn of the Screw* when next you can spare a few minutes for it.

4   Ridiculous? Of course, but can you say that you have never read a book in that fashion?

5   One of the advantages of reading is that it can be done in short spurts and under imperfect conditions. But how often do we read in conditions which are merely decent, not to speak of perfection? How often do we give a book a fair chance to make its effect with us?

△△

Further Reading:

Robertson Davies,
   A Voice from the Attic
   Fifth Business
   The Manticore
   World of Wonders

Structure:

1.   In discussing "duty-reading" that is best done at high speed, how does paragraph 1 prepare us for the main point?
2.   Where is the main point first stated?
3.   Paragraph 3 develops the *analogy* upon which this essay is based: listening to music as reading a book. Books have been

discussed in the introduction, but why are they not mentioned in the analogy itself?

4. Davies uses a standard technique in closing his essay: the asking of questions. Are these true questions that are open to debate, or are they rhetorical questions designed to make us agree with the author?

Style:

1. Why is this essay so much shorter than others you have read in this book? Has Davies failed to develop his point fully?

2. Why are paragraphs 1 and 3 so long while paragraphs 2 and 4 are so short?

3. What FIGURE OF SPEECH does Davies use in this sentence from paragraph 1: "Every kind of prose has its own speed, and the experienced reader knows it as a musician knows Adagio from Allegro"?

4. Is Davies entirely serious, as his elevated and dignified style would suggest? Or is humour important to his argument? Give examples.

Ideas for Discussion and Writing:

1. Is a desire to read fast like a desire to eat fast? To drive fast? To work fast? To live fast? Why is speed so highly regarded in our culture? Are you familiar with another culture that encourages a slower pace? If so, which do you prefer, and why?

2. Before writing was invented, all stories and poems were of course spoken aloud. What advantages do you think a listener has over a reader? What advantages do you think a reader has over a listener?

3. If you have read "A Tongue-Lashing for Deaf Ears," by Wendy Dennis, compare the distractions of the modern reader with those of the modern moviegoer.

4. Francis Bacon said, "Some books are to be tasted, others to be swallowed, and some few to be chewed and digested. . . ." Make a list of the five or ten books you have most recently read. Which did you "taste," which did you "swallow," and which did you "chew and digest"? What factors influenced your method in each case?

5. PROCESS IN WRITING: *In an essay based on analogy, tell how you "taste," "swallow," or "chew and digest" different kinds of music. First make notes for a week, whenever you listen to music on the radio or record player. Then put your best material into a brief outline before*

writing a first draft. Add plentiful examples, but cut any excess words. Read your final version aloud in class.

Note: See also the Topics for Writing at the end of this chapter.

June Callwood

The Country of the Poor*

One of the nation's most prolific journalists, June Callwood is also one of its leading social activists. In her long career she has never held a full-time job, yet as a freelance writer she has published thousands of newspaper and magazine articles, has produced regular columns, has ghostwritten the "autobiographies" of people as varied as Charles Mayo, Barbara Walters, Otto Preminger, and Bob White, and has published numerous widely read books of her own, such as The Law Is Not for Women *(with Marvin Zuker, 1976),* A Full Life *(1982),* Emotions *(1986), and* Twelve Weeks in Spring *(1986, an account of the last weeks in the life of a cancer victim). Her passionate social concerns are evident not only in her articles and books, but also in her other work as champion of the underdog. Siding with the weak and the poor, Callwood has helped to found over two dozen benevolent organizations, among them Digger House (a shelter for homeless youth in Toronto), Nellie's (a haven for battered women), Jessie's (a refuge for pregnant teenagers), and in 1987 Casey House (a residential treatment centre for people dying of AIDS). She also helped to found the Canadian Civil Liberties Association in 1965, and, as a writer, has fought strongly against censorship. Our selection "The Country of the Poor," Callwood's Toronto* Globe and Mail *column of November 21, 1987, is a characteristic sample of her work: an investigation of social injustice.*

Whatever else may unify a nation of such disparate pieces as this one, it is clear from a journey across the country that the poor have no regional boundaries. They occupy one country, poverty, and wherever they may happen to live, whatever their age or the language they speak, the similarities in their skewed lives unite them and make them one country, indivisible.

This was nowhere more striking than in Montreal, where the two solitudes, English and French, merge in the common misery of their predicament. While there are soup kitchens that ostensibly are English

*Editor's title.

179

and soup kitchens with French names, homeless people of both founding groups are lined up together, unified by the humiliating hunger they have in common.

3   The poor acquire citizenship in their country of the condemned in certain clichéd ways that are the same in Vancouver as in Halifax. Everywhere, the poor are growing younger as the country seems to have developed, simultaneously, an epidemic of grossly incapable parents, substitute care by the state that often serves only to intensify the child's wretchedness, and an economy that does not require unskilled youth — prostitutes excepted.

4   Everywhere the fastest-growing definable subgroup within the nationhood of poverty is the one that consists of young mothers and their children. Poverty strikes them most acutely in the shortage across the nation of affordable housing, with the consequence that their lives are precarious and unstable. Everywhere, their children have wild eyes and teachers worry.

5   Most poor women have been beaten by men on whom they depended. That truth has become banal, but the beatings are real nonetheless and convey a message of worthlessness which poverty exacerbates.

6   Many of the poor are addicted to drugs or alcohol, or both, though it is difficult to know whether they are really addicts or are merely making use of what in their environment is a congenial and effective, if temporary, escape.

7   Some of the poor are mad and stroll the streets shouting at their visions. The benign effect stable housing might have on their illness is only beginning to be explored.

8   Many of the poor are men who did what traditional males pride themselves on doing: fighting a war, working at back-bending hard labor. Something went wrong and couldn't be fixed: the war broke their hearts and their being; the jobs dried up; someone died or left and the grief of it could not be borne.

9   Everywhere, the poor live one day at a time with a fixed goal: to find at least one meal. In winter in this climate of killing cold they have a second — to keep from freezing.

10   The quest is so primitive and brutal that a person must deaden the soul to do it. In a soup kitchen somewhere last week a nattily dressed old man was eating daintily as he explained that he had spent the day painting a landscape. The room was so proud of him, so aware of what such a victory of the spirit represented, that it was a telling moment.

11   Also universal and interchangeable are the people who care. Every city in the country has one or 10 of them and they make a fine array. Though university-educated and articulate members of the upper middle class, they work for wages so debased their circumstances are little better than

those they strive to serve. What moved them initially to divert from more promising careers was compassion and respect for people they saw as essentially decent and valuable human beings in distress, as helpless as people caught in a mine cave-in. What keeps them at it, however, is the exhilaration of being at the centre of a good fight that might alter the face of poverty.

They wade rivers of bureaucratic bungling and political insensitivity and public indifference with determination because they have the right questions: Why does this affluent country need soup lines? How can it be that people live in cars and cardboard boxes? 12

A news release issued last August for the Canadian conference on homelessness that was held in Ottawa said that homelessness is "a much broader and deeper phenomenon than most Canadians believe." In communities across the country are signs that something is changing: housing for the poor is being developed with self-contained units; the concept of the need for supportive staff through transition periods is being acknowledged; food banks are being questioned, not for their present validity but for their apparent willingness to continue to exist forever. 13

Housing is seen everywhere as the key issue in the nation of the poor. Poverty will be relieved, the front-line people say, when housing is stable and affordable. They think the country is beginning to understand that. 14

However, no city in Canada yet has a sufficient supply of affordable permanent housing. There is therefore no hope for the homeless this winter, or for those who occupy vile rooming houses and hotels. 15

Some will die. The sick will get sicker, the well will become ill. In the spring, the survivors will be grateful for warmth. It will be safe again to sleep in the parks and on the riverbanks. Those are homeland in the country of the poor. 16

ΔΔΔΔΔΔΔΔΔΔΔΔΔΔΔΔΔΔΔΔΔΔΔΔΔΔΔΔΔΔΔΔΔΔΔΔΔΔΔΔΔΔΔΔΔΔΔΔΔΔΔΔΔΔΔΔΔΔ

Further Reading:

June Callwood,
Portrait of Canada
Emotions
Twelve Weeks in Spring

Structure:

1. Although Callwood's idea of poverty as a "country" is developed throughout, it is most sharply drawn in paragraphs 1–4 and 14–16. Why does she choose the beginning and end to most directly present her analogy?

2. In what way are the soup kitchens of Montreal effective as the opening example of Callwood's argument?

3. Toward the middle of her essay (par. 9 and 10) Callwood discusses poverty in winter, then in the final paragraph poverty in spring. Why this progression in time? What effect does it give to the closing?

Style:

1. Think of Callwood's audience: readers of the Toronto *Globe and Mail*. What are they like? Has Callwood succeeded or failed to adapt her approach to her readers, so they will accept her message? (Consider the essay's level of difficulty, diction, TONE, use of examples, etc.)

2. In addition to her overall analogy, Callwood uses smaller FIGURES OF SPEECH. To whom does she implicitly compare the "front-line people" of paragraph 14? In which other paragraph do we see the same METAPHOR in different words?

3. In paragraph 12 Callwood asks, "How can it be that people live in cars and cardboard boxes?" Point out at least three other places where she uses vivid IMAGES to reinforce her argument.

Ideas for Discussion and Writing:

1. Callwood sees housing as "the key issue in the nation of the poor" (par. 14). In your part of Canada, how high an income must a family have to rent an apartment? To rent a house? To buy a house?

2. Do you see more or fewer homeless people in your area than you saw a few years ago? Are most young or old? Male or female? Where do they eat? Where do they sleep? What proportion do you believe will someday escape from what many commentators now refer to as a permanent "underclass"?

3. In his famous *Essay on the Principle of Population* (1798), the English economist Thomas Malthus argued that, since geometric growth of population outstrips arithmetic growth of the food supply, we actually need poverty, disease, and starvation to restore the balance. While this theory was popular in the nineteenth century, very few would accept it today. Point out the major developments in science, economics, and government which, since the time of Malthus, have counteracted his argument.

4. If you have read "Suitcase Lady" by Christie McLaren,

compare the ways in which McLaren and Callwood depict poverty. Which is more effective, focussing on one person or surveying the larger picture?

5. **PROCESS IN WRITING:** *Develop your own essay of analogy entitled:*

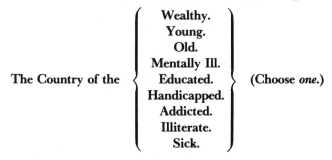

The Country of the ⎨ Wealthy. / Young. / Old. / Mentally Ill. / Educated. / Handicapped. / Addicted. / Illiterate. / Sick. ⎬ (Choose *one.*)

First take notes for a week, recording images of your subject. Then brainstorm or freewrite. Now do a first draft, exchange reactions with classmates, then revise to a final draft.

Note: See also the Topics for Writing at the end of this chapter.

Michael Ondaatje

Tabula Asiae

*In more than one way Michael Ondaatje is the least "Canadian" of our major
Canadian writers. He was born in 1943 in Ceylon (now Sri Lanka) to the family of
exuberant and eccentric aristocrats he later portrayed in his fictionalized
autobiography* Running in the Family. *And although he has since become one of
Canada's major poets, his works are often set outside our borders and are written in a
richly lyrical, often surreal, often cinematic style that suggests other places and other
influences. Ondaatje moved to England in 1954 and to Canada 1962. Here he took a
B.A. and an M.A. and began teaching, first at Western Ontario University, then since
1971 in the English Department of Glendon College, York University, in Toronto.
His first book of poetry,* The Dainty Monsters, *appeared in 1967. In 1969
appeared* The Man with Seven Toes, *in 1973* Rat Jelly, *and in 1979* There's a
Trick with a Knife I'm Learning to Do: Poems 1963–1978. *This last won
the Governor General's award, as had his 1970 book of poetry and prose,* The
Collected Works of Billy the Kid. *In 1976 appeared* Coming through
Slaughter, *his richly poetic novel about a jazz musician in New Orleans, and in
1987 his panoramic novel about Toronto in the 1930s,* In The Skin of a Lion.
*Ondaatje has also written literary criticism, edited anthologies, made films, and edited
for Coach House Press. Our selection, "Tabula Asiae,"° comes from* Running in
the Family *(1982).*

1   On my brother's wall in Toronto are the false maps. Old portraits of
Ceylon. The result of sightings, glances from trading vessels, the
theories of sextant. The shapes differ so much they seem to be
translations — by Ptolemy, Mercator, François Valentyn, Mortier, and
Heydt — growing from mythic shapes into eventual accuracy. Amoeba,
then stout rectangle, and then the island as we know it now, a pendant off
the ear of India. Around it, a blue-combed ocean busy with dolphin and

---

° *Tabula Asiae*: Map of Asia (in Latin; apparently the words Ondaatje sees on his brother's
old maps of Ceylon).

sea-horse, cherub and compass. Ceylon floats on the Indian Ocean and holds its naive mountains, drawings of cassowary and boar who leap without perspective across imagined 'desertum'° and plain.

At the edge of the maps the scrolled mantling depicts ferocious 2 slipper-footed elephants, a white queen offering a necklace to natives who carry tusks and a conch, a Moorish king who stands amidst the power of books and armour. On the south-west corner of some charts are satyrs, hoof deep in foam, listening to the sound of the island, their tails writhing in the waves.

The maps reveal rumours of topography, the routes for invasion and 3 trade, and the dark mad mind of travellers' tales appears throughout Arab and Chinese and medieval records. The island seduced all of Europe. The Portuguese. The Dutch. The English. And so its name changed, as well as its shape, — Serendip, Ratnapida ("island of gems"), Taprobane, Zeloan, Zeilan, Seyllan, Ceilon, and Ceylon — the wife of many marriages, courted by invaders who stepped ashore and claimed everything with the power of their sword or bible or language.

This pendant, once its shape stood still, became a mirror. It pretended 4 to reflect each European power till newer ships arrived and spilled their nationalities, some of whom stayed and intermarried — my own ancestor arriving in 1600, a doctor who cured the residing governor's daughter with a strange herb and was rewarded with land, a foreign wife, and a new name which was a Dutch spelling of his own. Ondaatje. A parody of the ruling language. And when his Dutch wife died, marrying a Sinhalese° woman, having nine children, and remaining. Here. At the centre of the rumour. At this point on the map.

ΔΔΔΔΔΔΔΔΔΔΔΔΔΔΔΔΔΔΔΔΔΔΔΔΔΔΔΔΔΔΔΔΔΔΔΔΔΔΔΔΔΔΔΔΔΔΔΔΔΔΔΔΔΔΔΔΔΔΔΔΔΔ

Further Reading:

Michael Ondaatje,
Running in the Family
In the Skin of a Lion
The Collected Works of Billy the Kid

Structure and Style:

1. Why is "Tabula Asiae" so much shorter than most selections in this book? Because it says less? Because it communicates

---

°desertum: empty land.
°Sinhalese (or Singhalese): the largest population group of Sri Lanka.

differently? If the latter, what are some techniques Michael Ondaatje has used that many contributors to this book have not?

2. Michael Ondaatje's usual form of writing is poetry. How CONCISE is most poetry compared to most PROSE? Why? Is there a sharp dividing line between poetry and prose, or can they draw on the same techniques? Can they ever resemble each other so closely that they almost merge? Where would you place "Tabula Asiae" in this respect, and why?

3. In paragraph 1 Ondaatje describes the shape of Ceylon in early "false maps" as an "amoeba" and a "stout rectangle." Would you call these comparisons METAPHORS or analogies? Why?

4. In paragraph 1 Ondaatje goes on to call Ceylon a "pendant off the ear of India." What FIGURE OF SPEECH is this? Does he develop it fully enough to make it an analogy?

5. In paragraph 3 Ondaatje calls Ceylon "the wife of many marriages." Explain his meaning. Also tell what FIGURE OF SPEECH he has used.

6. In paragraph 4 the "pendant" becomes a "mirror." In what sense? And again, is this image a METAPHOR or an analogy?

7. In what sense do the "false maps" of Ondaatje's brother in Toronto constitute an analogy of Ceylon?

8. "Serendip" is one of Sri Lanka's early names, as we are told in paragraph 3. In a desk-size or reference dictionary, find the connection between this name and the often-used word "serendipity."

Ideas for Discussion and Writing:

1. The Sri Lanka of "Tabula Asiae" — mysterious, romantic, and legendary — is not at all the Sri Lanka of the encyclopedia or the television newscast. Name all the reasons you can think of why Michael Ondaatje presents the land of his childhood in the SUBJECTIVE, poetic way he does.

2. "Tabula Asiae" is a chapter of Michael Ondaatje's autobiographical book *Running in the Family*. If you were to write the story of your own childhood and family, how far back in time could you begin? Who are your earliest known ancestors? When and where did they live? Do you think the homeland or personalities of your ancestors before your parents and grandparents had much influence in making you the person you are today?

3. Ondaatje's brother puts old maps of Ceylon on his wall in

Toronto. Do those who move to a new country do better to
cherish and preserve their past, as the Ondaatjes do, or to
forget the past in order to make a new life? If you or your
parents immigrated to Canada, which path have you taken,
and why? If English is your second language, do you intend to
retain your first? If so, how? Will you then teach it to your
children? Why or why not?

4. In paragraph 3 Ondaatje describes the early invaders of
    Ceylon who "stepped ashore and claimed everything with the
    power of their sword or bible or language." Have these
    three — sword, bible, and language — all been used as tools of
    conquest? If so, deliberately or accidentally? If you can, give
    examples, either from other countries or from Canada.

5. **PROCESS IN WRITING:** *Immigration has occurred at some point in the
    background of all Canadians, even those who are now called "native"
    peoples. Choose one of these topics:*
    — My ancestral homeland
    — The arrival of my ancestor(s) in Canada
    — My immigration to Canada
    *Select the one most appropriate to you. Focus it to fit your circumstances,
    knowledge, and interest. Now take a page of notes, perhaps consulting a
    parent, grandparent, or family records. Think about the importance, even
    the heroic, legendary, or mythic qualities you may see in this topic — then
    write your "discovery draft." In the next version heighten these overtones
    by clothing bare fact in the kinds of poetical devices Ondaatje has used in
    his account (see FIGURES OF SPEECH, and especially METAPHOR, in the
    Glossary). Test your prose by reading aloud, before writing the final
    draft.*

Note: See also the Topics for Writing at the end of this chapter.

Farley Mowat

The One Perfect House*

Farley Mowat is one of Canada's more flamboyant public figures. Soldier, traveller, writer, anthologist, storyteller, conservationist, and public gadfly, Mowat has always been more warmly received by the reading public than by the critics. He was born in 1921 in Belleville, Ontario. From 1940 to 1946 he served in the Canadian army in Europe, then after the war spent two years in the Arctic and in 1949 earned a B.A. at the University of Toronto. Since then Mowat has written or edited more than 25 books; his work has been translated into more than 20 languages and published in more than 40 countries. He is probably Canada's most widely read author. Among his works are children's books (Lost in the Barrens, 1956; The Dog Who Wouldn't Be, 1957; Owls in the Family, 1961), humour (The Boat Who Wouldn't Float, 1969), accounts of his experiences in the Arctic (People of the Deer, 1952; The Desperate People, 1959; Never Cry Wolf, 1963; Sibir, 1970), numerous anthologies, and a highly acclaimed account of his experiences at war (And No Birds Sang, 1979). In 1980 appeared an anthology of his selected works, The World of Farley Mowat. In books such as A Whale for the Killing (1972) and Sea of Slaughter (1984), Mowat's attention has turned more and more to the destructiveness of humankind towards nature. Our selection, "The One Perfect House," comes from People of the Deer, Mowat's study of the Ihalmiut among whom he stayed in the Arctic Barrens. These original Canadians, who called themselves "the People," have since vanished.

1   As I grew to know the People, so my respect for their intelligence and ingenuity increased. Yet it was a long time before I could reconcile my feelings of respect with the poor, shoddy dwelling places that they constructed. As with most Eskimos, the winter homes of the Ihalmiut are the snow-built domes we call igloos. (Igloo in Eskimo means simply "house" and thus an igloo can be built of wood or stone, as well as of snow.) But unlike most other Innuit, the Ihalmiut make snow houses which are cramped, miserable shelters. I think the People acquired the art of igloo

---

*Editor's title.

construction quite recently in their history and from the coast Eskimos. Certainly they have no love for their igloos, and prefer the skin tents. This preference is related to the problem of fuel.

Any home in the arctic, in winter, requires some fuel if only for cooking. The coast peoples make use of fat lamps, for they have an abundance of fat from the sea mammals they kill, and so they are able to cook in the igloo, and to heat it as well. But the Ihalmiut can ill afford to squander the precious fat of the deer, and they dare to burn only one tiny lamp for light. Willow must serve as fuel, and while willow burns well enough in a tent open at the peak to allow the smoke to escape, when it is burned in a snow igloo, the choking smoke leaves no place for human occupants.

So snow houses replace the skin tents of the Ihalmiut only when winter has already grown old and the cold has reached the seemingly unbearable extremes of sixty or even seventy degrees below zero. Then the tents are grudgingly abandoned and snow huts built. From that time until spring no fires may burn inside the homes of the People, and such cooking as is attempted must be done outside, in the face of the blizzards and gales.

Yet though tents are preferred to igloos, it is still rather hard to understand why. . . . Great, gaping slits outline each hide on the frame of a tent. Such a home offers hardly more shelter than a thicket of trees, for on the unbroken sweep of the plains the winds blow with such violence that they drive the hard snow through the tents as if the skin walls did not really exist. But the People spend many days and dark nights in these feeble excuses for houses, while the wind rises like a demon of hatred and the cold comes as if it meant to destroy all life in the land.

In these tents there may be a fire; but consider this fire, this smoldering handful of green twigs, dug with infinite labor from under the drifts. It gives heat only for a few inches out from its sullen coals so that it barely suffices to boil a pot of water in an hour or two. The eternal winds pour into the tent and dissipate what little heat the fire can spare from the cook-pots. The fire gives comfort to the Ihalmiut only through its appeal to the eyes.

However, the tent with its wan little fire is a more desirable place than the snow house with no fire at all. At least the man in the tent can have a hot bowl of soup once in a while, but after life in the igloos begins, almost all food must be eaten while it is frozen to the hardness of rocks. Men sometimes take skin bags full of ice into the beds so that they can have water to drink, melted by the heat of their bodies. It is true that some of the People build cook shelters outside the igloos but these snow hearths burn very badly, and then only when it is calm. For the most part the winds prevent any outside cooking at all, and anyway by late winter the willow supply is so deeply buried under the drifts, it is almost impossible for men to procure it.

7   So you see that the homes of the Ihalmiut in winter are hardly models of comfort. Even when spring comes to the land the improvement in housing conditions is not great. After the tents go up in the spring, the rains begin. During daylight it rains with gray fury and the tents soak up the chill water until the hides hang slackly on their poles while rivulets pour through the tent to drench everything inside. At night, very likely, there will be frost and by dawn everything not under the robes with the sleepers will be frozen stiff.

8   With the end of the spring rains, the hot sun dries and shrinks the hides until they are drum-taut, but the ordeal is not yet over. Out of the steaming muskegs come the hordes of bloodsucking and flesh-eating flies and these find that the Ihalmiut tents offer no barrier to their invasion. The tents belong equally to the People and to the flies, until midsummer brings an end to the plague, and the hordes vanish.

9   My high opinion of the People was often clouded when I looked at their homes. I sometimes wondered if the Ihalmiut were as clever and as resourceful as I thought them to be. I had been too long conditioned to think of home as four walls and a roof, and so the obvious solution of the Ihalmiut housing problem escaped me for nearly a year. It took me that long to realize that the People not only have good homes, but that they have devised the one perfect house.

10   The tent and the igloo are really only auxiliary shelters. The real home of the Ihalmio is much like that of the turtle, for it is what he carries about on his back. In truth it is the only house that can enable men to survive on the merciless plains of the Barrens. It has central heating from the fat furnace of the body, its walls are insulated to a degree of perfection that we white men have not been able to surpass, or even emulate. It is complete, light in weight, easy to make and easy to keep in repair. It costs nothing, for it is a gift of the land, through the deer. When I consider that house, my opinion of the astuteness of the Ihalmiut is no longer clouded.

11   Primarily the house consists of two suits of fur, worn one over the other, and each carefully tailored to the owner's dimensions. The inner suit is worn with the hair of the hides facing inward and touching the skin while the outer suit has its hair turned out to the weather. Each suit consists of a pullover parka with a hood, a pair of fur trousers, fur gloves and fur boots. The double motif is extended to the tips of the fingers, to the top of the head, and to the soles of the feet where soft slippers of harehide are worn next to the skin.

12   The high winter boots may be tied just above the knee so that they leave no entry for the cold blasts of the wind. But full ventilation is provided by the design of the parka. Both inner and outer parkas hang slackly to at least the knees of the wearer, and they are not belted in winter. Cold air does not rise, so that no drafts can move up under the parkas to reach the

bare flesh, but the heavy, moisture-laden air from close to the body sinks through the gap between parka and trousers and is carried away. Even in times of great physical exertion, when the Ihalmio sweats freely, he is never in any danger of soaking his clothing and so inviting quick death from frost afterwards. The hides are not in contact with the body at all but are held away from the flesh by the soft resiliency of the deer hairs that line them, and in the space between the tips of the hair and the hide of the parka there is a constantly moving layer of warm air which absorbs all the sweat and carries it off.

Dressed for a day in the winter, the Ihalmio has this protection over all parts of his body, except for a narrow oval in front of his face — and even this is well protected by a long silken fringe of wolverine fur, the one fur to which the moisture of breathing will not adhere and freeze. 13

In the summer rain, the hide may grow wet, but the layer of air between deerhide and skin does not conduct the water, and so it runs off and is lost while the body stays dry. Then there is the question of weight. Most white men trying to live in the winter arctic load their bodies with at least twenty-five pounds of clothing, while the complete deerskin home of the Innuit weighs about seven pounds. This, of course, makes a great difference in the mobility of the wearers. A man wearing tight-fitting and too bulky clothes is almost as helpless as a man in a diver's suit. But besides their light weight, the Ihalmiut clothes are tailored so that they are slack wherever muscles must work freely beneath them. There is ample space in this house for the occupant to move and to breathe, for there are no partitions and walls to limit his motions, and the man is almost as free in his movements as if he were naked. If he must sleep out, without shelter, and it is fifty below, he has but to draw his arms into his parka, and he sleeps nearly as well as he would in a double-weight eiderdown bag. 14

This is in winter, but what about summer? I have explained how the porous hide nevertheless acts as a raincoat. Well, it does much more than that. In summer the outer suit is discarded and all clothing pared down to one layer. The house then offers effective insulation against heat entry. It remains surprisingly cool, for it is efficiently ventilated. Also, and not least of its many advantages, it offers the nearest thing to perfect protection against the flies. The hood is pulled up so that it covers the neck and the ears, and the flies find it nearly impossible to get at the skin underneath. But of course the Ihalmiut have long since learned to live with the flies, and they feel none of the hysterical and frustrating rage against them so common with us. 15

In the case of women's clothing, home has two rooms. The back of the parka has an enlargement, as if it were made to fit a hunchback, and in this space, called the *amaut*, lives the unweaned child of the family. A 16 bundle of remarkably absorbent sphagnum moss goes under his backside and the child sits stark naked, in unrestricted delight, where he can look out on the world and very early in life become familiar with the sights and the moods of his land. He needs no clothing of his own, and as for the moss — in that land there is an unlimited supply of soft sphagnum and it can be replaced in an instant.

17   When the child is at length forced to vacate this pleasant apartment, probably by the arrival of competition, he is equipped with a one-piece suit of hides which looks not unlike the snow suits our children wear in the winter. Only it is much lighter, more efficient, and much less restricting. This first home of his own is a fine home for the Ihalmio child, and one that his white relatives would envy if they could appreciate its real worth.

18   This then is the home of the People. It is the gift of the land, but mainly it is the gift of Tuktu.°

∆∆

Further Reading:

Farley Mowat,
> *People of the Deer*
> *Never Cry Wolf*
> *And No Birds Sang*

Maurice Metayer, ed. and trans., *I, Nuligak* (autobiography)
John Robert Columbo, ed., *Poems of the Inuit*
S. Cole, ed., *We Don't Live in Snowhouses Now*

Structure:

1. In this selection, where does the *analogy* begin?
2. To what extent is the analogy developed? Point out all the ways in which the clothes of the Ihalmiut are described in terms of a house.
3. Why is this discussion of Eskimo clothing in terms of a house considered an analogy rather than a comparison and contrast?
4. Paragraphs 1–9 describe the qualities of the igloo and the tent. Is this passage an analogy or a comparison and contrast? Why?
5. In what way does Farley Mowat's discussion of the igloo and tent prepare us for his discussion of Eskimo clothing?

°Tuktu: the caribou

Style:

1. To what extent has Mowat used SENSE IMAGES to make this selection vivid? Give one example each of appeals to sight, hearing, touch, taste, and smell.
2. Hold your book at arm's length so that you have an overall view of the selection's appearance. Does Mowat's writing seem to consist mostly of long words or short words? What effect do you think his preference for long or for short words has upon his style?

Ideas for Discussion and Writing:

1. Dying cultures such as those of the Inuit are recorded by anthropologists, and dead cultures are reconstructed by archaeologists. Why do we study ways of life that are passing or past? Can such study in any way improve our present lives?
2. Over the last decades, the federal government has provided the Inuit of Canada with houses so that, except on hunting trips, they no longer need the igloos or tents described by Mowat. Do you agree with the government's actions? Did it make more sense to reduce physical hardship among the Inuit, or would it have made more sense to preserve at least some of their Stone Age culture? Would such preservation have been possible?
3. PROCESS IN WRITING: *Write an essay based on an extended analogy between a house and our planet Earth. First brainstorm or freewrite, because analogies demand free use of our imagination. Next write a rapid and free "discovery draft." Let it sit at least one day, then develop your concept through at least one more draft, adding the kinds of vivid IMAGES that Mowat used to spark his analogy.*

Note: See also the Topics for Writing at the end of this chapter.

Félix Leclerc

The Family House[*]

Translated from the French by Philip Stratford

Though as he got older his own music went out of style, Félix Leclerc (1914–1988), Quebec's original chansonnier, *set the example for a generation of popular singers who during the sixties and seventies were a vital force in Quebec's "Quiet Revolution." As singer Gilles Vigneault put it, Leclerc was "the father of us all." Referred to by the media simply as "Félix," honoured by the annual "Félix" music awards named after him, Leclerc spent his last years as unofficial poet laureate of Quebec, a sage to whom the public turned for words in time of crisis. When Quebec mourned the death of nationalist leader René Lévesque in 1987, it was Leclerc whose words were carved on the tomb: "The first page of Quebec's true and beautiful history has been turned. Now he takes his place among the few liberators of their people." And when Leclerc died soon after, those same words, in a cultural sense, might have described their own author. Leclerc was born in La Tuque. After announcing, acting, and writing for Radio-Canada in the thirties and early forties, he acted for several years with a theatre company. Then in 1951 he arrived at Paris, where, singing his own rough-hewn songs in music halls, he won instant acclaim as "Le Canadien." But despite his success as songwriter and singer, Leclerc viewed himself primarily as a writer. He published more than a dozen books, including poetry, plays, fables, stories, and novels. Among his most widely read have been* Adagio *(1943) and* Allegro *(1944), two collections of his fables and stories written for radio;* Pieds nus dans l'aube *(1946), the autobiographical novel from which our selection comes; and his novel* Le fou de l'île *(1958), translated by Philip Stratford in 1976 as* The Madman, the Kite and the Island.*

1 We were all, brothers and sisters alike, born in a long three-storey wooden house, a house as humped and crusty as a loaf of homemade bread, as warm and clean inside as the white of the loaf.

---

[*]Translator's title.

Roofed over with shingles, harbouring robins in its gables, it looked   2
itself like an old nest perched up there in the silence. Taking the north
wind over the left shoulder, beautifully adjusted to nature, from the
roadside one might also have mistaken it for an enormous boulder
stranded on the beach.

In truth it was a stubborn old thing, soaking up storms and twilight,   3
determined not to die of anything less than old age, like the two elms
beside it.

The house turned its back squarely on the rest of town so as not to see   4
the new subdivision with its shiny little boxes as fragile as mushrooms.
Looking out over the valley, highroad for the wild St. Maurice river, it
focused as if in ecstasy on the long caravan of blue mountains over there,
the ones that flocks of clouds and the oldest seagulls don't seem able to get
over.

With its rusty sides, its black roof and its white-trimmed windows, our   5
common cradle crouched over a heavy cement foundation sunk solidly in
the ground like a ship's anchor to hold us firm, for we were eleven children
aboard, a turbulent, strident lot, but as timid as baby chicks.

A big, robust, rough fieldstone chimney, held together by trowel-   6
smoothed mortar, began in the cellar near the round-bellied furnace just
above that drafty little iron door that sticking a mirror into you could see
the stars. Like the hub of a wheel it rose through the floors distributing
spokes of heat, then broke through to the outside as stiff as a sentinel with a
plumed helmet and smoked there with windswept hair, close to a grey
ladder lying along the roof. The grey ladder and the sooty little door, we
were told, were not for human use, but for an old man in red who in winter
jumped from roof to roof behind reindeer harnessed in white.

From top to bottom our home was inhabited: by us in the centre like the   7
core of a fruit; at the edges by parents; in the cellars and attics by superb
and silent men, lumberjacks by trade. In the walls, under the floors,
between the joists, near the carpets, and in the folds of the lampshades
lived goblins, gnomes, fairies, snatches of song, silly jokes and the echoes of
games; in the veins of our house ran pure poetry.

We had a chair for rocking in, a bench for saying prayers, a sofa to cry   8
on, a two-step staircase for playing trains. Also other fine toys that we
didn't dare touch, like the two-wired bird with its long beak and the bell
in its forehead that talked to the grown-ups. A flower-patterned linoleum
was our garden; a hook in the wall, a bollard to tie up our imaginary
boats; the staircases were slides; the pipes running up the walls our masts;
and armchairs miniature stages where we learnt with the hats, gloves and
overcoats of our elders how to make the same faces that we wear today but
without finding them funny.

A vast corridor divided the ground floor lengthwise. A few rung-backed   9 chairs made a circle in one corner; above them a row of hooks like question marks disappeared beneath the coats of visitors who came to consult Papa, the biggest timber merchant in the valley. The living room and a bedroom for visitors stood side by side. The living room, with its black piano, its net curtains, its big blue armchair, its gold-framed pictures, a few old-style chairs upholstered in satin (particularly a spring-rocker dressed up like an old lady out of the past with tassels on the hem of her dress) gave our lives a quality of Sunday celebration. Our parents' bedroom closed its door on impenetrable secrets. In its obscurity slumbered an old dresser full of camphor-scented sheets between which my mother hid mysterious notebooks, repositories of the exact hour of our birth, the names of godfathers and godmothers, and very private family events.

10   To the left of the hall a smoking room served as my father's study and as library for all of us. A door opened to the dining room — classroom would be more exact, for we only ate there once or twice a year. In the sewing room between the sewing machine and an enormous cupboard stood the sofa, ready to be cried on. At the back of the house, spreading the full width, was our gay and singing kitchen: the cast-iron stove with its built-in mirror, the red kitchen cupboards, the white muslin curtains hanging like fog in the narrow windows, and the patches of sunlight playing on the left of the long family table. There shone the ever-burning lamp, known to all people throughout all time as the soul of the home. There we were told of good news and bad. There Papa signed our school report cards. There in the high rocking chair we would often sit in silence to think of facts of creation discovered that day and ponder on the strange and marvellous world we had fallen into.

11   The first floor was lined with children's bedrooms. There were eight, I think, divided between girls and boys. In the girls' rooms it was cleaner, rosier, airier than the boys'. On the walls they pinned up tiny frames, graceful silhouettes and sprigs of flowers. On ours we stuck huge vulgar calendars, of hunters waiting for game and old gents smoking rubbed tobacco.

12   Our room, the most spacious on the floor, looked out on the garden, its black earth full as a cornucopia, and cut through with straight little paths that we walked down every evening, watering under the watching eyes of the cottontails.

13   We each had our own bed, a little white bed with a real straw mattress and iron bedposts ending in brass knobs where we hung our clothes, our slingshots, and our hands clasped in prayer.

14   On the second floor a screened veranda jutted out in a bow like a pilot-house. It was a veritable observation post dominating the waves of the valley like those of the sea: waves of snowstorms, waves of loggers in

springtime, waves of poor families gathering wild fruit, waves of falling leaves, of showers of sunshine, of the beating of birds' wings, of paths traced by children, hunters and fishermen. On hot nights we slept there above the waves on that wooden porch which was also the children's playroom. Soldiers, teddy bears, drums, little wooden shoes, dolls seated at table before empty china plates, all keeping good company together. A tin bridge built long ago by my eldest brother served as access to this cardboard world.

On the floor above, behind a bull's-eye window, stretched the attic, a   15
long deserted dusty cage, dormitory in winter for several lumberjacks. Between the three-legged chairs and the family portraits, these men on their mattresses, devoured by fatigue, tumbled headlong each night into sleep.

And like the crew of a happy ship, thinking neither of arrivals nor of   16
departures, but only of the sea that carries them, we sped through childhood all sails set, thrilled with each morning and every night, envying neither distant ports nor far cities, convinced that our ship was flying the best colours and that we carried on board all necessary potions to ward off pirates and bad luck.

The house we lived in was number 168, rue Claire-Fontaine.   17

△△

Further Reading:

Félix Leclerc,
The Madman, the Kite and the Island
Pieds nus dans l'aube (available only in French)
Philip Stratford, ed., *Chez nous* (anthology of writings from Quebec, translated into English)
Jacques Ferron, *Tales from an Uncertain Country* (short stories)

Structure:

1. This selection is filled with figures of speech — SIMILES, METAPHORS, and PERSONIFICATION — but only one is developed extensively enough to be called an *analogy*. What is it and which paragraphs develop it?
2. What is the main purpose of this selection, and where does Leclerc most openly state it?

Style:

1. Roughly how many METAPHORS and SIMILES appear in this selection as compared to the other selections in this book? Twice as many? Four times as many? Ten times as many? And

what effect does Leclerc achieve through such a concentration of FIGURES OF SPEECH?

2. Among his other achievements, Félix Leclerc was a poet and one of Quebec's best-loved singers. What relationship, if any, do you find between his experience as poet and singer and the approach he took to writing "The Family House"?

3. Point out at least ten SIMILES in this selection. Point out at least ten METAPHORS. Point out at least five examples of PERSONIFICATION. Do these figures of speech work together to build a dominant impression or do they seem to be used separately for their own sake?

4. Do you suppose "The Family House" was easy or difficult to translate from French to English? Is a perfect translation possible? If you know two languages, how easy or difficult is it to translate words and expressions from one to the other?

Ideas for Discussion and Writing:

1. In paragraph 8 Leclerc describes how he and his brothers and sisters imitated their elders, learning "how to make the same faces that we wear today but without finding them funny." Do you sense in this passage (and perhaps in the whole selection) a regret for lost childhood? Do you ever regret your own lost childhood? Do most people? If so, what might be the reasons?

2. Almost everything that Félix Leclerc published expresses the same happiness and security, the same goodwill towards the natural world and the people in it, that we see in "The Family House." Does a happy childhood such as the one he describes here lead inevitably to a happy adulthood? Can a happy adulthood follow an unhappy childhood? Give reasons and examples to support your answers.

3. "Coming of Age in Putnok" is the opening of George Gabori's autobiography, while "The Family House" is the opening of Félix Leclerc's autobiographical novel. If you have read both openings, compare them. Which gives more facts? Which gives more feeling? Which seems to give a greater insight into the author's background and personality? Do the two openings differ in TONE? And which would more strongly motivate a reader to finish the book?

4. If you have read "The One Perfect House," compare the ways in which Farley Mowat describes that "house" with the ways in which Leclerc describes the house of his childhood.

5. **PROCESS IN WRITING**: *Borrowing techniques from Leclerc, depict your own childhood home in such a way as to strongly convey the feelings you*

have toward it and toward the life you led there. First generate a page of
IMAGES such as SIMILES, METAPHORS, and SENSE IMAGES that convey
your early memories of home. Now search these notes for a common theme
such as Leclerc's idea of the house as a ship. Next write a "discovery
draft" that develops your analogy, *using pertinent images from your*
notes, and new ones that come as you write. In further drafts chop out
whatever does not contribute to the overall effect. Read your final version
aloud, with feeling, to the class.

Note: See also the Topics for Writing at the end of this chapter.

Topics for Writing

CHAPTER 6: ANALOGY AND RELATED DEVICES

Choose a topic from items 1–15, or choose a subject from items 16–30 and add an appropriate image to it. Then develop your choice into an extended analogy. (See also the guidelines that follow.)

1. Music as a drug
2. Prejudice as a wall
3. Human metabolism as fire
4. A career as a mountain to climb
5. Life as a road
6. A library as a brain
7. The playing field as a battlefield
8. The human race as a family
9. Addiction as a crutch
10. A paragraph as an essay in miniature
11. A career as war
12. The beehive as a city
13. Reading as programming a computer
14. A career as marriage
15. Dancing as life

16. Crime as ⎯⎯⎯⎯⎯⎯⎯⎯⎯⎯⎯⎯⎯⎯⎯
17. Wealth as ⎯⎯⎯⎯⎯⎯⎯⎯⎯⎯⎯⎯⎯⎯
18. A library as ⎯⎯⎯⎯⎯⎯⎯⎯⎯⎯⎯⎯⎯
19. Dating as ⎯⎯⎯⎯⎯⎯⎯⎯⎯⎯⎯⎯⎯⎯
20. Old age as ⎯⎯⎯⎯⎯⎯⎯⎯⎯⎯⎯⎯⎯⎯
21. Our legal system as ⎯⎯⎯⎯⎯⎯⎯⎯⎯⎯
22. A doctor as ⎯⎯⎯⎯⎯⎯⎯⎯⎯⎯⎯⎯⎯⎯
23. A teacher as ⎯⎯⎯⎯⎯⎯⎯⎯⎯⎯⎯⎯⎯
24. Religion as ⎯⎯⎯⎯⎯⎯⎯⎯⎯⎯⎯⎯⎯⎯
25. Divorce as ⎯⎯⎯⎯⎯⎯⎯⎯⎯⎯⎯⎯⎯⎯
26. Nuclear missiles as ⎯⎯⎯⎯⎯⎯⎯⎯⎯⎯
27. Health as ⎯⎯⎯⎯⎯⎯⎯⎯⎯⎯⎯⎯⎯⎯⎯
28. School as ⎯⎯⎯⎯⎯⎯⎯⎯⎯⎯⎯⎯⎯⎯
29. A book as ⎯⎯⎯⎯⎯⎯⎯⎯⎯⎯⎯⎯⎯⎯
30. The planet Earth as ⎯⎯⎯⎯⎯⎯⎯⎯⎯⎯

Note also the Process in Writing topic after each selection in this chapter.

Process in Writing: Guidelines

Follow at least some of these steps in writing your essay of analogy (your teacher may suggest which ones).

1. *Choose a topic you really like, because motivation is the single greatest factor in good writing.*

2. *If you complete one of the topics from 16 to 30, be sure to invent an analogy (with two items from different categories), not a comparison and contrast (with two items from the same category). Know which item is your real subject, and which one exists merely to explain the other.*

3. *Now freewrite on your topic, to achieve the spontaneity and originality that spark a good analogy.*

4. *Incorporate the best of this freewriting into your first draft. Let the ideas flow, not stopping now to revise or edit.*

5. *In your next draft add any more points of comparison that come to you (a strong analogy is fully developed). Read your prose aloud to detect awkward passages, and revise. Trim deadwood. Heighten TRANSITIONS.*

6. *Now edit for things like spelling and grammar.*

7. *Write and proofread your good copy. If you have used a computer, save the essay on disk in case your teacher suggests further revision.*

Classification

There are three kinds of them. . . .

Our world is so complex that without classification we would be lost. To call a friend we use an alphabetized phone book. To buy a steak we go to the meat section of the supermarket. To buy a used car we open our newspaper to the *classified* section. Putting things into categories is one of our most common methods of thought, both for good and for bad. Who would look through the whole dictionary when the word in question begins with "T"? What school child, *classified* into grade five, would look for the grade six *class*room?

Yet as Hitler and other bigots have demonstrated, classifying people by skin colour, race, or religion can lead to stereotypes and stereotypes can lead to violence. Ethnic jokes may seem innocent *(Why does it take two WASPs to change a light bulb? One makes the gin and tonics while the other calls the electrician)*. But such a characterization of a group makes it harder for others to view a member of that group as an individual. If all WASPs (or all Newfoundlanders or Torontonians or women or Jews or Indians or bankers or postal workers) are classified as the same, we have dehumanized them. Dislike and even persecution are now possible. Be

202

careful, then, not to let a classification become a stereotype. For example, you may have a practical reason to group people by age, but do leave room for individuals: not all teenagers are delinquents, not all 40-year-olds are getting a divorce, and not all retired people are ready for the rocking chair.

Whatever its subject, your essay of classification should have at least three categories, because only two would form a comparison and contrast. And it should have no more than you can adequately develop — perhaps six or seven at the most. To be logical your essay will follow these guidelines:

Classify all items by the same principle. An essay on sources of energy for home heating might include oil, natural gas, hydro, coal, wood, and solar heat. But it would not include insulation as a category, for insulation is not a *source* of energy but a means of *retaining* energy.

Do not leave out an obvious category. Would you discuss six artists in an essay about the Group of Seven?

Do not let categories overlap. An essay on the major types of housing might include the detached single-family house, the semidetached house, the row house, and the highrise apartment. The bungalow has no place in this list, though, because it *is* a detached single-family house. And rental units have no place in the list, because any of the above forms of housing can be rented.

Classifying is not easy; it is a real exercise in logic. Keep applying our three guidelines. Also observe the most important principle of any essay: *Know your purpose.* Is one form of housing cheaper, more pleasant, more appropriate to the city, more energy efficient, better suited to singles or to families or to retired people? Let that idea, whatever it is, underlie your classification so that your essay will emerge as a clear and unified message.

Note: For more examples of classification, see these essays in other chapters:

Judy Stoffman, "The Way of All Flesh," p. 238
Mavor Moore, "The Roar of the Greasepaint, the Smell of the Caucus," p. 143

Erika Ritter

Bicycles

*Playwright, humourist, and radio personality, Erika Ritter is well known to Canadians for her satirical views on urban life, and especially on what drama critic Martin Knelman called "her favourite subject — the dilemma of the modern woman whose twentieth-century political programmes and mastery of power dressing keep bumping against her nineteenth-century psyche" (*Saturday Night, *December 1986). Born in 1948 in Regina, Ritter studied literature at McGill, then drama at the University of Toronto. Though she declines the label of "feminist," her major plays,* The Splits *(1978),* Automatic Pilot *(1980),* The Passing Scene *(1982) and* Murder at McQueen *(1986), all examine the modern urban woman and her difficulty in maintaining relationships with men. In 1985 Ritter became the highly successful host of CBC Radio's* Dayshift, *a talk show, but in 1987 quit to spend more time writing.* Urban Scrawl *(1984) and* Ritter in Residence *(1987), her books of light satirical essays, indulge in slapstick humour, puns, and fantasy, yet still develop Ritter's investigation of the modern woman and of urban life in general. Our selection comes from* Urban Scrawl, *which Ritter dedicates to her mother — "who made the mistake of encouraging this kind of thing."*

1   It wasn't always like this. There was a time in the life of the world when adults were adults, having firmly put away childish things and thrown away the key.

2   Not any more. The change must have come about innocently enough, I imagine. Modern Man learning to play nicely in the sandbox with the other grown-ups. Very low-tension stuff.

3   Now, in every direction you look, your gaze is met by the risible spectacle of adults postponing adolescence well into senility by means of adult toys: running shoes, baseball bats, roller skates, and — bicycles!

4   But the attitude is no longer the fun-loving approach of a bunch of superannuated kids, and I'm sure you can envision how the evolution occurred. Jogging progressed from a casual encounter with the fresh air to

an intensive relationship, attended by sixty-dollar jogging shoes and a designer sweatband. Playing baseball stopped being fun unless you had a Lacoste (as opposed to low-cost) tee-shirt in which to impress your teammates. And where was the thrill in running around a squash court unless it was with a potentially important client?

As for bicycles — well, let's not even talk about bicycles. On the other hand, maybe we *should* talk about them, because there's something particularly poignant about how it all went wrong for the bicycle, by what declension this once proud and carefree vehicle sank into the role of beast of burden, to bear the weight of sobersided grown-ups at their supposed sport.   5

First, there was the earliest domestication of the North American bicycle *(cyclus pedalis americanus)* in the late Hippie Scene Era of the 1960s. This was the age of the no-nuke whole-grain cyclist, who saw in the bicycle the possibility of Making a Statement while he rode. A statement about pollution, about materialism, about imperialism, about militarism, about — enough already. You get the picture: two wheels good, four wheels bad.   6

Thus it was that the basic bicycle gradually evolved into a chunky three-speed number from China, bowed down under a plastic kiddie carrier, army surplus knapsacks, and a faded fender-sticker advising Make Tofu, Not War. And a rider clad in a red plaid lumber-jacket, Birkenstock sandals, and an expression of urgent concern for all living things.   7

Once the very act of bicycle riding had become an act of high moral purpose, it was an easy step to the next phase of the bicycle's journey along the path of post-Meanderthal seriousness.   8

I'm speaking of the era of the high-strung thoroughbred bicycle, whose rider had also made advances, from pedalling peacenik to a hunched and humorless habitué of the velodrome, clad in leather-seated shorts, white crash helmet, and fingerless gloves, whizzing soundlessly, and with no hint of joy, down city streeets and along the shoulders of super-highways, aboard a vehicle sculpted in wisps of silver chrome. A vehicle so overbred, in its final evolutionary stages, that it began to resemble the mere exoskeleton of a conventional cycle, its flesh picked away by birds of carrion.   9

Having been stripped of any connection with its innocent and leisurely origins, the bicycle now no longer bore the slightest resemblance to the happy creature it once had been. And in the mid-Plastic Scene Era, another crippling blow was struck by the upscale name-brand cyclist, who came along to finish what the fanatical velodromist had refined.   10

Namely, the complete transformation of an ambling and unhurried mode of transit into a fast, nerve-wracking, expensive, and utterly competitive display of high speed, high technology, and high status.

11   The Upscale Cyclist was looking for a twelve-speed Bottecchia that matches his eyes, something that he'd look trendy upon the seat of, when riding to the office (the office!), and he was ready to pay in four figures for it.

12   Not only that, he was also prepared to shell out some heavy bread for those status accessories to complete the picture: the backpack designed by the engineers at NASA, the insulated water-bottle to keep his Perrier chilled just right, the sixteen-track Walkman that would virtually assure him the envy of all his friends.

13   So much for the cyclist. What of his poor debased mount?

14   Not surprisingly, amongst the breed of bicycle, morale is currently low, and personal pride all but a thing of the past. And yet . . . and yet, there are those who say that *cyclus pedalis americanus* is an indomitable creature, and that it is the bicycle, not its rider, who will make the last evolution of the wheel.

15   In fact, some theorize that the present high incidence of bicycle thievery, far from being evidence of crime, is actually an indication that the modern bicycle has had enough of oppressive exploitation and man's joyless ways, and is in the process of reverting to the wild in greater and greater numbers.

16   There have always remained a few aboriginal undomesticated bicycles — or so the theory goes — and now it is these free-spirited mavericks, down from the hills at night, who visit urban bikeracks, garages, and back porches to lure tame bicycles away with them.

17   Costly Kryptonite locks are wrenched asunder, expensive accoutrements are shrugged off, intricate gear systems are torn away, and lo — look what is revealed! Unadorned, undefiled *cyclus* in all his pristine glory, unfettered and unencumbered once more, and free to roam.

18   A wistful fantasy, you might say? The maundering illusions of someone who's been riding her bicycle too long without a crash helmet? I wonder.

19   Just the other day, there was that piece in the paper about a bicycle that went berserk in a shopping centre, smashing two display windows before it was subdued. And did you hear about the recent sighting of a whole herd of riderless bicycles, all rolling soundlessly across a park in the night?

20   It all kind of gets you to thinking. I mean, do *you* know where your ten-speed is tonight?

ΔΔΔΔΔΔΔΔΔΔΔΔΔΔΔΔΔΔΔΔΔΔΔΔΔΔΔΔΔΔΔΔΔΔΔΔΔΔΔΔΔΔΔΔΔΔΔΔΔΔΔΔΔΔΔΔΔΔΔΔΔΔΔΔ

Further Reading:

Erika Ritter,
    The Splits
    Automatic Pilot
    Urban Scrawl
    Ritter in Residence

Structure:

1. In starting with the words "It wasn't always like this," what is Erika Ritter's opening strategy?
2. Ritter classifies the evolution of *"cyclus pedalis americanus"* into three main stages. Describe these three divisions of her *classification* and show where each begins and ends.
3. Have any categories of this classification overlapped? Have any obvious categories been left out?
4. Ritter marks each major change of subject with a transitional passage. Point out three of these transitions.
5. In concluding this selection, paragraphs 14–20 exploit the device discussed in our previous chapter, *analogy*. As the bicycle starts "reverting to the wild," to what is it compared? Point out at least ten words or phrases through this section that develop the analogy.
6. In closing, Ritter asks "do *you* know where your ten-speed is tonight?" To what does she allude here? Is the ALLUSION appropriate? Does it work as a closing?

Style:

1. Where did you first recognize the humorous TONE of this selection? Does Ritter's humour work?
2. What device of humour is exploited in paragraph 4, where baseball players wear "Lacoste (as opposed to low-cost)" tee-shirts?
3. What is Ritter doing when she refers to "the late Hippie Scene Era" (par. 6), "post-Meanderthal seriousness" (par. 8), and "the mid-Plastic Scene Era" (par. 10)?
4. Is Ritter's highly COLLOQUIAL style effective in this selection? Point out five or ten of her most strongly colloquial expressions.
5. In a piece that has so many colloquial expressions, why do we also find academic or even learned terms such as "risible" (par. 3), "superannuated" (par. 4), and "exoskeleton" (par. 9)? What is the total effect? Toward what kind of reader do you think Ritter has aimed this selection?

6. Does Ritter use CONCRETE detail effectively? From each of the three divisions of her classification, pick out the two or three details that say the most to you, and explain how they work.
7. In paragraph 9 the "thoroughbred" bicycle is described as so overbred "that it began to resemble the mere exoskeleton of a conventional cycle, its flesh picked away by birds of carrion." What FIGURES OF SPEECH do you find in this passage?

Ideas for Discussion and Writing:

1. Erika Ritter has been well known in Canada as both a playwright and a radio host. Do either of these professions seem reflected in the way she has written "Bicycles"?
2. How do you react when the humour of paragraphs 1–12 turns to fantasy in paragraphs 13–20? Has Ritter gone too far? Or can fantasy be a legitimate way to deal with a subject?
3. Is Ritter right? Do we sometimes go too far in "improving" products, such as the bicycle? Have we done so to any of the following? If so, describe how.

Automobiles
Motorcycles
Housing
Food
Clothes

4. Do you own a bicycle? Does it fit one of Ritter's categories? If so, how? If not, how does it differ?
5. Paragraphs 10–12 describe the bicycle as status symbol. What are your own major status symbols? Describe the qualities that give them — and therefore you — this status.
6. PROCESS IN WRITING: *Erika Ritter has classified the evolutionary stages of the bicycle. In an essay, either humorous or serious, do the same for one of these: the radio, the television set, the phonograph, the computer, the automobile, the airplane. First generate a page of notes, so you can decide on the stages of this "evolution." Now write a discovery draft, and look it over. Do categories overlap? Have you left out an obvious category? Is your TONE consistent? Have you supplied IMAGES, so the reader can "see" your subject? In the drafts that follow, develop any of these areas that need work.*

Note: See also the Topics for Writing at the end of this chapter.

Roderick Haig-Brown

Articles of Faith for Good Anglers

"If you want to catch a salmon, you must first learn to read," once observed Roderick Haig-Brown (1908–1976). Not only did he celebrate our long tradition of literature about fishing, but during his lifetime made a major contribution to it. In pure, direct, almost biblical prose, he shared with others both his techniques and his philosophy of angling, and in doing so gained a place as one of the nation's finest essayists. Haig-Brown was born in England to a cultivated family that early encouraged his reading and writing. Adventurous of spirit, and having lost his father in the war, he moved at age 17 to the state of Washington and then to British Columbia, where he worked as guide, logger, trapper, bounty hunter for cougars, semi pro boxer, and fisherman. Though he had not studied law, as one of the few highly literate people of the area he was appointed magistrate and judge at Campbell River, in 1941. He was sometimes late for court because of his fishing, but Haig-Brown served with distinction. He also never stopped writing. Of his 25 published books, over a dozen are still in print. The best-loved are his tetralogy: Fisherman's Spring *(1951),* Fisherman's Winter *(1954),* Fisherman's Summer *(1959) and* Fisherman's Fall *(1964). In 1960* Life *magazine published a version of our selection, but left out the parts that criticize industrial pollution. In 1981 Haig-Brown's daughter Valerie restored them and republished the essay in a collection of her father's works,* The Master and His Fish. *Our version follows hers.*

S ome twenty million angling licences a year are sold on the North 1
American continent and considerably more than twenty million people go fishing each year. There isn't a reason in the world to suppose that twenty million people really enjoy going fishing; a remarkably high proportion of them contribute vastly to the discomfort of others while finding little joy in the sport for themselves. This is sad but inevitable; it grows directly out of the misconception that anyone with two hands, a hook, and a pole, is equipped to go fishing. After all, the beloved fable has it that the boy with the worm on a bent pin always does far better than the master angler with his flies and intricate gear, so it follows logically that a state of blissful ignorance, combined with youthful clumsiness, is the

209

perfect formula for success. If the formula doesn't prove itself, the trouble is probably the weather.

2   Fishing is not really a simpleton's sport. It is a sport with a long history, an intricate tradition, and a great literature. These things have not grown by accident. They have developed by the devotion of sensitive and intelligent men and they make not only a foundation for rich and satisfying experience but the charter of a brotherhood that reaches around the world and through both hemispheres.

3   It is a brotherhood well worth joining. There are no papers to sign, no fees to pay, no formal initiation rites. All that is required is some little understanding of the sport itself and a decent respect for the several essentials that make it.

4   The first purpose of going fishing is to catch fish. But right there the angler separates himself from the meat fisherman and begins to set conditions. He fishes with a rod and line and hook — not with nets or traps or dynamite. From this point on, man being man, further refinements grow naturally and the sport develops. The fisherman is seeking to catch fish on his own terms, terms that will yield him the greatest sense of achievement and the closest identification with his quarry.

5   This establishes the first unwritten article of the brotherhood. Fishing is a sport, a matter of intimate concern only to fish and fisherman; it is not a competition between man and man. The man's aim is to solve by his own wits and skill the unreasoning reaction of the fish, always within the limits of his self-imposed conditions. Besides this, any sort of outshining one's fellow man becomes completely trivial. The fisherman is his own referee, umpire, steward, and sole judge of his performance. Completely alone, by remote lake or virgin stream, he remains bound by his private conditions and the vagaries of fish and weather. Within those conditions, he may bring all his ingenuity to bear, but if he departs from them or betrays them, though only God and the fish are his witnesses, he inevitably reduces his reward.

6   This total freedom from competitive pressure leads the fisherman directly to the three articles of faith that really govern the brotherhood: respect for the fish, respect for the fish's living space, and respect for other fishermen. All three are interrelated and, under the crowded conditions of today's fishing waters, all three are equally important.

7   Respect for other fishermen is simply a matter of common courtesy and reasonably good manners. The more crowded the waters the more necessary manners become and the more thoroughly they are forgotten. The rule can be expressed in a single golden-rule phrase: "Give the other guy the kind of break you would like to get for yourself." Don't crowd him, don't block him, don't push him. If he is working upstream, don't cut in above him; if he is working downstream, don't pile in directly below him.

If you see he is hooking fish along some favourite weed bed, don't force your boat in beside him and spoil it for both. Don't park all day in what you think is a favoured spot so that no one else can get near it — give it a fair try and move on.

On uncrowded waters a self-respecting fisherman always gives the other fellow first chance through the pool or the drift; as often as not the second time through is just as good. On crowded waters give whatever room and show whatever consideration you can and still wet a line; better still, try somewhere else. The crowds are usually in the wrong places anyway.   8

If you would be part of the brotherhood, be generous. Don't hide the successful fly or lure or bait; explain every last detail of it and give or lend a sample if you can. Show the next man along where you moved and missed the big one, make him aware of whatever little secret you may have of the river's pools or the lake's shoals or the sea's tides — but only if the other guy wants it. If he doesn't, be generous still and keep quiet. If he wants to tell you his secret instead of listening to yours, reach for your ultimate generosity and hear him out as long as you can stand it. Good things sometimes come from unlikely sources.   9

Respect for the fish is the real base of the whole business. He is not an enemy, merely an adversary, and without him and his progeny there can be no sport. Whatever his type and species, he has certain qualities that make for sport and he must be given a chance to show them to best advantage. He is entitled to the consideration of the lightest gear and the subtlest method the angler can use with a reasonable chance of success. Trout deserve to be caught on the fly; other methods may be necessary at times, but it is difficult to believe they give much joy to the fisherman. A northern pike or a muskie taken by casting is worth half a dozen taken by trolling. A black bass tempted to the surface is a far greater thrill than one hooked in the depths; an Atlantic salmon or summer steelhead risen to a floating fly is a memory that will live forever. If it takes a little time to learn such skills, there is no doubt the fish is worthy of them. And if the angler is any kind of a man he is unlikely to be satisfied with less.   10

Even in the moment of success and triumph, when the hooked fish is safely brought to beach or net, he is still entitled to respect and consideration: to quick and merciful death if he is wanted, to swift and gentle release if he is not. Killing fish is not difficult — a sharp rap on the back of the head settles most species. Releasing fish is a little, but only a little, more complicated. Fly-caught trout of moderate size are easy. Slide the hand down the leader with the fish still in the water, grip the shank of the hook, and twist sharply. Where it is necessary to handle the fish, a thumb and finger grip on the lower jaw does the least harm and is usually effective. If not, use dry hands and a light but firm grip on the body just   11 forward of the dorsal fin. Wet hands force a heavier grip which is extremely likely to injure vital organs. For heavily toothed fish like northern pike and muskies many fishermen use a grip on the eye sockets or the gill-covers. The first may be all right, but seems dangerous and unnecessarily cruel. The second is destructive. Fish up to ten pounds or so can be gripped securely on the body just behind the gill-covers and should not be harmed.

12   Larger fish that have fought hard are often in distress when released and need to be nursed in the water until they can swim away on their own. Generally little more is needed than to hold them on an even keel, facing upstream, while they take a few gulps of water through their gills. If they lack the strength for this, draw them gently back and forth through the water so that the gills will be forced to work; all but the most exhausted fish will recover under this treatment and swim smoothly away. Fish that have bled heavily or fish that have just swum in from salt water are less likely to recover and should be kept.

13   Respect for the fish's living space should be comprehensive. It includes the water, the bed of the stream or lake, the land on both sides of the water, and all the life that grows there, bird or mammal, plant or fish or insect. There isn't an excuse in the world for litter-leavers, tree-carvers, brush-cutters, flower-pickers, nest-robbers, or any other self-centered vandals on fishing waters. The fisherman comes at best to do some damage — to the fish — and the best he can do is keep it to that. He doesn't need to junk-heap the place with cartons and bottles and tin cans; he need not drop even so much as a leader case or cigarette pack; he can afford to remember that no one else wants to be reminded of him by his leavings.

14   These are elementary and negative points and if parents raised their children properly there would be no need to mention them in this context. A fisherman, any kind of a fisherman, should know better than to spoil the place that makes his sport. But a true share in the brotherhood calls for a little more. The fisherman is under obligation to learn and understand something about the life of his fish and the conditions it needs, if only so that he can take his little part in helping to protect them.

15   All fish need clean waters and all nations, if they know what is good for them, can afford to keep their waters clean. Pollution, whether from sewage or industrial wastes, starts as a little thing scarcely noticed and goes on to destroy all the life of the waters. Its damage can be repaired, slowly, painfully, expensively, but there is no excuse for it in the first place, though many are forthcoming.

16   Besides clean water for their own lives and the many living things they depend on, fish need special conditions for spawning and hatching and rearing. Migratory fish need free passage upstream and down. These

things and many others like them are worth understanding not merely because they suggest protections and improvements, but because knowledge of them brings the fisherman closer to the identification he seeks, makes him more truly a part of the world he is trying to share.

The old days and the old ways, when every stream was full of fish and empty of people, are long gone. They weren't as good as they sounded anyway. It took time and the efforts of good fishermen to learn what could be done and should be done to produce the best possible sport. North American angling has now come close to full development. No one is going to get what he should from the sport by simply buying some gear and going out on the water, nor can he achieve very much by sneering at better men than himself who do take the trouble to learn the delicate skills of the subtler methods. The real world of fishing is open to anyone, through the literature and the generosity of the brotherhood. Once entered upon, the possibilities are limitless. But even the casual, occasional fisherman owes the sport some measure of understanding — enough, shall we say, to protect himself and others from the waste and aggravations of discourtesy and bad manners that are so often based on ignorance. 17

In Winchester Cathedral, not far from a famous trout stream in Hampshire, England, is the tomb of William of Wykeham, a great fourteenth-century bishop and statesman who left a motto to a school he founded: "Manners makyth man." Within the same cathedral lie the bones of our father, Izaak Walton, who remarked three hundred years ago: "Angling is somewhat like poetry, men are to be born so." Perhaps Izaak's precept is for the inner circle of the brotherhood, but William's is certainly universal. It is just possible that nice guys don't catch the most fish. But they find far more pleasure in those they do get. 18

△△

Further Reading:

Roderick Haig-Brown, *Fisherman's Winter*
E. Bennet Metcalfe, *Haig-Brown: A Man of Some Importance*
Izaak Walton, *The Compleat Angler*

Structure:

1. Roderick Haig-Brown states four "articles of faith" for anglers, the first one serving as a general introduction to the three that "really govern the brotherhood" (par. 6). Point out all four articles of faith, specifying where each occurs.

2. Point out all the *contrasts* that you find in the first four paragraphs of the essay.

3. Which paragraphs make fullest use of *examples* as a means of development?
4. In the last paragraph, what does Haig-Brown achieve by quoting William of Wykeham's motto, "Manners makyth man"?
5. Can you think of a relevant "article of faith for good anglers" that Haig-Brown has omitted from his classification?

Style:

1. How FORMAL or INFORMAL would you judge the style of Haig-Brown's essay to be?
2. Largely because of his prose style, Haig-Brown is sometimes described as Canada's finest essayist. Analyze two especially good examples, paragraphs 5 and 9: In what ways is their STYLE effective?
3. Careful word choice is a central trait of Haig-Brown's style. In paragraph 10, why does Haig-Brown point out that the fish "is not an enemy, merely an adversary"?
4. In this 1960 essay, Haig-Brown continually uses expressions such as "brotherhood," "fisherman," "competition between man and man," "if the angler is any kind of a man," and so on, as if no woman has ever fished. If Haig-Brown were writing today, how do you think he would have phrased these passages?

Ideas for Discussion and Writing:

1. In our modern society, which produces food industrially and scientifically, why do people still hunt and fish?
2. According to a Chinese proverb, the time a person spends fishing is not subtracted from that person's life. Discuss the ways in which this philosophy may be true.
3. Many people consider overtly competitive and even violent sports, such as hockey and football, to be the best ones. Yet according to Haig-Brown, it is an absence of competition between anglers that contributes to the best qualities of fishing as a sport (par. 5). In your opinion, what makes a sport good? Is competition necessary? Is body contact or even violence desirable? Illustrate your answers by referring to sports you have played.
4. Haig-Brown writes, "Pollution, whether from sewage or industrial wastes, starts as a little thing scarcely noticed and goes on to destroy all the life of the waters" (par. 15). By the

1990s, pollution — mostly in the form of acid rain — had killed thousands of lakes in Canada and the United States, and it may kill hundreds of thousands more. Suggest specific ways in which we as individuals can reduce this damage, caused mainly by the fumes of oil refineries, chemical plants, smelters, coal-fired power plants, paper mills, factories, and the private automobile.

5. **PROCESS IN WRITING:** *Classify the practitioners of a sport or some other pastime that you enjoy: for example, kinds of soccer or hockey or squash players, weightlifters, dancers, hikers, runners, snowmobilers, etc. First try a cluster outline to establish your categories. Now place the items in a climactic order such as worst to best, least serious to most serious, etc. Are the items all classified by the same principle? Do any overlap? Have any obvious ones been left out? If so, revise your plan. Now write the first draft, let it "cool off," then add more examples and IMAGES to help us "see" the subject better. Test your prose by reading aloud before doing the final version.*

Note: See also the Topics for Writing at the end of this chapter.

W. P. Kinsella

How to Write Fiction

In the essay that follows, W. P. Kinsella recounts how for 20 years he got up at 5 a.m., ran water over his fingers so they would "make the typewriter keys work for an hour or two," then go off to his "hateful job." No longer does he sell life insurance, make pizza, or even teach creative writing: his 1982 novel Shoeless Joe *sold 150,000 copies, then brought in $295,000 for screen rights to a feature film,* Field of Dreams, *starring Kevin Costner. Now Kinsella is free to indulge the two passions of his life, baseball and writing. As a young boy in a log cabin in Alberta, he had relieved his isolation by imagining playmates. Soon he began to put these fantasies on paper, believing that someday he would be a writer. Kinsella's publications had already begun by the time he earned an M.F.A. at the Writer's Workshop of the University of Iowa, and they have continued apace. In* Born Indian *(1981),* The Moccasin Telegraph *(1983),* The Fencepost Chronicles *(1986), and other collections of humorous stories about life on a reservation in Alberta, Kinsella identifies with the Crees, who experience white society as bureaucratic and repressive. His other books of stories are about baseball; from one of these,* Shoeless Joe Jackson Comes to Iowa *(1980), grew Kinsella's first novel discussed above. In 1986 appeared his second,* The Iowa Baseball Confederacy. *In these works baseball is celebrated for its own sake, but is at the same time a metaphor for life — a myth of heroism, idealism, ritual, and purity, expressed in a blend of fact and fantasy that has been described as "magic realism." By contrast, in our selection, an essay from the* Globe and Mail *of April 27, 1985, Kinsella's advice is down-to-earth.*

1   The title, of course, is a lie, as fantastical as any of my fictional creations. I cannot teach anyone how to write fiction. No one can teach anyone how to write fiction.

2   What I can do, in my capacity as a professional fiction writer, is to smooth the road for those people I find who show talent as storytellers, to show them a few tricks of the trade — how to market their material, how to deal with publishers, editors, agents and the like.

3   I can never suggest what a would-be fiction writer should write about. If you don't have a few dozen ideas for stories floating around in your

head, stories that have to be told, then stick to your other hobbies and forget fiction writing.

But if you have your heart set on writing fiction, consider the following: fiction writing, I tell my students, consists of ability, imagination, passion and stamina. Let's consider each individually.   4

By "ability" I mean the ability to write complete sentences in clear, straightforward, standard English.   5

This will not pose a problem for most of the people in the Writers Union, but it is surprising how many university students are unable to write simple sentences. If you can't express yourself clearly, abandon hope unless you are prepared to take a remedial English course. I've been known to suggest to my university students that they get a Grade 5 grammar book and begin their study there.   6

"Imagination" involves the ability to create stories. Little children can create wonderful, uninhibited stories full of fanciful characters. But as the years pass, the regimens of school and community kill the storyteller that lives within each of us. To write fiction you have to dig deep and discover that storyteller.   7

Some writing instructors tell students to "write of what you know." I disagree with that. In 99 cases out of 100, writing about what you know will fill pages, but fill them with dull and uninteresting material.   8

Let's face it, for nine out of 10 of us our lives are so dull that no one would care in the least about them. The 10th person has a life so bizarre no one would believe it if it were written down. The secret of a fiction writer is to make the dull interesting by imagination and embellishment, and to tone down the bizarre until it is believable.   9

I belong to the nine. I live a very quiet life; I have a lovely wife who is a true helpmate and ultrasupportive of my career; we have a nice home on the ocean; we have the freedom to travel. In other words, we are very happy.   10

If I wrote about that I would soon be back selling life insurance, or something equally vile. People don't want to read about happy people. Conflict is an absolute must in every story or novel.   11

I think I clipped the following statement from an American Amateur Press Association publication a few years ago: "The master plot of all novels and stories is: 'An appealing character struggles against great odds to attain a worthwhile goal.'"   12

"Struggles against great odds" are the key words. Something must be at stake, and the character must take some action. What will the conflict be? What action will the appealing character take? That is up to the author. Authors spend half their time writing, and the rest looking at their story and saying, What if? What if? What if? What if I take the story this way? What if I take it that way?   13

14   "Passion" is an almost nebulous ingredient. It is what an author does to make you love a character. It takes very hard work to analyze it. When you find a novel or story in which you absolutely loved a character, where you had a sweet tear in your eye at the end of the story, or where you found yourself laughing uncontrollably, read it again for pleasure. Then re-read it 10 more times for business; analyze every line to learn how that author made you laugh or cry. When you learn the secret, use it in your next story.

15   Never forget that fiction writers are entertainers. Fiction writing comes from the days when the cavemen were gathered around a campfire and Ugh stood up, pounded his chest and said, "Listen to me! I want to tell you a story!" If his story wasn't interesting and suspenseful, his companions soon wandered off to their caves.

16   Fiction writers are not philosophers, or essayists, or pushers of causes religious or otherwise. And above all they are not navel-gazers. All of these are types of non-fiction, and should never be confused with storytelling.

17   One important point to remember is called Valgardson's Law (after B.C. writer W. D. Valgardson): Stories or novels are not about events, but about the people that events happen to. The fact that the Titanic is sinking or a skyscraper toppling — or even that the world is ending — is not important unless you have created an appealing character who is going to suffer if the dreaded event happens.

18   If you want to write fiction, cut out that paragraph and paste it on the wall in front of your typewriter. It will save you weeks, months, maybe even years of struggle.

19   The final ingredient is "stamina." Each of the others I have described is about 5 per cent of the writing process. Stamina is the final 85 per cent. Stamina is keeping your buns on the chair and writing even when you don't feel like it. I know it's a cliché, but though inspiration is nice, 98 per cent of writing is accomplished by perspiration.

20   Stamina is doing as I have done — sitting down to write my 50th short story, the previous 49 having been unpublishable, knowing that number 50 will also be unpublishable, but that it will be 2 per cent better than the previous 49.

21   Stamina is getting up at 5 a.m., running water over your fingers, so they will make the typewriter keys work for an hour or two before you go off to your hateful job. I did that for 20 years while I beat my head against the walls of North American literature.

22   If your head is still full of stories and you are still determined to write them down, lots of luck. You'll need that, too.

△△△

Further Reading:

W. P. Kinsella,
  Shoeless Joe
  The Iowa Baseball Confederacy
John Gardner, *The Art of Fiction*

Structure:

1. "The title, of course, is a lie," states Kinsella in his first line. Is this confession a good opening? What effects do it and the rest of the introduction achieve?
2. Where does Kinsella first announce the four categories of his classification?
3. Do you see a pattern in the way each division of Kinsella's classification is introduced? If so, what is it?
4. Do you think "ability," "imagination," "passion," and "stamina" appear in random order or in a logical progression? Explain.
5. Do any of Kinsella's categories overlap?
6. Do you find paragraphs 19 through 21 more forceful than most other parts of the essay? If so, why? What techniques give them power?
7. The next chapter of our book examines process analysis: the act of explaining how something is done. Would Kinsella's essay fit into that chapter? How fully, how clearly, and how usefully has Kinsella explained how to write fiction?

Style:

1. How FORMAL or INFORMAL is Kinsella's STYLE in this selection? Give evidence to support your answer.
2. In paragraph 19 Kinsella deliberately includes a CLICHÉ: writing as "perspiration" rather than "inspiration." Do you recognize any clichés elsewhere in the essay?

Ideas for Discussion and Writing:

1. In his opening sentence Kinsella implies that fiction can be a "lie." In what ways might this be true? In what ways can an invented plot and invented or embellished characters embody more "truth" than "lie"?
2. Do you agree with Kinsella's view that, since most of us live dull lives, we should avoid writing about what we know (par. 8–13)? Do any of your favourite authors write about what they know?

3. Picasso once said that he spent 50 years learning to paint as he could when he was a child. Is Kinsella right that "the regimens of school and community" (par. 7) kill children's imagination? If so, how? Did it happen to you? Is this process inevitable? Or might school and community take steps to preserve children's power of imagination? If so, what steps?

4. Write your own short story, following as much of Kinsella's advice as you can. Do an exploratory first draft very fast, then revise in further versions.

5. PROCESS IN WRITING: *Write an essay of classification that explains, one by one, the ingredients of success in writing any one of these: a poem of a certain kind, a love letter, a business letter, a lab report, a letter of application for a job, a letter to the editor. In your second draft, strengthen TRANSITIONS between the "ingredients." Sharpen your word choice. Cut deadwood. Finally, edit for things like spelling and grammar before making your good copy.*

Note: See also the Topics for Writing at the end of this chapter.

Hugh MacLennan

A Sound beyond Hearing*

Hugh MacLennan is one of the nation's best-known essayists and novelists, the author of over a dozen books, and the only writer to have won five Governor General's awards. His greatest distinction, though, is the debt of gratitude owed him by many younger writers who learned, from his example, that serious fiction need not be set outside the borders of their own country. MacLennan was born in 1907 in Glace Bay, Cape Breton, Nova Scotia, and studied at Dalhousie, Oxford and at Princeton, where he earned a Ph.D. in classics. From 1951 until his retirement in 1982, he taught in the English Department of McGill University. MacLennan has published several books of essays: Cross-Country *(1949),* Thirty and Three *(1954),* Scotchman's Return and Other Essays *(1960), and* The Other Side of Hugh MacLennan *(1978). Among his novels are* Each Man's Son *(1951),* The Watch that Ends the Night *(1959), and* Voices in Time *(1980).* Two Solitudes *(1945), which contrasts the French- and English-Canadian cultures, is his most widely read novel; but* Barometer Rising *(1941), from which our selection comes, is thought by many to be his best. In 1987 it was produced in a stage version at Halifax's Neptune Theatre. "A Sound beyond Hearing," MacLennan's account of an event he witnessed at age ten, is one of the best-known passages in Canadian literature. It describes the explosion that, on December 6, 1917, levelled much of Halifax and killed over 1600 people.*

T he *Mont Blanc* was now in the Narrows and a detail of men went into   1
her chains to unship the anchor. It would be dropped as soon as she
reached her appointed station in the Basin. A hundred yards to port were
the Shipyards and another hundred yards off the port bow was the blunt
contour of Richmond Bluff; to starboard the shore sloped gently into a
barren of spruce scrub. During the two minutes it took the *Mont Blanc* to
glide through this strait, most of Bedford Basin and nearly all its flotilla of
anchored freighters were hidden from her behind the rise of Richmond
Bluff.

---

*Editor's title.

2   Around the projection of this hill, less than fifty fathoms off the port bow of the incoming *Mont Blanc*, another vessel suddenly appeared heading for the open sea. She flew the Norwegian flag, and to the startled pilot of the munitioner the name *Imo* was plainly visible beside the hawse. She was moving at half-speed and listing gently to port as she made the sharp turn out of the Basin to strike the channel of the Narrows. And so listing, with white water surging away from her fore-foot, she swept across the path of the *Mont Blanc*, exposing a gaunt flank labeled in giant letters BELGIAN RELIEF. Then she straightened, and pointed her bow directly at the fore-quarter of the munitioner. Only at that moment did the men on the *Imo*'s bridge appear to realize that another vessel stood directly in their path.

3   Staccato orders broke from the bridge of the *Mont Blanc* as the two ships moved toward a single point. Bells jangled, and megaphoned shouts came from both bridges. The ships sheered in the same direction, then sheered back again. With a violent shock, the bow of the *Imo* struck the plates of the *Mont Blanc* and went grinding a third of the way through the deck and the forward hold. A shower of sparks splashed out from the screaming metal. The canisters on the deck of the *Mont Blanc* broke loose from their bindings and some of them tumbled and burst open. Then the vessels heeled away with engines reversed and the water boiling out from their screws as the propellers braked them to a standstill. They sprawled sideways across the Narrows, the *Mont Blanc* veering in toward the Halifax shore, the *Imo* spinning about with steerageway lost entirely. Finally she drifted toward the opposite shore.

4   For a fraction of a second there was intense silence. Then smoke appeared out of the shattered deck of the *Mont Blanc*, followed by a racing film of flame. The men on the bridge looked at each other. Scattered shouts broke from the stern, and the engine-room bells jangled again. Orders were half-drowned by a scream of rusty metal as some sailors amidships followed their own inclination and twisted the davits around to lower a boat. The scurry of feet grew louder as more sailors began to pour out through the hatches onto the deck. An officer ran forward with a hose, but before he could connect it his men were ready to abandon ship.

5   The film of flame raced and whitened, then it became deeper like an opaque and fulminant liquid, then swept over the canisters of benzol and increased to a roaring tide of heat. Black smoke billowed and rolled and engulfed the ship, which began to drift with the outgoing tide and swing in toward the graving-dock of the Shipyards. The fire trembled and leaped in a body at the bridge, driving the captain and pilot aft, and there they stood helplessly while the tarry smoke surrounded them in greasy folds and the metal of the deck began to glow under their feet. Both men glanced downward. Underneath that metal lay leashed an incalculable

energy, and the bonds which checked it were melting with every second the thermometers mounted in the hold. A half-million pounds of trinitrotoluol and twenty-three hundred tons of picric acid lay there in the darkness under the plates, while the fire above and below the deck converted the hollow shell of the vessel into a bake-oven.

If the captain had wished to scuttle the ship at that moment it would   6
have been impossible to do so, for the heat between decks would have roasted alive any man who tried to reach the sea-cocks. By this time the entire crew was in the lifeboat. The officers followed, and the boat was rowed frantically toward the wooded slope opposite Halifax. There, by lying flat among the trees, the sailors hoped they would have a chance when their ship blew up. By the time they had beached the boat, the foredeck of the *Mont Blanc* was a shaking rampart of fire, and black smoke pouring from it screened the Halifax waterfront from their eyes. The sailors broke and ran for the shelter of the woods.

By this time men were running out of dock sheds and warehouses and   7
offices along the entire waterfront to watch the burning ship. None of them knew she was a gigantic bomb. She had now come so close to the Shipyards that she menaced the graving-dock. Fire launches cut out from a pier farther south and headed for the Narrows. Signal flags fluttered from the Dockyard and the yardarms of ships lying in the Stream, some of which were already weighing anchor. The captain of the British cruiser piped all hands and called for volunteers to scuttle the *Mont Blanc*; a few minutes later the cruiser's launch was on its way to the Narrows with two officers and a number of ratings. By the time they reached the burning ship her plates were so hot that the seawater lapping the plimsoll line was simmering.

The *Mont Blanc* had become the center of a static tableau. Her plates   8
began to glow red and the swollen air inside her hold heated the cargo rapidly towards the detonation point. Launches from the harbour fire department surrounded her like midges and the water from their hoses arched up with infinite delicacy as they curved into the rolling smoke. The *Imo*, futile and forgotten, was still trying to claw her way off the farther shore.

Twenty minutes after the collision there was no one along the entire   9
waterfront who was unaware that a ship was on fire in the harbor. The jetties and docks near the Narrows were crowded with people watching the show, and yet no warning of danger was given. At that particular moment there was no adequate centralized authority in Halifax to give a warning, and the few people who knew the nature of the *Mont Blanc*'s cargo had no means of notifying the town or spreading the alarm, and no comfort beyond the thought that trinitrotoluol can stand an almost unlimited heat provided there is no fulminate or explosive gas to detonate it.

10   Bells in the town struck the hour of nine, and by this time nearly all normal activity along the waterfront had been suspended. A tug had managed to grapple the *Mont Blanc* and was towing her with imperceptible movement away from the Shipyards back into the channel of the Narrows. Bluejackets from the cruiser had found the bosun's ladder left by the fleeing crew, and with flesh shrinking from the heat, were going over the side. Fire launches surrounded her. There was a static concentration, an intense expectancy in the faces of the firemen playing the hoses, a rhythmic reverberation in the beat of the flames, a gush from the hose-nozzles and a steady hiss of scalding water. Everything else for miles around seemed motionless and silent.

11   Then a needle of flaming gas, thin as the mast and of a brilliance unbelievably intense, shot through the deck of the *Mont Blanc* near the funnel and flashed more than two hundred feet toward the sky. The firemen were thrown back and their hoses jumped suddenly out of control and slashed the air with S-shaped designs. There were a few helpless shouts. Then all movement and life about the ship were encompassed in a sound beyond hearing as the *Mont Blanc* opened up. . . .

12   Three forces were simultaneously created by the energy of the exploding ship, an earthquake, an air-concussion, and a tidal wave. These forces rushed away from the Narrows with a velocity varying in accordance with the nature of the medium in which they worked. It took only a few seconds for the earthquake to spend itself and three minutes for the air-expansion to slow down to a gale. The tidal wave traveled for hours before the last traces of it were swallowed in the open Atlantic.

13   When the shock struck the earth, the rigid ironstone and granite base of Halifax peninsula rocked and reverberated, pavements split and houses swayed as the earth trembled. Sixty miles away in the town of Truro windows broke and glass fell to the ground, tinkling in the stillness of the streets. But the ironstone was solid and when the shock had passed, it resumed its immobility.

14   The pressure of the exploding chemicals smashed against the town with the rigidity and force of driving steel. Solid and unbreathable, the forced wall of air struck against Fort Needham and Richmond Bluff and shaved them clean, smashed with one gigantic blow the North End of Halifax and destroyed it, telescoping houses or lifting them from their foundations, snapping trees and lamp posts, and twisting iron rails into writhing, metal snakes; breaking buildings and sweeping the fragments of their wreckage for hundreds of yards in its course. It advanced two miles southward, shattering every flimsy house in its path, and within thirty seconds encountered the long, shield-like slope of the Citadel which rose before it.

15   Then, for the first time since it was fortified, the Citadel was able to

defend at least a part of the town. The airwall smote it, and was deflected in three directions. Thus some of its violence shot skyward at a twenty-degree angle and spent itself in space. The rest had to pour around the roots of the hill before closing in on the town for another rush forward. A minute after the detonation, the pressure was advancing through the South End. But now its power was diminished, and its velocity was barely twice that of a tornado. Trees tossed and doors broke inward, windows split into driving arrows of glass which buried themselves deep in interior walls. Here the houses, after swaying and cracking, were still on their foundations when the pressure had passed.

Underneath the keel of the *Mont Blanc* the water opened and the harbor bottom was deepened twenty feet along the channel of the Narrows. And then the displaced waters began to drive outward, rising against the town and lifting ships and wreckage over the sides of the docks. It boiled over the shores and climbed the hill as far as the third cross-street, carrying with it the wreckage of small boats, fragments of fish, and somewhere, lost in thousands of tons of hissing brine, the bodies of men. The wave moved in a gigantic bore down the Stream to the sea, rolling some ships under and lifting others high on its crest, while anchor-chains cracked like guns as the violent thrust snapped them. Less than ten minutes after the detonation, it boiled over the breakwater off the park and advanced on McNab's Island, where it burst with a roar greater than a winter storm. And then the central volume of the wave rolled on to sea, high and arching and white at the top, its back glossy like the plumage of a bird. Hours later it lifted under the keel of a steamer far out in the Atlantic and the captain, feeling his vessel heave, thought he had struck a floating mine.

But long before this, the explosion had become manifest in new forms over Halifax. More than two thousand tons of red hot steel, splintered fragments of the *Mont Blanc*, fell like meteors from the sky into which they had been hurled a few seconds before. The ship's anchor soared over the peninsula and descended through a roof on the other side of the Northwest Arm three miles away. For a few seconds the harbor was dotted white with a maze of splashes, and the decks of raddled ships rang with reverberations and clangs as fragments struck them.

Over the North End of Halifax, immediately after the passage of the first pressure, the tormented air was laced with tongues of flame which roared and exploded out of the atmosphere, lashing downwards like a myriad blowtorches as millions of cubic feet of gas took fire and exploded. The atmosphere went white-hot. It grew mottled, then fell to the streets like a crimson curtain. Almost before the last fragments of steel had ceased to fall, the wreckage of the wooden houses in the North End had begun to burn. And if there were any ruins which failed to ignite from falling flames, they began to burn from the fires in their own stoves, onto which they had collapsed.

16

17

18

19   Over this part of the town, rising in the shape of a typhoon from the Narrows and extending five miles into the sky, was poised a cloud formed by the exhausted gases. It hung still for many minutes, white, glossy as an ermine's back, serenely aloof. It cast its shadow over twenty miles of forest land behind Bedford Basin.

ΔΔΔΔΔΔΔΔΔΔΔΔΔΔΔΔΔΔΔΔΔΔΔΔΔΔΔΔΔΔΔΔΔΔΔΔΔΔΔΔΔΔΔΔΔΔΔΔΔΔΔΔΔΔΔΔΔΔΔΔΔΔΔΔ

Further Reading:

Hugh MacLennan,
    Barometer Rising
    Two Solitudes
    The Other Side of Hugh MacLennan
Lesley Choyce, *December Six/The Halifax Solution: An Alternative to Nuclear War*
Elspeth Cameron, *Hugh MacLennan*

Structure:

1.   Which paragraph first names the three categories of Hugh MacLennan's *classification*? Are his categories mutually exclusive?

2.   Point out which paragraphs describe the "earthquake," which describe the "air-concussion" and other airborne effects, and which describe the "tidal wave." Does MacLennan give equal treatment to the three? Why or why not?

3.   In paragraph 12 MacLennan places the "media" of land, air, and sea in this order because the effects transmitted by land spend themselves first and those by sea last. But as he develops his description of each in the same order, why does he come back again to air, in paragraphs 17–19, at the end of this selection?

4.   To what extent does this selection *narrate*? To what extent does it *describe*? To what extent does it trace *cause and effect*? Argue why this selection might have appeared in one of those chapters instead of in this one. Does MacLennan's use of all these approaches at once confuse us, or do they all work smoothly together? Do you think he consciously planned all these interlocking methods? Would you attempt to combine methods as you plan a piece of writing? Would you resist them or welcome them if they appeared as you wrote?

Style:

1.   This explosion scene, from MacLennan's novel *Barometer Rising*,

is recognized as one of the most vivid passages in all of Canadian literature. One reason is the profusion of SENSE IMAGES. Point out one striking example each of appeals to sight, hearing, touch, and smell.

2. In paragraph 3 MacLennan uses the image of "screaming metal," and in paragraph 18 the image of "tongues of flame." Point out three other examples of PERSONIFICATION, in which an inanimate object is described in human terms.

3. In paragraph 17 MacLennan writes that fragments of red-hot steel "fell like meteors." Point out at least five other SIMILES.

4. In paragraph 15 MacLennan writes that "windows split into driving arrows of glass." Point out at least five other METAPHORS.

5. What do "port," "starboard," "hawse," "scuttle," and all the other nautical terms do for this selection? Would a reader's unfamiliarity with some of these specialized words detract from the effect? Why or why not?

Ideas for Discussion and Writing:

1. Name all the novels and films you can think of that are about disasters. Why is such entertainment popular? Do people like to be scared? If so, why?

2. The blast that killed over 1600 people in Halifax, on December 6, 1917, is said to be the world's most disastrous human-made explosion before the atomic bomb. If you have read about the atomic blast that destroyed Hiroshima, in Kildare Dobbs' essay "The Scar," compare these two events in their magnitude and their effect upon the inhabitants.

3. Do you sense moments of beauty in MacLennan's description of the disaster? If so, where? Is it appropriate or even moral to see beauty in destruction?

4. PROCESS IN WRITING: *Write about an environmental disaster that you have either witnessed or heard about recently in the news. First jot down notes on three blank pages, one entitled "Land," another "Air," and the third "Water." Now draw on these notes to classify, in an essay, the effects of the disaster in each of your three categories. Do not withhold frightening or even gross information, for it will show the reader the importance of your subject. In your second draft add more SENSE IMAGES and sharpen your TRANSITIONS. Read your final draft aloud to the class, keeping enough eye contact to judge which passages have the strongest effect.*

Note: See also the Topics for Writing at the end of this chapter.

Topics for Writing

CHAPTER 7: CLASSIFICATION

Develop one of the following topics into an essay of classification. (See also the guidelines that follow.)

1. Conversations
2. Television commercials
3. Crime
4. Music lovers
5. Wine
6. Martial arts
7. Roommates
8. Bosses
9. Horses
10. Grandparents
11. Education
12. Drugs
13. Novels
14. Lovers
15. Police officers
16. Landlords
17. Slang
18. Marriages
19. Readers
20. Salespersons
21. Handicapped people
22. Parties
23. Families
24. Teachers
25. Success

Note also the Process in Writing topic after each selection in this chapter.

Process in Writing: Guidelines

Follow at least some of these steps in writing your essay of classification (your teacher may suggest which ones).

1. *Write a short outline, since the logic of classifying can be difficult. Once you have chosen the principle on which to classify your topic, decide on the categories. Then ask: Do all relate to the same principle? If not, revise. Do any categories overlap? If so, revise. Have you left out an obvious category? Add it.*

2. *Write your thesis statement.*

3. *Now arrange the categories in some climactic order that supports your thesis: smallest to largest, least important to most important, worst to best, etc.*

4. *Write a rapid first draft, double-spaced, not stopping now to revise or edit.*

5. *When this draft has "cooled off," look it over. Does it follow the outline? If not, do the changes make sense? Does every part support the thesis? If not, revise.*

6. *In your second draft sharpen word choice. Add missing IMAGES or examples. Heighten TRANSITIONS. Cut deadwood.*

7. *Now edit for spelling and grammar, and write the good copy. If you have used a computer, save the essay on disk in case your teacher suggests further revision.*

Roberts/Miller Comstock Inc.

*In our early 20s, the lung capacity, the rapidity of motor responses and physical
endurance are at their peak. This is the athlete's finest hour.*

— *Judy Stoffman, "The Way of All Flesh"*

Process Analysis

Here's how it's done....

In the last quarter century, how-to-do-it books and magazines have flourished. Perhaps we have lost the skills we need to build a garage, grow cabbages, or bake bread, and need to look them up. Perhaps the increasing cost of labour has driven us to do our own work. Or perhaps increased leisure has led us to new hobbies. Whatever the reason, we are very familiar with the practical writing known as *process analysis*.

It is a sort of narrative, taking us from the beginning to the end of a task, usually in the strict time order required to build the garage, grow the cabbages, or make the bread. It includes every step, for each is necessary to the success of the whole project. And if it is written for the amateur, it includes *all* the details right down to the size of the nails, or the spacing and depth of seeds in the ground, or the amount of yeast or salt in the dough. A highly experienced cook might just say "Add some yeast" or "Put in a little salt," but the writer of a recipe tries to save us from failure by giving measurements. The main thing to remember in giving directions is to *keep your audience in mind*. If you are writing in your area of expertise, you'll be tempted to take short cuts, leaving out details the reader will be lost without. And you'll be tempted to load your writing with technical terms. But if you accurately estimate your reader's level of knowledge and write accordingly, your directions will stand a greater chance of working.

Another kind of process analysis satisfies not our practical needs but our curiosity. We may enjoy learning how a space satellite is launched, how stockholders are swindled, how liquor is distilled, how the Second World War was won or how a heart is transplanted — without ever doing these things ourselves. Of course, not every detail must be given in armchair reading such as this: only as many as it takes to clearly convey the information and to interest the reader.

Sometimes a writer will use process analysis not to instruct or inform, but for a totally different reason. When Stephen Leacock tells us "How to Live to Be 200," he advises us to eat cement — a strange way to reach the goal — until we see that his goal is not our longevity but laughs.

Whether you aim to help the reader accomplish a task, to satisfy the reader's curiosity, or even just to entertain, your process analysis will work only if you observe the most basic principle of writing any essay: know your purpose at the beginning and keep it firmly in mind as you write.

Note: For more examples of process analysis, see these essays in other chapters:

Stephen Leacock

How to Live to Be 200

During his lifetime Stephen Leacock became the world's best-known humourist writing in English, a Canadian successor to the American writer Mark Twain. Although he was for decades Canada's favourite author, Leacock has gradually slipped into an undeserved neglect. He was born in England in 1869, but at age 6 came with his family to Ontario. He studied at Upper Canada College, the University of Toronto, and the University of Chicago where, in 1903, he was awarded a Ph.D. In the same year McGill hired him to teach economics and political science, and from 1908 until his retirement in 1936, he served as head of his department. He died in 1944. Leacock wrote over sixty books, many on academic subjects, but of course it is for his books of humour that he is remembered. The best-loved have been Literary Lapses *(1910),* Nonsense Novels *(1911),* Sunshine Sketches of a Little Town *(1912),* Arcadian Adventures with the Idle Rich *(1914), and* My Remarkable Uncle and Other Sketches *(1942). Our selection, which comes from a later edition of* Literary Lapses, *is vintage Leacock: through exaggeration and incongruities, it reduces to absurdity a topic that many people, today as in Leacock's time, take seriously.*

Twenty years ago I knew a man called Jiggins, who had the Health Habit. 1

He used to take a cold plunge every morning. He said it opened his pores. After it he took a hot sponge. He said it closed the pores. He got so that he could open and shut his pores at will. 2

Jiggins used to stand and breathe at an open window for half an hour before dressing. He said it expanded his lungs. He might, of course, have had it done in a shoe-store with a boot stretcher, but after all it cost him nothing this way, and what is half an hour? 3

After he had got his undershirt on, Jiggins used to hitch himself up like a dog in harness and do Sandow exercises. He did them forwards, backwards, and hind-side up. 4

He could have got a job as a dog anywhere. He spent all his time at this kind of thing. In his spare time at the office, he used to lie on his stomach 5 on the floor and see if he could lift himself up with his knuckles. If he could, then he tried some other way until he found one that he couldn't do. Then he would spend the rest of his lunch hour on his stomach, perfectly happy.

6   In the evenings in his room he used to lift iron bars, cannon-balls, heave dumb-bells, and haul himself up to the ceiling with his teeth. You could hear the thumps half a mile.

7   He liked it.

8   He spent half the night slinging himself around the room. He said it made his brain clear. When he got his brain perfectly clear, he went to bed and slept. As soon as he woke, he began clearing it again.

9   Jiggins is dead. He was, of course, a pioneer, but the fact that he dumb-belled himself to death at an early age does not prevent a whole generation of young men from following in his path.

10   They are ridden by the Health Mania.

11   They make themselves a nuisance.

12   They get up at impossible hours. They go out in silly little suits and run Marathon heats before breakfast. They chase around barefoot to get the dew on their feet. They hunt for ozone. They bother about pepsin. They won't eat meat because it has too much nitrogen. They won't eat fruit because it hasn't any. They prefer albumen and starch and nitrogen to huckleberry pie and doughnuts. They won't drink water out of a tap. They won't eat sardines out of a can. They won't use oysters out of a pail. They won't drink milk out of a glass. They are afraid of alcohol in any shape. Yes, sir, afraid. "Cowards."

13   And after all their fuss they presently incur some simple old-fashioned illness and die like anybody else.

14   Now people of this sort have no chance to attain any great age. They are on the wrong track.

15   Listen. Do you want to live to be really old, to enjoy a grand, green, exhuberant, boastful old age and to make yourself a nuisance to your whole neighbourhood with your reminiscences?

16   Then cut out all this nonsense. Cut it out. Get up in the morning at a sensible hour. The time to get up is when you have to, not before. If your office opens at eleven, get up at ten-thirty. Take your chance on ozone. There isn't any such thing anyway. Or, if there is, you can buy a Thermos bottle full for five cents, and put it on a shelf in your cupboard. If your work begins at seven in the morning, get up at ten minutes to, but don't be liar enough to say that you like it. It isn't exhilarating, and you know it.

17   Also, drop all that cold-bath business. You never did it when you were a boy. Don't be a fool now. If you must take a bath (you don't really need to), take it warm. The pleasure of getting out of a cold bed and creeping

into a hot bath beats a cold plunge to death. In any case, stop gassing about your tub and your "shower," as if you were the only man who ever washed.

So much for that point.   18

Next, take the question of germs and bacilli. Don't be scared of them.   19
That's all. That's the whole thing, and if you once get on to that you never need to worry again.

If you see a bacilli, walk right up to it, and look it in the eye. If one flies   20
into your room, strike at it with your hat or with a towel. Hit it as hard as you can between the neck and the thorax. It will soon get sick of that.

But as a matter of fact, a bacilli is perfectly quiet and harmless if you are   21
not afraid of it. Speak to it. Call out to it to "lie down." It will understand. I had a bacilli once, called Fido, that would come and lie at my feet while I was working. I never knew a more affectionate companion, and when it was run over by an automobile, I buried it in the garden with genuine sorrow.

(I admit this is an exaggeration. I don't really remember its name; it   22
may have been Robert.)

Understand that it is only a fad of modern medicine to say that cholera   23
and typhoid and diphtheria are caused by bacilli and germs; nonsense. Cholera is caused by a frightful pain in the stomach, and diphtheria is caused by trying to cure a sore throat.

Now take the question of food.   24

Eat what you want. Eat lots of it. Yes, eat too much of it. Eat till you can   25
just stagger across the room with it and prop it up against a sofa cushion. Eat everything that you like until you can't eat any more. The only test is, can you pay for it? If you can't pay for it, don't eat it. And listen — don't worry as to whether your food contains starch, or albumen, or gluten, or nitrogen. If you are a damn fool enough to want these things, go and buy them and eat all you want of them. Go to a laundry and get a bag of starch, and eat your fill of it. Eat it, and take a good long drink of glue after it, and a spoonful of Portland cement. That will gluten you, good and solid.

If you like nitrogen, go and get a druggist to give you a canful of it at the   26
soda counter, and let you sip it with a straw. Only don't think that you can mix all these things up with your food. There isn't any nitrogen or phosphorus or albumen in ordinary things to eat. In any decent household all that sort of stuff is washed out in the kitchen sink before the food is put on the table.

And just one word about fresh air and exercise. Don't bother with   27
either of them. Get your room full of good air, then shut up the windows and keep it. It will keep for years. Anyway, don't keep using your lungs all

the time. Let them rest. As for exercise, if you have to take it, take it and put up with it. But as long as you have the price of a hack and can hire other people to play baseball for you and run races and do gymnastics when you sit in the shade and smoke and watch them — great heavens, what more do you want?

ΔΔΔΔΔΔΔΔΔΔΔΔΔΔΔΔΔΔΔΔΔΔΔΔΔΔΔΔΔΔΔΔΔΔΔΔΔΔΔΔΔΔΔΔΔΔΔΔΔΔΔΔΔΔΔΔΔΔΔΔ

Further Reading:

Stephen Leacock,
   Sunshine Sketches of a Little Town
   Literary Lapses
   My Remarkable Uncle and Other Sketches
Robertson Davies, *Stephen Leacock*
D. Staines, *Stephen Leacock: A Reappraisal*

Structure:

1. This essay is divided into two main parts. How do they differ from one another and where do we pass from one to the other?
2. Is the story of Jiggins explained in any particular order? And what effect is achieved at the end of his case (par. 9)?
3. Are Stephen Leacock's health instructions organized according to the order in which they should be applied?
4. What is our first clue that Leacock's *process analysis* is meant not to instruct but to entertain?

Style:

1. Leacock says "eat" seven times in the first half of paragraph 25. Read the passage aloud. Is this repetition accidental or deliberate? What effect does it achieve? Where else in the essay does Leacock use repetition?
2. In paragraph 25 Leacock writes: "That will gluten you, good and solid." What is the effect of the word "gluten" as used in this sentence?
3. In paragraph 21 Leacock writes: "I had a bacilli once, called Fido, that would come and lie at my feet while I was working." Analyze the sources of humour in this sentence.
4. Reduction to absurdity is a comic device often used by Leacock. One good example is the analogy of "bacilli" as insects being swatted or as a favourite dog being run over by a car. Where else in this essay is an idea reduced to absurdity?

Ideas for Discussion and Writing:

1. Do you have the "Health Habit," like Jiggins, or do you prefer comfort and luxury, like our narrator? Give reasons to justify your preference.

2. How would you update Leacock's essay for our times? Which aspects of the "Health Mania" would you drop from the argument, which would you keep, and which might you add?

3. PROCESS IN WRITING: *Write a* process analysis *on how to attain old age in good health. First brainstorm or freewrite. Then do a rapid "discovery draft," double-spaced. When it has "cooled off," analyze it: Are the steps in order? Are the instructions clear? Have you supplied examples? Revise accordingly in your second draft. Now sharpen word choice as well. Heighten TRANSITIONS. Cut deadwood. And test your prose by reading aloud, before writing the good version.*

Note: See also the Topics for Writing at the end of this chapter.

Judy Stoffman

The Way of All Flesh

Judy Stoffman has written and edited for several periodicals, including Today *magazine,* Canadian Living, *and the Toronto* Globe and Mail's *"Report on Business" magazine. She is now the Toronto* Star's *fashion editor. Born in Hungary, she came at age ten to Canada, where she grew up in Vancouver. Stoffman studied English literature at the University of British Columbia and at Sussex University, England, where she earned an M.A.; she studied also in France. Her future seemed decided as early as grade two: when a teacher read out to the class her composition on recess, Stoffman knew she wanted to be a writer. "I love the research and dread the writing," she says. "Before I start writing I have a kind of stage fright and from talking to other writers I know they have it too, but they persist because when the words finally start to flow there is an exhilaration nothing else can give." Our selection, "The Way of All Flesh," appeared in* Weekend Magazine *in 1979. Before writing it Stoffman did extensive research: she read ten books on aging and interviewed three gerontologists, a family doctor and a sex therapist. "Then," she says, "I tried to synthesize what I had learned, while exploring my own deepest fears. But you'll notice that I never used the word 'I.'" She has updated her essay for the present edition.*

1   When a man of 25 is told that aging is inexorable, inevitable, universal, he will nod somewhat impatiently at being told something so obvious. In fact, he has little idea of the meaning of the words. It has nothing to do with him. Why should it? He has had no tangible evidence yet that his body, as the poet Rilke said, enfolds old age and death as the fruit enfolds a stone.

2   The earliest deposits of fat in the aorta, the trunk artery carrying blood away from the heart, occur in the eighth year of life, but who can peer into his own aorta at this first sign of approaching debility? The young man has seen old people but he secretly believes himself to be the exception on whom the curse will never fall. "Never will the skin of my neck hang loose. My grip will never weaken. I will stand tall and walk with long strides as long as I live." The young girl scarcely pays attention to her clothes; she

scorns makeup. Her confidence in her body is boundless; smooth skin and a flat stomach will compensate, she knows, for any lapses in fashion or grooming. She stays up all night, as careless of her energy as of her looks, believing both will last forever.

In our early 20s, the lung capacity, the rapidity of motor responses and physical endurance are at their peak. This is the athlete's finest hour. Cindy Nicholas of Toronto was 19 when she first swam the English Channel in both directions. The tennis star Bjorn Borg was 23 when he triumphed at Wimbledon for the fourth time.   3

It is not only *athletic* prowess that is at its height between 20 and 30. James Boswell, writing in his journal in 1763 after he had finally won the favors of the actress Louisa, has left us this happy description of the sexual prowess of a 23-year-old: "I was in full glow of health and my bounding blood beat quick in high alarms. Five times was I fairly lost in supreme rapture. Louisa was madly fond of me; she declared I was a prodigy, and asked me if this was extraordinary in human nature. I said twice as much might be, but this was not, although in my own mind I was somewhat proud of my performance."   4

In our early 30s we are dumbfounded to discover the first grey hair at the temples. We pull out the strange filament and look at it closely, trying to grasp its meaning. It means simply that the pigment has disappeared from the hair shaft, never to return. It means also — but this thought we push away — that in 20 years or so we'll relinquish our identity as a blonde or a redhead. By 57, one out of four people is completely grey. Of all the changes wrought by time this is the most harmless, except to our vanity.   5

In this decade one also begins to notice the loss of upper register hearing, that is, the responsiveness to high frequency tones, but not all the changes are for the worse, not yet. Women don't reach their sexual prime until about 38, because their sexual response is learned rather than innate. The hand grip of both sexes increases in strength until 35, and intellectual powers are never stronger than at that age. There is a sense in the 30s of hitting your stride, of coming into your own. When Sigmund Freud was 38 an older colleague, Josef Breuer, wrote: "Freud's intellect is soaring at its highest. I gaze after him as a hen at a hawk."   6

Gail Sheehy in her book *Passages* calls the interval between 35 and 45 the Deadline Decade. It is the time we begin to sense danger. The body continually flashes us signals that time is running out. We must perform our quaint deeds, keep our promises, get on with our allotted tasks.   7

Signal: The woman attempts to become pregnant at 40 and finds she cannot. Though she menstruates each month, menstruation being merely the shedding of the inner lining of the womb, she may not be ovulating regularly.   8

9   Signal: Both men and women discover that, although they have not changed their eating habits over the years, they are much heavier than formerly. The man is paunchy around the waist; the woman no longer has those slim thighs and slender arms. A 120-pound woman needs 2,000 calories daily to maintain her weight when she is 25, 1,700 to maintain the same weight at 45, and only 1,500 calories at 65. A 170-pound man needs 3,100 calories daily at 25, 300 fewer a day at 45 and 450 calories fewer still at 65. This decreasing calorie need signals that the body consumes its fuel ever more slowly; the cellular fires are damped and our sense of energy diminishes.

10   In his mid-40s the man notices he can no longer run up the stairs three at a time. He is more easily winded and his joints are not as flexible as they once were. The strength of his hands has declined somewhat. The man feels humiliated: "I will not let this happen to me. I will turn back the tide and master my body." He starts going to the gym, playing squash, lifting weights. He takes up jogging. Though he may find it neither easy nor pleasant, terror drives him past pain. A regular exercise program can retard some of the symptoms of aging by improving the circulation and increasing the lung capacity, thereby raising our stamina and energy level, but no amount of exercise will make a 48-year-old 26 again. Take John Keeley of Mystic, Connecticut. In 1957, when he was 26, he won the Boston marathon with a time of 2:20. In 1979, fit and 48, he was as fiercely competitive as ever, yet it took him almost 30 minutes longer to run the same marathon.

11   In the middle of the fourth decade, the man whose eyesight has always been good will pick up a book and notice that he is holding it farther from his face than usual. The condition is presbyopia, a loss of the flexibility of the lens which makes adjustment from distant to near vision increasingly difficult. It's harder now to zoom in for a closeup. It also takes longer for the eyes to recover from glare; between 16 and 90, recovery time from exposure to glare is doubled every 13 years.

12   In our 50s, we notice that food is less and less tasty; our taste buds are starting to lose their acuity. The aged Queen Victoria was wont to complain that strawberries were not as sweet as when she was a girl.

13   Little is known about the causes of aging. We do not know if we are born with a biochemical messenger programed to keep the cells and tissues alive, a messenger that eventually gets lost, or if there is a 'death hormone,' absent from birth but later secreted by the thymus or by the mysterious pineal gland, or if, perhaps, aging results from a fatal flaw in the body's immune system. The belief that the body is a machine whose parts wear out is erroneous, for the machine does not have the body's capacity for self-repair.

14   "A man is as old as his arteries," observed Sir William Osler. From the

50s on, there's a progressive hardening and narrowing of the arteries due to the gradual lifelong accumulation of calcium and fats along the arterial walls. Arteriosclerosis eventually affects the majority of the population in the affluent countries of the West. Lucky the man or women who, through a combination of good genes and good nutrition, can escape it, for it is the most evil change of all. As the flow of blood carrying oxygen and nutrients to the muscles, the brain, the kidneys and other organs diminishes, these organs begin to starve. Although all aging organs lose weight, there is less shrinkage of organs such as the liver and kidneys, the cells of which regenerate, than there is shrinkage of the brain and the muscles, the cells of which, once lost, are lost forever.

For the woman it is now an ordeal to be asked her age. There is a fine 15
tracery of lines around her eyes, a furrow in her brow even when she smiles. The bloom is off her cheeks. Around the age of 50 she will buy her last box of sanitary pads. The body's production of estrogen and progesterone, which govern menstruation (and also help to protect her from heart attack and the effects of stress), will have ceased almost completely. She may suffer palpitations, suddenly break into a sweat; her moods may shift abruptly. She looks in the mirror and asks, "Am I still a woman?" Eventually she becomes reconciled to her new self and even acknowledges its advantages: no more fears about pregnancy. "In any case," she laughs, "I still have not bad legs."

The man, too, will undergo a change. One night in his early 50s he has 16
some trouble achieving a complete erection, and his powers of recovery are not what they once were. Whereas at 20 he was ready to make love again less than half an hour after doing so, it may now take two hours or more; he was not previously aware that his level of testosterone, the male hormone, has been gradually declining since the age of 20. He may develop headaches, be unable to sleep, become anxious about his performance, anticipate failure and so bring on what is called secondary impotence — impotence of psychological rather than physical origin. According to Masters and Johnson, 25 percent of all men are impotent by 65 and 50 percent by 75, yet this cannot be called an inevitable feature of aging. A loving, undemanding partner and a sense of confidence can do wonders. "The susceptibility of the human male to the power of suggestion with regard to his sexual prowess," observe Masters and Johnson, "is almost unbelievable."

After the menopause, the woman ages more rapidly. Her bones start to 17
lose calcium, becoming brittle and porous. The walls of the vagina become thinner and drier, sexual intercourse now may be painful unless her partner is slow and gentle. The sweat glands begin to atrophy and the sebaceous glands that lubricate the skin decline; the complexion becomes thinner and drier and wrinkles appear around the mouth. The skin,

which in youth varies from about one-fiftieth of an inch on the eyelids to about a third of an inch on the palms and the soles of the feet, loses 50 percent of its thickness betweeen the ages of 20 and 80. The woman no longer buys sleeveless dresses and avoids shorts. The girl who once disdained cosmetics is now a woman whose dressing table is covered with lotions, night creams and makeup.

18   Perhaps no one has written about the sensation of nearing 60 with more brutal honesty than the French novelist Simone de Beauvoir: "While I was able to look at my face without displeasure, I gave it no thought. I loathe my appearance now: the eyebrows slipping down toward the eyes, the bags underneath, the excessive fullness of the cheeks and the air of sadness around the mouth that wrinkles always bring. . . . Death is no longer a brutal event in the far distance; it haunts my sleep."

19   In his early 60s the man's calves are shrunken, his muscles stringy looking. The legs of the woman, too, are no longer shapely. Both start to lose their sense of smell and both lose most of the hair in the pubic area and the underarms. Hair, however, may make its appearance in new places, such as the woman's chin. Liver spots appear on the hands, the arms, the face; they are made of coagulated melanin, the coloring matter of the skin. The acid secretions of the stomach decrease, making digestion slow and more difficult.

20   Halfway through the 60s comes compulsory retirement for most men and working women, forcing upon the superannuated worker the realization that society now views him as useless and unproductive. The man who formerly gave orders to a staff of 20 now finds himself underfoot as his wife attempts to clean the house or get the shopping done. The woman fares a little better since there is a continuity in her pattern of performing a myriad of essential household tasks. Now they must both set new goals or see themselves wither mentally. The unsinkable American journalist I.F. Stone, when he retired in 1971 from editing *I.F. Stone's Weekly*, began to teach himself Greek and is now reading Plato in the original. When Somerset Maugham read that the Roman senator Cato the Elder learned Greek when he was 80, he remarked: "Old age is ready to undertake tasks that youth shirked because they would take too long."

21   However active we are, the fact of old age can no longer be evaded from about 65 onward. Not everyone is as strong minded about this as de Beauvoir was. When she made public in her memoirs her horror at her own deterioration, her readers were scandalized. She received hundreds of letters telling her that there is no such thing as old age, that some are just younger than others. Repeatedly she heard the hollow reassurance, "You're as young as you feel." But she considered this a lie. Our subjective reality, our inner sense of self, is not the only reality. There is also an

objective reality, how we are seen by society. We receive our revelation of old age from others. The woman whose figure is still trim may sense that a man is following her in the street; drawing abreast, the man catches sight of her face — and hurries on. The man of 68 may be told by a younger woman to whom he is attracted: "You remind me of my father."

Madame de Sévigné, the 17th-century French writer, struggled to rid herself of the illuson of perpetual youth. At 63 she wrote: "I have been dragged to this inevitable point where old age must be undergone: I see it there before me; I have reached it; and I should at least like so to arrange matters that I do not move on, that I do not travel further along this path of the infirmities, pains, losses of memory and the disfigurement. But I hear a voice saying: 'You must go along, whatever you may say; or indeed if you will not then you must die, which is an extremity from which nature recoils.' " 22

Now the man and the woman have their 70th birthday party. It is a sad affair because so many of their friends are missing, felled by strokes, heart attacks or cancers. Now the hands of the clock begin to race. The skeleton continues to degenerate from loss of calcium. The spine becomes compressed and there is a slight stoop nothing can prevent. Inches are lost from one's height. The joints may become thickened and creaking; in the morning the woman can't seem to get moving until she's had a hot bath. She has osteoarthritis. This, like the other age-related diseases, arteriosclerosis and diabetes, can and should be treated, but it can never be cured. The nails, particularly the toenails, become thick and lifeless because the circulation in the lower limbs is now poor. The man has difficulty learning new things because of the progressive loss of neurons from the brain. The woman goes to the store and forgets what she has come to buy. The two old people are often constipated because the involuntary muscles are weaker now. To make it worse, their children are always saying, "Sit down, rest, take it easy." Their digestive tract would be toned up if they went for a long walk or even a swim, although they feel a little foolish in bathing suits. 23

In his late 70s, the man develops glaucoma, pressure in the eyeball caused by the failure of the aqueous humour to drain away; this can now be treated with a steroid related to cortisone. The lenses in the eyes of the woman may thicken and become fibrous, blurring her vision. She has cataracts, but artificial lenses can now be implanted using cryosurgery. There is no reason to lose one's sight just as there's no reason to lose one's teeth; regular, lifelong dental care can prevent tooth loss. What can't be prevented is the yellowing of teeth, brought about by the shrinking of the living chamber within the tooth which supplies the outer enamel with moisture. 24

Between 75 and 85 the body loses most of its subcutaneous fat. On her 25

80th birthday the woman's granddaughter embraces her and marvels: "How thin and frail and shrunken she is! Could this narrow, bony chest be the same warm, firm bosom to which she clasped me as a child?" Her children urge her to eat but she has no enjoyment of food now. Her mouth secretes little saliva, so she has difficulty tasting and swallowing. The loss of fat and shrinking muscles in the 80s diminish the body's capacity for homeostasis, that is, righting any physiological imbalance. The old man, if he is cold, can barely shiver (shivering serves to restore body heat). If he lives long enough, the man will have an enlarged prostate, which causes the urinary stream to slow to a trickle. The man and the woman probably both wear hearing aids now; without a hearing aid, they hear vowels clearly but not consonants; if someone says "fat," they think they've heard the word "that."

26   At 80, the speed of nerve impulses is 10 percent less than it was at 25, the kidney filtration rate is down by 30 percent, the pumping efficiency of the heart is only 60 percent of what it was, and the maximum breathing capacity, 40 percent.

27   The old couple is fortunate in still being able to express physically the love they've built up over a lifetime. The old man may be capable of an erection once or twice a week (Charlie Chaplin fathered the last of his many children when he was 81), but he rarely has the urge to climax. When he does, he sometimes has the sensation of seepage rather than a triumphant explosion. Old people who say they are relieved that they are now free of the torments of sexual desire are usually the ones who found sex a troublesome function all their lives; those who found joy and renewal in the act will cling to their libido. Many older writers and artists have expressed the conviction that continued sexuality is linked to continued creativity: "There was a time when I was cruelly tormented, indeed obsessed by desire," wrote the novelist André Gide at the age of 73, "and I prayed, 'Oh let the moment come when my subjugated flesh will allow me to give myself entirely to. . . .' But to what? To art? To pure thought? To God? How ignorant I was! How mad! It was the same as believing that the flame would burn brighter in a lamp with no oil left. Even today it is my carnal self that feeds the flame, and now I pray that I may retain carnal desire until I die."

28   Aging, says an American gerontologist, "is not a simple slope which everyone slides down at the same speed; it is a flight of irregular stairs down which some journey more quickly than others." Now we arrive at the bottom of the stairs. The old man and the old woman whose progress we have been tracing will die either of a cancer (usually of the lungs, bowel or intestines) or of a stroke, a heart attack or in consequence of a fall. The man slips in the bathroom and breaks his thigh bone. But worse

than the fracture is the enforced bed rest in the hospital which will probably bring on bed sores, infections, further weakening of the muscles and finally, what Osler called "an old man's best friend": pneumonia. At 25 we have so much vitality that if a little is sapped by illness, there is still plenty left over. At 85 a little is all we have.

And then the light goes out.   29

The sheet is pulled over the face.   30

In the last book of Marcel Proust's remarkable work *Remembrance of*   31
Things Past, the narrator, returning after a long absence from Paris, attends a party of his friends throughout which he has the impression of being at a masked ball: "I did not understand why I could not immediately recognize the master of the house, and the guests, who seemed to have made themselves up, in a way that completely changed their appearance. The Prince had rigged himself up with a white beard and what looked like leaden soles which made his feet drag heavily. A name was mentioned to me and I was dumbfounded at the thought that it applied to the blonde waltzing girl I had once known and to the stout, white-haired lady now walking just in front of me. We did not see our own appearance, but each like a facing mirror, saw the other's." The narrator is overcome by a simple but powerful truth: the old are not a different species. "It is out of young men who last long enough," wrote Proust, "that life makes its old men."

The wrinkled old man who lies with the sheet over his face was once the   32
young man who vowed, "My grip will never weaken. I will walk with long strides and stand tall as long as I live." The young man who believed himself to be the exception.

△△△

Further Reading:

Gail Sheehy, *Passages*
Margaret Laurence, *The Stone Angel* (novel)
Roch Carrier, *No Country without Grandfathers* (novel)
Constance Beresford-Howe, *The Book of Eve* (novel)
Ernest Hemingway, *The Old Man and the Sea* (novella)
William Shakespeare, *King Lear*
Michel Tremblay, *Albertine, in Five Times* (theatre)

Structure:

1. "The Way of All Flesh" is a striking example of chronological order used to organize a mass of information. Point out at least

ten words, phrases, or sentences that signal the flow of time.

2. Does Judy Stoffman's *process analysis* tell the reader how to do something, how something is done by others, or how something happens?

3. How long would this essay be if all its examples were removed? How interesting would it be? How convincing would it be?

4. What device of organization underlies both paragraphs 14 and 16?

5. What effect does Stoffman achieve when, in the last paragraph, she refers to the first paragraph?

Style:

1. Why are paragraphs 29 and 30 so short?

2. To what extent does Stoffman rely on statistics? What do they do for her argument?

3. To what extent does Stoffman rely on quotations? Would you call this selection a research essay? Why or why not?

4. In a desk-size dictionary, look up the origins of the word "gerontologist" (par. 28). How is it related to the words "geriatrics," "Geritol," "gerontocracy," "astrology," and "zoology."

Ideas for Discussion and Writing:

1. Did this essay frighten or depress you? If so, was this effect a failure or a success on the part of the author?

2. Do you share the attitude of Stoffman's young man who "has seen old people" but who "secretly believes himself to be the exception on whom the curse will never fall" (par. 2)? What are the benefits of such an attitude? What are the dangers?

3. Jonathan Swift said, "Every man desires to live long, but no man would be old." How do you explain the apparent contradiction in this PARADOX?

4. In paragraph 21 Stoffman contrasts our "subjective" and "objective" realities. Which do you think is more important in forming our self-image? Which do you think *should* be more important, and why?

5. Is compulsory retirement at 65 good for the individual? For the company? For society? When would you retire if you had the choice, and why? Would you apply a standard other than age?

6. If you have read "The Firewood Gatherers," compare the description of old age given by Thierry Mallet with that given by Stoffman.

7. **PROCESS IN WRITING:** *Write a* process analysis *on one of these topics:*
— *How to stay physically fit past 30*
— *How to keep a feeling of self-worth in old age*
— *How to help parents and grandparents to be happy in their old age*
First fill a page with brief notes, then scan and sort to choose your points and the order in which they will appear. After a rapid first draft, add more TRANSITIONS to speed the chronology of your process. Are there enough IMAGES? Enough concrete examples? Share a draft with class members; do they think they could actually follow your directions? If not, clarify weak points. Finally, read your good copy aloud, slowly and clearly, to the whole class.

Note: See also the Topics for Writing at the end of this chapter.

Susanna Moodie

Dandelion Coffee*

Although Susanna Moodie (1803–1885) is now our most celebrated pioneer, an almost legendary woman who could raise crops, chase bears, and paddle a canoe, she began life in very different surroundings. Born in Suffolk, England, she spent her childhood in the gentility of her father's estate near Southwold. But when a poor investment took the family fortune, and when in 1831 she married a half-pay military officer, the only way to avoid poverty was to emigrate. In 1832 the couple joined Susanna's brother Samuel Strickland and her sister Catharine Parr Traill (see her selection on page 148 of this book) in the bush of Upper Canada. Moodie had published light fiction in England and continued to write for periodicals. But it was not till 1852, when the Moodies had left the wilds for town life in Belleville, that she told her whole story in the memoir that is now a Canadian classic: Roughing It in the Bush. *In this work she reveals ambiguous feelings: without the sunny optimism of her sister or brother, she detested her exile from polite society; yet her "Romantic" love for nature shines through her privations. Over a century later Margaret Atwood explored these ambiguities in her cycle of poems,* The Journals of Susanna Moodie *(1970), raising to almost mythic status this unwilling pioneer. Our own selection, which reveals Moodie's practical side, is from* Roughing It in the Bush.*

1   The first year we came to this country, I met with an account of dandelion coffee, published in the *New York Albion*, given by a Dr. Harrison, of Edinburgh, who earnestly recommended it as an article of general use.

2   "It possesses," he says, "all the fine flavour and exhilarating properties of coffee, without any of its deleterious effects. The plant being of a soporific nature, the coffee made from it when drunk at night produces a tendency to sleep, instead of exciting wakefulness, and may be safely used as a cheap and wholesome substitute for the Arabian berry, being equal in substance and flavour to the best Mocha coffee."

3   I was much struck with this paragraph at the time, and for several years

---

*Editor's title.

felt a great inclination to try the Doctor's coffee; but something or other always came in the way, and it was put off till another opportunity. During the fall of '35, I was assisting my husband in taking up a crop of potatoes in the field, and observing a vast number of fine dandelion roots among the potatoes, it brought the dandelion coffee back to my memory, and I determined to try some for our supper. Without saying anything to my husband, I threw aside some of the roots, and when we left work, collecting a sufficient quantity for the experiment, I carefully washed the roots quite clean, without depriving them of the fine brown skin which covers them, and which contains the aromatic flavour which so nearly resembles coffee that it is difficult to distinguish it from it while roasting.

I cut my roots into small pieces, the size of a kidney-bean, and roasted them on an iron baking-pan in the stove-oven, until they were as brown and crisp as coffee. I then ground and transferred a small cupful of the powder to the coffee-pot, pouring upon it scalding water, and boiling it for a few minutes briskly over the fire. The result was beyond my expectations. The coffee proved excellent — far superior to the common coffee we procured at the stores.

To persons residing in the bush, and to whom tea and coffee are very expensive articles of luxury, the knowledge of this valuable property in a plant scattered so abundantly through their fields, would prove highly beneficial. For years we used no other article; and my Indian friends who frequented the house gladly adopted the root, and made me show them the whole process of manufacturing it into coffee.

Experience taught me that the root of the dandelion is not so good when applied to this purpose in the spring as it is in the fall. I tried it in the spring, but the juice of the plant, having contributed to the production of leaves and flowers, was weak, and destitute of the fine bitter flavour so peculiar to coffee. The time of gathering in the potato crop is the best suited for collecting and drying the roots of the dandelion; and as they always abound in the same hills, both may be accomplished at the same time. Those who want to keep a quantity for winter use may wash and cut up the roots, and dry them on boards in the sun. They will keep for years, and can be roasted when required.

ΔΔΔΔΔΔΔΔΔΔΔΔΔΔΔΔΔΔΔΔΔΔΔΔΔΔΔΔΔΔΔΔΔΔΔΔΔΔΔΔΔΔΔΔΔΔΔΔΔΔΔΔΔΔΔΔΔΔΔΔΔ

Further Reading:

Susanna Moodie, *Roughing It in the Bush*
Margaret Atwood, *The Journals of Susanna Moodie* (poems)
Catharine Parr Traill, *The Backwoods of Canada*
Samuel Strickland, *Twenty-Seven Years in Canada West*
Marilyn Walker, *Harvesting the Northern Wild*

Structure:

1. In which paragraphs of this selection does Susanna Moodie rely most fully on *narration* to develop her *process analysis*?
2. Point out three passages where Moodie develops her subject of dandelion coffee through *comparison and contrast* with "common coffee."
3. Explain how *cause and effect* helps to develop paragraph 6.

Style:

1. How FORMAL is the style of this selection, especially in vocabulary, sentence length, and paragraph length? Give examples. How much less formal are this anthology's most recent selections than its pieces by earlier writers such as Roderick Haig-Brown, Thierry Mallet, Catharine Parr Traill, and Captain Thomas James? Is this change in level of formality in any way an improvement? Defend your answer with reasons.
2. Point out at least three SENSE IMAGES that help to bring alive Moodie's PROSE.

Ideas for Discussion and Writing:

1. Is Moodie's *process analysis* meant as directions? Is her recipe clear and exact enough for you to follow it?
2. Though from a background of privilege and luxury in England, Susanna Moodie soon learned the prime survival tactic of the North American pioneer: innovation. Have we lost this ability? Or is it still part of life in the 1990s?
3. With your present skills and knowledge, could you have made it as a pioneer in Upper Canada of the 1830s? Give a verbal process analysis of one act you could perform to help assure your survival.
4. In paragraph 2 Dr. Harrison praises dandelion coffee for putting us to sleep instead of "exciting wakefulness." Why do so many of us in the 1990s "excite wakefulness" with coffee, tea, or caffeinated soft drinks? Name at least three alternative, drug-free ways of staying alert.
5. PROCESS IN WRITING: *Write a process analysis of an act you perform to avoid depending on a commercial product or service, as Moodie avoided depending on commercial coffee. First take some notes, then use the best of them in your rough draft, double-spaced. Now in the spaces and margins add enough detail for your reader to successfully follow the directions. Have you specified measurements of time or size or quantity?*

Have you defined terms your reader may not know? Have you used time signals to highlight the progression of steps? Now share your directions with a small group of classmates, then revise any step they did not grasp. Finally, test your prose aloud before writing the finished version.

Note: See also the Topics for Writing at the end of this chapter.

Dian Cohen

The Commodities Game*

Dian Cohen represents the new invasion by women of an area traditionally dominated by men — economics. President of Cohen Couture Associates, financial editor of CTV News and frequent guest on Canada AM, member of the executive committee of the Economic Council of Canada, columnist for Maclean's magazine, and twice winner of the National Business Writing Award, Cohen is noted for commentary that goes right to the point. As business author Lyman MacInnis put it, "Dian Cohen is one of those rare individuals — an economist who speaks and writes in understandable language." These qualities are clearly demonstrated in our selection, which comes from her 1987 book on personal money management entitled, appropriately enough, Money.

> If you bet on a horse, that's gambling. If you bet you can make Three Spades, that's entertainment. If you bet cotton will go up three points, that's business. See the difference?
>
> — Blackie Sherrode

1   If gold is the bedrock of financial security, then commodities, with their promises of huge trading profits, are the will-o'-the-wisps dancing seductively above it. Yes, it is possible to lose money in gold, if you really work at it, and it is also possible to make a bundle in commodities trading. But over the long term, gold is literally safer than money in the bank, whereas in the commodities game, 85% of the players are losers, while only 15% are winners — about the same odds as horse-racing or gambling. This fact doesn't have to keep you out of commodities. But you have to remember that commodity trading is a technique — a tool — to help you reach your financial goals.

2   Commodities are basic goods produced by primary producers. They are the raw materials consumed by secondary producers such as

---

*Editor's title.

manufacturers. The most common examples of commodities include precious metals, like gold, silver, and platinum; other metals such as copper and nickel, produced by mine owners; agricultural goods such as wheat, corn, oats, soybeans, pork bellies (from which bacon is made), produced by farmers; and materials such as lumber and plywood, produced by sawmills.

There are three principal players involved in commodities markets: the producer, the consumer, and the commodities investor, or speculator. The attraction of commodities trading is the tremendous leverage that is possible. You don't put very much money down — 5% to 10% of the purchase price is average. In addition, there is no interest charged on the balance as there is with stock margins. With this kind of leverage, a very small change in the price of the commodity has a great effect on your profit or loss.   3

If you purchased $10,000 worth of a stock from your broker, and put up the full $10,000, then a $1,000 move in the value of that stock would increase or decrease your investment by 10%. If you margined the stock at 50%, and thus put up only $5,000, then the $1,000 gain or loss would be 20%. That's leverage. But if you put up only $500 for a $10,000 purchase, as with the commodities market, then a $1,000 move up would show a 200% gain, while a movement downward would lose you *double* your money. That's really leverage!   4

You don't actually buy the commodities, and though you have the right, you are not obligated to take delivery of them. You are trading *contracts* to buy or sell the commodities in the future. What you are assuming is that at some point in a specific period in the future, the price of the commodity will have changed. If you feel it will be higher then than it is now, you contract to buy; if you feel it will be lower, you contract to sell.   5

How do you contract to sell something you don't own? When you make the contract, you are not required to deliver until the future date specified. That gives you plenty of time to get the commodity. In practice, you will never have to, since your plan is to offset that contract before delivery is required. Offsetting is a procedure by which your contract to deliver a commodity is cancelled. You do this by selling what you have bought, or by buying what you have sold. When you are in a "long" position, that is, you own a contract to *buy* a commodity, you offset this by obtaining another contract to *sell* the same commodity. If you start out by buying someone else's contract to sell it, you are in a "short" position and must buy a contract, to offset your position.   6

There are a number of commodity futures exchanges which operate in a similar manner to stock exchanges. There is the Chicago Board of Trade, which deals chiefly in grains, plywood, broilers (chickens), and   7 silver; the Comex in New York, dealing only in metals; the Chicago Mercantile, which handles eggs, pork bellies, cattle, and lumber; the London Terminal Market, dealing in cocoa and sugar; and the London Metal Exchange for copper and silver. There are several others, including the Winnipeg Commodity Exchange which handles, among other things, canola and gold. These exchanges regulate the contracted amounts so that they are the same for all traders. This eliminates opportunities for big-time speculators to edge out the little guys. It also makes offsetting possible. The exchanges record and report the price during each day of trading. Unlike stocks, commodity futures prices are allowed to move only so far each day. This is to prevent trading activity from causing massive price moves. Once the price of a commodity future has moved to its permissible daily limit, no trading can take place outside that limit. It can still take place within the limit, however, and the next day it can move to a new limit. This regulates the futures market, but if spot prices — that is, the price at which the commodity is being bought and sold in the present — are extremely volatile, you may not be able to buy or sell your futures contract until the limited price movements catch up to the spot prices.

8   Consumers and producers of commodities are also active traders. Chocolate manufacturers, for example, trade in cocoa bean futures as a hedge against changes in the world price of cocoa, though they seldom take delivery. Nor are they as much interested in making money on the trade as they are in maintaining a uniform price for cocoa beans for manufacturing purposes. Thus, if world prices go up, and they hold a futures contract at a lower price, they can sell that contract, take their profit, and apply it to their operations back at the plant.

9   Producers hedge as well. The cocoa bean producer might be unsure of what his beans will bring on the market a year from now, and he would like to be assured of a reasonable price. So, he sells a contract at a price that will provide him with a profit, and insures him against a drop in world prices. Then he watches the market carefully, and hedges where he can.

10   How do you compete against these insiders? They may know chocolate, but like you, they don't know which way the price is going. All any of you can do is make an informed guess. Say a manufacturer calculates that to make his profit six months from now he needs to be able to buy cocoa at that time for 30 cents a pound. He will buy a contract to take delivery at that price on a specific date.

11   But the effect of that transaction is to establish the two sides of an argument. The buyer says that in six months time cocoa will be worth 30 cents a pound or higher. The seller says it will be worth 30 cents or lower. It will certainly be one or the other, and that's where the speculator enters

the picture. He backs one or the other by placing what is, in effect, a side bet with another speculator.

Some people feel that since they do not produce anything, speculators [12] must make their money on the misfortunes of those who do produce. Others feel that speculators are essential to trading, since they will often take risks that others won't. Suppose a farmer wants to sell his eggs for future delivery, and needs to make 40 cents a dozen to cover his costs and make a profit. He may find that none of the users around will pay him more than 35 cents. He would be losing money, and obviously wouldn't sell. Enter the speculator. He is betting that sooner or later a user will have to give in to the farmer's required price. He buys the eggs now at the 40-cent price, in the hope that when the users give in, the price will be 40 cents or higher. In that way, speculators serve a useful function in the market place.

Another theory says that speculators tend to drive prices up or down [13] out of all proportion to reality. For example, in the above case, the speculators may drive the price up to 50 cents. The farmer will see that the speculators are way off base, and rush in to sell, thereby getting more than he could otherwise expect. Other farmers will see what is happening and rush in too. This action will tend to drive prices down. Of course, the ideal theory holds that if all buyers and sellers are fully knowledgeable, the market will always find its proper level. But since people are never fully knowledgeable, especially about the future, the market sometimes does get out of whack with reality. Therein lies the challenge of commodity trading.

So, how does an amateur who knows little or nothing about a [14] particular industry get involved in commodities trading? Very carefully.

In order to trade successfully in the commodities market, you must [15] know when the price of a commodity is going to move up or down, and that's not easy. The best available knowledge about a commodity and its market is essential. Your broker might help. Watching what other traders are doing will give some indications as well. For example, if the further you look into the future, the progressively lower the price of a commodity gets, then the market, strangely enough, is tending to rise. Conversely, if the furthest futures price is progressively higher than the closest price, the market is tending to fall. These indicators are more clearly seen when a market is about to change from being a discounted (lower future price) to a premium (higher future price) market.

Qualifying as a bona fide trader depends on the amount of money you [16] have, and the tolerance threshold of your broker. Most houses won't touch you unless you have a net worth of $50,000 or more. But you can find brokers who will make transactions for you, even if you don't have more than $2,000 to trade. The best rule of thumb to follow is *never* put up more than you can afford to lose.

17   The cost of the commodity you wish to trade depends on the commodity, and on the exchange's policy that is in effect at that time. A contract for 5,000 bushels of wheat, or 40,000 pounds of cattle, costs about $1,500. A contract for 25,000 pounds of copper costs $1,300. The amount of money you stand to make also depends on the contract. A two-cent-per-bushel move upward in wheat will make you $100 — more than enough to cover the $65 commission. A one-cent-a-pound rise in copper amounts to $250, again more than enough to cover the $80 commission.

18   Like all highly-leveraged transactions, commodity trading is risky for speculators. But that's also why there are generous rewards. Commodities should be avoided unless the rest of your investment portfolio is in good shape, and you are prepared to lose everything you put into commodities. It is purely and simply highly-leveraged risk taking.

ΔΔΔΔΔΔΔΔΔΔΔΔΔΔΔΔΔΔΔΔΔΔΔΔΔΔΔΔΔΔΔΔΔΔΔΔΔΔΔΔΔΔΔΔΔΔΔΔΔΔΔΔΔΔΔΔΔΔΔΔΔΔΔΔΔ

Further Reading:

Dian Cohen, *Money*
Dian Cohen and Kristin Shannon, *The Next Canadian Economy*

Structure:

1. Dian Cohen prefaces her selection with an epigraph. Does it catch the reader's attention? Does it lead clearly to Cohen's subject?
2. Point out all the *comparisons and contrasts* through which Cohen introduces her subject in paragraph 1.
3. Cohen's *process analysis* is both informational and directional. Identify places where she gives background information to fill in the context. Identify other places where she instructs her audience how to play "the commodities game." How much sense would the specific directions make without the accompanying background?
4. Cohen's paragraphs are unusually direct in their organization, and are long enough to develop their point. Identify at least five paragraphs that open with a clearly identifiable topic sentence, and that go on to develop clearly the idea in that sentence.
5. Why is paragraph 14 so much shorter than all the others?

Style:

1. This selection first appeared in Cohen's book *Money*, an introduction to personal finance and investment. Describe her tactics for presenting a highly specialized subject to a general audience. For example, how does she resolve the problem of technical terms?

2. Identify all the FIGURES OF SPEECH that introduce Cohen's subject in paragraph 1.

Ideas for Discussion and Writing:

1. How clear and complete are Cohen's directions? If you had the money, could you begin the process today?

2. Does this selection entice you to play "the commodities game" or does it warn you away? Point out two or three passages that helped you decide.

3. In paragraph 12 Cohen writes, "Some people feel that since they do not produce anything, speculators must make their money on the misfortunes of those who do produce. Others feel that speculators are essential to trading, since they will often take risks that others won't." What is your view? Do commodities speculators help or hurt others? Defend your answer with examples from our selection.

4. Canadians are often portrayed as conservative money-under-the-mattress savers instead of aggressive speculators. Is this portrait a STEREOTYPE or is it the truth? Defend your answer with examples of people you know.

5. To some people "profit" is an obscene word, while to others it is the foundation of our whole way of life. Examine the profit motive: name three ways in which it is helping our society; name three other ways in which it is hurting our society.

6. PROCESS IN WRITING: *Today many people speculate in real estate, especially around large cities like Toronto and Vancouver. How is it done? Explain one approach, in an* informational, directional, *or* combined *process analysis. First consult a real estate agent or someone you know who has profited from real estate. Focus, then write a brief outline to establish the order of your process. Now do the first draft, double-spaced. Perhaps the act of writing has uncovered steps you had forgotten; add them. In your next draft make sure to define technical words your audience may not know, and add any missing TRANSITIONS between steps. Does a point lack a good example? Add it. Is a passage*

off-topic or a phrase or word unnecessary? Cross it out. Finally, test your prose aloud before writing the good copy.

Note: See also the Topics for Writing at the end of this chapter.

Captain Thomas James

Our Mansion House*

In May of 1631 Captain Thomas James (1593–1635) sailed with his crew from Bristol, England, in search of the fabled Northwest Passage. Such a route would speed merchant sailors to the Orient, to make their fortunes in trade without the danger and expense of sailing around Cape Horn. James never found the passage, for it did not exist. But in the process of looking, he explored and mapped the west coast of Hudson Bay. He and his crew also beached their ship, built shelter, and spent a harrowing winter encamped on Charlton Island, at the south end of the sea which was later named for him: James Bay. After a desperate struggle against pack ice, the men escaped Hudson Bay the next summer and arrived home in October, their ship "broken and bruis'd." King Charles I welcomed the captain of this failed but heroic expedition and commanded him to write his story. Our selection comes from The Dangerous Voyage of Capt. Thomas James, in His Intended Discovery of a North West Passage into the South Sea, *published in 1633 (our text follows the spelling, capitalization, and punctuation of the revised 1740 edition). In this passage James tells how he and his men built the shelter that saved their lives.*

When I first resolv'd to build a House, I chose the warmest and convenientest Place, and the nearest the Ship withal. It was among a Tuft of thick Trees, under a South Bank, about a slight Shot from the Sea Side. True it is, that at that Time we could not dig into the Ground, to make us a Hole, or Cave, in the Earth, which had been the best Way, because we found Water digging within two Foot; and therefore that Project fail'd. It was a white light Sand; so that we could, by no Means, make up a Mud-Wall. As for Stones, there were none near us; moreover, we were all now cover'd with the Snow. We had no Boards for such a Purpose; and therefore we must do the best we could, with such Materials as we had about us. 1

The House was square, about 20 Foot every Way; as much namely, as 2

---

*Editor's title.

our Main Course° could well cover: First, we drove strong Stakes into the earth, round about: which we wattel'd° with Boughs, as thick as might be, beating them down very close. This our first Work was six Foot high on both Sides, but at the Ends, almost up to the very Top. There we left two Holes, for the Light to come in at; and the same Way the Smoke did vent out also. Moreover, I caus'd at both Ends, three Rows of thick Bush Trees, to be stuck up, as close together as possible. Then at a Distance from the House, we cut down Trees; proportioning them into Lengths of 6 Foot, with which we made a Pile on both Sides, 6 Foot thick, and 6 Foot high; but at both Ends, 10 Foot high, and 6 Foot thick. We left a little low Door to creep into, and a Portal before that, made with Piles of Wood, that the Wind might not blow into it. We next fasten'd a rough Tree aloft over all: Upon which we laid our Rafters; and our Main Course over them again, which lying thwartways over all, reach'd down to the very Ground, on either Side. And this was the Fabrick of the Outside of it. On the Inside, we made fast our Bonnet Sails° round about. Then we drove in Stakes, and made us Bedstead Frames; about 3 Sides of the House, which Bedsteads were double, one under another, the lowermost being a Foot from the Ground: These, we first fill'd with Boughs, then we laid our spare Sails on that, and then our Bedding and Cloaths. We made a Hearth, in the Middle of the House, and on it made our Fire: Some Boards we laid round about our Hearth, to stand upon, that the cold Damp should not strike up into us. With our Waste Cloaths, we made us Canopies and Curtains; others did the like with our small Sails. Our second House was not past 20 Foot distant from this, and made for the Wattling much after the same Manner, but it was less,° and cover'd with our Fore-Course°: It had no Piles on the South Side; but in Lieu of that, we pil'd up all our Chests, on the Inside: And indeed the Reflex of the Heat of the Fire against them, did make it warmer than the Mansion House. In this House, we dress'd our Victuals; and the subordinate Crew did refresh themselves all Day in it. A third House, which was our Storehouse, about 29 Paces off from this; for fear of firing. This House was only a rough Tree fasten'd aloft, with Rafters laid from it to the Ground, and cover'd over with our new Suit of Sails. On the Inside, we had laid small Trees, and cover'd them over with Boughs; and so stored up our Bread, and Fish in it,

---

°Main Course: a large sail, the lowest on a square-rigged mast.

°wattel'd (wattled) with Boughs: Wattling is the process of weaving small branches or twigs into a framework of larger ones to produce a wall, roof, or fence.

°Bonnet Sails: a bonnet sail is an additional strip of canvas laced to the bottom of a foresail or jib.

°less: smaller.

°Fore-Course: on a square-rigged ship, the bottom sail of the mast nearest the bow.

about 2 Foot from the Ground, the better to preserve them. Other Things lay more carelessly.

Long before *Christmas*, our Mansion House was cover'd thick over with Snow, almost to the very Roof of it. And so likewise was our second House; but our Storehouse all over; by Reason we made no Fire in it. Thus we seem'd to live in a Heap, and Wilderness of Snow; forth of our Doors we could not go, but upon the Snow; in which we made us Paths middle deep in some Places; and in one special Place, the Length of ten Steps. To do this, we must shovel away the Snow first; and then by treading, make it something hard under Foot: The Snow in this Path, was a full Yard thick under us. And this was our best Gallery for the sick Men; and for mine own ordinary Walking. And both Houses and Walks, we daily accommodated more and more, and made fitter for our Uses.

3

∆∆

Further Reading:

Captain Thomas James, *The Dangerous Voyage of Capt. Thomas James. . . .*

H. P. Biggar, ed., *The Voyages of Jacques Cartier*

Joe Armstrong, *Champlain*

Structure:

1. In his *process analysis*, how closely does Captain James seem to follow the chronological order in which his "Mansion House" of Charlton Island would have been built?
2. Point out at least ten time signals (such as "next" or "then") which direct and speed the process analysis.
3. Do you think James left any important steps out of his process analysis? Did he leave any minor steps out?
4. Do you think the short accounts of building the second and third shelters contribute to this process analysis, or do they merely dilute the focus?

Style:

1. It is obvious that our language has changed since the time of Captain James. How do you react to the aspects of his STYLE listed below? Which aspects seem weaker than their replacements in contemporary English? Which seem stronger?
   A. Very long sentences joined with many commas, semicolons, and colons
   B. Much more extensive capitalization, almost always of nouns

    C. Variant spellings

    D. Shortened suffixes (as in "resolv'd," of sentence 1)

    E. Very long paragraphs

    F. A preference for short words (Hold the text at arm's length to judge the "look" of the page. Now do the same with five or ten pages from more recent selections in this book, and compare the proportion of short and long words.)

2.   Question 1 discusses some differences between our contemporary language and that of Captain James. Has our language changed radically? To what extent has it changed compared to changes in the following areas of life?

> **Transportation**
> **Physics**
> **Medicine**
> **Business**
> **Communications**

3.   Captain James dedicated his book to King Charles I, saying "Your Majesty will please to consider, That they were rough Elements, which I had to do withal; and will vouchsafe to pardon, if a Seaman's Stile be like what he most converseth with." Do you view James' STYLE as carefully worded and crafted? Or is it "like what he most converseth with"? Is James merely pretending humility or is he genuinely apologizing? And is a speech-like style necessarily bad?

Ideas for Discussion and Writing:

1.   How easy or difficult do you think it would be to follow James' directions? Explain.

2.   According to the rest of James' book, several of the crew died of scurvy, of drowning, of other accidents, or of weakness caused by the intense cold of winter on what was later called James Bay. And many times they all narrowly escaped death in the water, as rocks, pack ice, and even icebergs ground against their wooden ship. Do you think the planners of this expedition were wrong? Did the possible gains justify the cost in human misery and life?

3.   If you have read "The One Perfect House," compare the shelters of Thomas James and his crew with those of "the People" described by Farley Mowat.

4.   PROCESS IN WRITING: *Focus on something that you have made (for example a radio, a garment, a painting or sculpture, or a piece of furniture). Decide whether to just tell how you made it, or to give your*

reader actual directions. Now take a page of notes, then write a process analysis, *in chronological order. If these are directions, scrutinize them to see if they are clear and complete, then revise accordingly. Have you used terms your reader may not know? Have you supplied enough time signals to move the process along? Have you written in full sentences instead of in abbreviated recipe language? Have you read aloud to detect and revise wordiness and repetition? Finally, if a diagram will help, include it in your final copy.*

Note: See also the Topics for Writing at the end of this chapter.

Topics for Writing

CHAPTER 8: PROCESS ANALYSIS

Tell your reader how to perform one of these processes. (See also the guidelines that follow.)

1. How to avoid debt
2. How to survive driving in city traffic
3. How to windsurf
4. How the average person can help to reduce pollution
5. How to choose your style in clothing
6. How to avoid burnout in a high-pressure job
7. How to take a good picture
8. How a woman breaks into a male-dominated profession
9. How to find low-cost entertainment in the city
10. How to train a dog (or other pet)
11. How to get a raise from your employer
12. How to avoid criminal attack in the big city at night
13. How to decorate a room on a low budget
14. How to become a Canadian citizen
15. How to survive eating at the school cafeteria

Explain how one of these processes is performed, or how it occurs. (See also the guidelines that follow.)

16. How a piano works
17. How a fax machine works
18. How a television set works
19. How a transistor works
20. How paper is recycled
21. How the human circulatory system functions
22. How the human liver functions
23. How food is metabolized in the body
24. How a muscle functions
25. How animals hibernate
26. How a bird flies
27. How a plant synthesizes food
28. How hail is formed
29. How sedimentary rock is formed
30. How _____ *(If you choose your own topic in this final item, check it with your teacher before proceeding.)*

Note also the Process in Writing topic after each selection in this chapter.

Process in Writing: Guidelines

Follow at least some of these steps in writing your essay of process analysis (your teacher may suggest which ones).

1. *Choose the topic that most appeals to you, so your motivation will increase your performance.*

2. *Visualize your audience (see step 6 below), and choose the level of terminology accordingly.*

3. *Fill a page with brief notes. Scan and sort them to choose the steps of your process analysis, and their order.*

4. *Write a rapid first draft, double-spaced, not stopping now to revise or edit. If you do notice a word that needs replacing or a passage that needs work, underline it so you can find and fix it later.*

5. *A. When this draft has "cooled off," look it over. If you are giving actual directions (topics 1–15), are all steps there? Do TRANSITIONS introduce them? Have you defined any technical terms that may puzzle your audience? Revise accordingly.*

   B. In explaining how your process is carried out or occurs (topics 16–30), have you provided enough examples and IMAGES to interest your audience? Revise accordingly.

6. *Share the second draft with a small group of classmates. Do they think they could actually follow these directions? Or do they show interest in a process performed by others? Revise accordingly.*

7. *If you have consulted books or periodicals to write this paper, follow standard practice in quoting and in documenting your sources.*

8. *Now edit for spelling and grammar. Write the good copy and proofread word by word. If you have used a computer, save the essay on disk in case your teacher suggests further revisions.*

Roberts/Miller Comstock Inc.

*To think about thermonuclear war in the abstract is obscene. To think about any
kind of warfare with less than the whole of our mind and imagination is obscene.
This is the worst treason.*

— Kildare Dobbs, "The Scar"

Argumentation and Persuasion

Therefore. . . .

So far the essays in this book have taken many paths in developing their subject. They have narrated events, they have described, they have explained, and some have entertained. But you have surely realized that in one way or another, whatever else they do, almost all the selections have tried to make a point. After all, an essay without a point is "pointless." The very use of a thesis statement implies a main idea or opinion. In this final chapter, we now focus more closely on how the writer makes that point. The process takes two complementary forms: *argumentation* and *persuasion*.

ARGUMENTATION

This word has a broad set of meanings, but here we will consider it the writer's attempt to convince the reader *through logic*. This stance implies respect: it considers the reader a mature individual capable of independent thought. It assumes the reader will also respect the thoughts of the writer, if those thoughts are presented in a logical way. In summary, the writer and reader are *partners*: since the writer does not play on the reader's emotions, the reader considers the argument with a more open mind. If the logic makes sense, the reader may be convinced. Argumentation through logic takes two opposite forms, *deduction* and *induction*. Let's look at each.

Deduction

Deduction accepts a general principle as true, then applies it to specific cases. For over two thousand years logicians have expressed this process in a formula called the *syllogism*. Here's a well-known example:

> **Major premise: All men are mortal.**
> **Minor premise: Socrates is a man.**
> **Conclusion: Socrates is mortal.**

This chain of reasoning is about as foolproof as any: since no human in the history of the world has yet lived much longer than a century, we feel safe in assuming that no one ever will; therefore "all men are mortal." And since all historical records about Socrates portray him as a man — not, say, as a rock or horse or tree — we accept the minor premise as well. Logic tells us that if both the major and minor premises are true, then the conclusion will inevitably be true as well.

But now let's look at a syllogism whose logic is not as clear:

> **Major premise: Progress is good.**
> **Minor premise: The automobile represents progress.**
> **Conclusion: The automobile is good.**

At first glance the argument may seem all right: it certainly reflects values common in our society. But let's examine the major premise, the foundation on which all the rest is built: is it true that "progress is good"? Well, how do we know until we define "progress"? Is it more jobs? More production? More cars? Higher sales? More consumption? A rising stock market? Or are all these the opposite of "progress" because our natural resources are dwindling, our highways are choked with traffic, our lakes and forests are dying of acid rain, the greenhouse effect is already disrupting our climate, and around the world two species of life per hour are becoming extinct? Our values will determine our response.

If we cannot agree on what "progress" is, how can we say that it is "good"? And how could we go on to our minor premise, saying that "the automobile represents progress"? How could we build even further on this shaky foundation, claiming in our conclusion that "the automobile is good"? Within its own framework the argument may be "valid" (or logical). But only those who accept the original premise will view the conclusion as true. Those who do not will reject it as false.

And that is the problem with deduction: not always can we agree on premises. Five hundred years ago society ran on deduction: the King or the Church or our parents told us what to believe, and we simply applied those principles to any case that came up. But in the 20th century many of us dislike being told what to think. Not only do many people now question systems of belief such as Marxism or codes of religion, but scientists even question the previously accepted "laws" of nature. How is a person to know what is true? It is therefore no coincidence that most contemporary essays argue not through deduction but through induction.

Induction

We have discussed how deduction applies a general rule to explain particular cases. Induction is the opposite: it first observes particular cases, then from them formulates a general rule. This is the basis of the scientific way, the procedure that enables humans to conquer disease, multiply food production, and travel to the moon. It can produce faulty results, just like deduction, but the open mind required to use it appeals to our modern sensibilities. Let's take an example.

> After a summer in the factory Joan thought she could afford a car, so the week before school began she bought a sporty red three-year-old Japanese model. Speeding around town with the stereo turned up was so much fun that she didn't mind the $500-a-month payments. But when the insurance company hit her for $2500 as a new driver, her savings took a dive. Each month she found herself paying $100 for gas and $150 for parking. A fall tuneup set her back $200, and new tires $400. Then came the repairs: $250 for brakes, $350 for a clutch, and $225 for an exhaust system. In desperation Joan took a part-time job selling shoes. That helped her bankbook but took her study time. Two weeks after exams, holding a sickly grade report in her hand, Joan decided to sell the car. Nobody could have told her to, since, like most people, she likes to make up her own mind. But the long string of evidence did the teaching: now Joan knows, through *induction*, that as a student she cannot afford a car.

Induction is not infallible. Conceivably Joan's next car might never need a repair. Next year insurance might somehow drop from $2500 to, say, $75. Gas stations might sell premium for 10¢ a litre, and on Boxing Day a good tire might cost $1.99. Anything is possible. But Joan feels that the consistency of her results — the steady high cost of her car ownership — will *probably* not change. Likewise, the scientist believes that her or his years of research have yielded results that will not be disproven by the very next experiment. But in all humility both writer and scientist must consider the new principle not a fact, not an unchangeable law, but simply an idea with a very high probability of being true.

Finally, suppose that Joan analyzes her experience in an essay. If she sets up her paper as most essayists do, we will read her thesis statement near the beginning — even though the principle it states is the *result* of the evidence to come next. This tactic is not a flaw of logic: Joan simply *introduces* the main idea so we can see where we are going, then tells us how she arrived at it, letting her evidence lead inductively toward the main point which will be restated at the end. You will find this pattern at work in several of this chapter's inductive essays, for example the one by Margaret Atwood.

You will also find that, although deduction and induction represent opposite methods of logic, sometimes both are used in the same argument — as in the essay by Wendy Dennis. This does not necessarily mean weakness in logic either. Another link between these opposites is that most principles which we accept as true, and upon which we base our own deductions, originated in someone else's induction. (Newton arrived inductively at his theory of gravity, through evidence such as the famous apple that fell on his head; almost all of us now believe Newton and his theory without waiting for an apple, or anything else, to fall on our own heads.) Similarly, a conclusion we derive from our own induction could become the premise of someone else's deduction — a link in an ongoing chain of logic. To keep this chain from breaking, the individual has a double task: to check over any links provided by others, then to make his or her own link as strong as possible.

PERSUASION

We have just seen how *argumentation* seeks to convince through logic. But, whether deductive or inductive, is logic enough? Now let's look at the complementary approach of persuasion, which attempts to convince through emotion. A century of inductive research into psychology has shown that we humans are seldom rational. Even when we think we are "reasoning," we are often building arguments merely to justify what we thought or felt already. It is possible to write an argumentative essay with enough restraint to be almost purely logical. But to most people the effort is difficult and unnatural, requiring a great deal of revision, and the result may seem cold and uninviting to those who have not spent years reading the pure argumentation of scholarly journals. Most professional writers would say that a little feeling and a little colour can help an essay. But how do we take this approach without slipping into dishonesty? Let's look now at the major techniques of *persuasion* — both their uses and abuses.

Word choice: Is a person "slim," "thin," or "skinny"? Is a governmental expenditure an "investment," a "cost," a "waste," or a "boondoggle"? Is an oil spill an "incident," an "accident," a "mistake," a "crime," or an "environmental tragedy"? Essayists tend to choose the term that reflects their feeling and the feeling they hope to encourage in the readers. While deliberate choice of words is one of the central tasks of all writers, including essayists, let's not abuse the process. Bertrand Russell once quipped, "I am firm; you are stubborn; he is pig-headed." If too many of your word choices follow the model of "pig-headed," you will alarm an alert reader and unfairly overwhelm a careless one.

Example: Although examples form the basis of logical induction, they can also add colour and feeling to a persuasive essay. Choose vivid ones. An attempt to show old people as active may be helped by the example of your grandmother who skis. But avoid dubious cases like that of the man in Azerbaijan who is said to have ridden a horse at age 155.

Repetition: Although we try to cut accidental repetition from our writing (as in the case of one student who used the word "tire" 55 times in an essay about, you guessed it, tires), intentional repetition can build feeling. Stephen Leacock builds emphasis by using the word "eat" over and over in paragraph 25 of his essay (see p. 233) and in paragraphs 14–17 of her selection (see p. 316) Joy Kogawa builds feeling by starting a whole string of sentences with the contraction "it's."

Hyperbole (exaggeration): If your essay is objective in tone, stay strictly with the truth. For example, in her factual investigation of child abuse, Michele Landsberg writes that Brazil has 30 million street children; if she had stretched that figure to 50 million, we would perceive it as a lie. But when in his satirical essay Charles Gordon describes an Ottawa High school as having 15,000 students, we "feel" his exaggeration as an ironic jab at the rulers of his "Cutback World."

Analogy and figures of speech: You have seen in Chapter 6 how we can suggest a point by comparing one thing with another from a different category: prose with music, clothing with housing, or a house with a ship at sea. Analogies, and their shorter cousins similes and metaphors, are powerful tools of persuasion; avoid abusing them through name-calling. Think twice before casting a political party as a dinosaur, entrepreneurs as piranhas, or police officers as gorillas. Remember, above all, that neither analogies nor figures of speech are logical proof of anything.

Irony: When in Chapter 4 Franklin Russell shows the capelin's multitude of population as the reason for its population crash, when in Chapter 8 Judy Stoffman shows us the once-young athlete dying of old age, and when in this chapter Pierre Berton shows us the gold he had so painfully extracted from the earth being returned underground at Fort Knox, we feel the power of irony. A writer can use this device for a lifetime without exhausting its emotional power; yet irony lends itself less easily to abuses than do many tools of persuasion, for both its use and its appreciation demand a certain exercise of intelligence.

Appeal to authority or prestige: Campaigners against nuclear weapons love to quote Albert Einstein on their dangers; after all, since his discoveries made this hardware possible, he should know. We also invite our reader to believe what a famous economist says about money, what a judge says about law, or what an educator says about education. This approach appeals to our reader's ethical sense: he or she believes these people know the facts and tell the truth. But avoid the common abuse of quoting people on matters outside their competence — Wayne Gretzky on baseball, Hulk Hogan on communism, a disgraced politician on honesty, or a convicted murderer on religion.

Fright: You can be sure that a frightened reader is an interested reader, for fright is personal: what you say in your essay could be important! Avoid cheap effects, though. Frighten a reader only with facts that really are scary (such as the number of times computer error has nearly launched a Third World War).

Climax: Whatever your argument, don't trail off from strong to weak. After a good introduction, drop to your least important or least dramatic point, then progress upward to your strongest. This very rise produces an emotion in the reader, like that of the concertgoer who thrills to the final chords of the "Hallelujah Chorus."

PLAYING FAIR IN ARGUMENTATION AND PERSUASION

We have looked at some abuses both of argumentation and of persuasion. Now read the following communication, an actual chain letter that arrived one day in the mail. What attempts does it make at *deduction* or *induction*? Are they logical? What attempts does it make at *persuasion*? Are they fair? (For your information, the person who received this letter did not send it on. So far he has not died or lost his job — but then, neither has he won a lottery!)

KISS SOMEONE YOU LOVE WHEN YOU GET THIS LETTER AND
MAKE SOME MAGIC

This paper has been sent to you for good luck. The original copy is in New England. It has been around the world nine times. The luck has sent it to you. You will receive good luck within four days of receiving this letter, provided you send it back out. THIS IS NO JOKE. You will receive it in the mail. Send copies to people that you think need good luck. Don't send money as fate has no price. Do not keep this letter. It must leave your hands within 96 hours. An R.A.F. officer became a hero. Joe Elliot received $40,000, and lost it because he broke the chain. While in the Philippines, Gene Welch lost his wife six days after receiving this letter. He failed to circulate the letter. However, before her death she had won $50,000.00 in a lottery. The money was transferred to him four days after he decided to mail out this letter. Please send twenty copies of this letter and see what happens in four days. The chain came from Venezuela and was written in South America. Since the copy must make a tour of the world you must make copies and send them to your friends and associates. After a few days you will get a surprise. This is true even if you are not superstitious. Do note the following: Constantine Dias received the chain in 1953. He asked his secretary to type twenty copies and send them out. A few days later he won a lottery of $2,000,000. Aria Daddit, an office employee, received the letter and forgot that it had to leave his hands within 96 hours. He lost his job. Later, finding the letter again, he mailed out twenty copies. A few days later he got a better job. Dalen Fairchild received the letter and not believing, threw it away. Nine days later he died.

PLEASE SEND NO MONEY. PLEASE DON'T IGNORE THIS. IT WORKS!

Note: No essay in this chapter adopts a stance of pure logic to the exclusion of emotion, or of pure emotion to the exclusion of logic. The eight essays represent different proportions of both elements, and are arranged in approximate order from most argumentative to most persuasive.

For more examples of argumentation and persuasion, see these essays in other chapters:

Kildare Dobbs

The Scar*

Kildare Dobbs was born in Meerut, Uttar Pradesh, India in 1923, was educated in Ireland, then during the Second World War spent five years in the Royal Navy. After the war he worked in the British Colonial Service in Tanganyika and, after earning an M.A. at Cambridge, came in 1952 to Canada. Dobbs has been a teacher, editor for Macmillan, managing editor of Saturday Night, *and book editor of the* Toronto Star. *He was one of the founders, in 1956, of the* Tamarack Review. *He is also the author of several books:* Running to Paradise *(essays, 1962, winner of the Governor General's Award);* Canada *(an illustrated travel book, 1964);* Reading the Time *(essays, 1968);* The Great Fur Opera *(a comic history of the Hudson's Bay Company, 1970);* Pride and Fall *(short fiction, 1981);* Historic Canada *(1984); and* Away from Home: An Anthology of Canadian Travel-Writing *(1986). Our selection is from* Reading the Time. *It is about an event that Dobbs did not witness, yet the vivid details with which he supports his argument recreate all too clearly what that event must have been like.*

1   This is the story I was told in 1963 by Emiko Okamoto, a young Japanese woman who had come to live in Toronto. She spoke through an interpreter, since at that time she knew no English. It is Emiko's story, although I have had to complete it from other sources.

2   But why am I telling it? Everyone knows how terrible this story is. Everyone knows the truth of what von Clausewitz said: "Force to meet force arms itself with the inventions of art and science." First the bow-and-arrow, then Greek fire, gunpowder, poison-gas — and so on up the lethal scale. These things, we're told, should be considered calmly. No sweat — we should think about the unthinkable, or so Herman Kahn suggests, dispassionately. And he writes: "We do not expect illustrations in a book of surgery to be captioned 'Good health is preferable to this kind of cancer'. Excessive comments such as 'And now there is a lot of blood' or

---

*Editor's title.

'This particular cut really hurts' are out of place. . . . To dwell on such things is morbid." Perhaps the answer to Herman Kahn is that if surgeons hadn't dwelt on those things we wouldn't now have anaesthetics, or artery forceps either, for that matter.

To think about thermonuclear war in the abstract is obscene. To think 3 about any kind of warfare with less than the whole of our mind and imagination is obscene. This is the worst treason.

Before that morning in 1945 only a few conventional bombs, none of 4 which did any great damage, had fallen on the city. Fleets of U.S. bombers had, however, devastated many cities round about, and Hiroshima had begun a program of evacuation which had reduced its population from 380,000 to some 245,000. Among the evacuees were Emiko and her family.

"We were moved out to Otake, a town about an hour's train-ride out of 5 the city," Emiko told me. She had been a fifteen-year-old student in 1945. Fragile and vivacious, versed in the gentle traditions of the tea ceremony and flower arrangement, Emiko still had an air of the frail school-child when I talked with her. Every day, she and her sister Hideko used to commute into Hiroshima to school. Hideko was thirteen. Their father was an antique-dealer and he owned a house in the city, although it was empty now. Tetsuro, Emiko's thirteen-year-old brother, was at the Manchurian front with the Imperial Army. Her mother was kept busy looking after the children, for her youngest daughter Eiko was sick with heart trouble, and rations were scarce. All of them were undernourished.

The night of August 5, 1945, little Eiko was dangerously ill. She was not 6 expected to live. Everybody took turns watching by her bed, soothing her by massaging her arms and legs. Emiko retired at 8:30 (most Japanese people go to bed early) and at midnight was roused to take her turn with the sick girl. At 2 a.m. she went back to sleep.

While Emiko slept, the *Enola Gay*, a U.S. B-29 carrying the world's first 7 operational atom bomb, was already in the air. She had taken off from the Pacific island of Iwo Jima at 1:45 a.m., and now Captain William Parsons, U.S.N. ordnance expert, was busy in her bomb-hold with the final assembly of Little Boy. Little Boy looked much like an outsize T.N.T. block-buster but the crew knew there was something different about him. Only Parsons and the pilot, Colonel Paul Tibbets, knew exactly in what manner Little Boy was different. Course was set for Hiroshima.

Emiko slept. 8

On board the *Enola Gay* co-pilot Captain Robert Lewis was writing up 9 his personal log. "After leaving Iwo," he recorded, "we began to pick up some low stratus and before very long we were flying on top of an under-cast. Outside of a thin, high cirrus and the low stuff, it's a very beautiful day."

10   Emiko and Hideko were up at six in the morning. They dressed in the uniform of their women's college — white blouse, quilted hat, and black skirt — breakfasted and packed their aluminum lunch-boxes with white rice and eggs. These they stuffed into their shoulder bags as they hurried for the seven-o'clock train to Hiroshima. Today there would be no classes. Along with many women's groups, high school students, and others, the sisters were going to work on demolition. The city had begun a project of clearance to make fire-breaks in its downtown huddle of wood and paper buildings.

11   It was a lovely morning.

12   While the two young girls were at breakfast, Captain Lewis, over the Pacific, had made an entry in his log. "We are loaded. The bomb is now alive, and it's a funny feeling knowing it's right in back of you. Knock wood!"

13   In the train Hideko suddenly said she was hungry. She wanted to eat her lunch. Emiko dissuaded her: she'd be much hungrier later on. The two sisters argued, but Hideko at last agreed to keep her lunch till later. They decided to meet at the main station that afternoon and catch the five-o'clock train home. By now they had arrived at the first of Hiroshima's three stations. This was where Hideko got off, for she was to work in a different area from her sister. "Sayonara!" she called. "Goodbye." Emiko never saw her again.

14   There had been an air-raid at 7 a.m., but before Emiko arrived at Hiroshima's main station, two stops farther on, the sirens had sounded the all-clear. Just after eight, Emiko stepped off the train, walked through the station, and waited in the morning sunshine for her streetcar.

15   At about the same moment Lewis was writing in his log. "There'll be a short intermission while we bomb our target."

16   It was hot in the sun. Emiko saw a class-mate and greeted her. Together they moved back into the shade of a high concrete wall to chat. Emiko looked up at the sky and saw, far up in the cloudless blue, a single B-29.

17   It was exactly 8:10 a.m. The other people waiting for the streetcar saw it too and began to discuss it anxiously. Emiko felt scared. She felt that at all costs she must go on talking to her friend. Just as she was thinking this, there was a tremendous greenish-white flash in the sky. It was far brighter than the sun. Emiko afterwards remembered vaguely that there was a roaring or a rushing sound as well, but she was not sure, for just at that moment she lost consciousness.

18   "About 15 seconds after the flash," noted Lewis, 30,000 feet high and several miles away, "there were two very distinct slaps on the ship from

the blast and the shock wave. That was all the physical effect we felt. We turned the ship so that we could observe the results."

When Emiko came to, she was lying on her face about forty feet away 19 from where she had been standing. She was not aware of any pain. Her first thought was: "I'm alive!" She lifted her head slowly and looked about her. It was growing dark. The air was seething with dust and black smoke. There was a smell of burning. Emiko felt something trickle into her eyes, tasted it in her mouth. Gingerly she put a hand to her head, then looked at it. She saw with a shock that it was covered with blood.

She did not give a thought to Hideko. It did not occur to her that her 20 sister who was in another part of the city could possibly have been in danger. Like most of the survivors, Emiko assumed she had been close to a direct hit by a conventional bomb. She thought it had fallen on the post-office next to the station. With a hurt child's panic, Emiko, streaming with blood from gashes in her scalp, ran blindly in search of her mother and father.

The people standing in front of the station had been burned to death 21 instantly (a shadow had saved Emiko from the flash). The people inside the station had been crushed by falling masonry. Emiko heard their faint cries, saw hands scrabbling weakly from under the collapsed platform. All around her the maimed survivors were running and stumbling away from the roaring furnace that had been a city. She ran with them toward the mountains that ring the landward side of Hiroshima.

From the *Enola Gay*, the strangers from North America looked down at 22 their handiwork. "There, in front of our eyes," wrote Lewis, "was without a doubt the greatest explosion man had ever witnessed. The city was nine-tenths covered with smoke of a boiling nature, which seemed to indicate buildings blowing up, and a large white cloud which in less than three minutes reached 30,000 feet, then went to at least 50,000 feet."

Far below, on the edge of this cauldron of smoke, at a distance of some 23 2,500 yards from the blast's epicentre, Emiko ran with the rest of the living. Some who could not run limped or dragged themselves along. Others were carried. Many, hideously burned, were screaming with pain; when they tripped they lay where they had fallen. There was a man whose face had been ripped open from mouth to ear, another whose forehead was a gaping wound. A young soldier was running with a foot-long splinter of bamboo protruding from one eye. But these, like Emiko, were the lightly wounded.

Some of the burned people had been literally roasted. Skin hung from 24 their flesh like sodden tissue paper. They did not bleed but plasma dripped from their seared limbs.

The *Enola Gay*, mission completed, was returning to base. Lewis sought 25 words to express his feelings, the feelings of all the crew. "I might say," he wrote, "I might say 'My God! What have we done?' "

26   Emiko ran. When she had reached the safety of the mountain she remembered that she still had her shoulder bag. There was a small first-aid kit in it and she applied ointment to her wounds and to a small cut in her left hand. She bandaged her head.

27   Emiko looked back at the city. It was a lake of fire. All around her the burned fugitives cried out in pain. Some were scorched on one side only. Others, naked and flayed, were burned all over. They were too many to help and most of them were dying. Emiko followed the walking wounded along a back road, still delirious, expecting suddenly to meet her father and mother.

28   The thousands dying by the roadside called feebly for help or water. Some of the more lightly injured were already walking in the other direction, back towards the flames. Others, with hardly any visible wounds, stopped, turned ashy pale, and died within minutes. No one knew then that they were victims of radiation.

29   Emiko reached the suburb of Nakayama.

30   Far off in the *Enola Gay*, Lewis, who had seen none of this, had been writing, "If I live a hundred years, I'll never get those few minutes out of my mind. Looking at Captain Parsons, why he is as confounded as the rest, and he is supposed to have known everything and expected this to happen. . . ."

31   At Nakayama, Emiko stood in line at a depot where riceballs were being distributed. Though it distressed her that the badly maimed could hardly feed themselves, the child found she was hungry. It was about 6 p.m. now. A little farther on, at Gion, a farmer called her by name. She did not recognize him, but it seemed he came monthly to her home to collect manure. The farmer took Emiko by the hand, led her to his own house, where his wife bathed her and fed her a meal of white rice. Then the child continued on her way. She passed another town where there were hundreds of injured. The dead were being hauled away in trucks. Among the injured a woman of about forty-five was waving frantically and muttering to herself. Emiko brought this woman a little water in a pumpkin leaf. She felt guilty about it; the schoolgirls had been warned not to give water to the seriously wounded. Emiko comforted herself with the thought that the woman would die soon anyway.

32   At Koi, she found standing-room in a train. It was heading for Otake with a full load of wounded. Many were put off at Ono, where there was a hospital; and two hours later the train rolled into Otake station. It was around 10 p.m.

33   A great crowd had gathered to look for their relations. It was a nightmare, Emiko remembered years afterwards; people were calling

their dear kinfolk by name, searching frantically. It was necessary to call them by name, since most were so disfigured as to be unrecognizable. Doctors in the town council offices stitched Emiko's head-wounds. The place was crowded with casualties lying on the floor. Many died as Emiko watched.

The town council authorities made a strange announcement. They said a new and mysterious kind of bomb had fallen in Hiroshima. People were advised to stay away from the ruins. 34

Home at midnight, Emiko found her parents so happy to see her that they could not even cry. They could only give thanks that she was safe. Then they asked, "Where is your sister?" 35

For ten long days, while Emiko walked daily one and a half miles to have her wounds dressed with fresh gauze, her father searched the rubble of Hiroshima for his lost child. He could not have hoped to find her alive. All, as far as the eye could see, was a desolation of charred ashes and wreckage, relieved only by a few jagged ruins and by the seven estuarial rivers that flowed through the waste delta. The banks of these rivers were covered with the dead and in the rising tidal waters floated thousands of corpses. On one broad street in the Hakushima district the crowds who had been thronging there were all naked and scorched cadavers. Of thousands of others there was no trace at all. A fire several times hotter than the surface of the sun had turned them instantly to vapour. 36

On August 11 came the news that Nagasaki had suffered the same fate as Hiroshima; it was whispered that Japan had attacked the United States mainland with similar mysterious weapons. With the lavish circumstantiality of rumour, it was said that two out of a fleet of six-engined trans-Pacific bombers had failed to return. But on August 15, speaking for the first time over the radio to his people, the Emperor Hirohito announced his country's surrender. Emiko heard him. No more bombs! she thought. No more fear! The family did not learn till June the following year that this very day young Tetsuro had been killed in action in Manchuria. 37

Emiko's wounds healed slowly. In mid-September they had closed with a thin layer of pinkish skin. There had been a shortage of antiseptics and Emiko was happy to be getting well. Her satisfaction was short-lived. Mysteriously she came down with diarrhoea and high fever. The fever continued for a month. Then one day she started to bleed from the gums, her mouth and throat become acutely inflamed, and her hair started to fall out. Through her delirium the child heard the doctors whisper by her pillow that she could not live. By now the doctors must have known that ionizing radiation caused such destruction of the blood's white cells that victims were left with little or no resistance against infection. 38

39   Yet Emiko recovered.

40   The wound on her hand, however, was particularly troublesome and did not heal for a long time.

41   As she got better, Emiko began to acquire some notion of the fearful scale of the disaster. Few of her friends and acquaintances were still alive. But no one knew precisely how many had died in Hiroshima. To this day the claims of various agencies conflict.

42   According to General Douglas MacArthur's headquarters, there were 78,150 dead and 13,083 missing. The United States Atomic Bomb Casualty Commission claims there were 79,000 dead. Both sets of figures are probably far too low. There's reason to believe that at the time of the surrender Japanese authorities lied about the number of survivors, exaggerating it to get extra medical supplies. The Japanese welfare ministry's figures of 260,000 dead and 163,263 missing may well be too high. But the very order of such discrepancies speaks volumes about the scale of the catastrophe. The dead were literally uncountable.

43   This appalling toll of human life had been exacted from a city that had been prepared for air attack in a state of full wartime readiness. All civil-defence services had been overwhelmed from the first moment and it was many hours before any sort of organized rescue and relief could be put into effect.

44   It's true that single raids using so-called conventional weapons on other cities such as Tokyo and Dresden inflicted far greater casualties. And that it could not matter much to a victim whether he was burnt alive by a fire-storm caused by phosphorus, or by napalm or by nuclear fission. Yet in the whole of human history so savage a massacre had never before been inflicted with a single blow. And modern thermonuclear weapons are upwards of 1,000 times more powerful and deadly than the Hiroshima bomb.

45   The white scar I saw on Emiko's small, fine-boned hand was a tiny metaphor, a faint but eloquent reminder of the scar on humanity's conscience.

△△

Further Reading:

Kildare Dobbs, *Reading the Time*
John Hershey, *Hiroshima*
Jonathan Schell, *The Fate of the Earth*
Lesley Choyce, *December Six/The Halifax Solution: An Alternative to Nuclear War*

Structure:

1. Identify Kildare Dobbs' THESIS STATEMENT, the principle from which all the rest of his argument is deduced. In what very direct way does the rest of this selection teach us to apply that principle?
2. "The Scar" is developed mostly through *narrative*, in fact through two parallel narratives. How do the stories of Emiko and of Captain Lewis complement each other? How does each help to explain nuclear war?
3. Dobb's argument is arranged as a short essay split in the middle to accommodate a long narrative. Why? How does his plan work? Identify the places where he moves from each part to the next.

Style:

1. In his log, Captain Lewis writes "it's a very beautiful day" (par. 9), and in paragraph 11 Dobbs writes "It was a lovely morning." What effect do these pleasant words have in the context of the situation? What literary device underlies their power?
2. Captain Lewis writes in his log, "There'll be a short intermission while we bomb our target" (par. 15). Do these words seem peculiar? If so, why?
3. In referring to the first operational nuclear bomb as "Little Boy" (par. 7), what does Dobbs add to the force of his narrative?
4. Paragraphs 23, 24, 27, and 36 are filled with gruesome details that illustrate the effects of "Little Boy." Do these details help or hurt the purpose of the argument? Do they encourage in the reader an opposition to nuclear weapons? Or, in their dreadfulness, do they encourage the reader merely to drop the subject and think of other things?
5. In what sense is the scar on Emiko's hand a METAPHOR, and what qualifies this metaphor to end our selection?

Argumentation and Persuasion:

1. Dobbs' argument is *deductive*, based on his opening premise that "To think about thermonuclear war in the abstract is obscene. To think about any kind of warfare with less than the whole of our mind and imagination is obscene. This is the worst treason" (par. 3). Identify at least five passages where he shuns abstraction to dwell on the CONCRETE, immediate, personal

experience of nuclear war. Has he applied his own thesis by using "the whole of [his] mind and imagination"?

2. Point out at least three passages where Dobbs portrays Captain Lewis' more "abstract" view of nuclear war as "obscene." Does the *contrast* between Lewis' bird's-eye view and Emiko's ground-level view help to develop Dobbs' premise?

3. Does Dobbs make his point mostly through *argumentation* or *persuasion*? To what extent has he argued through objective logic, fact, and example? To what extent has he persuaded through IRONY, loaded words, fright, or other appeals to our emotions?

4. What effect does Dobbs achieve when, at the end, he shifts from specific examples to generalizations and statistics (par. 42–44)?

Ideas for Discussion and Writing:

1. According to the Washington, D.C. research group World Priorities (quoted by Michele Landsberg in the *Globe and Mail*, February 1, 1986), the world spends an average of $162 per person per year on the military; it spends 6¢ per person per year on peacekeeping. What is your response to these figures?

2. It has been estimated that the Soviet Union has enough nuclear warheads to destroy the United States 25 times over, and that the United States has enough nuclear warheads to destroy the Soviet Union 50 times over. What is your response to these figures?

3. Do you think that civilians around the world should be trained in civil defence against a nuclear attack? Would it save lives? Or on the other hand, would it make such an attack more acceptable to military leaders and thus more likely?

4. To what extent do you believe the "Cold War" between East and West has thawed? To what extent has the danger of nuclear war decreased? Will the trend continue? Can you imagine the Soviet Union and the United States becoming allies, as they once were? What can Canada, as a middle power, do to encourage friendship between major powers?

5. PROCESS IN WRITING: *Politicians often state that one letter received from a citizen is worth a thousand votes. Decide whether you think Canada is spending too little or too much on the military. Now write a letter to the Minister of Defence, arguing your point deductively. Apply your premise to a specific example or examples, such as tanks, fighter planes, destroyers, submarines, etc. As you look over your "discovery*

draft," see whether you have specialized in either argumentation *or* persuasion. *If your treatment seems too extreme, modify it in your second draft with a dose of the other approach, to produce a combined treatment like that of Dobbs. In your final draft, edit for conciseness (the best letters to politicians are short). Finally, you need no stamp to mail a letter to any member of parliament.*

Note: See also the Topics for Writing at the end of this chapter.

Michele Landsberg

West Must Confront Anonymous Misery of the World's Children

Michele Landsberg's career as a journalist could be summed up in the words Women & Children First, *the title of her 1978 book. In it she collects some of her best newspaper columns on problems such as rape and domestic violence, but also on the joys of family life such as birth, holiday rituals, graduation, and marriage. This split focus illustrates Landsberg's position as a feminist: while on the one hand she fights to end the inequalities traditionally suffered by women, on the other hand she strongly believes in marriage and family life. Her attempts to bridge the gap between these sometimes opposing values lend an often dramatic power to her essays. Landsberg was born in 1939 in Toronto, and studied at the University of Toronto. Since then she has written for the Toronto* Globe and Mail, Chatelaine, *and the* Toronto Star, *winning National Newspaper Awards for both her columns and feature articles. In 1986 her family interests led her to publish* Michele Landsberg's Guide to Children's Books. *And, living in New York City as wife of Canada's ambassador to the United Nations, Stephen Lewis, Landsberg wrote a series of columns for the Toronto* Globe and Mail *about New York and about international issues at the U.N. One of these is our selection, which appeared November 7, 1987.*

1   International Declarations come in for a lot of derision. Any hostile observer at the United Nations Commission on Human Rights in Geneva, for example, might well snicker as delegates lengthily debate each parenthesis, comma, word, in the draft Convention on the Rights of the Child.

2   The process has gone on for years, and will not come to fruition for several more. Can the verbiage really make that much difference to the millions of the world's children who suffer and die in anonymous misery?

3   Yes. Ten years ago, the mere phrase "children's rights" was, to most people, a joke, a ludicrous extension of the "rights" frenzy of the '70s. Today it has entered our consciousness as a legitimate and forceful claim. The Declaration process itself (now pressing forward more rapidly under

the leadership of Poland and Canada), involving hundreds of volunteer organizations and government officials, has turned many governments' attention, some for the first time, to the agony of their children.

An essential part of social change is the forcing of this attention. What   4
newspaper, a decade ago, wrote about child labor in the Third World? Now, in recent weeks and months, well-researched documents — from the Christian Science Monitor, the Cox Newspaper Service, the International Defence and Aid Fund, the United Nations sub-commission on the prevention of discrimination against minorities — have heaped up on my desk.

They catalogue a horror that has been invisible to most of us.   5

They tell of Gypsy children who are kidnapped or sold from Yugoslavia   6
to criminal gangs in Italy, where they are beaten into performing as thieves and beggars.

Thirteen- and 14-year-old girls work 17-hour days at their sewing   7
machines in Manila sweatshops. The pay: 13 cents an hour.

That's better than the one cent a day earned by 5-year-olds who weed   8
the tea plantations in Sri Lanka.

In the Ashanti Goldfields (jointly owned by the Government of Ghana   9
and a company called Lonrho International), 11-year-old boys labor naked in pools of cyanide to extract gold from rock.

Girls as young as 4 are virtual slaves in Moroccan carpet factories,   10
crouched on their benches for 12-hour days, sleeping on the floor next to their looms at night, breathing air thick with fluff and fibre.

They compete with Indian carpet-makers for the North American   11
market. In New York department stores like Bloomingdale's, the luscious glowing colors of the carpets fetch prices in the thousands. But the small Indian and Moroccan weavers themselves earn a pittance of pennies an hour.

World Health Organization officials are researching the trauma of   12
children as young as 7, in countries like Kenya, who drudge through 15-hour days as household servants. They weep at night, refuse to speak, wet their beds. They mind the babies, scrub dishes, floors and laundry, live like little household animals.

Brazil has 30 million street children; many more are actually sold for   13
forced labor. On rice plantations, children of 6 or 7 are primed with alcohol in the pre-dawn to get ready for work. Their beds are the bare ground, their wages a plate of rice; little girls are used as prostitutes by their overseers. On Brazil's tea plantations, 10,000 children ages 5 to 13 wade through pesticide muck. They get 15 cents for every 52-pound sack of tea they pick and carry.

You'll switch to cocoa? Thousands of Nigerian children are   14
kidnapped — some as young as 5 or 6 — to slave in cocoa plantations.

15   In Mozambique and Angola, 375 of every 1,000 infants die — the highest infant mortality rate in the world — because of devastation caused by South African armed aggression.

16   Thailand has at least 30,000 child prostitutes. In one Bangkok house, owned by a prominent man active in charity, the little girls crawl through a hole in the wall at the sound of the madame's whistle, and sit on benches wearing numbered shirts, to be picked by customers. Their faces, in Cox News photographs, are ravishingly lovely, shatteringly sad.

17   In most of these countries, governments are struggling to overcome the kind of poverty that makes child labor a condition of life. Much of the poverty is caused by debt. Third World countries are economically strangled by the high interest rates on the money they owe to us First Worlders.

18   In some countries, however, it is the government that orchestrates the horror. South African news censorship means that we no longer see the sudden, irrational descent of gun-wielding police from their armored cars to shoot at random as black children scatter, terrified, in the dusty township streets. But volunteer organizations doggedly collect the evidence. They tell us that last year, 59,000 children were detained by South African police.

19   Children as young as 7 and 8 are cross-questioned for hours in court, denied lawyers or visits from parents. They are so small that all we can see of them over the edge of the dock are their troubled, panicky eyes.

20   Fathers tell of finding their broken, tortured children lying on concrete floors of police stations, trembling and speechless and sometimes dying. Children in jail are routinely beaten and whipped; many have been tear-gassed, scarred with boiling water, hosed, electric-shocked, raped, beaten into permanent brain damage or death.

21   Can a United Nations Convention on children's rights make a difference? The people at work in the field say yes. When enough people absorb the idea that all children have fundamental rights, we lucky ones in the West will begin to accept responsibility. We buy the carpets, the cocoa, the rice, the cheap shirts, the pornography, the South African gold. One day we'll buy the idea that we can, through our foreign policy, help the children.

ΔΔΔΔΔΔΔΔΔΔΔΔΔΔΔΔΔΔΔΔΔΔΔΔΔΔΔΔΔΔΔΔΔΔΔΔΔΔΔΔΔΔΔΔΔΔΔΔΔΔΔΔΔΔΔΔΔΔΔΔΔΔ

Further Reading:

Michele Landsberg, *Women & Children First*
Alison Acker, *Children of the Volcano*

Structure:

1. Michele Landsberg opens her argument with a question (in par. 2) and closes it with another question (in par. 21). Both have the same answer. Analyze the effects of these parallels.
2. What proportion of Landsberg's essay is devoted to *examples*? Has she given enough? Too many? Compare her use of examples to that of Ray Guy in "Outport Menu": Do you prefer his use of almost pure example throughout, or her use of generalization at beginning and end to interpret her examples? Why?
3. Explore the parallelism of the words "we buy" in Landsberg's final two sentences: How does it help to engineer her closing?
4. What rhetorical principle has Landsberg used in placing "children" as the very last word of her argument?

Style:

1. Analyze how Landsberg employs IRONY in each of these examples: the wages of carpet makers compared to the price of their carpets (par. 10–11), our use of tea vs. our use of cocoa (par. 13–14), and the case of the man active in charity who owns a house of child prostitution (par. 16).
2. Has Landsberg achieved a good proportion of content to length? Has her great number of examples just led her into wordiness, or have they fostered CONCISENESS? Explain.

Argumentation and Persuasion:

1. In this INDUCTIVE argument Landsberg makes heavy use of evidence: the many examples of exploited children, found in the many documents "heaped up" on her desk (par. 4). To what conclusion or conclusions does all this evidence lead her?
2. Point out the several kinds of statistics Landsberg uses. In what ways and to what extent do they support her argument?
3. Landsberg's massive use of examples, bolstered by statistics, is typical of ARGUMENTATION: her pattern implies a logical, OBJECTIVE stance. But to what extent has she also employed PERSUASION, in using more SUBJECTIVE, emotional appeals? In particular, examine her vocabulary: How frequently do you see emotionally loaded words? Point them out. What is their total effect?

Ideas for Discussion and Writing:

1. Why does Landsberg not include examples from our own country? Is the First World free of the problems she cites in the Third World?

2. At the time Landsberg wrote this column, her husband Stephen Lewis was Canada's ambassador to the United Nations. Does this mean that we should consider her opinions as more trustworthy than those of others? Or should we judge her argument strictly on its own innate worth?

3. In her closing paragraph, Landsberg links our shopping habits to the plight of Third-World children. Add to her suggestions: What else can we do in Canada, besides selective shopping, to reduce misery among the world's young? In particular, how might we carry out Landsberg's idea of using our foreign policy to help the children?

4. Choose a troubled Third-World country to research. Read and take notes. Focus. Then write an INDUCTIVE argument, like Landsberg's, in which evidence leads to a conclusion explaining some aspect of that country's problems. Before you begin your first draft, choose deliberately the proportion of ARGUMENTATION and PERSUASION you think will best represent your case.

5. PROCESS IN WRITING: *For one week read the international section of your favourite daily newspaper, paying special attention to reports that have implications for Third-World children. Choose one event or issue that arouses either your approval or your indignation, then respond to it in a letter to the editor. Using evidence in the article, make an* INDUCTIVE *argument for your point. Use* ARGUMENTATION *and* PERSUASION *in the proportion you think most effective. If this is a class assignment, show a rough draft to your teacher before writing and mailing your final draft. To increase the chances of publication, keep your letter short.*

Note: See also the Topics for Writing at the end of this chapter.

Pierre Berton

The Dirtiest Job in the World

Few people are better known to Canadians than Pierre Berton — journalist, humourist, social critic, popular historian, and television personality. He was born in 1920 in Whitehorse, Y.T., and studied at the University of British Columbia. In 1942 he began his career in journalism at the Vancouver News-Herald. *After wartime service in the Canadian Information Corps, Berton returned to journalism as a feature writer for the* Vancouver Sun, *moved in 1947 to an editorial position at* Maclean's, *then in 1958 became a daily columnist for the* Toronto Star. *For decades Berton has appeared regularly on television series such as* Front Page Challenge, The Great Debate, *and* My Country, *and since 1954 has written over 30 books, many of them bestsellers. His most widely read have been* The National Dream *(1970) and* The Last Spike *(1971), the massively researched and highly readable two-volume history of the CPR that in 1974 was serialized on the CBC with Berton as narrator.* The Invasion of Canada, 1812–13 *appeared in 1980,* Flames across the Border *in 1981,* The Promised Land *in 1984, his bestselling* Vimy *in 1986, and in 1987 his autobiography* Starting Out. *More of a popularizer than a scholar, Berton is a Canadian nationalist and social critic. Whatever his subject, his writing is vivid, opinionated, full of human interest and concern for social justice. Nowhere are these traits more evident than in our selection,* "The Dirtiest Job in the World," *which appeared in Berton's 1968 book* The Smug Minority.

On my seventeenth birthday, which fell on July 12, 1937, one of the worst years of the Depression, I went to work for pay and there was jubilation among my friends and relatives. In an era when jobs were scarce I had a job; and having a job was the goal of everyone in those days. Having a job in the Thirties was a bit like having a swimming pool in the Sixties; it conferred status. It didn't really matter what the job was. It could be unrewarding, mindless, foolish, unproductive, even degrading — no matter: it set you apart as a paying member of a society whose creed was that everyone must work at something, and the harder the better, too.

2   My job was in a mining camp in the Yukon some 1,500 miles from my home in Victoria, B.C. I worked ten hours a day, seven days a week, and I was paid $4.50 a day plus my board. Almost everybody who learned about my job had the same thing to say about it: "It will make a man out of you!" And when the job came to an end at the start of my university term, almost every adult I knew examined my hands to note with satisfaction the heavy callouses. Back-breaking work was considered to be a high form of human endeavour. A man who worked hard couldn't be all bad, whether he was a convict breaking rocks in a prison yard or an executive neglecting his family by toiling weekends at the office.

3   I worked for three summer seasons at that same job and it was commonly held that I was "working my way through college," another laudable endeavour in a society which believed, and still believes, that every individual must pay his own way regardless of position, health, mental ability, or physical condition.

4   The first year I worked on a construction gang; the following years I worked on the thawing crew, engaged in preparing the ground for the actual gold mining that was to follow. Thawing permafrost with cold water is a fascinating process to almost everyone except those actually employed in it. As far as I know, it is the world's muddiest job, involving as it does the pumping of millions of gallons of cold water into the bowels of the earth.

5   In earlier days steam had been used to thaw the permanently frozen ground so that the dredges could reach the gold; but the lovely, verdant valleys had long since been denuded of their timber and no fuel was left to operate the old-time boilers. So now a new process had been devised to tear the valley apart and convert it into a heaving sea of mud.

6   On Dominion Creek in the Klondike watershed, where I toiled those three Depression summers, the gold lay hidden in crevices of bedrock some twenty or thirty feet beneath the surface. The valley was perhaps a mile wide at this point and it was being ripped to pieces so that man might reach this gold. First, every shred of plant life was sheared off by a bush-cutting crew. Then all the black topsoil, most of it frozen hard as granite, was sluiced away by giant nozzles flinging water against the banks at a pressure so high it could cut a man in half. By the time the thawing crew arrived, the sinuous valley, misty green each spring, flaming orange each fall, had been reduced to a black, glistening scar.

7   It was our task to dam the creek anew to build up water pressure and then introduce a spider web of pipes across the newly ravaged valley floor. From these pipes at sixteen-foot intervals there protruded an octopus-like tangle of hoses. On to each hose was fastened a ten-foot length of pipe, known as a "point," because of the chisel-bit at the end. This point was

driven into the frozen soil by means of a slide hammer. When it was down the full ten feet, an extension pipe was screwed onto the end and this was driven down, too, inch by painful inch. If necessary, further extensions were added. And all the time, without cessation, ice cold water was being pumped through every pipe at high pressure. In this way an underground lake was created beneath the valley floor and, though its waters were only a few degrees above freezing, that small change in temperature was enough to thaw the permafrost.

And so we toiled away, up to our ankles, our knees, and sometimes even our hips in a pulsating gruel of mud and ice-water. The men who drove those points into the rock-like soil were soaking wet most of the time, for it was difficult to add extensions or withdraw a point without water spurting in all directions. All day long they laboured, with their fingers curled around the handles of their slide hammers, their torsos rising and falling as they drove each pipe inch by inch into the earth. When a point became plugged it had to be hauled up and unplugged while the ice-water squirted in their faces. Each man was logged on the amount of footage he had driven in a day, and if that footage was seen to be too low he could expect to draw his time slip that evening. There was a story current in my day that the general manager had come out from Dawson on a tour of inspection and seen a man standing immobile in the distance. "Fire that man!" he cried. "I've been watching him and he hasn't moved for half an hour." Later it was discovered that he *couldn't* move; he was up to his hips in mud.

8

As the water continued to flow into the ground, the floor of the valley began to go to pieces. Immense craters ten or twenty feet deep began to appear. Whole sections fell away, sometimes taking men with them. The mud grew thicker. The pipeline supports toppled as the soil crumbled, and the pipes themselves — mainlines and feeder lines — began to buckle and break and to shoot icy fountains in every direction. When this occurred it was the job of the pipeline crew, of which I was a member, to replace the pilings, drive new pipes and repair leaks. Sometimes the sun was out and we stripped to our shorts; sometimes a bone-chilling wind swept down the valley accompanied by a sleety rain. It did not matter. We worked our ten hours (later it was reduced to a merciful nine) day in and day out, without a holiday of any kind.

9

When you work for ten hours at hard labour, whether you are seventeen or fifty-seven, there is precious little time or energy left for anything else. We rose at six, performed our swift ablutions, wolfed an enormous breakfast, and headed off for the job which had to begin at seven. At noon we started back up the valley slopes through the mud to the messhall, wolfed another vast meal, and finished it just in time to head back once more. At six we were finished, in more ways than one. I have

10

seen men so tired they could not eat the final meal of the day which was always consumed in silence and at top speed. (It was said that any man who stumbled on the messhall steps on the way in found himself trampled by the rush coming out.) When this was over, large numbers of men of varying ages simply lay down on their bunks, utterly fagged out, and slept. There was nothing else to do anyway: no library, no recreation hall, no lounge, no radio or films — nothing but a roadhouse five miles distant where you could buy bootleg rum. Civilization was represented by Dawson, forty miles away; we never visited it. We were like men in a prison camp, except that we worked much harder.

11   Under such conditions any kind of creative act or thought is difficult. I remember one man, a German immigrant, who was trying to learn to draw by correspondence. He had some talent but in the end he had to give it up. He was too tired to draw. I had brought along a pile of books required in my university course for summer reading, but most of the time I found I was too tired to read. Those who did not immediately go to sleep after supper spent their spare time washing their work clothes or lying in their bunks indulging in verbal sexual fantasies. I often wondered if this was what the adults meant when they said that mining camp life would make a man of me. Certainly I learned a great deal more from these sexual bull sessions than I had at my mother's knee. It was not until many years later that I discovered most of it was wrong.

12   It is difficult to describe the absolute dreariness and hopelessness of this kind of job. The worst thing about it was that there was no respite, since — in a seven-day-a-week job — there were no breaks of any kind to look forward to until the coming of winter rendered further toil impossible. There was one wit among us who used to leap from his bunk once a week, when the bull cook banged the triangle at 6:00 a.m., crying jubilantly: "Thank God, it's Sunday!" This always provoked a bitter laugh. Without any change of pace, time moves sluggishly; without any break in the routine, a kind of lethargy steals over the mind. The blessed winter seemed eons away to all of us.

13   Yet for me, in my late teens, life in this mining camp was immeasurably easier than it was for the others. There were men here in their sixties who had lived this way all their lives. There were men in their prime with wives and children to support — families they did not see for half of every year. There were all kinds of men here and few who were really stupid. I worked with immigrants from Austria, Germany, Switzerland, Italy, Sweden, Norway, and Denmark, as well as with Canadians. Most were intelligent and a great many were extremely sharp and able. All were industrious. Each had displayed enough courage and independence to somehow make his way several thousand miles to the one corner of North America where a job of sorts was comparatively easy to get. But all had one thing in

common: according to my observation, none had been educated up to his ability.

There were many men in that mining camp easily capable of obtaining   14
a university degree; and there were many more who might have completed high school and then gone on to technical school. I saw them each evening, lying on their bunks and trying to force their hands open — hands that had been curled into almost permanent positions around cold pipes; I saw them each morning, shambling down to that grotesque mud-pie of a valley; during the day I saw them — scores of ant-like figures, bent double over their slide hammers, struggling in the gumbo, striving and groaning; and the thought that came to my mind was ever the same: "What a waste of human resources!"

For this "job," which everybody had congratulated me upon getting,   15
which was supposed to be so ennobling, which was to make a man of me, was actually degrading, destructive, and above all useless. It was degrading because it reduced men to the status of beasts. There was one wag who went around with his zipper purposely undone and his genitals exposed. "If I'm working like a horse, I might as well look like one," he'd say. It was destructive because it reduced a glorious setting to a black obscenity. And it was useless because the gold, which was mined at such expense and human cost, was melted into bars and shipped to Fort Knox in the United States where it was once again confined below ground. Every manjack of us knew this; it was the subject of much bitter banter and wisecracking; each of us, I think, was disturbed by the fact that we were engaged in an operation which was essentially unproductive. If we'd been growing wheat, we would at least have had the satisfaction of knowing our labours were useful. The whole, vast, complicated operation seemed to me to be pointless: even the stockholders failed to profit by it greatly; for years the company was forced to pass its dividends. Would we or the nation have been worse off if we had stayed drunk all summer?

For myself, as a teenager, there were certain minor advantages that   16
did not apply to those older men who worked out of necessity and desperation. Certainly it was healthy enough. Certainly I got to know a bit more about my fellow men. It occurs to me now, however, that both these goals could have been achieved in a pleasanter and more productive fashion. As for the financial gain, much of that was illusory. After I paid for my equipment and my return fare home, there was precious little left. The first year I scarcely broke even. In succeeding seasons I was able to pay my university tuition but not much more. Like my fellow students, I could say that I was working my way through college, but like most of them I could not have continued a university career had I not been able to board at home and take money for clothing and extras from my parents. During four years at university, I met only a handful of students who were

able to support themselves wholly through summer employment.

17   The one valuable asset that I recovered from my mining camp experience was status. It allows me to use a line in my official biography which I notice is seized upon joyfully by those who have to introduce me when I make after-dinner speeches: "During the Thirties, he worked in Yukon mining camps to help put himself through university." When that line is uttered the audience is prepared to forgive me almost anything: outlandishly radical opinions, dangerous views on matters sexual, alarming attitudes toward religion. I am pronounced worthy because, in that one sentence, is summed up the great Canadian myth: that work — *any* work — is the most important thing in life, and that anybody who is willing to work hard enough can by his own initiative get as far as he wants.

ΔΔΔΔΔΔΔΔΔΔΔΔΔΔΔΔΔΔΔΔΔΔΔΔΔΔΔΔΔΔΔΔΔΔΔΔΔΔΔΔΔΔΔΔΔΔΔΔΔΔΔΔΔΔΔΔΔΔΔΔΔΔΔΔ

Further Reading:

Pierre Berton,
> *Klondike* (history)
> *Drifting Home* (autobiography)

Peter Such, *Fallout* (novel)

Tom Wayman, ed., *Going for Coffee: An Anthology of Contemporary North American Working Poems*

Structure:

1. Point out all the ways in which Pierre Berton uses chronological order to organize his argument.
2. In which paragraphs does Berton give us a straight *process analysis* of how he performed his job?
3. Berton both begins and ends his argument by showing Canadian society's reverence of "work — *any* work." Point out all the ways in which this view is a *contrast* to his own experiene in the middle of the essay. Also explain why he chose the opening and closing as the locations of this contrast.
4. In paragraph 15 Berton employs a powerful rhetorical device again and again to hammer home his point. What is this device? Point out each example of its use in this passage, and describe the effect.

Style:

1. In paragraph 5 Berton describes the valley as "a heaving sea of mud." Find at least five more FIGURES OF SPEECH and explain the effect of each.

2. In paragraph 10 the crew "wolfed an enormous breakfast" and later "wolfed another vast meal." Have you heard this expression before? Would you use it in an essay? Name several other CLICHÉS often heard in speech or seen in writing.

Argumentation and Persuasion:

1. What is the proportion of *argumentation* to *persuasion* in this essay? Point out three paragraphs where objectivity and reason seem to dominate. Point out three others where emotion seems to dominate. Which approach is more prominent in the essay as a whole?
2. Berton's argument is clearly *inductive*: society has told him of its reverence for "work — *any* work," but after seeing a great deal of evidence, himself, Berton rejects that view and formulates his own. Point out at least five major pieces of evidence which help lead Berton to his own conclusion.
3. If Berton's argument is inductive, why does he imply his own view already in paragraph 1?
4. Analyze Berton's use of *induction* in paragraphs 13 and 14: What is his evidence in this section and what does he conclude from it?
5. SARCASM, an extreme of IRONY, is one of the most overtly SUBJECTIVE tools of persuasion. Analyze how Berton exploits it in paragraphs 8, 12, and 15.

Ideas for Discussion and Writing:

1. Do we still believe, or did we ever believe, in what Berton calls "the great Canadian myth: that work — *any* work — is the most important thing in life, and that anybody who is willing to work hard enough can by his own initiative get as far as he wants"?
2. Is work necessary for human happiness? How are prisoners, pensioners, the unemployed, and the rich affected by large amounts of leisure time? Give examples from the experience of people you know.
3. To what extent does our society still believe that "every individual must pay his own way regardless of position, health, mental ability, or physical condition" (par. 3)?
4. Berton seems to view education as the means of escape from "back-breaking work" (see par. 14). Was that view correct during the Depression, in which the essay is set? Was it correct in 1968, when the essay was first published? Is it correct now?

5. How much did Berton learn from his experience in the gold fields? How large a part of your own education has come from summer or part-time work?

6. "It will make a man out of you!" people said of young Berton's job. Define what you think they meant by "man." Do we still hear this expression? Identify any STEREOTYPES you sense behind these words.

7. PROCESS IN WRITING: *Think of a job you have had. Write a page of rough notes about it, then, looking these over, decide how socially useful or useless the job was. Now write an* inductive *argument showing the evidence for your conclusion. After a rapid first draft, examine what you have said: Do the examples support your THESIS? If not, change your thesis to reflect what you have discovered while writing. Are your examples fully enough explained to make sense to the reader? If not, elaborate. Or is there deadwood? Trim it out. Read your second-to-last version aloud to help fine-tune its style. Read the final version aloud to the class.*

Note: See also the Topics for Writing at the end of this chapter.

Bonnie Laing

An Ode to the User-Friendly Pencil

"Anyone can write," says Bonnie Laing, "it's the rewrites that kill you." She gave her own essay three drafts, on the very computer whose behaviour she describes below. Laing is a freelance advertising copywriter who also publishes essays and fiction (her short stories have appeared in Fiddlehead, Quarry, *and* Montreal, *and her humorous articles in* Toronto Life, *the* Toronto Star, *and* Canadian Living*). Originally from Montreal, Laing did an Honours B.A. in English at Queen's, then, as she states, was a hippie for two years in England. But once arrived in Toronto, she quickly entered advertising. As a "social marketer" of food and other "lifestyle products," Laing needs a keener sense of audience than even the essayist; in producing "target-specific" text, she says, you have to keep asking yourself "Who is this person I'm writing for?" Although she did have publication in mind, the audience of "An Ode to the User-Friendly Pencil" was herself: she vented her frustrations, felt better, then found that others liked the piece too. The* Toronto Globe *and* Mail *had already published three of her essays in its "Mermaid Inn" column. It published this fourth on April 29, 1989.*

R ecently I acquired a computer. Or perhaps I should say it acquired 1
me. My therapist claims that acknowledging the superior partner in a destructive relationship is the first step toward recovery. I should point out that prior to this acquisition, my idea of modern technology at its best was frozen waffles. My mastery of business machines had advanced only as far as the stapler.

I was persuaded to make this investment by well-meaning friends who 2
said the word-processing capacity of a computer would (a) make me a better writer (b) make me a more productive writer and (c) make me a richer writer. I pointed out that Chaucer was a pretty good writer even though he used a quill, and Dickens managed to produce 15 novels and numerous collections of short stories without so much as a typewriter. But I have to admit that option C got to me, even if I couldn't figure out how spending $3,000 on a piece of molded plastic was going to make me wealthier.

3   To date, my association with the computer has not been too successful. It has proved to be very sensitive to everything but my needs. At the last breakdown (its, not mine) the service man commented that it should have been called an Edsel, not an Epson, and suggested an exorcist be consulted. Needless to say, I am not yet in a position to open a numbered Swiss bank account.

4   But they say hardship teaches you who your friends are. And so, my computer experience has forced me to spend a lot more time with an old friend, the pencil. Its directness and simplicity have proven to be refreshing. In fact, the more I wrestled with my microchips (whatever they are), the more convinced I became that the pencil is superior to the computer. Allow me to cite a few examples.

5   To start with the purchase decision, you don't have to ask for a bank loan to buy a pencil. Since most pencils are not manufactured in Japan, you don't feel you're upsetting the nation's balance of trade by buying one.

6   In fact, pencils are constructed in part from that most Canadian of natural resources — wood. By buying pencils you create employment and prosperity for dozens of people in British Columbia. Well, a few anyway.

7   Of course, like most people I rarely *buy* a pencil, preferring to pick them up free from various places of employment, in the mistaken belief that they are a legitimate fringe benefit. It's best not to make that assumption about office computers.

8   Operationally, the pencil wins over the computer hands down. You can learn to use a pencil in less than 10 seconds. Personally, at the age of 2, I mastered the technology in 3.2 seconds. To be fair, erasing did take a further 2.4 seconds. I've never had to boot a pencil, interface with it or program it. I just write with it.

9   Compared to a computer, a pencil takes up far less space on a desk and it can be utilized in a car, bathroom or a telephone booth without the aid of batteries. You can even use one during an electrical storm. Pencils don't cause eye strain and no one has ever screamed, after four hours of creative endeavor, "The - - - - pencil ate my story!"

10   Pencils are wonderfully singleminded. They aren't used to open car doors, make the morning coffee or remind you that your Visa payment is overdue. They're user-friendly. (For the uninitiated, see comments on vocabulary.)

11   Of course, the technologically addicted among you will argue that the options of a pencil are rather limited. But the software of a pencil is both cheap and simple, consisting of a small rubber tip located at one end of the unit. A pencil is capable of producing more fonts or typefaces than any word processor, depending on the operator's skill.

Its graphic capability is limited only by the operator's talent, an 12
element referred to as the Dürer or Da Vinci Factor. Backup to a pencil
can usually be found in your purse or pocket. Although a pencil has
no memory, many of us who write badly consider that to be an
advantage.

But it's in the area of maintenance that the pencil really proves its 13
superiority. Should a pencil break down, all you have to do to render it
operational again, is buy a small plastic device enclosing a sharp metal
strip, a purchase that can be made for under a dollar. A paring knife, a
piece of broken glass or even your teeth can be used in an emergency. For
the more technically advanced, an electronic pencil sharpener can be
obtained, but I should point out that these devices don't run on electrical
power but by devouring one-third of the pencil.

You never have to take a pencil to a service department located on an 14
industrial site on the outskirts of Moose Factory. Neither do you have to
do without them for two weeks before discovering that the malfunction is
not covered by the warranty and that the replacement part is on a boat
from Korea.

What finally won me over to the pencil was its lack of social pretension. 15
For instance, very few people suffer the nagging doubt that their
intelligence is below that of a pencil. No one has ever claimed that a pencil
put them out of a job. And the pencil has not created a whole new class of
workers who consider themselves superior to, let's say, crayon operators.
At parties, you meet very few people who will discuss pencils with a fervor
normally found only at student rallies in Tehran. Fewer people boast
about being 'pencil literate.'

Of course, the pencil is not without its flaws. It has a nasty habit of 16
hiding when most needed. If located beside a telephone, it will break
spontaneously if a caller wishes to leave a message. Those aspiring to be
professional writers should note that editors are unreasonably prejudiced
against submissions in pencil.

But a pencil won't argue with you if you wish to write more than 50 17
lines to the page. It won't insist on correcting your whimsical use of
grammar, and it won't be obsolete 10 seconds after you mortgage your
first-born to buy one. Just in case you remain unconvinced, I ask you, can
you imagine chewing on a computer while balancing your cheque book?
And what do computer operators use to scratch that place in the middle of
the back where they can't reach? The defence rests.

ΔΔΔΔΔΔΔΔΔΔΔΔΔΔΔΔΔΔΔΔΔΔΔΔΔΔΔΔΔΔΔΔΔΔΔΔΔΔΔΔΔΔΔΔΔΔΔΔΔΔΔΔΔΔΔΔΔ

Further Reading:

Heather Menzies, *Women and the Chip*
Henry David Thoreau, *Walden*

Structure:

1. Bonnie Laing begins her whole essay of *contrast* with a series of shorter contrasts. Identify each in paragraph 1, and tell how it prepares us for the argument that follows.
2. Identify Laing's THESIS STATEMENT.
3. Identify the sentence of TRANSITION that moves us from Laing's introduction to the body of her argument.
4. Laing's argument in favour of the "user-friendly pencil" is an exceptionally clear example of *comparison and contrast*. Does she proceed "point by point" or by "halves"?
5. The body of Laing's argument has four parts (par. 5–7, 8–12, 13–14, and 15). To organize her first draft she gave each part a heading, then later removed it. Restore those headings, labelling each division of her argument.
6. What techniques of closing does Laing use in her final two paragraphs?

Style:

1. In paragraph 2 Laing dismisses her computer as a $3000 "piece of molded plastic." Point out five other IMAGES calculated to further her point of view.
2. In paragraph 4 Laing spends "a lot more time with an old friend, the pencil." Point out three other examples of PERSONIFICATION in her essay.
3. In paragraph 11 the pencil's "software" is its eraser. What device of humour has Laing used here?
4. In paragraph 8 Laing states, "I've never had to boot a pencil, interface with it or program it. I just write with it." Point out all the elements of repetition in this passage, and their effects. Are these effects accidental or deliberate?

Argumentation and Persuasion:

1. Laing's essay is a *comparison and contrast* as clearly organized and developed as any in the "Comparison and Contrast" chapter of this book. How well does the pattern lend itself to her *argumentative* and *persuasive* purpose? Are essayists free to use any pattern that supports their purpose?
2. Is Laing's argument *deductive* or *inductive*? If it is deductive, point out its major and minor premises. If it is inductive, point out five major pieces of evidence that lead to the author's conclusion.

3. To what extent is Laing's essay based on *argumentation*? To what extent on *persuasion*? Defend your answer with examples.
4. Laing's TONE is rich in IRONY. As an example, point out every irony of paragraph 15. What is the overall effect?

Ideas for Discussion and Writing:

1. Are you a technophobe, like Laing? Or do you rejoice in high technology? Defend your answers with examples.
2. Do you write with a word processor? If so, tell all the contrasts you have personally experienced between "high-tech" and "low-tech" writing. Give specific examples.
3. The American writer and philosopher Henry David Thoreau, who left town life for his cabin by Walden Pond, wrote, "Our life is frittered away by detail. . . . Simplify, simplify." In your opinion, has high technology simplified or complicated our lives? Defend your answer with personal examples.
4. PROCESS IN WRITING: *Choose one high-tech invention that you have used, and write an* inductive *essay that praises or condemns it. First freewrite on your subject for at least five minutes — automatically, never letting your user-friendly pencil stop — then look over what you have produced in order to learn your point of view. Now take more notes, gathering examples. Arrange these in order from least to most important, and from this rough outline write a draft. In the second draft adjust your tone: Is your whole argument serious and objective? Is it* argumentative? *Or is it more like Laing's essay: humorous, subjective, and therefore* persuasive? *Whichever it is, be consistent. Now read your argument aloud to family members or classmates, revise any part that fails to work on your audience, then write the final version.*

Note: See also the Topics for Writing at the end of this chapter.

Margaret Atwood

Canadians: What Do They Want?

Long respected by critics for her poetry, and now internationally celebrated for her novels, Margaret Atwood has emerged as the nation's major literary star. She was born in Ottawa in 1939, and spent much of her childhood with her parents in the wilderness of the Canadian North, where her father did biological research. After studies at the University of Toronto and at Radcliffe, Atwood published several books of poetry in which she explored the inability of language to express reality, and the alienation of women in society. Her feminist vision has found even broader scope in numerous volumes of short fiction and in her novels, such as The Edible Woman *(1969),* Surfacing *(1972),* Life before Man *(1979),* Bodily Harm *(1981), and especially* The Handmaid's Tale *(1985), which became an international bestseller and was made into a feature film. Set in Boston, it portrays a future America, devastated by nuclear pollution, in which a right-wing theocracy has reduced women to the status of slaves. Like the black slaves of American Civil War times fleeing north to freedom, the narrator flees towards Canada, but she is caught near the border. Atwood has published many essays as well.*

She wrote our selection for the American political journal Mother Jones, *which in 1982 wished to know why so many Canadians were anti-American. In the 1990s her answers now contrast starkly to new times: with the free trade agreement passed by a pro-American government, Canada's economy, social services, and some would say even its culture, are rapidly adjusting to blend with those of the America Atwood accused of being an empire. Is Atwood's view obsolete, a mere historical record of times past? Is our country's move toward economic partnership merely the new wisdom and realism of our time? Or are we risking our national sovereignty? Are we hastening towards cultural or even political assimilation by the "empire" of which Atwood writes? As we reread Atwood's argument in the 1990s, these questions are worth some thought; they represent the major ongoing debate in Canadian public life.*

1   Last month, during a poetry reading, I tried out a short prose poem called "How to Like Men." It began by suggesting that one start with the feet. Unfortunately, the question of jackboots soon arose, and things

went on from there. After the reading I had a conversation with a young man who thought I had been unfair to men. He wanted men to be liked totally, not just from the heels to the knees, and not just as individuals but as a group; and he thought it negative and inegalitarian of me to have alluded to war and rape. I pointed out that as far as any of us knew these were two activities not widely engaged in by women, but he was still upset. "We're both in this together," he protested. I admitted that this was so; but could he, maybe, see that our relative positions might be a little different.

This is the conversation one has with Americans, even, uh, *good*   2
Americans, when the dinner-table conversation veers round to Canadian-American relations. "We're in this together," they like to say, especially when it comes to continental energy reserves. How do you *explain* to them, as delicately as possible, why they are not categorically beloved? It gets like the old Lifebuoy ads: even their best friends won't tell them. And Canadians are supposed to be their best friends, right? Members of the family?

Well, sort of. Across the river from Michigan, so near and yet so far,   3
there I was at the age of eight, reading *their* Donald Duck comic books (originated, however, by one of *ours*; yes, Walt Disney's parents were Canadian) and coming at the end to Popsicle Pete, who promised me the earth if only I would save wrappers, but took it all away from me again with a single asterisk: Offer Good Only in the United States. Some cynical members of the world community may be forgiven for thinking that the same asterisk is there, in invisible ink, on the Constitution and the Bill of Rights.

But quibbles like that aside, and good will assumed, how does one go   4
about liking Americans? Where does one begin? Or, to put it another way, why did the Canadian women lock themselves in the john during a '70s "international" feminist conference being held in Toronto? Because the American sisters were being "imperialist," that's why.

But then, it's always a little naive of Canadians to expect that   5
Americans, of whatever political stamp, should stop being imperious. How can they? The fact is that the United States is an empire and Canada is to it as Gaul was to Rome.

It's hard to explain to Americans what it feels like to be a Canadian.   6
Pessimists among us would say that one has to translate the experience into their own terms and that this is necessary because Americans are incapable of thinking in any other terms — and this in itself is part of the problem. (Witness all those draft dodgers who went into culture shock when they discovered to their horror that Toronto was not Syracuse.)

Here is a translation: Picture a Mexico with a population ten times   7
larger than that of the United States. That would put it at about two

billion. Now suppose that the official American language is Spanish, that 75 percent of the books Americans buy and 90 percent of the movies they see are Mexican, and that the profits flow across the border to Mexico. If an American does scrape it together to make a movie, the Mexicans won't let him show it in the States, because they own the distribution outlets. If anyone tries to change this ratio, not only the Mexicans but many fellow Americans cry "National chauvinism," or, even more effectively, "National socialism." After all, the American public prefers the Mexican product. It's what they're used to.

8   Retranslate and you have the current American-Canadian picture. It's changed a little recently, not only on the cultural front. For instance, Canada, some think a trifle late, is attempting to regain control of its own petroleum industry. Americans are predictably angry. They think of Canadian oil as *theirs*.

9   "What's mine is yours," they have said for years, meaning exports; "What's yours is mine" meaning ownership and profits. Canadians are supposed to do retail buying, not controlling, or what's an empire for? One could always refer Americans to history, particularly that of their own revolution. They objected to the colonial situation when they themselves were a colony; but then, revolution is considered one of a very few home-grown American products that definitely are not for export.

10   Objectively, one cannot become too self-righteous about this state of affairs. Canadians owned lots of things, including their souls, before World War II. After that they sold, some say because they had put too much into financing the war, which created a capital vacuum (a position they would not have been forced into if the Americans hadn't kept out of the fighting for so long, say the sore losers). But for whatever reason, capital flowed across the border in the '50s, and Canadians, traditionally sock-under-the-mattress hoarders, were reluctant to invest in their own country. Americans did it for them and ended up with a large part of it, which they retain to this day. In every sellout there's a seller as well as a buyer, and the Canadians did a thorough job of trading their birthright for a mess.

11   That's on the capitalist end, but when you turn to the trade union side of things you find much the same story, except that the sellout happened in the '30s under the banner of the United Front. Now Canadian workers are finding that in any empire the colonial branch plants are the first to close, and what could be a truly progressive labor movement has been weakened by compromised bargains made in international union head-quarters south of the border.

12   Canadians are sometimes snippy to Americans at cocktail parties. They don't like to feel owned and they don't like having been sold. But

what really bothers them — and it's at this point that the United States and Rome part company — is the wide-eyed innocence with which their snippiness is greeted.

Innocence becomes ignorance when seen in the light of international affairs, and though ignorance is one of the spoils of conquest — the Gauls always knew more about the Romans than the Romans knew about them — the world can no longer afford America's ignorance. Its ignorance of Canada, though it makes Canadians bristle, is a minor and relatively harmless example. More dangerous is the fact that individual Americans seem not to know that the United States is an imperial power and is behaving like one. They don't want to admit that empires dominate, invade and subjugate — and live on the proceeds — or, if they do admit it, they believe in their divine right to do so. The export of divine right is much more harmful than the export of Coca-Cola, though they may turn out to be much the same thing in the end. 13

Other empires have behaved similarly (the British somewhat better, Genghis Khan decidedly worse); but they have not expected to be *liked* for it. It's the final Americanism, this passion for being liked. Alas, many Americans are indeed likable; they are often more generous, more welcoming, more enthusiastic, less picky and sardonic than Canadians, and it's not enough to say it's only because they can afford it. Some of that revolutionary spirit still remains: the optimism, the 18th-century belief in the fixability of almost anything, the conviction of the possibility of change. However, at cocktail parties and elsewhere one must be able to tell the difference between an individual and a foreign policy. Canadians can no longer afford to think of Americans as only a spectator sport. If Reagan blows up the world, we will unfortunately be doing more than watching it on television. "No annihilation without representation" sounds good as a slogan, but if we run it up the flagpole, who's going to salute? 14

We *are* all in this together. For Canadians, the question is how to survive it. For Americans there is no question, because there does not have to be. Canada is just that vague, cold place where their uncle used to go fishing, before the lakes went dead from acid rain. 15

How do you like Americans? Individually, it's easier. Your average American is no more responsible for the state of affairs than your average man is for war and rape. Any Canadian who is so narrow-minded as to dislike Americans merely on principle is missing out on one of the good things in life. The same might be said, to women, of men. As a group, as a foreign policy, it's harder. But if you like men, you can like Americans. Cautiously. Selectively. Beginning with the feet. One at a time. 16

ΔΔΔΔΔΔΔΔΔΔΔΔΔΔΔΔΔΔΔΔΔΔΔΔΔΔΔΔΔΔΔΔΔΔΔΔΔΔΔΔΔΔΔΔΔΔΔΔΔΔΔΔΔΔΔΔΔΔΔΔ

Further Reading:

Margaret Atwood,
> *The Handmaid's Tale*
> *Surfacing*
> *Bodily Harm*

Al Purdy, ed., *The New Romans* (essays)
Pierre Berton, *Hollywood's Canada: The Americanization of Our National Image*
Richard Rohmer, *Exxoneration* (novel)
Donald Creighton, *Takeover* (novel)

Structure

1. Analyze the ANECDOTE that begins this essay: Does it stir the reader's interest? Does it clearly introduce Margaret Atwood's subject?
2. How do the opening and closing of this essay complement each other? Upon what rhetorical pattern are both based?
3. What proportion of her argument does Atwood devote to *examples*? Has she used enough? Too many?
4. Atwood's economic "translation" in paragraph 7 is a *comparison* of American control over Canada with a hypothetical Mexican control over the United States. What purpose does this passage serve for the AUDIENCE it was meant to instruct?

Style:

1. How FORMAL or INFORMAL is Atwood's TONE in this essay? Defend your answer with examples.
2. Why does Atwood close her essay with a series of four sentence fragments? Read the final paragraph aloud, to help you both feel and analyze the effects.

Argumentation and Persuasion:

1. In Atwood's argument, evidence leads *inductively* not just to one conclusion but to two related conclusions. The first is that America is an "empire." What is the second?
2. If Atwood is arguing *inductively*, why does she state as early as paragraph 5 that "the United States is an empire and Canada is to it as Gaul was to Rome"? Can an inductive argument introduce its conclusion before the evidence? If so, how do we distinguish such an arrangement from *deduction*?
3. Point out at least seven *examples* used inductively as evidence

that America is, in Atwood's view, an "empire." Are these examples also *causes* of the anti-Americanism Atwood was asked to explain?

4. To what extent is Atwood's essay *argumentative*, based on fact and reason? To what extent is it *persuasive*, based on appeals to our emotions? Defend your answer with examples.

5. One of Atwood's trademarks as a writer, whether in poetry, fiction or essays, is heavy use of IRONY. Point out the most dramatic examples of this approach in her essay. To what extent do they increase the degree of *persuasion* that we feel?

Ideas for Discussion and Writing:

1. How well do you think this essay, written for an audience of Americans, communicates to Canadians?

2. In paragraph 13 Atwood writes that "empires dominate, invade and subjugate — and live on the proceeds. . . ." Do you agree with her that the United States is an "empire"? And if so, to what extent has it dominated, invaded, and subjugated Canada? Defend your response with specific examples.

3. What degree of American influence do you detect in these aspects of Canadian life?

Computer software	Interest rates
Eating habits	Language
Fashions	Pollution
Film distribution	Popular music
Foreign policy	Social services
Hockey	Television programming
Inflation	Textbooks

4. Atwood states in paragraph 13 that Americans are "ignorant" of Canada. Attack or defend her view *inductively*, citing examples from your own experiences with Americans.

5. Point out the similarities and/or differences that you have noticed between Americans and Canadians as individuals. Give specific details.

6. PROCESS IN WRITING: *You have probably studied the Canadian-American free trade pact in other courses, and have heard a great deal about it in the media. Will it ultimately strengthen or weaken our nation? Brainstorm to produce a page of notes, especially examples, in no particular order. Now group your evidence into subtopics, and let them lead inductively to your conclusion. Base a first draft on this rough outline, but whenever the act of writing uncovers a new idea, consider*

adding it. When this draft has "cooled off," check and adjust your organization. Does every example lead to the same overall conclusion? Are there enough examples? Have you made transitions between them? Now check the TONE: whether you lean more towards argumentation or persuasion, are you consistent enough to avoid confusing your audience? Finally, test your prose aloud before writing the final version.

Note: See also the Topics for Writing at the end of this chapter.

Charles Gordon

A Guided Tour of the Bottom Line

"Laughter can be more persuasive than outrage in making a point," states Charles Gordon. As a columnist for both the Ottawa Citizen and MacLean's magazine, he practises this philosophy of persuasion: in an outwardly light and entertaining prose, he makes serious points about politics and other aspects of our national life — as in our selection, which appeared June 9, 1986 in MacLean's. He describes the piece as "an attempt to show the consequences of governmental spending cuts without being preachy about it." Born in New York City in 1940, Gordon grew up there and in Tokyo, Cairo, Rome, and Beirut, because of his Canadian father's work with the United Nations. After a degree in political science at Queen's, he spent a decade at the Brandon Sun before joining the Ottawa Citizen in 1974, where he has been editorial writer and city editor, as well as columnist. Gordon's book of political satire, The Governor General's Bunny Hop, was published in 1985, and in 1987 he developed it into 12 episodes of a comedy series, Not My Department, broadcast by the CBC. Author Sandra Gwyn wrote, of Gordon's approach in this book, "his dry, sly, deadpan wit transforms all that official Ottawa holds dear . . . into theatre of the absurd." Our selection takes a similar approach.

Welcome to Cutback World, ladies and gentlemen. We hope you enjoyed your flight. Sorry you had to walk so far in the rain, but spending reductions have made it possible for us to operate the same number of airplanes with fewer unloading ramps. You will notice complimentary newspapers on some of the seats of this bus. We hope you don't mind sharing them. While we wait to begin our tour, you might like to read some of the stories, just to get an introduction to the place we call home. 1

If you'll turn to page 1, you'll see the little item about what we are doing for our homeless citizens. We have provided 300 beds for them in this city alone. According to the most recent estimates, this means that at least 10 per cent of our homeless citizens will be able to find a bed tonight. So across the country, only 20,000 to 40,000 people are sleeping on the streets. 2

3   For those of you unfamiliar with our streets, many of them are very nice, although the garbage is not collected as frequently as it used to be.

4   Looking out the window, you can see that there will be a slight delay while we try to find somebody to open the gate, so you might like to turn the page to the story about our services for mentally disturbed adolescents. "Data collected by a committee examining adolescent bed demand in Toronto found that 85 per cent of all requests for admission were considered appropriate, but places could be found for only 41 per cent."

5   Perhaps we can have questions on that later, but I see that our bus tour is about to get under way. Be sure you have your seat belts fastened. Traffic accidents are up a bit since we discovered we could save money by not painting white lines down the middle of the road. Those of you for whom seat belts have not been provided can hang on to the seat in front of you.

6   The first thing you'll see, as we leave the airport area, is one of our factories. It is operating very efficiently now since the layoffs. Soon the robots will arrive and even fewer workers will be necessary. This improves productivity, and improved productivity improves profits and improved profits make possible future investment in new technology. Eventually, it will be possible to operate this entire factory with no human beings in it at all.

7   On the right there, you'll see one of our city buses. You'll notice it is mostly empty. Since we began running the buses once every two hours and raised the fare to $2, it is much easier to find a seat. Furthermore, increases in the transit system deficit have diminished as we began running fewer and fewer buses.

8   That empty building on the left was once a school. Here in Cutback World we have discovered that the educational system operates far more efficiently if schools are not open. You should not conclude from this that we have closed all our schools. That would be foolish. There *is* a school downtown somewhere. Every city of at least 100,000 people in Cutback World is entitled to have a school. Ours has 15,000 students in it, which enables it to offer a full range of courses. When we pass it, you might notice some students hanging out the open windows. We regard this as a sign that classroom space is being fully utilized.

9   We also have a university, and there is no restriction on who can attend. Any kid who can afford it can go. When the government stopped sending money to the university and the university hiked the fees, it helped to separate out those who were not sincere about getting an education.

10   Over there are the former drop-in centre and the former neighborhood

clinic. That vacant lot to the left is where we started to build low-cost housing before we changed our minds. That was when we decided to give bonuses to bureaucrats who cut spending, which has been a very successful program. Up ahead is one of the hospitals we were able to shut down in the big consolidation last year, after the lottery money didn't come in.

We'll stop here for a minute. This traffic light hardly ever works, but 11 there should be a policeman along any minute to get things sorted out. The police department budget is a lot trimmer these days. Some of you might like to get off the bus while we're waiting and visit the information booth. They can answer just about any of your questions for only a nominal fee.

Thanks for your patience. We're just coming up now to the arts centre. 12 Many of you may not be aware that it is possible to make the arts more cost-efficient. This is done by putting on only those shows that are likely to make money. I see there's a bingo on tonight, and some of you may want to drop in.

I hope you've enjoyed our bus tour so far and that the mosquitos 13 haven't bothered you too much. In answer to a question, no, we're not going to be able to see the Bottom Line today. They used to bring it out twice a week during the tourist season, and all the people liked to come look at it. But you can understand the security problems that caused. People don't mean any harm: they just want to touch it. But with our reduced police budget, it became increasingly difficult to provide the kind of security we needed. So now we only bring it out once a month. However, color photographs are available at our next stop, which should be the highlight of our visit.

There they are now, our parliament buildings. Quite something, aren't 14 they? I should point out that the grass will be cut next week, and we turn the fountains on every Saturday night during the tourist season. Gas for the eternal flame should be made available from the proceeds of the next lottery.

Now I'd like to warn you before we go inside that there are likely to be 15 debates going on and that interruptions from the public galleries are not permitted. We are very proud of our politicians here, particularly the way they have refurbished and dusted off the Bottom Line to make it the major spiritual force and tourist attraction it is today.

It would have been easy for them to throw money at problems and earn 16 the appreciation of the public, but they decided to devote their energies to improving conditions for the Bottom Line and let the problems look after themselves. Instead of earning the appreciation of the people, they have earned the appreciation of bankers and editorial writers.

17   And yet you can see what a job they have done. The fountains are beautiful when they're on, fewer than 40,000 people are homeless and our credit rating in New York is Triple-A.

ΔΔΔΔΔΔΔΔΔΔΔΔΔΔΔΔΔΔΔΔΔΔΔΔΔΔΔΔΔΔΔΔΔΔΔΔΔΔΔΔΔΔΔΔΔΔΔΔΔΔΔΔΔΔΔΔΔΔΔΔΔΔΔ

Further Reading:

The Canadian Encyclopedia, 2nd ed., "Public Debt, Public Expenditure" and "Public Finance" (pp. 1780–1782, illustrated with graphs)
J. Lorimer, *How Ottawa Spends*
Darrell Delamaide, *Debt Shock: The Full Story of the World Credit Crisis*

Structure:

1. Defend or attack Charles Gordon's choice of *narration* as the underlying organizational pattern of his argument. Give reasons for your view.
2. What percentage of this selection is given to *examples*? Does Gordon use them as profusely as Ray Guy does in "Outharbor Menu"? Is any part of Gordon's argument *not* an example?
3. To what extent can Gordon's whole argument be seen as *cause and effect*? What is the overall cause?
4. Gordon's paragraphing is unusually methodical and clear: virtually every paragraph develops one example or related set of examples. Identify five paragraphs that follow this pattern. Identify one that does not, and analyze why it is different.
5. Why does Gordon close his tour of Cutback World by stating in the very last sentence that "our credit rating in New York is Triple-A"?

Style:

1. The way Gordon reduces our METAPHOR of "the bottom line" to absurdity and CLICHÉ is reminiscent of Stephen Leacock's humour (see "How to Live to Be 200"). Explain how Gordon does it (in par. 13–15).
2. Identify three examples of HYPERBOLE in Gordon's argument.
3. In paragraph 14 the "eternal" flame is out, until new lottery money pays for the gas. What literary device powers this example?

Argumentation and Persuasion:

1. Paragraph 16 is a THESIS that generalizes upon the string of examples preceding it; in other words, this paragraph is the

conclusion of an *inductive* argument. Identify at least five
examples that you agree would earn "the appreciation of
bankers and editorial writers" rather than of the public.

2. Our "tour" of Ottawa is apparently a mixture of fact and
   fiction. For example, the statistics of paragraphs 2 and 4 seem
   realistic, while those of paragraph 8 are so outrageously
   exaggerated as to be SATIRE or even SARCASM. Does this mixed
   approach strengthen or weaken Gordon's case? Do you respond
   to his sometimes strong *persuasion* or do you miss a more
   objective *argumentation*?

3. Has Gordon gone too far in stacking the cards to favour his
   viewpoint? Should he at least have mentioned the dangers of
   our national debt, and other reasons why politicians cut back
   services? Is an essayist obligated to show both sides of an
   argument?

Ideas for Discussion and Writing:

1. Canadians who want more government had their way in the
   sixties and seventies, while those who want less government are
   having their way now. Which view do you favour, and why?
   Do you believe cutbacks and privatization are enhancing or
   threatening your wellbeing in the present? In the future?
   Defend your view with examples.

2. The 1980s and 1990s have seen a massive shift of college and
   university students from arts programs to business and
   engineering. Are we finally realizing that we have to make a
   living? Or are we abandoning higher pursuits in a desire for
   material gain?

3. In paragraph 9 Gordon states that "When the government
   stopped sending money to the university and the university
   hiked the fees, it helped to separate out those who were not
   sincere about getting an education." Is it fair that society now
   subsidizes college and university students, the very people who
   will make the most money later on? Or do you believe that
   society must do so, or else few could rise above the economic
   class into which they were born?

4. In paragraph 12 a bingo is on at the "arts centre," because in
   Cutback World "only those shows that are likely to make
   money" are produced. Explore this idea: What kinds of
   cultural activities pay for themselves? What kinds have to be
   subsidized by governmental agencies such as the Canada
   Council? In what ways do the arts affect our daily lives? Our

attitudes about ourselves and others? Our national sovereignty?

5. **PROCESS IN WRITING:** *Choose one example of governmental spending which has been or soon will be "cut back." Produce a page of notes, then conclude from them whether you favour or oppose the cutback. Now write an inductive essay to support your opinion. Apply at least three of the nine techniques of persuasion listed on pp. 270–272. After a quick "discovery draft," check to see if you have left out any good points from your notes. Has writing led you to discover new points? If they are good, add them. In further drafts, revise for CONCISENESS, CONCRETE language, and consistent TONE. Test your prose aloud before writing the final version.*

Note: See also the Topics for Writing at the end of this chapter.

Joy Kogawa

Grinning and Happy*

*With three published books of poetry to her credit — The Splintered Moon (1967).
A Choice of Dreams (1974), and Jericho Road (1977) — Joy Kogawa had
become a respected minor poet. But in 1981 she created a sensation with her first novel.
Obasan represented a new step for Kogawa as a writer and as a person: in it she
explores her own past and one of the most dubious events of Canadian history. Born in
Vancouver in 1935, Kogawa was a child during the Second World War when the
federal government classified Japanese Canadians as "enemy aliens." Her parents'
house in Vancouver was seized, and the family was moved first to a relocation camp in
Slocan, B.C., then to the sugar-beet fields of southern Alberta, which are the setting of
our selection from the novel. Our narrator is modelled after Kogawa herself, Stephen is
the narrator's brother, Obasan is the narrator's silent and suffering aunt, and "Aunt
Emily" is modelled after Muriel Kitagawa, a Japanese-Canadian activist whose
letters Kogawa studied in the National Archives in Ottawa. Kogawa now lives in
Toronto.*

There is a folder in Aunt Emily's package containing only one   1
newspaper clipping and an index card with the words "Facts about
evacuees in Alberta." The newspaper clipping has a photograph of one
family, all smiles, standing around a pile of beets. The caption reads:
"Grinning and Happy."

Find Jap Evacuees Best Beet Workers   2
Lethbridge, Alberta, Jan. 22.

    Japanese evacuees from British Columbia supplied the labour for   3
65% of Alberta's sugar beet acreage last year, Phil Baker, of
Lethbridge, president of the Alberta Sugar Beet Growers' Association,
stated today.
    "They played an important part in producing our all-time record   4
crop of 363,000 tons of beets in 1945," he added.

---

*Editor's title.

5   Mr. Baker explained Japanese evacuees worked 19,500 acres of beets and German prisoners of war worked 5,000 acres. The labour for the remaining 5,500 acres of Alberta's 30,000 acres of sugar beets was provided by farmers and their families. Some of the heaviest beet yields last year came from farms employing Japanese evacuees.

6   Generally speaking, Japanese evacuees have developed into most efficient beet workers, many of them being better than the transient workers who cared for beets in southern Alberta before Pearl Harbor. . . .

7   Facts about evacuees in Alberta? The fact is I never got used to it and I cannot, I cannot bear the memory. There are some nightmares from which there is no waking, only deeper and deeper sleep.

8   There is a word for it. Hardship. The hardship is so pervasive, so inescapable, so thorough it's a noose around my chest and I cannot move any more. All the oil in my joints has drained out and I have been invaded by dust and grit from the fields and mud is in my bone marrow. I can't move any more. My fingernails are black from scratching the scorching day and there is no escape.

9   Aunt Emily, are you a surgeon cutting at my scalp with your folders and your filing cards and your insistence on knowing all? The memory drains down the sides of my face, but it isn't enough, is it? It's your hands in my abdomen, pulling the growth from the lining of my walls, but bring back the anaesthetist turn on the ether clamp down the gas mask bring on the chloroform when will this operation be over Aunt Em?

10   Is it so bad?

11   Yes.

12   Do I really mind?

13   Yes, I mind. I mind everything. Even the flies. The flies and flies and flies from the cows in the barn and the manure pile — all the black flies that curtain the windows, and Obasan with a wad of toilet paper, spish, then with her bare hands as well, grabbing them and their shocking white eggs and the mosquitoes mixed there with the other insect corpses around the base of the gas lamp.

14   It's the chicken coop "house" we live in that I mind. The uninsulated unbelievable thin-as-a-cotton-dress hovel never before inhabited in winter by human beings. In summer it's a heat trap, an incubator, a dry sauna from which there is no relief. In winter the icicles drip down the inside of the windows and the ice is thicker than bricks at the ledge. The only place that is warm is by the coal stove where we rotate like chickens on a spit and the feet are so cold they stop registering. We eat cloves of roasted garlic on winter nights to warm up.

15   It's the bedbugs and my having to sleep on the table to escape the nightly attack, and the welts over our bodies. And all the swamp bugs and

the dust. It's Obasan uselessly packing all the cracks with rags. And the muddy water from the irrigation ditch which we strain and settle and boil, and the tiny carcasses of water creatures at the bottom of the cup. It's walking in winter to the reservoir and keeping the hole open with the axe and dragging up the water in pails and lugging it back and sometimes the water spills down your boots and your feet are red and itchy for days. And it's everybody taking a bath in the round galvanized tub, then Obasan washing clothes in the water after and standing outside hanging the clothes in the freezing weather where everything instantly stiffens on the line.

Or it's standing in the beet field under the maddening sun, standing   16
with my black head a sun-trap even though it's covered, and lying down in the ditch, faint, and the nausea in waves and the cold sweat, and getting up and tackling the next row. The whole field is an oven and there's not a tree within walking distance. We are tiny as insects crawling along the grill and there is no protection anywhere. The eyes are lidded against the dust and the air cracks the skin, the lips crack, Stephen's flutes crack and there is no energy to sing any more anyway.

It's standing in the field and staring out at the heat waves that waver   17
and shimmer like see-through curtains over the brown clods and over the tiny distant bodies of Stephen and Uncle and Obasan miles away across the field day after day and not even wondering how this has come about.

There she is, Obasan, wearing Uncle's shirt over a pair of dark baggy   18
trousers, her head covered by a straw hat that is held on by a white cloth tied under her chin. She is moving like a tiny earth cloud over the hard clay clods. Her hoe moves rhythmically up down up down, tiny as a toothpick. And over there, Uncle pauses to straighten his back, his hands on his hips. And Stephen farther behind, so tiny I can barely see him.

It's hard, Aunt Emily, with my hoe, the blade getting dull and   19
mud-caked as I slash out the Canada thistle, dandelions, crab grass, and other nameless non-beet plants, then on my knees, pulling out the extra beets from the cluster, leaving just one to mature, then three hand spans to the next plant, whack whack, and down on my knees again, pull, flick flick, and on to the end of the long long row and the next and the next and it will never be done thinning and weeding and weeding and weeding. It's so hard and so hot that my tear glands burn out.

And then it's cold. The lumps of clay mud stick on my gumboots and   20
weight my legs and the skin under the boots beneath the knees at the level of the calves grows red and hard and itchy from the flap flap of the boots and the fine hairs on my legs grow coarse there and ugly.

I mind growing ugly.   21

I mind the harvest time and the hands and the wrists bound in rags to   22 keep the wrists from breaking open. I lift the heavy mud-clotted beets out of the ground with the hook like an eagle's beak, thick and heavy as a nail attached to the top of the sugar-beet knife. Thwack. Into the beet and yank from the shoulder till it's out of the ground dragging the surrounding mud with it. Then crack two beets together till most of the mud drops off and splat, the knife slices into the beet scalp and the green top is tossed into one pile, the beet heaved onto another, one more one more one more down the icy line. I cannot tell about this time, Aunt Emily. The body will not tell.

23   We are surrounded by a horizon of denim-blue sky with clouds clear as spilled milk that turn pink at sunset. Pink I hear is the colour of llama's milk. I wouldn't know. The clouds are the shape of our new prison walls — untouchable, impersonal, random.

24   There are no other people in the entire world. We work together all day. At night we eat and sleep. We hardly talk anymore. The boxes we brought from Slocan are not unpacked. The King George/Queen Elizabeth mugs stay muffled in the *Vancouver Daily Province*. The camera phone does not sing. Obasan wraps layers of cloth around her feet and her torn sweater hangs unmended over her sagging dress.

25   Down the miles we are obedient as machines in this odd ballet without accompaniment of flute or song.

26   "Grinning and happy" and all smiles standing around a pile of beets? That is one telling. It's not how it was.

△△

Further Reading:

Joy Kogawa, *Obasan*

Barry Broadfoot, *Years of Sorrow, Years of Shame: The Story of Japanese Canadians in World War II*

Ken Adachi, *The Enemy That Never Was: A History of the Japanese Canadians*

Ann Sunahara, *The Politics of Racism: The Uprooting of Japanese Canadians during the Second World War*

Structure:

1. Joy Kogawa refers to the newspaper clipping "Grinning and Happy" in both the opening and the closing of her argument. What purpose does this "framing" of her argument at both ends achieve? How does it help her make her point?

2. How important to Kogawa's argument is the device of *contrast*? Explain.

3. What percentage of this selection do you estimate consists of *examples* that illustrate Kogawa's point?

4. To what extent is this selection based on *description*?

5. Most THESIS STATEMENTS are placed toward the beginning of an argument; why is Kogawa's placed in the very last line?

Style:

1. Until the publication of *Obasan*, Joy Kogawa was best known as a poet. What poetical qualities do you find in this selection of her PROSE?

2. To what extent has Kogawa used SENSE IMAGES to make this selection vivid? Give one example each of appeals to sight, hearing, touch, taste, and smell.

3. Kogawa's poetic prose is filled with FIGURES OF SPEECH. Point out at least three good examples each of SIMILE and METAPHOR.

4. In paragraphs 14 through 17, how many times do you find the contraction "it's" at or near the beginning of a sentence? Is this repetition accidental or deliberate? What is its effect?

5. How many words long is the first sentence of paragraph 19? How many times does it use the word "and"? Is this run-on sentence accidental or deliberate? What is its effect?

Argumentation and Persuasion:

1. As a member of a persecuted minority, Kogawa's narrator strongly rejects a *deductive* stance. She shuns the official "telling" of the newspaper article, and instead produces her own eyewitness "telling." Point out at least ten pieces of evidence that lead *inductively* to her own conclusion that the newspaper's version of the truth is "not how it was."

2. Does Kogawa rely more heavily on *argumentation* or on *persuasion*? To what extent does she communicate through reason? To what extent through emotion?

3. Analyze Kogawa's tools of *persuasion*: point out at least five loaded words, five SENSE IMAGES, and five FIGURES OF SPEECH that build emotion. Identify one case of deliberate repetition, and one of extreme sentence length, that both build emotion. Does all this persuasion put you on guard? Or does it convince you?

Ideas for Discussion and Writing:

1. How often are you, like Kogawa's narrator, caught between two or more views of the truth? Cite one recent example. Did you proceed *deductively*, by accepting an established view held by yourself or others, or did you proceed *inductively* to a new conclusion?

2. The narrator of "Grinning and Happy" and her immediate family are Canadian citizens of Japanese descent, removed by the federal government from the coast of British Columbia during the Second World War for fear they would betray Canada to enemy Japan. They were separated from other family members and their property was taken, never to be returned. Discuss the wisdom of our government's action against the Japanese-Canadians, who are accurately represented by this fictitious family. Did anything like it happen before the Second World War? Has anything like it happened since? Under what circumstances can you imagine it happening again and to what group or groups?

3. During the Second World War the Canadian government confiscated an island off the coast of British Columbia from its owner, a Japanese-Canadian, paying him $2000 in compensation. Two generations later his granddaughter, a student at Ryerson Polytechnical Institute in Toronto, estimated the worth of this property at 200 million dollars. In 1988 the Canadian government officially apologized to the Japanese-Canadian community and offered each survivor of the epoch $21,000. Has the wrong been righted? Attack or defend our government's action.

4. *You are* the student mentioned in question 3 above. Write a letter to the prime minister, arguing either *deductively* or *inductively* that the valuable island be restored to the heirs of its original owner.

    Or *you are* a present owner of this property. Write a letter to the prime minister, arguing either *inductively* or *deductively* that your land should not be confiscated and given to the descendants of the man who once owned it.

5. **PROCESS IN WRITING:** *Identify a group that you believe has been poorly treated by Canadian society (for example the handicapped or disabled, the elderly, native peoples, farmers, immigrants, refugees, single parents, etc.). Take notes, then write an* inductive *argument in which you present the evidence that led to your belief. In your next draft revise to seek an effective balance of argumentation and persuasion. Now share this draft in small groups at school, and apply your classmates'*

best advice. At home, read aloud to detect wordiness and awkwardness. Edit. Finally, read your good version aloud to the whole class, and be prepared to answer questions.

Note: See also the Topics for Writing at the end of this chapter.

Wendy Dennis

A Tongue-Lashing for Deaf Ears

Wendy Dennis is an editor and freelance writer. Born in 1950, she has lived in Toronto all her life. After attending York University and the University of Toronto, she taught high school English for seven years, then, "terminally bored with that line of work," discovered a deeper interest while attending Ryerson Polytechnical Institute's journalism program. Since that time she has published extensively in periodicals such as Maclean's, Toronto Life, City Woman, Homemaker's, Chatelaine, Ontario Living, *and* New Woman. *She also contributes to the CBC radio program* Later the Same Day. *Dennis sometimes writes in an analytical, objective, argumentative vein, but says her readers respond with more letters when she takes the personal, subjective, persuasive approach of our selection. "A Tongue-Lashing for Deaf Ears" is still one of her favourites. "It was a joy to write that piece," she says, "because I was so angry and frustrated." She suggests to other writers that "the best place to start is with something you have felt or observed strongly, because the thinking will follow naturally from the writing." Her essay appeared in 1981 in the "Podium" column of* Maclean's.

1   The last time I went to the movies and got stuck beside a motor-mouth whose IQ bore an uncanny resemblance to his shoe size, I vowed, like Peter Finch in *Network*, that I was mad as hell and I wasn't going to take it anymore. That night I dreamt that my own rage-twisted face was projected in cinemascopic grandeur on the screen, while my Charlton Heston voice boomed hideous warnings in Dolby sound at foolish would-be noisemakers. No longer would I smile sweetly and apologize for the unusual craving I had to follow the plot without a Howard Cosell play-by-play; no longer would I stand miserably by while some pimply-faced prefect with a flashlight solemnly asked the buffoon on my right to please stop belching through the love scenes. It was time to retaliate.

2   I considered my options carefully. I thought of Nancy Reagan, who reportedly sleeps with "a tiny little gun" beside her bed, and had to admit that her solution, like the First Lady herself, possessed a certain clean elegance. But I didn't require a lethal weapon. A canister of tear gas

maybe? Or a branding iron? Perhaps one of those guns they use to stun cattle before transforming them into the neat little cellophane packages you find under the red lights at supermarkets. I liked the poetic justice of that. Stun the beast and call four of those scrubbed choirboys theatres inevitably hire as ushers to deposit him under the marquee, where he would symbolize the long-overdue revolt of the Silent Movie Majority.

Noisy invasion of public spaces by yahoos is hardly a new problem but, unless my experience has been atypical, it seems to be nearing epidemic proportions. And the brutes are branching out. No longer content merely to destroy the sweet holy silence of the movie houses, like nasty malignant cells, they're now everywhere — and they're out for blood. I see them on subway platforms, where their infernal amplified radios bring demented stares to other passengers' faces but never seem to rouse the offenders from their somnambulant stupor. I've pulled up beside roving packs of them at red lights, where they stare like zombies, blithely unaware that the decibel level of their tape decks is precipitating anxiety attacks in passers-by for miles. I've come face to face with them as close to home as a campsite in Algonquin Park and as far away as a surf-washed beach in Bali; recently I've even encountered them at live theatre. All of which convinces me there's something awry in the land.

But to blame it entirely on a lapse in good manners is, I think, to miss the whole point. It has to do with something much larger and scarier than rudeness. What brought it all home to me was an incident that occurred in a Grade 12 English class I was teaching a few years ago. While we discussed a movie everyone had seen, I saw a wonderful opportunity to interject a few comments about my pet obsession — the invasion of movies by morons. Before I could sermonize, one of the boys said, "I know just what you're going to say and it bugs me too." Delighted I'd be preaching to the converted, I tried to continue, but he interrupted me again: "It really burns me when I go to the movies with my friends and we're horsing around and some jerk turns around and asks us to be quiet." When my berserk ravings had melted into a whimpering whine, I was struck by an overwhelming sadness — the kind of sadness one feels when a familiar touchstone has been lost. Here was someone I knew to be quite normal, sometimes even thoughtful, explaining how people who requested quiet in movies constituted an invasion of *his* rights. There was no doubt about it — something was certainly rotten.

I blame television. Though TV is a convenient whipping boy, what else could have so warped that boy's perception of what a movie ought to be? Like the tube he switches on for company the moment he gets home, the movie screen is just supposed to be there — several dollars worth of objective background noise for *his* performance. Add to that insidious ethic a healthy dose of egocentricity, and you begin to understand the value system of the radio-schleppers too. If they travel in hermetically sealed vacuum-packed capsules of indifference, so must everyone else. Sadly then, all the reliable approaches to solving such a problem, like asking the offenders to quieten down, no longer work. What's worse, it has been my experience that *any* approach tends to evoke obscene remarks or the verbal equivalent of two longs and a short. Perhaps soon the home video revolution will keep them safely locked up and they will venture into the public domain only spasmodically to cart away armloads of tapes from the corner video outlet. Until then, however, this travesty demands a little noisemaking from the rest of us.

6   Now I've never been one to shirk a struggle, but I'll admit this one is getting me down. I'm weary of paying to see a film and getting a rumble instead. I'm tired of cowardly theatre managers who won't throw the bums out. But most of all I'm sick of this rabid Canadian disease of deferential politeness — even to neanderthals who deserve nothing better than to have their eyes burned out with projector bulbs. I figure we've got one chance only. If, in a few short years, the nonsmokers could make us feel like social lepers for lighting up in public, maybe we can do the same to the noise polluters. Is anybody out there listening?

△△

Further Reading:

Environmental Health Directorate, *Noise Hazard and Control*
Anthony Burgess, *A Clockwork Orange* (novel)

Structure:

1. How effective are the *examples* with which Wendy Dennis introduces her essay?
2. Roughly what proportion of the whole essay consists of examples? How effective would the argument be without them? Choose the best example and tell what it achieves.
3. Paragraph 5 blames the epidemic on television and "egocentricity." Why do you think Dennis waits until almost three-quarters of the way through her argument to analyze these *causes*? What is the effect of this strategy?
4. Point out all the *comparisons and contrasts* that Dennis uses in paragraph 6 to heighten the force of her closing.
5. "Is anybody out there listening?" asks Dennis in the last line. What does this question attempt to achieve? Does it succeed?

Style:

1. Dennis tells us in her opening sentence that she is "mad as hell." What other COLLOQUIAL or SLANG expressions do you find in her essay? Could she have expressed her feelings as vividly in more FORMAL language?

2. What FIGURE OF SPEECH does Dennis use in paragraph 3 when she says that noise polluters are "like nasty malignant cells"? Point out five more SIMILES or METAPHORS in this selection.

3. The term "yahoos" (par. 3) is an ALLUSION to the semi-human monsters of Jonathan Swift's book *Gulliver's Travels*. To what does "the Silent Movie Majority" of paragraph 2 allude? What is the effect of this allusion? In what way can allusions help to create a CONCISE STYLE?

Argumentation and Persuasion:

1. Dennis tells us throughout her argument that noise pollution has increased. Point out all the evidence in paragraphs 1, 3, and 4 that leads *inductively* to this conclusion.

2. In never questioning her view that others *should* be quiet in the movie house and other public places, Dennis also reasons *deductively*. Put this view into the major premise of a syllogism, then add Dennis' minor premise and conclusion.

3. In this essay of persuasion, to what extent does Dennis also use *argumentation*? Point out at least three passages that rely strongly on logic.

4. Dennis hints as early as her title, "A Tongue-Lashing for Deaf Ears," that she will specialize in *persuasion*. Point out at least five of her persuasive techniques, giving examples.

Ideas for Discussion and Writing:

1. There is no doubt that Wendy Dennis is angry. Why, then, does she also give her essay a humourous TONE, as in paragraph 1? Is anger a good motivation for writing? In what ways may it help? In what ways may it harm? In your opinion, what is the overall effect of Dennis' anger on the quality of her argument?

2. Has Dennis gone too far in so heavily favouring *persuasion* over *argumentation*? Has her shoot-from-the-lip approach convinced you of her view, or has it alienated you?

3. Do you agree with Dennis that noise in public places is disagreeable? That it is a real problem? If so, give two or three

examples from your own experience. Or are you on the side of the "noise polluters"? Is Dennis unjustly trying to stop your legitimate fun? If so, explain why you should be allowed to talk in "the sweet holy silence of the movie houses," or play your radio on the beach.

4. Explain the meaning of "touchstone" (par. 4) using a dictionary if necessary. Through her encounters with people who make noise, Wendy Dennis has lost one of her "familiar touchstones." Name a few of your "familiar touchstones." Have you "lost" any in your lifetime so far? If so, which, and how? And how has the "loss" affected you?

5. Have you noticed the "rabid Canadian disease of deferential politeness" that Dennis laments in her final paragraph? Are we too tolerant toward those who violate social norms? Or even toward other countries that violate our national norms? If so, give examples. If not, explain why not.

6. PROCESS IN WRITING: *Wendy Dennis' "pet obsession" is noise in public places. What is yours? In an essay developed mostly through persuasion, denounce the object of your scorn, and, like Dennis, propose a solution. First write the name of your "obsession" in the middle of a page, then near it write other words that it calls to mind. Connect related items with lines, then apply the best of this cluster outline as you write the first draft. In your next draft add more tools of persuasion: vivid word choice, SENSE IMAGES, FIGURES OF SPEECH, and examples that support your view. But don't go overboard; respect both the intellect and the emotions of your reader. Have you used TRANSITIONS to speed your prose? Have you cut deadwood? Have you worked toward a climax? Read your final version aloud to the class, with expression, and be prepared to answer questions.*

Note: See also the Topics for Writing at the end of this chapter.

Topics for Writing

CHAPTER 9: ARGUMENTATION AND PERSUASION

Develop one of the following topics into an essay of argumentation and/or persuasion, choosing the side you wish to take. (See also the guidelines that follow.)

1. Companies (should/should not) be held liable for their own pollution.
2. Adopted children (should/should not) be told who their "birth parents" are.
3. The government (should/should not) require less foreign programming on television.
4. Compulsory retirement at 65 should be (continued/abolished).
5. Pit bulls should be (legal/illegal).
6. "Streaming" of students in the high schools should be (increased/maintained/reduced/abolished).
7. Canadian foreign aid should be (increased/maintained/decreased).
8. The government (should/should not) require that all plastic containers be biodegradable.
9. The minimum driving age should be (raised/maintained/lowered).
10. Private ownership of handguns should be (allowed/prohibited).
11. Free trade between Canada and the United States will (increase/decrease) opportunities in the career I hope to enter.
12. Racism in Canada is (increasing/decreasing).
13. Canada should (permit/prohibit) irradiation of food.
14. Municipal recycling should be (optional/required).
15. Car insurance (should/should not) cost the same for males and females.
16. There (is/is not) life in outer space.
17. The Canadian Senate should be (maintained/changed/abolished).
18. Public transit (should/should not) be free.
19. Canada should (increase/maintain/decrease) its level of immigration.
20. Chemical additives to food (should/should not) be allowed.
21. The minimum drinking age should be (raised/maintained/lowered).

22. Medical experimentation on animals (should/should not) be permitted.
23. Official censorship of films should be (increased/maintained/ decreased/abolished).
24. Canada should (increase/maintain/decrease/abolish) passenger rail service.
25. Stores (should/should not) be required to close on Sundays.

Note also the Process in Writing topic after each selection in this chapter.

Process in Writing: Guidelines

Follow at least some of these steps in writing your essay of argumentation and/or persuasion (your teacher may suggest which ones).

1. *Choose a good topic, then go to either 2 or 3 below.*

2. DEDUCTION: *Do you already know your point of view because of a moral or intellectual principle you hold? First examine that principle, the foundation of your argument: Is it extreme, or is it reasonable enough (and clear enough) that your* AUDIENCE *can accept it? If the latter, proceed. Make notes, then write a rapid and double-spaced first draft showing how the principle supports your point.*
   OR

3. INDUCTION: *Did experience or observation teach you the point you wish to make? First generate a page of notes. Then put these experiences or observations into the order that led you to your conclusion. Now transfer this argument to a rapid, double-spaced first draft.*

4. *You have probably organized your draft through a pattern we studied in an earlier chapter.* Cause and effect *is a natural for either deduction or induction, and so is* comparison and contrast *(in this chapter see Margaret Atwood for the former and Bonnie Laing for the latter). You have probably used* examples, *perhaps* narrating *or* describing *them. You might also have* classified *your subject, or cast your logic in a* process analysis. *Apart from* analogy, *which appeals more to emotion than to logic, all the approaches we have studied so far can serve deduction or induction. Use whatever works. If your first draft makes partial use of a major pattern, consider revising to extend the pattern and strengthen its effect.*

5. *As you look over your first draft, add any missing examples, especially if your argument is inductive (the more evidence, the better). Heighten your logic with signals such as "however," "therefore," "as a result," and "in conclusion."*

6. *Now judge how* argumentative *or* persuasive *your approach has been so far. Does your cold logic need a little colour and life? If so, add it, consulting pp. 270–272 on techniques of persuasion. Or do your emotional appeals, like those of Wendy Dennis in this chapter, dominate your argument? Do they even encourage the audience not to think? If so, revise towards a more blended stance in your second draft.*

7.   *Now cut all deadwood. Check for details of spelling and grammar. Write your good copy, then proofread it word by word. If you have used a computer, save the essay on disk in case your teacher suggests further revision.*

Glossary

Glossary

Abstract Theoretical, relying more on generalities than on specific facts. Abstract writing tends to lack interest and force, because it is difficult to understand and difficult to apply. *See also* the opposite of abstract, CONCRETE.

Allegory In poetry or PROSE, a passage or an entire work that has two levels of meaning: literal and symbolic (*see* SYMBOL). Like a parable, an allegory draws such numerous or striking parallels between its literal subject and its implied subject that, without ever stating "the moral of the story," it leads us to perceive a moral or philosophical truth. An allegory, however, is longer and more complex than a parable. It also differs from an analogy in that it does not openly identify and compare the two subjects.

Allusion An indirect reference to a passage in literature or scripture, an event, a person, or anything else with which the reader is thought to be familiar. An allusion is a device of compression in language, for in a few words it summons up the meaning of the thing to which it refers, and applies that meaning to the subject at hand. Critics of big government, for example, will often allude to Big Brother, the personification of governmental tyranny in George Orwell's novel *1984.*

Anecdote A short account of an interesting and amusing incident. An anecdote can be a joke or a true story about others or oneself and is often used as an example to introduce an essay, close an essay, or illustrate points within an essay.

Audience The reader or readers. One of the essayist's crucial tasks is to match the level and strategy of an argument with the needs and qualities of the particular audience that will read it. *See* the section "Who is my audience?" in this book's introductory essay, "The Act of Writing," p. xxxv.

Bias words Terms which, either subtly or openly, encourage strong value judgements. SUBJECTIVE language is a vital ingredient of much good writing, especially in description and in persuasion; to avoid it altogether would be both impossible and undesirable. The important thing is to avoid blatantly loaded language in an essay: words like "Commie," "slob," "cretin," "Newfie," "ex-con," or "broad" will inflame an uncritical reader and offend a critical one. Note that many bias words are also SLANG.

Cliché A worn-out expression that takes the place of original thought: "to make a long story short," "sadder but wiser," "bite the bullet," "hustle and bustle," "by hook or by crook," "as different as night and day," and "hit the nail on the head." Most clichés were once effective, but like last year's fad in clothing or music have lost their appeal and may even annoy.

Climax In an essay, the point at which the argument reaches its culmination, its point of greatest intensity or importance. The closing of an essay tends to be most effective as a climax; if it is not, it may give the impression of trailing feebly off into nothingness.

Colloquial Speech-like. Colloquial expressions like "cop," "guy," "kid," "nitty gritty," and "okay" are often used in conversation but are usually avoided in essays, especially FORMAL essays. Although they are lively, colloquialisms are often inexact: "guy," for example, can refer to a person or a rope, and "kid" can refer to a child or a goat. *See also* SLANG.

Conciseness The art of conveying the most meaning in the fewest words. A concise essay does not explain its topic less fully than a wordy one; it just uses words more efficiently. Concise writers get straight to the point and stay on topic. They are well enough organized to avoid repeating themselves. They give CONCRETE examples rather than pages of ABSTRACT argument. They use a short word unless a long one is more exact. And most concise writers, to achieve these goals, revise extensively.

Concrete Factual and specific, relying more on particular examples than on abstract theory. Concrete language makes writing more forceful, interesting, and convincing by recreating vividly for the reader what the writer has experienced or thought. SENSE IMAGES, ANECDOTES, FIGURES OF SPEECH, and CONCISENESS all play a part in concrete language and are generally lacking in its opposite, ABSTRACT language.

Deduction A kind of logic that accepts a general principle as true, then uses it to explain a specific case or cases. *See* "Deduction," p. 268.

Dialogue The quoted conversation of two or more people. Normally a new paragraph begins with each change of speaker, to avoid confusion as to who says what. A certain amount of dialogue can lend colour to an essay, but heavy use of it is normally reserved for fiction and drama.

Economy See CONCISENESS.

Epigram A short, clever, and often wise saying. The best-known epigrams are proverbs, such as "What can't be cured must be endured" and "To know all is to forgive all."

Epigraph A short introductory quotation prefixed to an essay or other piece of writing.

Essay Derived from the French term *essai,* meaning a "try" or "attempt," the word "essay" refers to a short composition in which a point is made, usually through analysis and example. While most essays are alike in being limited to one topic, they may vary widely in other ways. The *formal essay,* for example, is objective and stylistically dignified, while the *familiar essay* is subjective, anecdotal, and colloquial.

Euphemism A polite expression that softens or even conceals the truth: "pass away" for "die," "senior citizens" for "old people," "low-income neighbourhood" for "slum," "gosh darn" for "God damn," "perspire" for "sweat," "eliminate" for "kill," and "de-hire" or "select out" for "fire." Euphemisms are becoming more and more common in uses ranging from personal kindness to advertising to political repression.

Fiction Imaginative literature written in PROSE. Consisting mainly of novels and short stories, fiction uses invented characters and plots to create a dramatic story; most essays, by contrast, rely on literal fact and analysis to create an argument. There is of course an area of overlap: some fiction is very factual and some essays are very imaginative.

Figures of speech Descriptive and often poetic devices in which meaning is concentrated and heightened, usually through comparisons:
A. **Simile**: A figure of speech in which one thing is said to be *like* another. ("With its high buildings on all sides, Bay Street is like a canyon.")
B. **Metaphor**: A figure of speech, literally false but poetically true, in which one thing is said to *be* another. ("Bay Street is a canyon walled by cliffs of concrete.")
C. **Hyperbole**: Exaggeration. ("The office buildings rise miles above the city.")
D. **Personification**: A figure of speech in which a non-human object is described as human. ("At night the empty buildings stare from their windows at the street.")

Formal Formal writing is deliberate and dignified. It avoids partial sentences, most contractions, colloquial expressions, and slang. Instead its vocabulary is standard and its sentences are often long and qualified with dependent clauses. In general it follows the accepted rules of grammar and principles of style. *See also* INFORMAL.

Hyperbole *See* FIGURES OF SPEECH.

Image In literature, a mental picture triggered by words. Because they strongly stimulate thought and feeling, yet take little space, well-chosen images are vital ingredients of writing that is CONCRETE and has CONCISENESS. *See also* SENSE IMAGES.

Induction A kind of logic that derives a general principle from the evidence of specific examples. *See* "Induction," p. 269.

Informal Informal writing resembles speech and, in fact, is often a representation of speech in writing. It may contain partial sentences, many short sentences, contractions, COLLOQUIAL expressions, and sometimes SLANG. *See also* FORMAL.

Irony A manner of expression in which a statement that seems literally to mean one thing in fact means another. "That's just great!" is a literal statement when said by a dinner guest enjoying the fondue but is an ironic complaint when said by a driver who has backed into a tree. In a larger sense, *irony of situation* is a contrast between what is expected to happen and what does happen. It is this that creates our interest in the national leader who is impeached, the orphan who becomes a millionaire, or the evangelist convicted of tax fraud. Irony is a powerful tool of argument and especially of SATIRE.

Jargon Technical language or language that seeks to impress by appearing difficult or technical. Specialized terms can hardly be avoided in technical explanations: How could two electricians discuss a radio without words like "capacitor," "diode," and "transistor"? But these same words may need definition when used in an essay for the general reader. Other jargon uses technical-sounding or otherwise difficult words to seem important. An honest essayist will try to avoid "input," "output," "feedback," "interface," "knowledgeable," "parameters," and other ugly words of this sort when writing for the general reader.

Juxtaposition The deliberate placing together of two or more thoughts, IMAGES or other elements that emphasize each other, usually by contrast.

Metaphor See FIGURES OF SPEECH.

Neologism A newly invented word. Some new terms are accepted into our standard vocabulary. For example, a word like "laser" tends to become standard because it is needed to label a new and important invention. Most newly minted words are nuisances, though, for they are meaningless to the great majority of readers who do not know them.

Objective The opposite of SUBJECTIVE. In objective writing the author relies more on hard evidence and logical proof than on intuitions, prejudices, or interpretations.

Onomatopoeia A poetical device in which language sounds like what it means. Some onomatopoetic words, such as "boom," "bang," and "crash," are out-and-out sound effects; others, such as "slither," "ooze," and "clatter," are more subtle. Onomatopoeia can be achieved not only through word choice but also through larger aspects of style. A series of short sentences, for example, gives an impression of tenseness and rapidity.

Paradox A statement that seems illogical but that in some unexpected way may be true. The Bible is full of paradoxes, as in "Blessed are the meek, for they shall inherit the earth."

Personification *See* FIGURES OF SPEECH.

Prose Spoken or written language without the metrical structure that characterizes poetry. Conversations, letters, short stories, novels, and essays are all prose.

Pun A play on words. A pun is based either on two meanings of one word or on two words that sound alike but have different meanings. Often called the lowest form of humour, the pun is the basis of many jokes. (Why did the fly fly? Because the spider spider.)

Quotation The words of one person reproduced exactly in the writing or speech of another person. A well-chosen quotation can add force to an argument by conveying the opinion of an authority or by presenting an idea in words so exact or memorable that they could hardly be improved upon. Quotations should be reproduced exactly, and of course should be placed in quotation marks and attributed to their source.

Reduction to absurdity A technique of SATIRE in which the subject is belittled through being portrayed as absurd. A favourite device of humourists.

Sarcasm Scornful and contemptuous criticism, from the Greek word *sarkazein* ("to tear flesh").

Satire Humorous criticism meant to improve an individual or society by exposing abuses. In TONE, satire can range from light humour to bitter criticism. Its chief tools are wit, IRONY, exaggeration, and sometimes SARCASM and ridicule.

Sense images Descriptive appeals to one or more of the reader's five senses: sight, hearing, touch, taste, and smell. Sense images are vital in helping the reader to experience, at second-hand, what the writer has experienced in person. CONCRETE language has many sense images; ABSTRACT language does not.

Simile See FIGURES OF SPEECH.

Slang Racy, unconventional language often limited to a certain time, place, or group. Slang is the extreme of colloquial language, terminology used in conversation but hardly ever in an essay except for dialogue or special effects. One reason to avoid a slang term is that not everyone will know it: expressions like "swell," "square," and "far out" have gone out of use, while expressions like "bug juice," "croaker," "jointman," and "rounder" are known to only one group — in this case, convicts. *See also* COLLOQUIAL.

Stereotype An established mental image of something. Most stereotypes are of people and are based on their sex, race, colour, size or shape, economic or social class, or profession. Jokes about mothers-in-law, "Newfies," absent-minded professors, "woman drivers," or short people are all examples of stereotyping. While they may provoke humour, stereotypes are anything but harmless: they hinder recognition of people's individuality and they encourage prejudices which, at their extreme, can result in persecution like that of the Jews in Nazi Germany.

Style In general, the way something is written, as opposed to what it is written about. Style is to some extent a matter of TONE — light or serious, INFORMAL or FORMAL, ironic or literal. It is also a matter of technique. Word choice, FIGURES OF SPEECH, level of CONCISENESS, and character-istics of sentence structure and paragraphing are all ingredients of style. Although a writer should pay close attention to these matters, the idea that one deliberately seeks out "a style" is a mistake that only encourages imitation. An individual style emerges naturally as the sum of the writer's temperament, skills, and experience.

Subjective The opposite of OBJECTIVE. In subjective writing the author relies more on intuitions, prejudices, or interpretations than on hard evidence and logical proof.

Symbol One thing that stands for another, as in a flag representing a country, the cross representing Christianity, or a logo representing a company. Symbols appear frequently in poetry, drama, fiction, and also essays. For example, in Charles Gordon's satirical essay, the "bottom line" is an object shown to tourists, but it also represents the government's policy about spending public money. Like many symbols, it is a tangible thing representing an intangible thing.

Thesis statement The sentence or sentences, usually in the introduction, which first state the main point and restrict the focus of an essay.

Tone The manner of a writer toward the subject and reader. The tone of an essay can be light or serious, INFORMAL or FORMAL, ironic or literal. Tone is often determined by subject matter; for example, an essay about cocktail parties is likely to be lighter and less formal than one about funerals. An innovative writer, though, could reverse these treatments to give each of the essays an ironic tone. The identity of the reader also influences tone. An essay for specialists to read in a technical journal will tend to be more OBJECTIVE and serious than one written for the general reader. The main point for the writer is to choose the tone most appropriate to a particular essay, then maintain it throughout.

Transition A word, phrase, sentence, or paragraph that moves the reader from one part of the essay to the next. Transitions even as short as "next," "then," "as a result," "on the other hand," "in conclusion," or "finally" are crucial not only to moving the argument along, but also to pointing out its logic.

cut here

STUDENT REPLY CARD

In order to improve future editions, we are seeking your comments on *The Act of Writing: Canadian Essays for Composition,* Revised Third Edition, by Ronald Conrad.

After you have read this text, please answer the following questions and return this form via Business Reply Mail. *Thanks in advance for your help!*

Name of your college or university: _____

Major program of study: _____

Are there any sections of this text that were *not* assigned as course reading? If so, please specify those chapters or portions:

How would you rate the overall accessibility of the content? Please feel free to comment on reading level, writing style, terminology, and layout and design features.

cut here

fold here

What selections did you like *best* in this book?

What selections did you like *least*?

If you would like to say more, we'd love to hear from you. Please write to us at the address shown on the reverse of this card.

------------------------------ cut here ------------------------------

------------------------------ fold here ------------------------------

Postage will be paid by

MAIL ⤳ POSTE

Canada Post Corporation / Société canadienne des postes

Postage paid
if mailed in Canada

Port payé
si posté au Canada

**Business
Reply**

**Réponse
d'affaires**

0183560299   01

cut here

0183560299-L1N9B6-BR01

Attn.: Sponsoring Editor
College Division

MCGRAW-HILL RYERSON LIMITED
300 WATER ST
WHITBY ON   L1N 9Z9

tape shut